The State of
Working America
2008/2009

The State of Working America
2008/2009

LAWRENCE MISHEL

JARED BERNSTEIN

HEIDI SHIERHOLZ

Economic
Policy
Institute

ILR Press
an imprint of Cornell University Press
Ithaca and London

ISBN 978-0-8014-4754-9 (cloth: alk. paper)
ISBN 978-0-8014-7477-4 (paper: alk. paper)

Printed in the United States of America

Recommended citation for this book is as follows: Mishel, Lawrence, Jared Bernstein, and Heidi Shierholz, *The State of Working America 2008/2009*. An Economic Policy Institute Book. Ithaca, N.Y.: ILR Press, an imprint of Cornell University Press, 2009

Cornell University Press strives to use environmentally responsible suppliers and materials to the fullest extent possible in the publishing of its books. Such materials include vegetable-based, low-VOC inks and acid-free papers that are recycled, totally chlorine-free, or partly composed of nonwood fibers. For further information, visit our website at www.cornellpress.cornell.edu.

Cloth printing   10 9 8 7 6 5 4 3 2 1
Paperback printing   10 9 8 7 6 5 4 3 2 1

PRINTED IN U.S.A.

To my newly broadened family who make me a very happy man: my wife,
Ellen Kurlansky; my two newest children, Calla and Isaac Brown (and fiancée
Holly Scavone); and Eli and Julia Simon-Mishel. My cup runneth over.
To my brother, Henry, who is my oldest, dearest friend. I am his greatest admirer.
- LAWRENCE MISHEL

To Senator Edward M. Kennedy, a tireless fighter
for the economic rights of working families.
- JARED BERNSTEIN

To my exceedingly supportive parents.
-HEIDI SHIERHOLZ

Visit epi.org and StateofWorkingAmerica.org
The Economic Policy Institute's Web sites contain current analysis of issues
addressed in this book. The State of Working America.org Web site presents
up-to-date historical data series on incomes, wages, employment, poverty, and
other topics. It also includes graphic image files of every figure and table in
this volume. The data can be viewed online or downloaded as spreadsheets.

Acknowledgments

The preparation of this publication requires the intense work of many people on EPI's staff and many contributions from other researchers on the topics covered in the text.

Emily Garr and James Lin provided extensive and enormously valuable research assistance in all of the areas covered in this book by collecting and organizing data and creating tables and graphs. Jin Dai provided extensive computer programming and data analysis.

Among EPI staffers (past and present), Josh Bivens, Elise Gould, John Irons, Monique Morrissey, and Liana Fox provided extensive insights and guidance in many areas, including research on outsourcing, trade and employment, international comparisons, and analysis of capital and labor incomes. We thank all of our previous co-authors—Jacqueline Simon, David Frankel, John Schmitt, Heather Boushey, and Sylvia Allegretto—for their lasting input. Our development staff, headed by Noris Weiss Malvey, provided valuable help in raising funds for this work.

EPI's Publications Director Joe Procopio directs the book's production with Ellen Levy, Sylvia Saab, and Pat Watson. Their careful editing and layout under considerable time pressure is greatly appreciated. Our readers are the true beneficiaries of their work, as they make us look like far better writers. Nancy Cleeland, Nancy Coleman, and Karen Conner work to provide a large audience for our work. We deeply appreciate the energy and creativity they bring to their work.

Many experts were helpful in providing data or their research papers for our use. We are particularly grateful to Ed Wolff for the provision of special tabulations. Others who provided data, advice, or their analysis include: Greg Acs, Elaine Ditsler, Henry Farber, Thesia Garner, Jacob Hacker, Steven Sabow, Arloc Sherman, and Kathleen Short.

We are grateful to the Annie E. Casey Foundation, the Ford Foundation, the Joyce Foundation, the Charles Stewart Mott Foundation, the Open Society Institute, the Public Welfare Foundation, and the Bernard and Audre Rapoport Foundation for providing support for the research and publication of this volume.

Table of Contents

Executive summary

The promises and the pitfalls of the new economy

When the job market began to contract in 2008, it drew the curtains on a recovery that had seen strong productivity gains that never translated into adequate income growth for most workers. As a result, working families are seeing extraordinary economic challenges. In the first half of 2008 alone, the economy has lost over 400,000 jobs. Unemployment has jumped to 5.5% by mid-2008, up from 4.4% in March 2007, pushing an additional 1.8 million persons onto the jobless rolls. This weakness in the job market has taken a further toll on already lackluster worker earnings, with most paychecks actually losing ground after inflation.

These recent problems have correctly been linked to a confluence of events. The sharp spike in energy costs—up 25% since the middle of last year—is taking a huge bite out of family budgets (and at a time when wage growth is weakening). The bursting of the housing bubble (see Chapter 5) has undercut home values, shutting down a significant source of household wealth. This in turn is fueling millions of defaults on home loans, often followed by foreclosure. Spillovers from the housing crisis have wracked financial markets and frozen credit markets. In turn, diminished borrowing, including home equity lines of credit, is choking off one of the main sources of consumer spending growth in the 2000s.

Yet working Americans are more productive than ever. Putting aside the current cyclical downturn, the men and women who routinely keep this country running have been working harder and smarter. Since the mid-1990s, the growth of output per hour—or productivity—has undergone a resurgence, and the folks responsible are the 140 million Americans who go to work every day.

When it comes to efficient, profitable production, the men and women of the American workforce have a lot to be proud of. But when it comes to being rewarded for

the work they do, the skills they have sharpened, and the contributions they make…
well, that's a different story. Their paychecks have been frozen, their health coverage
is being cut back, their jobs are at risk of being shipped overseas, and their pensions
are more precarious than ever.

For the first time since the Census Bureau began tracking such data back in the
mid-1940s, the real incomes of middle-class families are lower at the end of this
business cycle than they were when it started. This fact stands as the single most
compelling piece of evidence that prosperity is eluding working families.

Where has all that productivity growth been going? As this book extensively documents, it has gone to the top of the income scale, and the higher up you started out,
the better you did. From 1947 to 1979, the top sliver of wage earners made about 20
times that of the bottom 90%. By 2006, that ratio had catapulted to 77 times more.

Now, there are some smart, hard-working, and creative people up there in that
rarified end of the economic stratosphere, and some deserve large returns for their
labors. But they cannot possibly be the only ones whose living standards should be
boosted in a growing economy. Productivity growth is a result of the efforts of the
whole workforce, not just the fortunate few. Yes, it reflects the work of the CEOs and
CFOs at the top of the corporate ladder. But it also reflects the work of the waitperson
who serves those executives their lunch, the construction worker who builds their
homes, the manufacturer who forges the steel that girds their corporate headquarters,
the home health aid who cares for their aging parents, the cop who protects their beat,
and the teacher who educates their kids.

Earlier editions of this book began to explore this split between the promise of productivity growth and the realities of stagnant living standards. But the business cycle
of the 2000s was ongoing and thus prevented a conclusive evaluation of how these
dynamics would ultimately play out. After all, the 1990s cycle began with a jobless and
wageless recovery, too, yet the productivity gains in the latter half of the decade were
eventually shared. In fact, the late 1990s was the only time of broad-based gains for
American workers since the early 1970s.

This edition, however, will be able to examine the full business cycle of the 2000s
and compare it to earlier cycles. The findings show that the 2000s cycle was one of great
promise in terms of productivity growth, but the promise of better living standards such
growth implied was never realized.

Family income

Family income is the core building block of American living standards. It is through
their income that families meet their material needs as well as their aspirations. The
income that families receive through work, government benefits, or return on investments enables them to provide for their households, raise their children, and invest
in their futures. Income not consumed flows into wealth, enabling families to finance
longer-term investments, like a home, or to offset a period wherein the income flow is
interrupted. This chapter provides a detailed look into how this key living-standards
determinant has evolved, both recently and over the long term.

The analysis reveals two related points that are central to understanding the evolution of income growth in America. First, the most recent business cycle the 2000s—was unique: despite significant productivity growth in the overall economy, most families experienced stagnant or falling real incomes. The American workforce is working harder, smarter, and more efficiently, yet failing to share fairly in the benefits of the growth they themselves are creating. In fact, with data going back to the mid-1940s, it appears that the real income of a typical, middle-income family (i.e., the median) was lower at the end of the 2000s cycle than at the beginning.

That has never happened before. Yes, middle-income families lose ground in a recession, and lately such losses continue for a number of years after the official recession ends. But before the cycle ends—before the next downturn takes hold—real median incomes usually start to grow, and ultimately surpass their prior peak. Yet in the 2000s, the longest jobless recovery on record hurt families earnings' capacity, while increased inequality meant that the growth that did occur bypassed the middle class.

Second, this sharp rise of income inequality has meant that the link between economic growth and broadly shared income gains is broken. The most comprehensive data on inequality reveal this stark imbalance. Data on income concentration going back to 1913 show that the top 1% of wage earners now hold 23% of total income, the highest inequality level in any year on record, bar one: 1928. In the last few years alone, $400 billion of pretax income flowed from the bottom 95% of earners to the top 5%, a loss of $3,660 per household on average in the bottom 95%.

Note that these inequality developments are all based on market outcomes, or pretax measures. Recent changes to the tax system have exacerbated the problem, by lowering the tax liabilities of those at the top of the income scale much more so than those in the middle or at the low end. In 2008, the impact of the Bush tax cuts had virtually no effect on low-income families and lowered the tax liabilities of middle-income families by around $1,000. Families in the top 1% of the income scale, conversely, saw tax reductions of over $50,000.

Another important observation woven through Chapter 1 is that there are persistent gaps in income between white and African American and Hispanic families. Certainly, discrimination plays a role here, as do the lower average levels of educational achievement among minority populations relative to whites (of course, discrimination is in play here too; Chapter 2 adds perspective to these differences by examining educational opportunity and income mobility by race). It is also the case that minority families' incomes, particularly those of African Americans, tend to be more responsive to overall economic trends, both positively and negatively. The downsides of this heightened responsiveness are worrisome, particularly given the current economic downturn. But it is critically important for living standards analysts interested in racial differences to also remain mindful of the upside of this relationship: full employment provides a strong boost to minority incomes. We stress this point both in historical terms and with reference to the most recent period of full employment: the latter 1990s. In those years, the pace of minority families' income growth surpassed that of white families, (average annual income growth from 1995-2000 was 2.9% for black families and 2.1% for white families) and the racial income gap shrunk to historically low levels. In the ensuing downturn and weaker 2000s recovery, much of this valuable ground has been lost (with average annual income growth from 2000-06 at -0.2% for white families and -0.5% for black families).

Amidst the troubling results of the labor market of the 2000s, it is important to scan the historical record for periods where living standards outcomes were much different. In fact, there are a few periods over both the distant and recent past when family incomes were distributed much more equally, leading to living standards improvements across the board, not just at the top. There is one characteristic—alluded to in the above discussion on minority incomes—that these periods shared, whether it was the 1950s or the latter 1990s: very tight labor markets. Full employment, where the unemployment rate is low enough such that employers must share the benefits of growth in order to get and keep the workforce they need, is absolutely a necessary condition for reconnecting the overall economy and with the income of the working families that propel it forward.

Income-class mobility

Chapter 2 documents the historically large increase in income inequality in recent years, reaching levels of concentration not seen since the latter 1920s. Such analysis essentially takes a snapshot of the distribution of family income at one point in time and compares it to another of different families, years later. As the chapter reveals, these pictures present important information about the extent of economic inequality at two points in time. But they say nothing about how individuals themselves have fared over their own lifetimes. For that, one must switch from "snapshots" to "movies." That is the purpose of the Income-class Mobility chapter.

What do we learn from this "movie" approach compared to the snapshots of the previous chapter? If the data were to show, for example, that many families were likely to move from the bottom fifth of the income distribution to the top over time, or that children of wealthy families might switch places with middle-class kids when they became adults, then one could conclude that the benefits of growth were more broadly shared than suggested by the profound inequality displayed in the snapshots of Chapter 1.

The evidence, however, does not find this degree of mobility. Of course, some families do move up and down the income scales, but most maintain their relative positions, meaning that relative to other families in their cohort, they remain at or near the income or wealth position in which they started out. For example, one recent study finds that about 60% of families that start in the bottom fifth are still there a decade later. At the other end of the income scale, 52% of families that start in the top fifth finish there at the end of the decade.

Given its dynamic component, mobility can be a more ambiguous concept than others explored thus far. Simply put, Chapter 2 examines the extent to which your economic position today determines your position tomorrow. If where you start out in the income scale has a strong influence on where you end up, then the rate of economic mobility is low. If, on the other hand, where you start out is largely unrelated to where you end up, mobility is high. In fact, Chapter 2 reports significant correlations between parents and their children, implying that income mobility is at least some-what restricted as one generation's position in the income scale is partially dependent on their parents' position. For example, one recent study finds the correlation between parents and children to be 0.6 (Mazumder 2005). This finding is significant because it implies that it would take a poor family of four with two children approximately nine to 10 generations—over 200 years—to achieve the income of the middle-income four-person family.

In other words, the extent of income mobility across generations plays a determinant role in the living standards of American families. It is, for example, a key determinant of how many generations a family will be stuck at the low end of the income scale, or snugly ensconced at the high end. American folklore often emphasizes the rags-to-riches Horatio Alger stories, which suggest that anyone with the gumption and smarts to prevail can lift themselves up by their bootstraps and transverse the income scale in a generation. Reality, however, shows much less mobility.

Still, popular wisdom would suggest that there is probably more mobility in America compared with the advanced economies in Europe or Scandinavia. Shouldn't their more-extensive social protections and less-freewheeling approach to economic policy dampen the entrepreneurial spark that gives birth to the American rags-to-riches paradigm? To the contrary: one of the most surprising findings of this research is that the opposite is true. Parents' economic positions in these countries are less correlated with their children's later income, meaning there is more intergenerational mobility there than in the United States.

What explains this lack of mobility? Certainly unequal education opportunities and historical discrimination play a role. For example, there are very steep mobility barriers facing African Americans, both in their own chances of moving up, and especially when compared to whites. One study shows that almost two-thirds (63%) of black children who start out in the bottom fourth of the income scale remain there as adults, compared to half that share for white children. Another deeply disturbing study finds that 45% of African American children who start out in middle-income families experience significant downward mobility, ending up in poor families (in the bottom fifth of the income scale) as adults, compared to 16% for whites.

In fact, opportunity itself appears to be unequally distributed, leading to one of the central conclusion of Chapter 2, one that ties the findings of this chapter to those of Chapter 1. It is often said that Americans do not object to unequal outcomes, only to unequal opportunities. But what if unequal outcomes themselves lead to diminished opportunities? If growth flows mostly to those at the top of scale (higher inequality), it is possible that children from these fortunate households will have greater access to quality education relative to children from less well-placed families. If inequality means that some neighborhoods get parks and libraries while others do not, this too restricts opportunity. If quality health care is more accessible to the haves than the have-nots, the latter face a mobility barrier born of inequality.

If income concentration leads to a level of political influence that tilts against the have-nots, this too will reduce opportunity and ultimately lower the rate of economic mobility. If, for example, as has occurred in recent federal budgets, opportunity enhancing programs for disadvantaged children, like Head Start or subsidized health care (State Children's Health Insurance Program), are cut in order to maintain high-end tax cuts, the likelihood that economically disadvantaged children will experience significant mobility is diminished.

While these connections are logical, at this point, research has not generally identified the determinants of mobility in this or other countries. One important exception, however, is higher education. Here, the data do show that children from wealthy families have much greater access to top-tier universities than kids from low-income families, *even when controlling for innate skills*.

This educational barrier places profound limits on income mobility. Of those adults who grew up in low-income families but managed to earn a college degree, only 16% ended up in the bottom fifth of the income scale as adults. But for those who failed to graduate college, the share that started out and ended up in the bottom fifth was 45%. In other words, among children who grew up in low-income families, those who failed to graduate college were almost three times more likely to still be in the bottom fifth as adults compared to children who completed college.

Wages

Because wages and salaries make up roughly three-fourths of total family income (the proportion is even higher among the broad middle class), wage trends are the driving force behind income growth and income inequality trends. Chapter 3 examines and explains the trends in wage growth and wage inequality during the last few decades up through 2007, with a particular focus on the business cycle from 2000 to 2007.

The major development in the labor market in recent years has been the stunning disconnect between the possibilities for improved pay provided by rapid productivity growth and the reality of stunted paychecks, especially in the recent recovery. Productivity grew 11% in the recovery, a faster growth than any recovery since the 1970s. Yet, hourly compensation for the median worker (either the overall median, or of workers with either a high school or college degree) did not grow at all in the recovery despite historically high productivity growth.

The wage momentum from the late 1990s into the 2000s is important to understand when looking at trends over the just completed business cycle, the 2000-07 period; all of the wage growth in the 2000-07 cycle occurred within the first two years. The poor job creation and increased job shortages during the early 2000s recession and lackluster recovery eventually knocked wage growth down so that prices rose at least as fast. This was the case even in 2007, when the unemployment rate was at 4.6%. Since 2000, wage growth among the bottom 70% has been modest at 3.0% or less; at the median, growth of 2.6% over the 2000-07 period was just one-third that of the 1995-2000 period. Wage growth among higher-wage workers was also slower in recent years than in the 1995-2000 period. Wage deceleration, then, has been pervasive.

Digging a little deeper into these trends, we find that women are much more likely to earn poverty-level wages than men. In 2007, 31.4% of women earned poverty-level wages or less, significantly more than the share of men (21.8%). The proportion of minority workers earning low wages is substantial—34.0% of black workers and 41.8% of Hispanic workers in 2007. Overall, 26.4% of workers, over one in every four, earned poverty-level wages in 2007. There was momentum in reducing poverty-wage jobs in the late 1990s that continued until 2002 and then dissipated. There has been no progress in reducing the share of workers with low earnings over the 2002-07 recovery; this is true for all race/ethnic groups and for both genders.

There are three key elements of wage inequality. One is the "bottom half" gap between middle-wage (median-wage earners) and low-wage workers. Another is the "top half" gap between high-wage (90th or 95th percentile wage earners) and middle-wage earners. The third element is the gap at the very top, that is, the growth of wages for those in the upper 1% and even the upper 0.1%, including chief executive officers (CEOs). These three elements have had differing historical trajectories. The gap at the bottom grew in the 1980s but has been stable or declining ever since, whereas the "top half" wage gap has persistently grown since the late 1970s. The very highest earners have done considerably better than other workers for at least 30 years, but they have done extraordinarily well over the last 10 years.

Explaining these shifts in wage inequality requires attention to several factors that affect low-, middle-, and high-wage workers differently. The experience of the late 1990s is a reminder of the great extent to which a low unemployment rate benefits workers, especially low-wage earners. Correspondingly, the high levels of unemployment in the early and mid-1980s and in recent years disempowered wage earners and provided the context in which other forces—specifically, a weakening of labor market institutions and globalization—could drive up wage inequality. Significant shifts in labor market policies and institutions, such as the severe drop in the minimum wage and deunionization, can explain one-third of growing wage inequality. Similarly, the increasing globalization of the economy—immigration, trade, and capital mobility—and the employment shift toward lower-paying service industries (such as retail trade) and away from manufacturing can explain, in combination, at least another third of the total growth in wage inequality. Macroeconomic factors also played an important role: high unemployment in the early 1980s greatly increased wage inequality, the low unemployment of the late 1990s reduced it, and the slack labor market of the 2000s has fueled further inequalities.

The shape of wage inequality shifted in the late 1980s as the gap at the bottom—that is, the 50/10 gap between middle-wage workers at the 50th percentile and low-wage workers at the 10th—began to shrink. However, over the last few years, this progress against wage inequality at the bottom has been growing among both men and women. This reversal is partially the effect of the jobless recovery and the still-remaining shortage of jobs and partially a result of the continued drop in the real value of the minimum wage, at least until 2007. The greatest increase in wage inequality at the bottom occurred among women and corresponded to the fall in the minimum wage over the 1980s, the high unemployment of the early 1980s, and the expansion of low-wage retail jobs. The positive trend in this wage gap over the 1990s owes much to increases in the minimum wage, low unemployment, and the slight, relative contraction in low-paying retail jobs in the late 1990s. The wage gap at the top half—the 90/50 or 95/50 gap between high- and middle-wage earners—continued its steady growth in the 1990s and the 2000s (except the last few years) but at a slightly slower pace than in the 1980s. The continuing influence of globalization, deunionization, and the shift to lower-paying service industries ("industry shifts") can explain the continued growth of wage inequality in the top half.

The top 1% of earners in 2006 had average annual earnings of $576,000 (in 2007 dollars). The top earners' share of earnings was relatively stable from 1947 into the 1970s but nearly doubled from 7.3% in 1979 to 13.6% in 2006 (the latest year of available data). This is the consequence of earnings growth of 144.4% from 1979 to 2006 for the top 1% compared with just 15.6% for the bottom 90%. Those in the upper 0.1% of earners (the top one-thousandth) fared far better, seeing their annual earnings grow 324% since 1979 to reach over $2.2 million in 2006. Consequently, the earnings of the top 0.1% grew to be 77 times the earnings of the bottom 90% in 2006 whereas they were just 21 times as much in 1979.

The erosion of the extent and quality of employer-provided benefits, most notably pensions and health insurance, is an important aspect of the deterioration in job quality for many workers. Employer-provided health care coverage eroded from 1979 until 1993-94, when it stabilized, and then began falling again after 2000 through 2006 (the latest data): coverage dropped from 69.0% in 1979 to 55.0% in 2006, with a 3.9 percentage-point fall since 2000. Employer-provided pension coverage tended to rise in the 1990s but receded by 2.8 percentage points from 2000 to 2006 to 42.8%, 7.8 percentage points below the level in 1979. Pension plan quality also receded as the share of workers in defined-benefit plans fell from 39% in 1980 to just 18% in 2004. Correspondingly, the share of workers with a defined-contribution plan (and no other plan) rose from 8% to 31%.

Young workers' prospects are a barometer of the strength of the labor market: when the labor market is strong for workers the prospects for young workers are very strong, and when the labor market is weak their prospects are very weak. Wages were stagnant or fell among every entry-level group, both high school and college-educated workers and both men and women in the period of sluggish wage growth since 2000. For instance, the entry-level hourly wage of a young male high school graduate in 2007 was 18.2% less than that for the equivalent worker in 1979, a drop of $2.62 per hour. Among women, the entry-level high school wage fell 11.2% in this period, with a 6.3% loss since 2000 standing out. Entry-level wages fell among both female and male college graduates from 2000 to 2007, 3.2% among men and 1.7% among women. This contrasts to the extremely strong wage growth for each of these groups from 1995 to 2000, when wages rose roughly 10% for entry-level high school men and women and 20.9% for entry-level college men, 11.7% for college women.

Unionized workers earn higher wages than comparable non-union workers and also are 18.3% more likely to have health insurance, 22.5% more likely to have pension coverage, and 3.2% more likely to have paid leave. The erosion of unionization (from 43.1% in 1978 to just 19.2% in 2005) can account for 65% of the 11.1 percentage-point growth of the blue-collar/white-collar wage gap among men over the 1978-2005 period.

Until it was raised in 2007, the real value of the minimum wage fell steadily in real terms from 2000, thereby causing the earnings of low-wage workers to seriously fall behind those of other workers and contributing to rising wage inequality in this period. The legislated increases in the minimum wage through 2009 benefits workers who make important contributions to their family's economic well-being: over half of those benefiting from the current increases in the minimum wage work full-time and another 31% work more than 20 hours weekly. While minorities are disproportionately represented among minimum wage workers, 61% are white. These workers also tend to be women (59% of the total) and concentrated in the retail and hospitality industries (46% of all minimum wage earners are employed there, compared to just 21% of all workers).

The 1980s, 1990s, and 2000s have been prosperous times for top U.S. executives, especially relative to other wage earners. Over the 1989 to 2007 period, the median CEO saw pay rise by 106.8%, and the average CEO pay rose 167.3%. During that same period a typical worker's wage grew by just 10%, and mostly in the late 1990s. In 1965, U.S. CEOs in major companies earned 24 times more than an average worker; this ratio grew to 298 at the end of the recovery in 2000, fell due to the stock market decline in the early 2000s and recovered to 275 in 2007. In other words, in 2007 a CEO earned more in one workday (there are 260 in a year) than the typical worker earned all year.

Finally, an analysis of employment projections shows that jobs of the future will require greater education credentials, but not to any great extent. In 2006 the occupational composition of jobs required that 27.7% of the workforce have a college degree or more. This share will rise by just 1 percentage point, to 28.7%, by 2016.

Jobs

The job market is the primary mechanism through which the county's economic growth reaches working families. So following a recession, a robust job market—one with enough job creation to fully utilize the labor force's workers and their skills—is a critical component of a strong, lasting, and equitable recovery. By that measure, the recovery following the recession of 2001 fell short.

The recession of 2001 was followed by nearly two years of continued job loss, and it took an unprecedented *four years* to re-attain the number of jobs the economy supported prior to the recession. The first few years of the recovery of the 2000s have been aptly coined the "jobless" recovery—meaning that the recession of 2001 was officially over, but the economy was still not generating job growth. Looking over the whole cycle, from 2000 to 2007, average annual job growth was 0.6%, well below the 1.8% job growth of the 1990s cycle. This historically weak job creation was costly for working families. The resulting lower rates of employment and consequent lack of upward pressure on wages translated into lost output and forgone increases in living standards. Poor job growth is one of the important factors underlying the ongoing divergence of overall economic growth and the wages and income of working families shown in earlier chapters.

In addition to weak job creation, the business cycle of the 2000s was lackluster by other relevant employment indicators. The unemployment rate increased by 0.7 percentage points from March 2001 (the peak of the last business cycle) to December 2007, despite the fact that the average age of workers increased and the labor force participation rate shrank—both of which should have put downward pressure on the rate of unemployment. Furthermore, if unemployed, a worker's likelihood of being unemployed long-term grew dramatically. In 2000, 11.4% of the unemployed had been so for more than six months, but in 2007, that number was 17.5%. Underemployment also grew particularly quickly—from 7.0% in 2000 to 8.3% in 2007—with, for example, a significantly higher percentage of workers working "involuntarily" part time in 2007 than in 2000.

The employment rate was also disappointing—it decreased by 1.5 percentage points over the 2000s cycle, in contrast to the 2.6 percentage-point average *increase* over prior cycles. The departure from previous cycles was especially dramatic for women, who saw their employment rates decrease by 1.8 percentage points after decades of dramatic increases. The one group that saw significant gains in employment over this period were workers aged 55 and over, as older workers were more likely to need to work to cover health care costs and to bolster retirement income.

Employment is the foundation of family income and economic well-being. The great American jobs machine is arguably the most powerful mechanism in the economy for achieving broadly shared prosperity. But the faltering of that machine in the 2000s, as it produced the weakest jobs recovery on record, has left lingering adversity for workers and their families. When jobs are plentiful, not only are workers more likely to find employment that matches their skills and experience, they are also in a better position to search for higher-paid employment and are in a better bargaining position with respect to their employer to ask for higher levels of compensation. Job growth, however, was too tepid over the business cycle of the 2000s to boost living standards for most workers—even as the economy expanded and labor productivity posted impressive gains.

In other words, for most working families, the "recovery" of the 2000s felt like anything but. And by virtually all measures, the recovery has ended, and the economy is now heading into a potentially severe economic downturn. Without the cushion that a robust jobs expansion may have afforded them, many families are now facing a substantial threat to their living standards.

Wealth

Like wages and income, wealth has a crucial effect on a family's standard of living. Wealth—particularly liquid assets such as checking account balances, stocks, and bonds—can help families cope with financial emergencies related to unemployment or illness. Wealth also makes it easier for families to invest in education and training, start a small business, or fund retirement. More tangible forms of wealth, such as cars, computers, and homes, can directly affect a family's ability to participate fully in work, school, and community life. Chapter 2 touches on the fact that in the United States there is a high degree of correlation in wealth across generations—children of poor parents are much more likely to be poor, and children of wealthy parents are much more likely to be wealthy—pointing to the existence of class barriers that violate a core American principal of equal opportunity for all.

Chapter 5 further investigates wealth in America, uncovering some important features. First, wealth distribution is highly unequal—much more so than the distribution of wages and income that are the focus of other chapters. In 2004 (the most recent data available), the wealthiest 1% of all households controlled a larger share of national wealth than the entire bottom 90%. Average wealth held by the top 1% was close to $15 million, while it was $81,000 for households in the middle fifth of the wealth distribution. The ownership of stocks is particularly unequal, with most Americans having no meaningful stake in the stock market.

Moreover, wealth has become more concentrated at the top over time. Over the 1962-2004 period, the share of wealth held by the bottom 80% of the wealth distribution fell from 19.1%—already an extremely small share—to 15.3%. The decline in wealth share being held by the bottom 80% shifted to the wealthiest 5% over this period.

As the wealthiest continue to thrive, many households are left behind with little or nothing in the way of assets, and often with significant debt. Approximately 30% of households have a net worth of less than $10,000, and approximately one in six households have zero or negative net wealth. Furthermore, only households at the top of the income distribution are likely to be adequately prepared for retirement. For over a quarter of American households, income from Social Security, pensions, and personal savings are expected to replace less than half of their pre-retirement income.

That wealth differs considerably by race is another important observation of this analysis. Median wealth of white households is 10 times that of black households. Home ownership rates also vary considerably by race—less than half of black and Hispanic household own their homes, whereas almost three-quarters of white households do. Many more black households than white households (29.4% vs. 13.0%) have zero or negative net wealth.

Finally, for the typical household, debt has grown much faster than income in the last decade, fueled by increases in mortgages and home equity loans. In 2007, debt was over 140% of disposable personal income. As housing prices collapse, the associated loss of home equity combined with large debt burdens are endangering the economic security of many Americans. Furthermore, for the vast majority of homeowners, home equity is the main source of wealth. For many homeowners approaching retirement, a decline in home equity means the loss of retirement security. The extent of the effects of the bursting of the housing bubble on wealth levels of the typical homeowner remains to be seen, but high average debt levels along with plunging home prices suggest that the damage will be severe and long lasting.

Poverty

While other chapters discuss income, wealth, and mobility trends affecting families of all income classes, Chapter 6 focuses exclusively on families with low incomes.

The first challenge in this analysis is definitional. Dividing lines between income groups are, of course, somewhat arbitrary, and there are many ways to define "low income." The most common definition in American income analysis uses the official poverty line of the U.S. government. While there is some value to this measure—it is consistent over time, and many useful time series employ the official measure—it is widely considered to be an inadequate measure of the concept of poverty.

The concept of poverty, or inadequate income to meet the basic needs given societal norms, involves two basic measurement challenges: defining income and defining the threshold below which families are judged to be poor. Chapter 6 presents measures using various alternative definitions of both income and poverty thresholds. For example, some of the evidence Chapter 6 tracks uses twice the official poverty line as a threshold. While this measure will lead to higher shares of low-income persons compared to the official measure, evidence on basic-needs family budgets suggests it is a much more realistic measure of material well-being.

Chapter 6 also presents measures that adjust income in common sense ways. For example, the official measure ignores the value of food stamps, a near-cash benefit received by some low-income families. Some of the analysis below corrects that, adding the cash value of this benefit back into income. Better measures also subtract taxes paid and add tax credits, since poverty is best understood as a post-tax measure (because families provide for themselves with post-tax income).

Analyzing both the official series, enhanced by a broad set of better, alternative measures, establishes a number of revealing facts about poverty in America:

- Under the official poverty measure, 12.3% of the population, over 36 million people (including 12.8 million children), were poor in 2006. But under an updated, comprehensive measure that corrects the shortcomings of the official measure, many millions more people would be classified as poor. In 2006, the poverty rate was 17.7%, compared to 12.3% under the official measure. That is an extra 16 million poor persons, compared to the official undercount.

- Under either an official or more accurate alternative measure, a larger share of the population was poor or low-income in 2006 than in 2000, despite the economic recovery that occurred over those years. While the 2000s business cycle was not the first in which poverty increased (poverty rose over the 1980s cycle, too), the increase is especially problematic because it occurred despite significantly faster productivity growth than in earlier periods.

- An analysis of the factors responsible for the increase in poverty in the 2000s suggests that greater inequality of income explains almost all of the full percentage-point increase.

- The backsliding against poverty in the 2000s is most notable among the least advantaged, who happened to be the same groups that made the most progress in the 1990s. One particularly disheartening example is young (less than six years old) African American children. Almost half were officially poor in 1995, going down to one-third in 2000. That share has since climbed back up to 38.4%.

- Similarly, the poverty of mother-only families increased significantly over the 2000s. Evidence regarding their incomes and work in the paid labor market suggests that the anti-poverty safety net in the United States has been less counter-cyclical, that is, less effective in reducing economic hardship when the economy and job market are underperforming.

• As low-income policy has come to depend more on paid work as the main pathway out of poverty, the quality of jobs in the low-wage labor market, along with work-supports (public benefits tied to work), have become more important determinants of poverty outcomes. The fact that one-fourth of the labor force earns low wages by one widely used measure thus poses a binding constraint on progress against low incomes.

Health

Much of this book focuses on wages, income, and wealth across the population. Chapter 7, however, examines another important measure of workers' living standards—health care, particularly employer-provided health insurance, life expectancy, and health care costs.

Vast improvements have been made in health insurance coverage and health status over the last half century. Living standards are better in general, and Americans have the advantage of a more-extensive and far-reaching health care system than ever before. These improvements, though true on average, do not reflect the inequality ·in the U.S. health care system. While Americans, on average, are healthier and living longer, many are left without adequate insurance coverage or access to the great advances of our health care system. Nowhere are these disparities clearer than in life expectancies, where the gap between the socioeconomically best- and worst-off grew from 2.8 years in 1980 to 4.5 years in 2000.

Chapter 7 begins with trends in employer-provided health insurance over the 2000s. Since the previous peak, the findings indicate losses in this valuable benefit (down 5.4 percentage points), particularly among the less educated and lower income. Children experienced the greatest declines in employer-provided coverage (down 6.5 percentage points), although they have the greatest advantage of the public health insurance safety net, which has kept many of them from becoming uninsured.

The data suggest growing disparities in access to insurance, health security, and health outcomes by income, race, and education. Other chapters demonstrate the great divide between those at the top of the income distribution and those in the middle and at the bottom. Here, we reveal how those inequalities play out in the health care landscape. While average life span in the United States has grown, much of the increase is due to large gains at the top and minimal gains at the bottom. Disparities also remain by race: the infant mortality rate of blacks is 2.3 times higher than whites.

One area that affects everyone in the United States is rising health costs. The costs to employers and workers of purchasing healthcare coverage and services are growing much faster than overall inflation and wages. Premiums increased 115% from 1999 to 2007 as compared to 29% and 24% increases in workers' earnings and wages, respectively. Rising expenses are shown to incur an increasing burden on working families even for those lucky enough to have insurance on the job.

Chapter 7 concludes with a comparison of health care in the United States with that in several peer countries. While the United States is the only one of its peers without universal health insurance, it spends by far the highest percentage of its GDP on health care. Furthermore, the high spending in the United States does not produce better overall health outcomes relative to other developed countries—for example, the United States has the lowest life expectancy and the highest infant mortality rates of its peers.

International comparisons

Preceding chapters examine current U.S. economic outcomes using historical U.S. outcomes as a benchmark. Chapter 8 compares U.S. economic performance to 19 other industrialized countries belonging to the Paris-based Organization for Economic Cooperation and Development (OECD). These countries are the global peers of the United States—economies facing the same global conditions with respect to trade, investment, technology, the environment, and other factors that shape economic opportunities. The comparison thus provides an independent yardstick for gauging the strengths and weaknesses of the U.S. economy. It also sheds light on the advisability of exporting the "U.S. model" to other economies—specifically, features of the U.S. economy such as weaker unions, lower minimum wages, less-generous social benefits, and lower taxes—as a strategy for addressing the economic problems, real or perceived, among its global peers.

Two dominant themes emerge from Chapter 8. First, while the United States is a very rich country—currently second only to Norway in per capita income—much less of the vast income of the United States is reaching the lower end of the income distribution. The United States has the highest level of inequality of its peers, whether measured in terms of Gini coefficients or the ratio of earnings of high earners (90th percentile) to low earners (10th percentile). The United States also has the highest rate of poverty among its peers, including child poverty—with a child poverty rate over twice as high as the average of the comparison countries. While it is true that many families in the United States are well-off, a great many are not, especially when compared to low- and moderate-income families in other advanced countries.

Second, it is far from a foregone conclusion that economies that have strong welfare states and labor protections are also necessarily less productive, less employment-generating, and less "flexible" than the U.S. economy. Many peer countries with strong unions, high minimum wages, generous social benefits, and high taxes have caught up with, and in many cases surpassed, U.S. productivity while achieving low unemployment levels. Both Norway and the Netherlands, for example, have higher productivity than the United States and lower unemployment rates. It is an important point that so many peer countries have been successful and productive within very different economic models.

Other important insights in Chapter 8:

• The employment rate in the United States was the 10th highest (out of 20 countries).

- A breakdown of per capita income shows that, while U.S. productivity is an important determinant of its high per capita income, an equally significant factor is that Americans simply work more annual hours.

- Vacation time is mandated in every other peer country, whereas there is no mandated vacation time in the United States. On average, full-time employees in the United States work over four weeks more per year than full-time workers in peer countries.

Conclusion

In the popular media, economic experts will endlessly debate the dynamics and causes of the current downturn. They will parse the minutia of the data, with some claiming the worst is over while others argue it is yet to come. Sadly, most of these debates will likely have very little to do with the real economic challenges facing working families today.

The men and women of the American workforce have worked harder and smarter to make the United States a world-class economy. In particular, when considering the 2000s, the U.S. workforce has chalked up some of the most impressive productivity growth rates in decades. And the mantra among economists and policy makers is that, as grows productivity, so shall living standards improve.

Would it were so. The results highlighted in this volume regarding the income of middle-class families, the poverty of low-income families, and the historically off-the-charts measures of inequality tell a very different story. That is, they *describe* a different story. The story behind these unsettling trends—the chain of events and policy changes that brought them about—is more complex than the tale told by a few tables and graphs.

That story has to do with the diminished bargaining power of the American worker. Not simply the story of the factory workers facing competition from cheap imports. Not simply that of the disempowered worker trying to form a union while facing stiff political opposition from above, nor simply the tale of the minimum wage worker facing a sinking real wage floor.

The diminished ability of American workers to claim their fair share of the economy's growth—growth they themselves are creating—includes all of these stories and much more.

The full explanation would also encompass the gifted child whose family's income constraints bar her from any college, much less a top tier one. It includes the willing workers who couldn't find a good job during the expansion and can't find one at all in the downturn. It includes college graduates whose work can now be digitized and sent offshore. It includes workers throughout the pay scale absorbing evermore of the costs and risks of their pension and health care coverage, risks that used to be carried by the employer.

Behind these changes lies the rise of YOYO economics, the "You're-on-Your-Own" philosophy that has guided economic policy makers for too long. The YOYOs are market fundamentalists. They believe that unfettered market outcomes are always the best outcomes, and to nudge the invisible hand is to invite doom (unless you're nudging it toward your well-endowed friends). The YOYOs want to replace Social Security with private retirement accounts, kill the minimum wage, weaken unions, and force everyone to buy health insurance in the individual market. Anything else, they argue, will create the "wrong incentives."

As this book goes to press, we are in a unique position to judge the efficacy of an economic model based on reduced worker bargaining power and YOYO economics. Recent years have provided something rare in economics: a natural experiment. The past few decades, and especially the past few years, reveal the impact of this approach on the living standards of working families. The results are unequivocal: families are ill-served by this set of policies. For the first time in the history of the data going back to 1947, middle-income families were left no better off at the end of this business cycle in 2007 than they were in 2000. Similarly, a smaller share of the adult population was working at the end of this cycle than at the beginning. Despite the YOYO's label of "ownership society" for their set of policies, home-ownership rates are falling, along with net worth. And after making historically rapid progress against minority poverty in the latter 1990s, poverty rates are higher now than in 2000, especially for the least-advantaged among us.

The macro-economy is in serious disrepair, beset by the spillovers from the bursting of a massive housing bubble, high energy prices, and unsustainable levels of household indebtedness. Policy makers are doing some things to stem the damage—rebate checks for households and massive, federally administered liquidity injections to the financial markets (revealingly, the YOYOs turn to government quite aggressively when their backs are against the wall). But unless these policy makers change the underlying notions that have guided their policy making (or lack thereof), these will all be temporary patches.

The State of Working America series has never been a policy manifesto. Elsewhere, we and others have worked to craft the set of ideas designed to reconnect growth and broadly shared prosperity (see the Economic Policy Institute's Agenda for Shared Prosperity for the results of such efforts). But, if we have succeeded in our purpose, this book will stand as a powerful motivator for the type of change we believe these new policies will engender.

The hundreds of graphs and tables that follow paint a portrait of working America. Some sections of the portrait are bright and optimistic, documenting the prodigious efforts of the men and women who keep the biggest and richest economy in the world moving forward. But other sections are less hopeful, as too few of those worker's contributions are fairly rewarded. Some sections even show despairing families, left behind in ways that will painfully reverberate for generations.

We present the whole of the portrait—*The State of Working America 2008-2009*—to you in the pages that follow. We hope it informs, motivates, and inspires you to press for an economy that works best, not for a select few, but for all of us.

Introduction
The promises and the pitfalls of the new economy

When the job market began to contract in 2008, it drew the curtains on a recovery that had seen strong productivity gains that never translated into adequate income growth for most workers. As a result, working families are seeing extraordinary economic challenges. In the first half of 2008 alone, the economy has lost over 400,000 jobs. Unemployment has jumped to 5.5% by mid-2008, up from 4.4% in March 2007, pushing an additional 1.8 million persons onto the jobless rolls. This weakness in the job market has taken a further toll on already lackluster worker earnings, with most paychecks actually losing ground after inflation.

These recent problems have correctly been linked to a confluence of events. The sharp spike in energy costs—up 25% since the middle of last year—is taking a huge bite out of family budgets (and at a time when wage growth is weakening). The bursting of the housing bubble (see Chapter 5) has undercut home values, shutting down a significant source of household wealth. This in turn is fueling millions of defaults on home loans, often followed by foreclosure. Spillovers from the housing crisis have wracked financial markets and frozen credit markets. In turn, diminished borrowing, including from home equity lines of credit, is choking off one of the main sources of consumer spending growth in the 2000s.

Yet working Americans are more productive than ever. Putting aside the current cyclical downturn, the men and women who routinely keep this country running have been working harder and smarter. Since the mid-1990s, the growth of output per hour—or productivity—has undergone a resurgence, and the folks responsible are the 140 million Americans who go to work every day.

When it comes to efficient, profitable production, the men and women of the American workforce have a lot to be proud of. But when it comes to being rewarded for the work they do, the skills they have sharpened, and the contributions they make…well, that's a different story. Their paychecks have been frozen, their health coverage is being cut back, their jobs are at risk of being shipped overseas, and their pensions are more precarious than ever.

For the first time since the Census Bureau began tracking such data back in the mid-1940s, the real incomes of middle-class families are lower at the end of this business cycle than they were when it started. This fact stands as the single most compelling piece of evidence that prosperity is eluding working families.

Where has all that productivity growth been going? As this book extensively documents, it has accrued to the top of the income scale, and the higher up you started out, the better you did. From 1947 to 1979, the top sliver of wage earners made about 20 times that of the bottom 90%. By 2006, that ratio had catapulted to 77 times more.

Yes, there are some smart, hard-working, and creative people up there in that rarified end of the economic stratosphere, and some deserve large returns for their labors. But they cannot possibly be the only ones whose living standards should be boosted in a growing economy. Productivity growth is a result of the efforts of the *whole workforce*, not just the fortunate few. Yes, it reflects the work of the CEOs and CFOs at the top of the corporate ladder. But it also reflects the work of the waitperson who serves those executives their lunch, the construction worker who builds their homes, the manufacturer who forges the steel that girds their corporate headquarters, the home health aide who cares for their aging parents, the cop who protects their beat, and the teacher who educates their kids.

Earlier editions of this book began to explore this split between the promise of productivity growth and the realities of stagnant living standards. But the business cycle of the 2000s was ongoing and thus prevented a conclusive evaluation of how these dynamics would ultimately play out. After all, the 1990s cycle began with a jobless and wageless recovery, too, yet the productivity gains in the latter half of the decade were eventually shared. In fact, the late 1990s was the only time of broad-based gains for American workers since the early 1970s.

This edition, however, will be able to examine the full business cycle of the 2000s and compare it to earlier cycles. The findings show that the 2000s cycle was one of great promise in terms of productivity growth, but the promise of better living standards such growth implied was never realized.

The 2000s: The economy did well, except for the people in it

Table 1 shows a set of indicators regarding economic growth in the 2000s, from the peak cyclical year of 2000 to the most recent cycle's peak in 2007 (data availability permitting). Both real gross domestic product (GDP) and productivity, the main indicators of overall growth, were up solidly by almost 20%. In fact, productivity actually grew faster over the 2000s cycle than over the 1990s (2.5% annually in the 2000-07 period vs. 2.0% in the 1990s).

But once we move below these top-line statistics, the key indicators affecting working families are much less impressive. Job growth was a miserly 4.0%. Note that this is the

TABLE 1 The major indicators of the 2000s economy from the perspective of working families

	2000	2007	Change
GDP (billions of dollars)	$9,817	$11,567	18.0%
Productivity	116	138	19.0%
Jobs (in thousands)	131,785	137,626	4.0%
Unemployment rate	4.0%	4.6%	0.6
Underemployment rate	7.0%	8.3%	1.3
Labor force participation rate	67.1%	66.0%	-1.1
Annual hours*	3,207	3,121	-3.0%
Median weekly earnings of full-time workers+	$694	$695	0.2%
Median income of working-age households+	$58,555	$56,545	-3.4%
Poverty rate	11.3%	12.5%	1.2
Inequality**	21.5	22.9	1.4

+ 2007 dollars.
* Last data point: 2006.
** The share of national income (including cap gains) going to the top 1%.

Source: Authors' analysis of BEA (2008), BLS (2008b), BLS (2008c), CPS March Supplement and U.S. Bureau of Census data.

lowest growth rate on record for a business cycle lasting more than a few months, and one of the main factors behind the weak wage and income growth over the cycle. The unemployment rate was higher in 2007 than in 2000, and the underemployment rate—a more comprehensive measure of joblessness—had doubled.

The 1.1 percentage-point decline in the labor force participation rate—that is, the share of the population working or officially unemployed—is also historically unprecedented over a business cycle. The fact that a smaller share of the population was in the labor force at the end of the cycle has two important implications. First, the unemployment rate would have been higher had more folks not left the job market due to weak job creation (the official jobless rate only counts active job seekers, so those who give up looking are not counted). Second, it implies that the pool of potential workers was significantly underutilized over this cycle. By never regaining the peak levels of labor force participation that prevailed since the latter 1990s, the economy produced less growth and less opportunity for improved living standards than it had in the past.

The fall-out from such job deficits show up clearly in the disappointing wage and income results. Median weekly earnings for full-time workers rose all of $1.00 between 2000 and 2007, creating a huge gap between earnings and productivity growth. Annual hours worked actually declined for middle-income families, and this combination of stagnant earnings and falling hours drove poverty up while income fell for working-age

FIGURE A Job growth: 2000s cycle versus average of past cycles

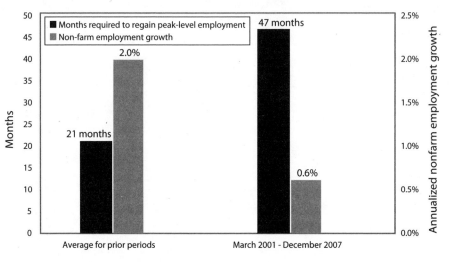

Source: Authors' analysis of BLS (2008b) data.

households. Of course, the growth in national income shown in the first two lines had to go somewhere, and as detailed in a later section, it bypassed the middle of the income scale and flowed almost exclusively to those at the top.

As noted, to understand the disappointing income trends in the 2000s, one has to begin with the economy's unusually weak job growth. Although the official recovery began in late 2001, there ensued a period dubbed the "jobless recovery" in which payrolls did not begin to grow until the autumn of 2003. **Figure A** shows two measures of this weakness: the number of months it took to regain the prior payroll peak, and the yearly rate of job growth. The figure shows that, prior to the 2000s, it took an average of 21 months to regain peak-level employment after a recession, but during the most recent recovery it took over twice that long—nearly four years. It also shows that prior to the 2000s, average employment growth over a business cycle was 2.0% per year, but in the 2000s employment growth averaged only 0.6% annually, well below the rate needed simply to keep up with an ever-increasing population. If the economy had added as many jobs from March 2001 to December 2007 (a period of 81 months) as it had in the first 81 months of the 1990s business cycle (July 1990 to April 1997), it would have added almost *7 million* more jobs than it did.

Weakness in the job market results in weaker income growth. **Table 2** makes this clear by decomposing real middle-family income growth into both earnings and non-labor income (that is, income from capital sources, such as interest, stock dividends, or government transfers in the form of Social Security, unemployment insurance, etc.). Earnings growth can be further broken down into hourly wage rates and annual hours worked in the paid job market. For example, the real income of the middle fifth

TABLE 2 Middle-income growth in the 1990s and 2000s: Earnings and hours

1989-2000

Income growth	10.6%
Earnings	8.8
Annual hours	4.1
Hourly wage	4.7
Other income	1.8

2000-06

Income growth	-1.1%
Earnings	-1.3
Annual hours	-2.2
Hourly wage	1.0
Other income	0.1

Source: Authors' analysis of CPS March Supplement data.

of families grew 10.6% in the 1989-2000 period. Earnings growth explains 8.8% of that 10.6% growth, while other income growth contributed 1.8%. Furthermore, the 8.8% annual earnings growth can be further decomposed: 4.1% came from the growth in annual hours and 4.7% from that of hourly wages.

The differences between the two cycles are stark. Over the 1990s, real middle incomes grew by 10.6%, lifted by increases in both hours of work and by faster hourly wage growth.

The cost to family income from the weak job market of the 2000s is apparent in the bottom panel of Table 2. The slight decline (1.1%) in real family income in the 2000s is more than explained by the decline in hours worked, which shaved 2.2% off of the growth of middle incomes. Had annual hours worked simply remained flat for these groups, their incomes would have risen slightly; had their hours grown as much as in the 1990s, their incomes would have grown by 5.0%, an increase of $3,800 over their actual income in this period.

These results for the 2000s led to a historically unique outcome. For the first time since this data series began in the mid-1940s, it appears based on preliminary estimates that median family income for working-age household failed to regain its prior peak. That is, despite hundreds of billions of dollars of added growth to the economy, the real value of the median family's income was lower at the end of this cycle than at the beginning. (Even if our forecast is off by as much as a few percent, real median family income would only regain or slightly surpass its prior peak, an extremely unsatisfactory benchmark, especially in the productivity-rich recovery of the 2000s.)

FIGURE B Jobs and joblessness, January 2007-June 2008

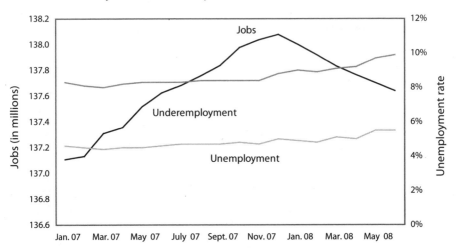

Source: BLS (2008b, 2008c) data.

The downturn's effect on working families

As shown in **Figure B**, the total number of jobs is down by over 400,000 since peaking in December 2007, and unemployment is up to 5.5% from its low point of 4.4% in March of 2007, an addition of 1.8 million to the jobless rolls. The lack of job creation has led to longer spells of joblessness, a problem that persisted throughout this expansion (as discussed in Chapter 4). By June 2008, 18% of the unemployed had been so for at least half of a year.

Unfortunately, the unemployment rate is an inadequate gauge of labor market weakness right now for two reasons. First, by mid-2008, many employers were adjusting their workforces more by cutting back on hours rather than by layoffs, a trend the unemployment rate doesn't take into account. Second, recall that the unemployment rate fails to count those jobless persons who give up looking for work. This is important in the current context, because as shown in Table 1 above, the labor force participation rate never regained its prior peak over the recent cycle. This decline suggests that the unemployment rate was misleading because jobless individuals simply left the labor market and thus were not factored into the unemployment rate.

The underemployment rate (shown above the unemployment rate in Figure B) not only takes into account the unemployed, but also includes the large number—over five million in mid-2008—of part-time workers who would rather have full-time jobs but cannot find them. It also includes so-called discouraged workers, a group that gave up looking for work due to slack job opportunities. As shown in the figure, underemployment has risen faster than unemployment, and was just about 10% in June 2008.

These weaknesses in the job market, in tandem with energy-induced spikes in inflation, are taking a further toll on wage growth. **Figure C** shows the annual growth rates by three wage measures. The first bar is the average hourly wage of the 80% of the workforce in blue-collar or non-managerial jobs; the second bar is this group's weekly paycheck; and the third bar is a measure of average compensation—wages plus benefits—for all workers. As of late 2007, all three series are falling in real terms. Note that weekly earnings—the middle bar—are falling more quickly than hourly earnings, due to declining weekly hours worked. Also, total compensation is falling particularly quickly, as both wages and benefits are lagging inflation going into this downturn.

Much is made of the fact that as of this writing, the economy has only recorded one quarter in which real GDP contracted (2007q4), while the unofficial definition of recession is two consecutive quarters of real GDP declines. But as long as the economy is growing below trend—that is, real GDP is growing less than a 3% annual rate, as has been the case since the last quarter of 2007 and as is likely to continue until at least mid-2009—unemployment will continue to rise. One forecast, by the investment bank Goldman Sachs (2008), expects the unemployment rate to climb to 6.4% by the end of 2009.

Historically, such increases in joblessness have translated into declining incomes, due to job losses and diminished hours of work and due to a slackening of pressure on wage growth.

FIGURE C Real paychecks falling in the downturn

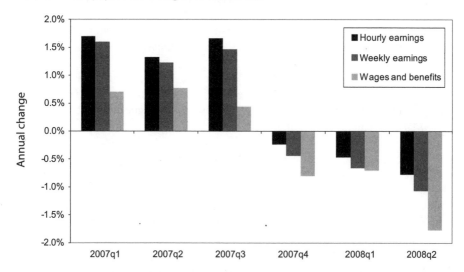

Source: Authors' analysis of BLS (2008b, 2008d) data.

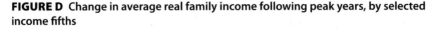

FIGURE D Change in average real family income following peak years, by selected income fifths

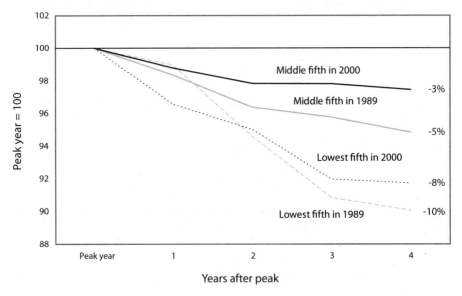

Source: Authors' analysis of U.S. Census Bureau data.

Figure D shows how this dynamic has played out in the last two recessions. The figure plots the percentage losses for low- and middle-income families in the first few years of each recession. The horizontal axis marks the years out from the peak. Thus, for the 1990-91 recession, the "peak year" was 1989, and for the 2001 recession the peak year was 2000.

Percentage losses were larger for low-income families than for middle-income families. In the early 1990s downturn, average income fell 10% for the bottom fifth over these years (1989-93) and about half that for the middle fifth. In the 2000s (2000-04), the pattern was similar, with real income losses of about 8% for the lowest fifth and 3% for the middle.

Economists have quantified the relationship between rising unemployment and falling real incomes for the various income classes shown in the Figure D. Applying those estimates to the unemployment forecast of 6.4% noted above reveals real predicted income losses that follow the historical pattern, with incomes in the bottom fifth dropping about 5%, and middle incomes falling about 4% (**Figure E**).

We stress that we cannot know how accurate these predictions will turn out to be, but they do closely follow the historical patterns of the toll that recessions take on family incomes. We are especially confident of the *relative magnitudes* of these losses: the most economically vulnerable families take the biggest recessionary hits.

FIGURE E Forecasted real income losses given rising unemployment, 2006-09

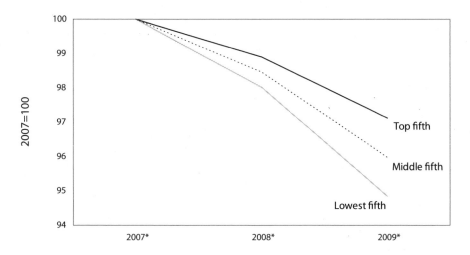

* Forecast based on rising unemployment rates.

Source: Authors' analysis of U.S. Census data.

Income flowed uphill?

Although the typical family's income failed to improve over the last business cycle, this was not the case for better-off families. In fact, most of the income growth has flowed to those at the very top of the income scale, and this has been true for each of two types of market-based incomes: wages and salaries from employment, and capital incomes (e.g., dividend, capital gain, and interest income) from wealth. Moreover, the higher returns flowing to wealth have expanded the importance of capital incomes overall, a trend that fuels greater income inequality because the vast majority of capital income accrues to the very best-off families.

Often, economists analyze income trends by dividing families up into equal fifths by income level, and tracking the shares of income going to each fifth. Chapter 1 does this, and finds that the share going to the richest fifth of families in 2007 was 47.3%, scholarly research undertaken over the last few years has revealed that the growth in inequality has been driven not by the families in the top 20%, but by those in the very highest reaches of the top fifth. It turns out that it is the top 1%—and even the top one-thousandth (or 0.1%) that are scooping up the income.

Table 3 presents the average income levels and income shares of the various groups comprising the upper 10% of the income distribution, the 14.8 million households (of 148.4 million in the nation) who earned over $107,666 in 2006 (shown in 2007 dollars) and received over half the nation's income that year. Of particular note is **Table 3**'s detailed breakdown of those in the upper 1% (exceeding $393,000, and averaging about $1.3 million), including the upper one of 1,000 households (the sum of the last two columns), and the upper one of 10,000 families (i.e., the last column, 99.99 to 100.0).

Over the longest period shown, from 1979 to 2006 those in the 90-95th percentiles saw their incomes grow a considerable 32.0%, but that was less than one-sixth the 203.7% income growth for the top 1%. When you break that top 1% down even further, the upper-most reaches (the top 1/10,000) had incomes grow by 425% to $30.5 million in 2006. This pattern of growth led the top 1% to more than double their share of income from 10.0% in 1979 to 22.9% in 2006, with the top-most sliver expanding

TABLE 3 Income growth and income shares of the top 10% of earners, 1979-2006

Year	Bottom half of top 10% 90th-95th	Next 4% 95th-99th	Top 1% 99th-99.5	99.5-99.9	99.9-99.99	99.99-100	Total
Incomes (thousands of $2007)*							
1979	$95.4	$137.2	$241.0	$387.9	$971.0	$5,805.8	$421.1
1989	104.6	159.3	308.8	575.4	1,784.8	11,123.4	656.5
2000	124.6	213.6	460.7	931.6	3,653.3	28,738.5	1,219.2
2002	117.5	190.1	382.8	712.2	2,333.1	15,712.2	843.4
2006	125.9	216.6	478.6	984.1	3,801.6	30,478.8	1,278.8
1979-2006	32.0%	57.9%	98.6%	153.7%	291.5%	425.0%	203.7%
1989-2006	20.4	36.0	55.0	71.0	113.0	174.0	94.8
2000-06	1.0	1.4	3.9	5.6	4.1	6.1	4.9
2000-02	-5.7	-11.0	-16.9	-23.5	-36.1	-45.3	-30.8
2002-06	7.1	13.9	25.0	38.2	62.9	94.0	51.6
Income shares							
1979	11.3	13.0	2.8	3.7	2.1	1.4	10.0
1989	11.5	14.1	3.4	5.1	3.5	2.5	14.5
2000	11.0	15.1	4.1	6.6	5.8	5.1	21.5
2006	11.3	15.5	4.3	7.0	6.1	5.5	22.9
Change 1979-2006	0.0	2.5	1.4	3.4	4.1	4.1	13.0

* Incomes as reported on tax returns such as wages and salaries, pensions received, profits from businesses, capital income such as dividends, interest, or rents, and realized capital gains; but excluding government transfers such as Social Security retirement benefits or unemployment compensation.

Source: Authors' analysis of Pikkety and Saez (2003) updates.

their income share nearly four-fold from 1.4% to 5.5%. In contrast, households below the 95th percentile saw no change, and those below the 90th percentile saw a decline in their income shares. *In other words, there has been a huge income redistribution from the bottom 90% to the upper 5%, particularly to the upper 1%.* The majority of the gains to the upper 1% actually accrued to the upper 0.1%, whose income shares grew by 8.2 percentage points from 1979-2006. This *increase* in the share of total income gained by the upper 0.1% represents more income than the entire bottom fifth of households earns in a year (see Chapter 1) and equals one in every six dollars earned by the bottom 90% of households.

This unbalanced pattern of income growth began in the 1980s and prevailed into the 1990s (though the latter part of this decade was the only time over the last 30 years in which incomes grew for all groups). The incomes of the very well-off reached remarkable levels by 2000, fueled by the stock market boom. The bursting of the stock market bubble and the fall-off in stock options (some of which are measured as "wages") caused the incomes at the top to tumble from 2000 to 2002 (see the row 2000-02 in (**Table 3**). The rapid 51.6% income growth for the top 1% in the recovery from 2002 to 2006 allowed this group to return to and exceed the very high incomes they reached at the end of the 1990s. And remember, while all of these gains were made by the top-most sliver, the typical family ended up with *lower income* at the end of the business cycle in 2007 than in 2000.

Another way to portray the unbalanced income growth is to present, as **Table 4** does for the 1989-2006 period, the shares of the income growth that each group received. The table also lists each group's income share in 1989 as a benchmark because receiving a larger share of the income growth than your current income share indicates that a group's overall share of income will rise. For instance, the top 10% received 90.9% of all of the income growth in this period, more than double their 40.1% share of income at the start in 1989. More impressive is that the top 1% received 59% of all

TABLE 4 Share of income growth by income group, 1989-2006

	Share of income growth, 1989-2006	Income share in 1989
Top 10%	90.9%	40.1%
Top 1.0%	59.0	14.5
Top 0.1%	35.6	6.0
Remaining top 1% (99.0-99.9)	23.6	8.5
Next 4%	21.7	14.1
Next 5%	10.1	11.5
Bottom 90%	9.1	59.9

Source: Authors' analysis of Pikkety and Saez (2003) update.

FIGURE F Growth in annual earnings by wage group, 1979-2006

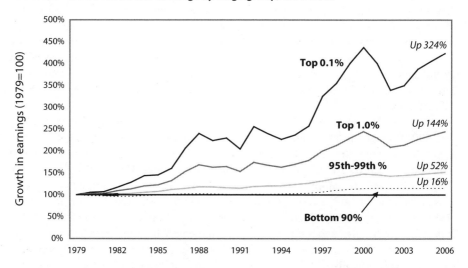

Source: Authors' analysis of Social Security wage data and Kopczuk, Saez, and Song (2007).

FIGURE G Ratio of wages of highest earners to those of bottom 90%, 1947-2006

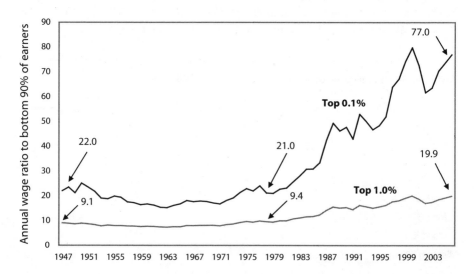

Source: Authors' analysis of Social Security wage data and Kopczuk, Saez, and Song (2007).

of the income growth from 1989 to 2006 even though this group had only 14.5% of all income in 1989. The top sliver of 0.1%, the top 1/1,000th (148,000 households) received more than a third of all the income growth in this period.

As noted at the outset, this trend reflects how income from wealth (i.e., capital income) has grown much faster than that from employment. Two trends relating to capital income have contributed to this disparity. One is that the receipt of capital income has become far more concentrated, according to the Congressional Budget Office. Whereas the top 1% received 34.2% of all capital income in 1979, that share rose to 58.6% by 2000, and again to 65.3% in 2005 (the latest year for these data). Thus, the top 1% roughly doubled its share of capital income between 1979 and 2005. Correspondingly, the share of capital income going to the bottom 90% declined from 36.7% in 1979 to just 15.1% in 2005.

The second trend is that higher rates of return to wealth have expanded the share of capital income among personal income, which in turn reflects the greater capital income (profits and interest) generated in the corporate sector. For instance, capital income such as interest and dividend income and from realized capital gains (the sale of assets) comprised 18.0% of personal market-based income in 1979 but a heftier 24.2% by 2007. This necessarily generates greater income inequality because most capital income is received by those who are well-off. Likewise, the share of income in the corporate sector going to capital income in the recent recovery was the highest in nearly 40 years: in the 2004-07 recovery, capital income accounted for 22.3% of corporate income, a jump from its 19.2% share in the 1976-79 recovery. The share going to compensation was correspondingly at a low point. The resulting historically high returns to capital are associated with the average worker's compensation being 4.4% lower and the equivalent of transferring $206 billion dollars annually from labor compensation to capital incomes.

There has also been extraordinarily unequal growth of wage and salary incomes, as is explored in Chapter 3. An analysis of social security data on annual earnings (**Figure F**) shows that the bottom 90% of wage earners saw their annual earnings grow by a total of 15.6% from 1979 to 2006, with almost all of that growth occurring in the interval between 1995 and 2000. In contrast, the earnings of the upper 1% of earners rocketed upward 144.4%, despite a dip in the early 2000s (reflecting the lower realized stock options that are counted as "wages"). Whereas the upper 1% earned an annual salary (in 2007 dollars) of $235,141 in 1979, their salary grew to $576,141 by 2006. Slicing the workforce even more thinly, one can see that the top 0.1% fared even better, raising their 1979 wages of $525,000 by 323.6% to $2,224,000 in 2006.

Figure G shows the contrasting wage growth between the very highest earners and the vast majority of workers by showing the ratios of the earnings of the top 1% and top 0.1% to those of the bottom 90%. The ratio of the wage income of the top 1% of earners to the wage income of the bottom 90% more than doubled between 1979 and 2006 from 9.4 to 19.9-to-1. In contrast there was relatively little change in that ratio over the period from 1947 to 1979. The ratio of the wages of the top 0.1% to those of the bottom 90% has grown even faster: in 2006 the upper one-thousandth earned 77.0 times as much as the average person in the bottom 90%, a ratio that was just 21.0 in 1979. In other words,

FIGURE H Productivity and compensation: Four recoveries

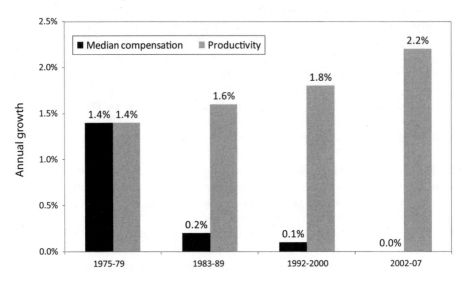

Source: BLS and authors' analysis of BLS and BEA (2008) data.

in 1979 it took the highest paid earners 12.4 days to earn what an average earner did in a year, but by 2006 that feat was accomplished in just 3.4 days.

Figure H shows another dimension of the evolution of earnings inequality by comparing the annual growth rate of productivity and real median compensation over four economic recoveries. Though the productivity/wage gap has been evolving since the 1980s, the gap in the 2002-07 recovery was the largest. Over the 1970s recovery, both productivity and median compensation grew apace, at 1.4% per year. The gap then steadily grew over each ensuing recovery until the most recent case—2002-07— when median compensation was flat and productivity grew 2.2% per year. It is a stark example of the extent to which pay *and* benefits eluded middle-earning workers in the 2000s, even as they posted solid efficiency gains.

Income inequality and income mobility

Inequality at the levels detailed above poses a major economic problem
First, there is the productivity/income split. If growth eludes all but those at the top, the actual living standards of many other families will fall, even as the economy is expanding. Besides failing to keep up with rising costs, these families may lack the resources to invest in their children's future. It is no coincidence that over this very period, the challenge of paying for a college education has been identified as a prominent factor behind the middle-class squeeze.

This aspect of inequality poses a high potential cost for families and society. It is often said that Americans do not object to unequal outcomes, only to unequal opportunities. But what if unequal outcomes themselves lead to diminished opportunities?

If some people are a lot more economically successful than others—either because they work harder, make better choices, or are just plain smarter—so be it. We may, as a society, choose to adjust those outcomes through taxes and transfers, but most would not consider such outcomes unjust. But if an economy favors those who are not necessarily more meritorious but are instead born wealthier, more connected, more powerful, whiter, male, etc., then this seems like a violation of the basic American value of equal opportunity. If growth flows mostly to those at the top of the scale, then it is possible that children from these fortunate households will have greater access to quality education relative to children from less well-placed families. If inequality means that some neighborhoods get parks and libraries while others do not, this too restricts opportunity. If quality health care is more accessible to the haves than to the have-nots, then the latter face a mobility barrier born of inequality.

If income concentration leads to a level of political influence that tilts against the have-nots, this too will reduce opportunity and lower the rate of economic mobility. If, to take a recent example, opportunity-enhancing programs for disadvantaged children— such as Head Start or the State Children's Health Insurance Program (SCHIP)—are cut

FIGURE I How likely is it that a son of a low-wage father will attain higher earnings?

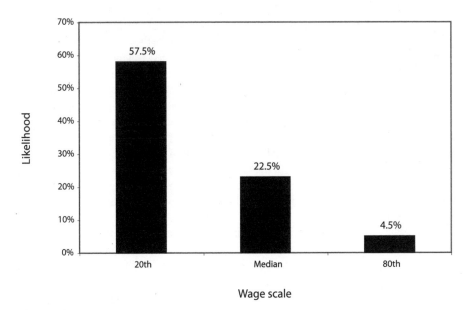

Source: Unpublished data provided by Gary Solon.

in order to maintain high-end tax cuts, then it chips away that much more at the prospect of economic mobility.

Some interesting research has been brought to bear on these concerns. One strain of this work asks about intergenerational mobility: to what extent are one generation's economic outcomes predicted by their parent's? Two main findings from this research are that, first, significant correlations exist—that is, your economic position is not random but rather linked to your parents' position—and, second, that there is less generational mobility in America than in other advanced economies.

One recent study cited in Chapter 2 examines the correlation between parents and children in the United States and finds that it would take a poor family of four with two children approximately nine to 10 generations—over 200 years—to achieve the income of the middle-income four-person family. Were the correlation half that size, meaning income differences were half as persistent across generations, it would still take four to five generations, on average, for the poor family to catch up to the middle.

The results from a similar study cited in Chapter 2 are shown in **Figure I**, which shows the likelihood of a son of a low-earning father ending up in a higher earnings class as an adult. There is considerable persistence between the earnings of fathers and sons. For example, there is almost a 60% chance that the son of a low-earning father would end up in the lowest fifth of the wage scale, and less than a 5% chance that he would end up with earnings above the 80th percentile.

Of course, educational opportunities play a role in shaping these intergenerational outcomes, and the evidence is clear: children from wealthy families have much greater access to top-tier universities than kids from low-income families, *even when controlling for innate skills*. Each set of bars in **Figure J** shows the probability of completing college for children based on both family income and their math test scores in eighth grade. For example, the first set of bars (for the students with the lowest test scores) shows that 3% of students with both low scores and low incomes completed college, while 30% of low-scoring children from high-income families managed to complete college.

The fact that each set of bars has an upward gradient shows that the current system is far from a pure meritocracy: at every level of test scores, higher income led to higher completion rates. The first set of bars, for example, shows that even among the highest-scoring students in eighth grade, only 29% of those from low-income families finished college, compared with 74% of those wealthiest families. In fact, this 29% share is about identical to the completion rates of low-scoring, high-income students (30%), shown in the third set of bars. Simply put, high-scoring children from low-income families are no more likely to complete college than low-scoring, wealthy children.

This educational barrier places profound limits on income mobility. Of those adults who grew up in low-income families but managed to earn a college degree, only 16% ended up in the bottom fifth of the income scale as adults. But for those who failed to graduate college, the share that started out and ended up in the bottom fifth was 45%. In other words, among children who grew up in low-income families, those who failed to graduate college were almost three times more likely to still be in the bottom fifth as adults compared to the children who completed college.

FIGURE J College completion by income status and test scores

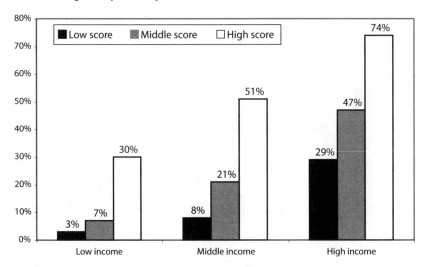

Source: Fox, Connolly, and Snyder (2005).

Thus, the extent of income mobility across generations clearly helps determine the living standards of American families. It is a key determinant of how many generations a family will be stuck at the low end of the income scale, or snuggly ensconced at the high end. American folklore often emphasizes the rags-to-riches, Horatio Alger stories, which suggest that anyone with the gumption and smarts to prevail can lift themselves up by their bootstraps and climb the income scale in a generation. In the real world, there is much less mobility.

Still, popular wisdom would suggest that there is probably more mobility in America compared with the advanced economies in Europe. Shouldn't their more-extensive social protections and less-freewheeling approach to economic policy dampen the entrepreneurial spark that gives birth to the American rags-to-riches cliché? To the contrary: one of the most surprising findings of this research is that the opposite is true. Parents' economic positions in these countries are less correlated with their children's later income, meaning there is more intergenerational mobility there than in the United States (**Figure K**).

Figure K shows the same earnings correlations between fathers and sons discussed above, but for various countries (unfortunately, much less research has been done with regards to daughters; we show this research also in Chapter 2). Only the United Kingdom has a slightly higher correlation. In all of the other countries, children's ultimate economic position is less dependent on that of their family of origin.

What explains the United States' relative lack of mobility? Certainly unequal education opportunities and historical discrimination play a role. For example, there are

FIGURE K Intergenerational correlations, father and son, U.S. and Europe

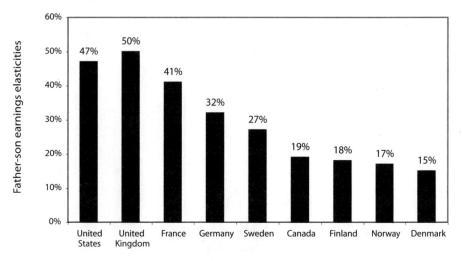

Source: Corak (2006).

very steep mobility barriers facing African Americans in their own chances of moving up the income ladder, especially when compared to whites. One study shows that almost two-thirds (63%) of black children who start out in the bottom fourth of the income scale remain there as adults, compared to half that share for white children. Another deeply disturbing study finds that 45% of African American children who start out in middle-income families experience significant downward mobility, ending up in poor

TABLE 5 Economic indicators for African Americans, Hispanics, and all workers, 1989-2006/7

	All		African American		Hispanic	
Change in:	*1990s*	*2000s*	*1990s*	*2000s*	*1990s*	*2000s*
Unemployment rate	-1.3%	0.6%	-3.8%	0.7%	-2.3%	-0.1%
Employment-to-population ratio	1.4	0.4	4.0	-2.5	3.5	-0.8
Median income	10.6	-1.7	24.3	-0.1	9.6	-2.2
Poverty rate, all	-1.5	1.2	-8.2	1.8	-4.7	0.0
Poverty rate, kids under 6	-5.3	3.4	-16.9	6.7	-9.9	2.2

Source: Authors' analysis of U.S. Census Bureau and BLS data.

families (in the bottom fifth of the income scale) as adults, compared to 16% for whites. (See Chapter 2 for a further discussion.)

It also seems clear that inequality itself is playing an important role in reducing opportunity and thus, mobility. As income and wealth become more concentrated in American society, so do access to higher education, to political power, to good neighborhoods with good schools, to decent health care, and ultimately, to opportunity itself. The previous figure offers strong support for this hypothesis, because the countries with the most-aggressive policies to offset market inequalities, such as the Scandinavian countries, also have the most mobility.

If, as we suspect, the United States' excessively high levels of inequality are reducing opportunity and thus constricting mobility, then the structure of our economy is actively violating a core American principle: that of fair opportunity for all. If market forces are failing to provide fair opportunities, and there is ample evidence to support this claim, then policy intervention to reset the balance is essential.

The racial and ethnic dimension

This section continues to examine the stark difference in outcomes for minorities, particularly how they have fared in the 2000s, and how their experience in the current downturn might differ from the past.

Table 5 examines changes in a few key variables, comparing the 1990s cycle with that of the 2000s for all persons, African Americans, and Hispanics. In every case, outcomes in the 2000s were less favorable, particularly for African Americans. As noted earlier, unemployment rose in the 2000-07 period, after falling, as usual, in the 1990s. But the changes for minorities are quite a bit larger than for the overall group. For example, unemployment rose about the same amount for blacks as for everyone else in the 2000s, but the decline in the jobless rate was much greater for blacks in the 1990s: -3.8 points vs. -1.3. This progress mostly occurred in the second half of the 1990s, as the economy moved towards full employment. In fact, a persistent finding throughout this book is that truly tight labor markets make a large, positive difference in the economic outcomes of minorities.

Employment rate comparisons reveal that, while the share of the population employed expanded by 1.4 percentage points over the 1990s cycle, it fell back by that same amount in the weaker jobs cycle of the 2000s. But for blacks and Hispanics, the differences are much larger. In fact, the black employment rate in 2000—60.9%—was the highest on record going back to the early 1970s, underscoring the notion that there are many more job opportunities for minorities in full employment job markets. Similarly, the Hispanic employment rate of 65.7% was also a historical peak. For African Americans, however, the decline in employment in the 2000s was more severe than for all or for Hispanics.

The same patterns are evident for real median income trends and poverty rates. Note, in particular, the historically very large growth in median income for African American families in the 1990s, a trend explored in greater detail in Chapter 1. Once again, the gains reversed in the 2000s.

The table breaks out the poverty of young children because poverty is such a devastating factor for this population, with troubling long-term consequences (explored further in Chapter 6). Quite dramatic progress was made against poverty in the 1990s, especially for blacks and Hispanics. For young black children, for example, poverty fell from about 50% in 1989 to about 33% in 2000. Now, we fully recognize that ending up with a third of young children in poverty is not exactly a success story, but those years saw true income progress and the trend moving in the right direction. Yet, for these highly economically vulnerable children, one-third of that dramatic progress was erased in the 2000s.

Sociologist Algernon Austin has examined the potential impact of the current downturn of African Americans. His work suggests that, as the downturn proceeds, unemployment will likely continue rising, as layoffs occur and labor force growth proceeds apace, while job creation remains stalled. One must also keep in mind that minority rates are consistently above the overall rate. For example, while the overall rate was 4.6% in 2007, black unemployment was 8.3%, and the white rate was 4.1% (the black rate tends to consistently be twice that of whites). Using these historical relationships between overall rates and those of African Americans, the forecasts of an overall rate of 6.4% in 2009 suggests that black unemployment will jump to 11.0%.

As shown in Figure E, this increase in unemployment is expected to lead to declines in income. Since unemployment is a lagging indicator—that is it follows in the wake of some other indicators—it tends to recover well after a recession is over (unemployment rose for over a year and a half after the last recession ended in late 2001). This dynamic means incomes also take awhile to reverse course and begin rising in real terms. As a result, median family income could easily fall 4% in the coming downturn. For African Americans, however, the decline would be about 6%, leaving the average African American family $2,400 poorer.

Conclusion

In the popular media, economic experts will endlessly debate the dynamics and causes of the current downturn. They will parse the minutia of the data, with some claiming the worst is over while others argue it is yet to come. Sadly, most of these debates will likely have very little to do with the real economic challenges facing working families today.

As we have documented in this introduction and in the chapters that follow, the men and women of the American workforce have worked harder and smarter to make the United States a world-class economy. In particular, when considering the 2000s, the U.S. workforce has chalked up some of the most impressive productivity growth rates in decades. And the mantra among economists and policy makers is that, as grows productivity, so shall living standards improve.

Would it were so. The results highlighted in this volume regarding the income of middle-class families, the poverty of low-income families, and the historically off-the-charts measures of inequality tell a very different story. That is, they *describe* a different story. The story behind these unsettling trends—the chain of events and policy changes that brought them about—is more complex than the tale told by a few tables and graphs.

That story has to do with the diminished bargaining power of the American worker. Not simply the story of the factory workers facing competition from cheap imports. Not simply that of the disempowered worker trying to form a union while facing threats and hostility from above, nor simply the tale of the minimum wage worker facing a sinking real wage floor.

The diminished ability of American workers to claim their fair share of the economy's growth—growth they themselves are creating—includes all of these stories and much more.

The full explanation would also encompass the gifted child whose family's income constraints bar her from any college, much less a top tier one. It includes the willing workers who couldn't find a good job during the expansion and can't find one at all in the downturn. It includes college graduates whose work can now be digitized and sent offshore. It includes workers throughout the pay scale absorbing ever more of the costs and risks of their pension and health care coverage, risks that used to be carried by the employer.

Behind these changes lies the rise of YOYO economics, the "You're-on-Your-Own" philosophy that has guided economic policy makers for too long. The YOYOs are market fundamentalists. They believe that unfettered market outcomes are always the best outcomes, and to nudge the invisible hand is to invite doom (unless you're nudging it toward your well-endowed friends). The YOYOs want to replace Social Security with private retirement accounts, kill the minimum wage, weaken unions, and force everyone to buy health insurance in the individual market. Anything else, they argue, will create the "wrong incentives."

As this book goes to press, we are in a unique position to judge the efficacy of an economic model based on reduced worker bargaining power and YOYO economics. Recent years have provided something rare in economics: a natural experiment. The past few decades, and especially the past few years, reveal the impact of this approach on the living standards of working families. As shown above and in much greater detail throughout this edition, the results are unequivocal: families are ill-served by this set of policies. For the first time in the history of the data going back to 1947, working-age middle-income families were left no better off at the end of this business cycle in 2007 than they were at its start in 2000. Similarly, a smaller share of the adult population was working at the end of this cycle than at the beginning. Despite the YOYO's label of "ownership society" for their set of policies, home-ownership rates are falling, along with net worth. And after making historically rapid progress against minority poverty in the latter 1990s, poverty rates are higher now than in 2000, especially for the least-advantaged among us.

The macro-economy is in serious disrepair, beset by the spillovers from the bursting of a massive housing bubble, high energy prices, and unsustainable levels of household indebtedness. Policy makers are doing some things to stem the damage—rebate checks for households and massive, federally administered liquidity injections to the financial markets (revealingly, the YOYOs turn to government quite aggressively when their backs are against the wall). But unless these policy makers change the underlying notions that have guided their policy making (or lack thereof), these will all be temporary patches.

The State of Working America series has never been a policy manifesto. Elsewhere, we and others have worked to craft a set of ideas designed to reconnect growth and broadly shared prosperity (see the Economic Policy Institute's *Agenda for Shared Prosperity* for the results of such efforts). But, if we have succeeded in our purpose, this book will stand as a powerful motivator for the type of change we believe these new policies will engender.

The hundreds of graphs and tables that follow paint a portrait of working America. Some sections of the portrait are bright and optimistic, documenting the prodigious efforts of the men and women who keep the biggest and richest economy in the world moving forward. But other sections are less hopeful, as too few of those worker's contributions are fairly rewarded. Some sections even show despairing families, left behind in ways that will painfully reverberate for generations.

We present the whole of the portrait—*The State of Working America 2008/2009*—to you in the pages that follow. We hope it informs, motivates, and inspires you to press for an economy that works best, not for a select few, but for all of us.

Documentation and methodology

Documentation

The comprehensive portrait presented in this book of changes over time in incomes, taxes, wages, employment, wealth, poverty, and other indicators of economic performance and well-being relies almost exclusively on data in the tables and figures. Consequently, the documentation of our analysis is essentially the documentation of the tables and figures. For each, an abbreviated source notation appears at the bottom, and complete documentation is contained in the Table Notes and Figure Notes found at the back of the book. This system of documentation allows us to omit distracting footnotes and long citations within the text and tables.

The abbreviated source notation at the bottom of each figure and table is intended to inform the reader of the general source of our data and to give due credit to the authors and agencies whose data we are presenting. We have three categories of designations for these abbreviated sources. In instances where we directly reproduce other people's work, we provide an "author/year" reference to the bibliography. Where we present our own computations based on other people's work, the source line reads "Authors' analysis of author (year)." In these instances we have made computations that do not appear in the original work and want to hold the original authors (or agencies) blameless for any errors or interpretations. Our third category is simply "Authors' analysis," which indicates that the data presented are from our original analysis of microdata (such as much of the wage analysis) or our computations from published (usually government) data. We use this source notation when presenting descriptive trends from government income, employment, or other data, since we have made judgments about the appropriate time periods or other matters for the analysis that the source agencies have not made.

Time periods

Economic indicators fluctuate considerably with short-term swings in the business cycle. For example, incomes tend to fall in recessions and rise during expansions. Therefore, economists usually compare business cycle peaks with other peaks and compare troughs with other troughs so as not to mix apples and oranges. In this book, we examine changes between business cycle peaks. The initial year for many tables is 1947, with intermediate years of 1967, 1973, 1979, 1989, and 2000, all of which were business cycle peaks (at least in terms of having low unemployment). We also present data for the latest full year for which data are available (2007, when available) to show the changes over the recent business cycle, which we assume ended in 2007 (at least using annual data).

In some tables, we also separately present trends for the 1995-2000 period in order to highlight the differences between those years and those of the early 1990s (or, more precisely, 1989-95) and the recent business cycle. This departs from the convention of presenting only business-cycle comparisons (e.g., comparing 1979-89 to 1989-2000 trends) or comparisons of recoveries. We depart from the convention because there was a marked shift in a wide variety of trends after 1995, and it is important to understand and explain these trends.

Growth rates and rounding

Since business cycles differ in length, we usually present the annual growth rates in each period rather than the total growth. We also present compound annual growth rates rather than simple annual rates. Compound annual growth rates are just like compound interest on a bank loan: the rate is compounded continuously rather than yearly. In some circumstances, as noted in the tables, we have used log annual growth rates. This is done to permit decompositions. In presenting the data we round the numbers, usually to one decimal place, but we use unrounded data to compute growth rates, percentage shares, and so on. Therefore, it is not always possible to exactly replicate our calculations by using the data in the table. In some circumstances, this leads to an appearance of errors in the tables. For instance, we frequently present shares of the population (or families) at different points in time and compute changes in these shares. Because our computations are based on the "unrounded" data, the change in shares presented in a table may not match the difference in the actual shares. Such rounding errors are always small, however, and never change the conclusions of the analysis.

Adjusting for inflation

In most popular discussions, the Consumer Price Index for All Urban Consumers (CPI-U), often called simply the consumer price index, is used to adjust dollar values for inflation. However, some analysts hold that the CPI-U overstated inflation in the late 1970s and early 1980s by measuring housing costs inappropriately. The methodology for the CPI-U from 1983 onward was revised to address these objections. Other changes were introduced into the CPI in the mid-1990s but not incorporated into the historical series. Not all agree that these revisions are appropriate. We chose not to use the CPI-U so as to avoid any impression that this report overstates the decline in wages and understates the growth in family incomes over the last few decades.

Instead of the CPI-U, we adjust dollar values for inflation using the CPI-U-RS index. This index uses the new methodology for housing inflation over the entire 1967-2007 period and incorporates the 1990s changes into the historical series (though not before 1978, which makes economic performance in the years after 1978 falsely look better than the earlier years). The CPI-U-RS is now used by the Census Bureau in its presentations of real income data. Because it is not available for years before 1978, we extrapolate the CPI-U-RS back to earlier years based on inflation as measured by the CPI-U.

In our analysis of poverty in Chapter 6, however, we generally use the CPI-U rather than the CPI-U-RS, since Chapter 6 draws heavily from Census Bureau publications that use the CPI-U. Moreover, the net effect of all of the criticisms of the measurement of poverty is that current methods understate poverty. Switching to the CPI-U-RS without incorporating other revisions (i.e., revising the actual poverty standard) would lead to an even greater understatement and would be a very selective intervention to improve the poverty measurement. (A fuller discussion of these issues appears in Chapter 6.)

Household heads

We often categorize families by the age or the race/ethnic group of the "household head," that is, the person in whose name the home is owned or rented. If the home is owned jointly by a married couple, either spouse may be designated the household head. Every family has a single household head.

Hispanics

Unless specified otherwise, data from published sources employ the Census Bureau's designation of Hispanic persons. That is, Hispanics are included in racial counts (e.g., with blacks and whites) as well as in a separate category. For instance, in government analyses a white person of Hispanic origin is included both in counts of whites and in counts of Hispanics. In our original analyses, such as the racial/ethnic wage analysis in Chapter 3, we remove Hispanic persons from other racial (white or black) categories; using this technique, the person described above would appear only in counts of Hispanics.

CHAPTER 1

Family income
Historic failure to grow in 2000s business cycle

Family income is the core building block of American living standards. It is through income that families meet their material needs as well as their aspirations. The income that families receive through work, government benefits, or return on investments enables them to provide for their households, raise their children, and invest in their futures. Income not consumed flows into wealth, enabling families to finance longer-term investments, like a home, or to offset a period in which the income flow is interrupted. This chapter provides a detailed look into how this key determinant of living standards has evolved, both recently and over the longer term.

The analysis reveals two related points that are central to understanding the evolution of income growth in America. First, the most recent business cycle—the 2000s—was historically unique: despite significant productivity growth in the overall economy, most of those families experienced stagnant or falling real incomes. The American workforce is working harder, smarter, and more efficiently, yet failing to share fairly in the benefits of the growth they are creating. In fact, for the first time on record, based on an analysis of data going back to the mid-1940s, it appears that the real income of the typical, middle-income family (i.e., the median) will be lower at the end of a business cycle than it was at the beginning.

The 2000s was not the first time that middle-income families lost ground in a recession, nor was it the first time that such losses continued for a number of years after the official recession ended. But before a cycle ends—before the next downturn takes hold—real median incomes usually start to grow and ultimately surpass their prior peak. Yet in the 2000s, the longest jobless recovery on record hurt families' earnings capacity, while increased inequality meant that the growth that did occur bypassed the middle class.

The second point arising from this analysis of family income is that the sharp rise of income inequality has broken the link between economic growth and broadly shared income gains.The most comprehensive data on inequality reveal this stark imbalance. Data on income concentration going back to 1913 show that the top 1% now holds 23% of total income, the highest inequality level in any year on record, bar one: 1928. In the last few years alone, $400 billion of pretax income flowed from the bottom 95% to the top 5%, a loss of $3,660 per household in the bottom 95%.

Note that these inequality developments are all based on market outcomes, or pre-tax measures. Recent changes to the tax system have exacerbated the problem by lowering the tax liabilities of those at the top of the income scale much more so than those in the middle or at the low end. In 2008, the impact of the Bush tax cuts had virtually no impact on low-income families and lowered the tax liabilities of middle-income families by around $1,000. Families in the top 1% of the income scale, however, saw tax reductions of over $50,000.

Amidst these troubling results, it is important to scan the historical record for periods in which living standards outcomes were different than those discussed above. In fact, there are a few periods over both the distant and recent past when family incomes were distributed much more equally, leading to living standards improvements across the board, not just at the top. The one characteristic these periods shared, whether it was the 1950s or the latter 1990s, was tight labor markets. Full employment, at which the unemployment rate is low enough so that employers must share the benefits of growth in order to get and keep the workforce they need, is a necessary condition for reconnecting the economy and the working families that propel it forward.

Income in the 2000s: the weakest cycle on record?

In terms of the income of the typical, or median, family, the 2000s were historically unique. By one measure—the Census Bureau's long-time series of median family income (**Figure 1A**)—this is the first time on record that over the course of a business cycle the median family income failed to surpass its prior peak. Before examining the factors behind that dubious distinction, let us look more closely at this historical record.

As can be seen in Figure 1A, inflation-adjusted median income is a cyclical variable: it falls in downturns (shaded in the figure) and rises in recoveries. But along with this predictable cyclical pattern, a structural shift has also occurred: real median family income has grown a lot more slowly since the mid-1970s. This slowdown corresponds with a number of developments, including slower overall growth and productivity, along with a factor we explore extensively in this chapter: the increase in income inequality. As inequality grew, less growth reached middle-income families, even as many spent considerably more time working in the paid labor market (these issues are also explored in detail later in the chapter).

The slower growth in family income meant that it took longer to make up losses from recessions. This pattern is clear in **Figure 1B**, in which each bar represents how many years it took in each business cycle for median income to regain its peak from the last cycle. Over time, as real income growth has slowed, it has taken considerably longer to make up recessionary losses, from two years in the 1950s, to seven years in the 1980s, 1990s, and 2000s cycles.

FIGURE 1A Real median family income, 1947-2007

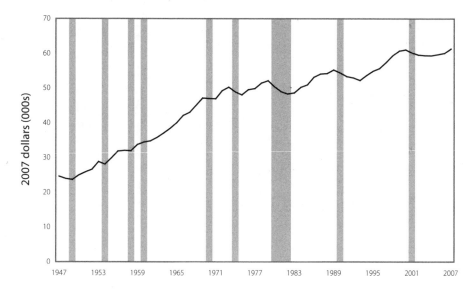

Source: Authors' analysis of U.S. Census Bureau data.

FIGURE 1B Years for median family income to regain prior peak

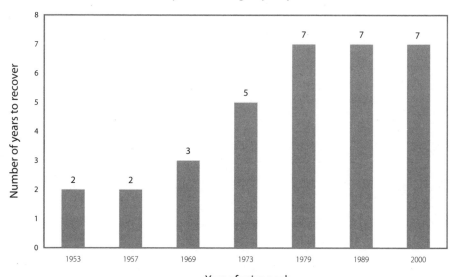

Year of prior peak

Source: Authors' analysis of U.S. Census Bureau data.

With regard to the latest cycle, economic indicators show that a recession took hold in late 2007 or early 2008, suggesting that the income peak for the 2000s cycle occurred in 2007 (these income data are available only on an annual basis). Data on median family income are available only through 2006 (as of press time), but by using data on key real income determinants, including inflation and hours worked, we can make a reliable forecast of median family income for 2007. According to this forecast, shown as the dotted line segment in Figure 1A, median family income failed to regain its prior peak before the most recent business cycle ended.

Note that this assessment depends on a few assumptions: first, that 2007 was indeed the peak year of the recovery that began in 2001 and, second, that income did not grow significantly faster than in our forecast. But even if this forecast is off by as much as a few percent, real median family income will simply regain or only slightly surpass its prior peak, an extremely unsatisfactory benchmark against which to judge income growth, especially in the productivity-rich recovery of the 2000s. **Table 1.1** shows total and annualized growth rates of median family income across previous cycles.

TABLE 1.1 Median family income,* 1947-2007 (2007 dollars)

	Median family income*
1947	$24,612
1973	50,268
1979	52,135
1989	55,238
1995	54,863
2000	61,083
2007	61,355

Changes	Annual growth rates	Total growth
1947-73	2.8%	na
1973-79	0.6	3.7%
1979-89	0.6	6.0
1989-2000	0.9	10.6
1989-95	-0.1	-0.7
1995-2000	2.2	11.3
2000-07	0.1	1.4

* Income includes all wage and salary, self-employment, pension, interest, rent, government cash assistance, and other money income.

Source: Authors' analysis of U.S. Bureau of the Census data.

TABLE 1.2 Income growth in the 1990s and 2000s and the roles of earnings, hours, and hourly wages

	Bottom fifth	Middle fifth	Top fifth
1989-2000			
Income growth	14.2%	10.6%	23.3%
Earnings	14.3	8.8	21.7
Annual hours	7.3	4.1	-0.5
Hourly wage	7.0	4.7	22.2
Other income	-0.1	1.8	1.5
2000-06			
Income growth	-3.2%	-1.1%	2.1%
Earnings	-1.1	-1.3	1.9
Annual hours	-3.5	-2.2	-1.5
Hourly wage	2.4	1.0	3.4
Other income	-2.2	0.1	0.3

Source: Authors' analysis of ASEC data.

Besides confirming the clear impression of Figure 1A regarding the post-1970s negative structural shift in growth, the table shows the increasing cost of this dynamic in terms of diminished cyclical gains. Median family income grew only 6% over the 1970s and 1980s, and was essentially flat in the 2000s. Real income growth in the 1990s, however, was up about 11%, and this growth all occurred in the latter 1990s, a period of uniquely full employment.

What explains the especially weak 2000s result? As examined in detail below, inequality is an obvious culprit, but another important (and related) factor has to do with earnings opportunities. One reason income follows the cyclical pattern shown in Figure 1A is that the income growth of most working-age families depends on their opportunities in the job market. The first years of the 2000s business cycle was the longest jobless recovery on record, and, after that, job growth was uniquely weak. This slack in the job market took a serious toll on family income growth.

This impact is quantified in **Table 1.2**, which breaks down family income growth into earnings and other income (non-labor income comes from capital sources, like interest and dividends, and government transfers, like Social Security or unemployment insurance). Earnings growth can be further broken down into hourly wage rates and annual hours worked. For example, the real income of the middle-fifth of families grew 10.6% during 1989-2000. Earnings growth explains 8.8% of that 10.6% growth, while other income growth contributed 1.8% (8.8%+1.8%=10.6%). The 8.8% annual earnings growth can be further decomposed: 4.1% came from the growth in annual hours and 4.7% from hourly wages.

The differences between the two cycles are stark. Over the 1990s incomes grew for low-, middle-, and high-income families, and grew faster at the low end than in the middle (as discussed later in this chapter, the growth almost exclusively occurred in the latter half of the 1990s). For families in the bottom half, the growth in both annual hours of work and hourly wages contributed equally to the growth in family incomes. The hours worked among high-income families were flat due in large part to the "ceiling effect" (discussed below), that is, hours for this group had little room to grow. By contrast, the 2000s period (through 2006, the last year of available data) saw a decline in hours worked, and this drop shaved 3.5% off of the lowest incomes and 2.2% off of middle incomes. Had hours simply remained flat for these groups, their incomes would not have fallen.

A final question with regard to family income and the latest business cycle is the impact of the recession that appeared to be in effect by early 2008. Real incomes tend to fall across the income spectrum in a downturn, as higher unemployment and slower wage growth drive incomes down. But since lower-income families are more dependent on labor income (and less so on capital income, such as interest and capital gains), recession-induced losses are larger for lower-income than higher-income families. For example, analysis by economist Tim Bartik finds that, for each one percentage-point increase in unemployment, average income falls 1.8% for the bottom fifth of families, 1.4% for the middle fifth, and 1.0% for the top fifth.

FIGURE 1C Change in average real family income following peak years, by selected income quintiles

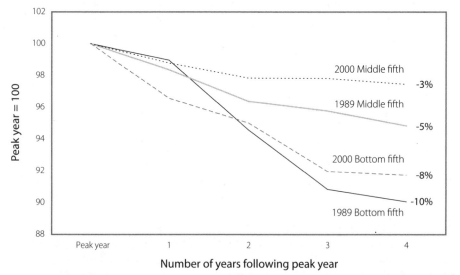

Number of years following peak year

Source: Authors' analysis of Census Bureau data.

Evidence for this differential impact of a recession on income groups can be seen in **Figure 1C**, which plots the percentage losses for low- and middle-income families in the first few years of the last two downturns (in both of these cases, unemployment kept rising after the recession ended; see Chapter 4). Following the path of the lines as they progress from left to right illustrates that, even four years after the prior peak, incomes had failed to rise for these families. Bartik's work has shown that the percentage losses were larger for low-income families than for middle-income families. In the early 1990s downturn, average income fell 10% for the bottom fifth over these years (1989-93) and about half that for the middle fifth. In the 2000s (2000-04), the pattern was similar, with real income losses of about 8% for the lowest fifth and 3% for the middle.

Using Bartik's findings of the relationship between the decline in real income and the increase in unemployment by income fifth, along with a forecast for unemployment over the next few years, allows an estimate of the losses for low-, middle-, and high-income families. Forecasters at Goldman Sachs predict that unemployment will rise from 4.6% in 2006-07 to 5.7% in 2008 and 6.4% in 2009. Applying those predictions yields the income paths shown in **Figure 1D**. The losses follow the historical pattern shown in the previous figure, with real incomes in the bottom fifth down about 5%, middle incomes down about 3%, and top-fifth incomes down 2%.

These predictions are based, of course, on a variety of assumptions that could change, but they closely follow the historical patterns of the toll that recessions take on family incomes. In any case the relative differences, with the most economically

FIGURE 1D Forecasted real income losses given predicted unemployment,* 2006-09

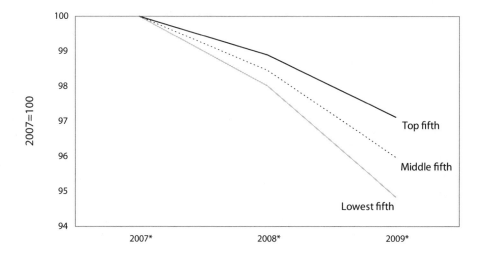

* Forecast based on rising unemployment rates.

Source: Authors' analysis of U.S. Census data.

50

THE STATE OF WORKING AMERICA

vulnerable families taking the biggest recessionary hits, can be predicted with a great degree of confidence.

Family income by race, ethnicity, and native/foreign birth

As with almost every variable measuring living standards, there are persistent gaps between white, African American, and Hispanic families. Certainly, discrimination plays a role here, as do the lower average levels of educational achievement among minority populations relative to whites (of course, discrimination is in play here too; the next chapter adds perspective to these differences by examining educational opportunity and income mobility by race). It is also the case that minority families' incomes, particularly those of African Americans, tend to be more responsive to overall economic trends, both positively and negatively. The downsides of this heightened responsiveness are worrisome, given the downturn discussed above. But it is critically important that

TABLE 1.3 Median family income by race/ethnic group, 1947-2007(2007 dollars)

Year	White	Black*	Hispanic**	Share of white family income: Black	Hispanic
1947	$25,635	$13,106	n.a.	51.1%	n.a.
1967	44,693	26,461	n.a.	59.2	n.a.
1973	52,537	30,321	$36,352	57.7	69.2%
1979	54,403	30,807	37,714	56.6	69.3
1989	58,083	32,628	37,854	56.2	65.2
1995	57,612	35,084	33,192	60.9	57.6
2000	63,849	40,547	41,469	63.5	64.9
2007	64,427	40,143	40,566	62.3	63.0

Annual growth rate

1947-67	2.8%	3.6%	n.a.		
1967-73	2.3	2.0	n.a.		
1973-79	6.0	0.3	6.0%		
1979-89	0.7	0.6	0.0		
1989-2000	0.9	2.0	0.8		
1995-2000	2.1	2.9	4.6		
2000-07	0.1	-0.1	-0.3		

* Prior to 1967, data for blacks include all non-whites.
** Persons of Hispanic origin may be of any race.

Source: Authors' analysis of U.S. Bureau of the Census data.

living standards analysts interested in racial differences remain mindful of the upside of this relationship: full employment provides a strong boost to minority incomes. Such was definitely the case during the most recent period of full employment in the latter 1990s. In those years, the pace of minority families' income growth surpassed that of white families, and the racial income gap shrank to historically low levels. In the ensuing downturn and weaker 2000s recovery, much of this valuable ground was lost.

Table 1.3 shows that, during periods of low unemployment, income growth of families headed by African American and Hispanics tended to outpace that of whites, thus helping to narrow the racial income gap. For example, the black/white median income ratio went from 51.1% to 59.2% between 1947 and 1967, and from 56.2% to 63.5% from 1989 through 2000. The Hispanic gap also closed significantly over the latter 1990s. This last point is also relevant in that the 1990s was a period of fast immigrant inflows, yet the income growth of both African Americans and Hispanics surpassed that of whites, suggesting that immigrant competition did not prevent favorable minority income trends. For African Americans, income growth in the 1990s was the fastest in a generation.

These relative income gains by minority families are illustrated in **Figure 1E**, which plots black and Hispanic median income relative to white (Hispanic data are available only for 1972 and later; note also that the data for white families include Hispanics who identify their race as white. Data on non-Hispanic whites are available from 1972 forward; using this series for whites does not change the trends shown in the figure). Throughout the 1960s, the median income of black families increased

FIGURE 1E Ratio of black and Hispanic to white median family income, 1947-2007

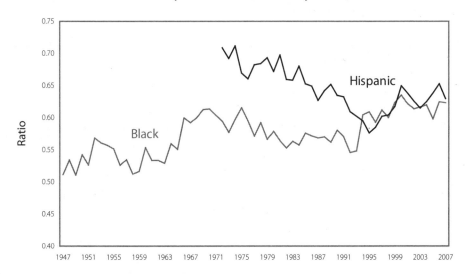

Source: Authors' analysis of U.S. Census Bureau data.

relative to that of whites, with the ratio peaking in the mid-1970s. The relative gains by African Americans were partly driven by geographic and industry shifts, as many African American families migrated north and found employment in manufacturing. In fact, by 1970, the share of black men working in manufacturing surpassed that of whites. As manufacturing employment contracted over the 1980s and especially the latter 1990s, this sector ceased to be a venue for relative gains by minorities. Over the 1980s, African American families lost ground relative to whites, but this trend was reversed in the full employment period of the 1990s, when the black/white ratio rose to its highest level on record (63.5% in 2000).

A closer look at full employment and African American incomes

The relationship between full employment and African American income growth can be examined in greater detail by using the Congressional Budget Office's estimates of the so-called natural rate of unemployment (the rate associated with stable price growth). Comparing this rate to the actual unemployment rate allows a measure of whether the job market was above or below full employment (i.e., whether it was slack, meaning lots of job seekers and too few jobs, or taut, meaning a tight match between the number of workers and the number of jobs).

The first column of **Table 1.4** accumulates the annual percentage-point differences between the natural rate and the actual rate over the 1949-73 and 1973-2006 time periods. If CBO's natural rate was 5% and the actual jobless rate was 4.5%, the per-centage-point difference would be -0.5. Between 1949 and 1973, the unemployment rate was often below the natural rate, cumulatively 19 percentage points. This happens to be about the same number of points that unemployment was above this rate in the latter period. In other words, in the first period, job markets were typically much tighter than in the second period.

When job markets were much tighter—when the unemployment rate averaged 4.8%—the incomes of black families grew at an average annual rate of 3.7%, compared to less than 1% in the latter period, when unemployment averaged 6.2%. Of course, many other factors were in play here. As shown above, every group's income grew

TABLE 1.4 Full employment, African American family income, unemployment, and inflation, 1949-2006

Year	Cumulative points below or above full employment	Real annual growth in median income, African American families	Average unemployment	Inflation*
1949-73	-19.1%	3.7%	4.8%	2.4%
1973-2006	20.7%	0.8%	6.2%	3.7%

* Post-1973 comparison leaves out 1979-82 to avoid upward bias. Including these years gives an average of 4.3%.

Source: CBO NAIRU estimates; Census Bureau, median family income (RS deflator); BLS, unemployment; BLS, CPI-RS deflator.

more slowly in the latter period. The early progress of blacks grew off of a very low base, making it easier for this group to post large percentage gains. Also, a larger share of black families was headed by single parents in the latter period, and this contributed to the income slowdown. But less favorable job market conditions surely played an important role as well. Thus, tight labor markets, persistently below the supposed natural rate, have been associated with much better income growth for African American families.

The last column in the table addresses the commonly made argument that tight job markets generate unacceptably high levels of inflation. This simple comparison shows that inflation was lower when job markets were tighter.

The 2000s were an important reminder of the impact on minorities of less-than-full employment. Even when the "jobless" part of the recovery ended in the fall of 2003, employment growth remained weak, and the low unemployment rate partially masked other problems (like declining employment rates) that depressed the bargaining power of minority workers. As shown in the last row of Table 1.3, black real median income fell more quickly than that of whites during 2000-07, and the black/white income gap fell from 63.5% to 62.3%.

Income by native/foreign birth
One line of argument holds that immigrant families bring down the trends in income figures such as those above. Since many immigrant families, especially in recent years,

FIGURE 1F Income growth for middle-income immigrant and non-immigrant families

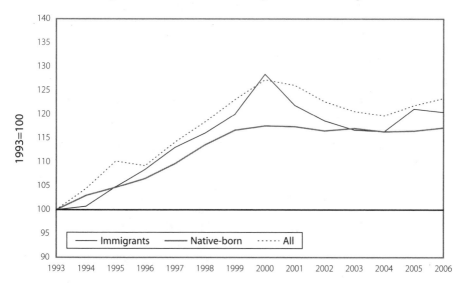

Source: Authors' analysis of Census ASEC data.

have lower earnings profiles, data series like those shown above might suffer from a composition effect, wherein the addition of families with especially low incomes brings down the average income for all families..

One simple way to test this theory is to examine the trends of native-born families and immigrants separately. If adding immigrants brings down the average, then taking them out of the data series should show above-average growth for families headed by native-born persons. **Figure 1F** uses data on the average income of middle-income families from 1993 to 2006 (the years for which we can perform such analyses) to illustrate the findings of this exercise. It shows that the real incomes of both immigrant and native-born middle-income families followed similar growth patterns, rising in the 1990s and remaining flat in the 2000s. If anything, immigrant incomes were more responsive to the economy's ups and downs; they grew faster in the 1990s and slower in the 2000s. But the native-born average does not grow faster when we remove the immigrants. To the contrary, it grows a bit more slowly. Thus, it appears that the addition of more immigrants to the economy was not responsible for the poor income growth in recent years. Real family income trends were flat, regardless of the place of birth of the family head.

Of course, this test is very simple. If immigrant competition were placing downward pressure on the incomes of native-born families, simply removing immigrants from the data would not offset this effect (since it's embedded in native outcomes). Yet, the similarity of the trends for native-born and immigrant families suggests that factors other than native-immigrant competition are likely in play. For example, regardless of the place of birth of the family head (or race/ethnicity, as shown above), middle-incomes grew smartly in the 1990s and stagnated in the 2000s. A more likely hypothesis is that roughly similar forces were at play on all middle-income families, including changes in number and quality of employment opportunities and inequality.

Income by age and family type

Along with race and ethnicity, income also varies across the age scale. Young families, just starting out, usually have lower income than older families, who tend to have both higher earning capacity and greater wealth. As families retire and spend down their assets, income tends to decline. In fact, as shown in any year in **Table 1.5**—median income levels by age of the head of the family—the pattern of median family income by age follows an inverted U in any given year. As families age, their working members typically gain more years of labor market experience, leading to higher income levels. In retirement, however, this trend reverses.

Table 1.5 reveals that median family income losses in the 2000s were concentrated among both younger (under 25) and prime-age families, that is, those headed by someone 25-54. These are typically peak earning years, so the impact of these losses on living standards over the life cycle are by no means trivial. Older workers fared better, with gains of about 1% per year, or almost 8% over the full seven-year period. Interestingly, as shown in Chapter 4, older workers were the only group whose employment rates rose significantly in these years. As longevity gains and various

TABLE 1.5 Median family income by age of householder, 1979-2007 (2007 dollars)

Year	Under 25	25-34	35-44	45-54	55-64	Over 65	45-54 compared to 25-34 relative incomes
1979	$34,632	$51,392	$60,990	$67,341	$58,331	$30,136	1.31
1989	27,550	49,845	64,907	74,431	60,776	37,268	1.49
1995	25,338	48,661	62,855	74,340	61,149	38,233	1.53
2000	32,456	54,631	69,939	81,684	66,756	40,156	1.50
2007	31,283	52,291	67,849	77,440	72,286	41,851	1.48
Annual growth rate							
1979-89	-2.3%	-0.3%	0.6%	1.0%	0.4%	2.1%	1.3%
1989-2000	1.5	0.8	0.7	0.8	0.9	0.7	0.0
1995-2000	5.1	2.3	2.2	1.9	1.8	1.0	-0.4
2000-07	-0.5	-0.6	-0.4	-0.8	-1.1	0.6	-0.1

Source: Authors' analysis of U.S. Bureau of the Census data.

economic factors (such as the loss of pensions and health care) keep older families spending more years in the paid job market, the income/age profile may well change, with less of a dip in older years.

Table 1.5 breaks out the latter 1990s to reinforce the point made above regarding full employment. Earlier, we discussed the responsiveness of income growth for minority workers to tight job markets. Here, we see a similar pattern of income gains by age, revealing that tight job markets gave a larger boost to younger relative to older families. For example, prime-age workers realized gains of 2% or higher per year, and younger families had even higher growth rates compared to older families. The median income of families who were early in their earning years (headed by someone age 25-34) grew 12% from 1995 to 2000 compared to 9% for families headed by a 55-64-year-old.

The final column in the table shows the impact of increasing returns to experience over the past few decades. That is, over the longer term incomes of older families have been growing more quickly than those of younger families. For example, in real terms, the income level of families headed by a 25-34-year-old was about the same in 2007 as in 1979, while that of families headed by a 45-54-year-old was up about 15%. This pattern of growth differences by age means that the living standards of today's working families are improving less quickly as they age compared to the experience of families in earlier periods. We explore these and other related dynamics in the next chapter, which examines the extent of income mobility by persons and families as they grow older.

Income changes by family type

Both the composition and the labor market participation of American families have changed in important ways over time. In the late 1940s, married-couple families accounted for almost 90% of all families; now they account for 75%. At the same time, single-parent families have gone from a 13% to a 25% share, and married women have steeply increased their participation in the paid job market, though this trend appears to have hit a ceiling over the past decade. We explore these trends, and their impact on income growth, in this section.

TABLE 1.6 Median family income by family type, 1973-2007 (2007 dollars)

Year	Total	Married couples		Single		All families
		Wife in paid labor force	Wife not in paid labor force	Male-headed	Female-headed	
1973	$54,343	$63,557	$47,627	$44,807	$24,181	$50,268
1979	57,038	66,173	47,128	44,738	26,298	52,135
1989	62,235	73,083	46,413	44,960	26,546	55,238
1995	63,578	75,413	43,736	41,012	26,601	54,863
2000	71,157	83,361	48,140	45,425	30,963	61,083
2007	72,589	86,435	47,329	44,358	30,296	61,355
Labor force						
1973-79	1.2%	1.1%	0.2%	0.4%	1.8%	1.0%
1979-89	0.9	1.0	-0.2	0.0	0.1	0.6
1989-2000	1.2	1.2	0.3	0.1	1.4	0.9
1989-95	0.4	0.5	-1.0	-1.5	0.0	-0.1
1995-2000	2.3	2.0	1.9	2.1	3.1	2.2
2000-07	0.3	0.5	-0.2	-0.3	-0.3	0.1
Share of families						
1951*	87.0%	19.9%	67.1%	3.0%	10.0%	100.0%
1979	82.5	40.6	41.9	2.9	14.6	100.0
1989	79.2	45.7	33.5	4.4	16.5	100.0
2000	76.7	47.4	29.4	5.8	17.5	100.0
2007	75.0	46.3	28.7	6.6	18.5	100.0

* Earliest year available for wives' work status.

Source: Authors' analysis of U.S. Bureau of the Census data.

Table 1.6 shows median family incomes and population shares for various family types (we use the Census Bureau's definition of family, which excludes single-person households). Looking first at the most recent period, only married-couple families with both spouses working saw their real median incomes rise in the 2000s, by 0.3% per year (about 2% overall). Real losses accrued to single-parent families. Note that this is a sharp reversal from the latter 1990s, when single-mother families experienced the fastest growth of all family types (we look more closely at these families' income trends in Chapter 6).

Turning to the longer-term trend of median income growth over the full period covered by the table, only two family types experienced significant growth: married-couple families where both spouses work (up 36%), and mother-only families (up 25%). As discussed in detail later, due to the long-term deterioration in the earnings of middle-income men, the prime mechanism through which married-couple families could experience income growth over the past few decades was through married women's increased work in the paid job market. In that regard, the apparent "topping out" of married women's labor supply—their share has been relatively constant since the late 1980s—may explain these families' weaker performance in the 2000s and may well place an important constraint on future growth.

Middle-income single-mother families have experienced two periods of solid income growth over these years: the 1970s cycle and the latter 1990s (note that they gained nothing during 1989-95, before the job market tightened significantly). These families' income trends are particularly sensitive to employment conditions.

Growing inequality of family income

Thus far, this chapter has restricted its focus primarily to trends among families in the middle of the income range. In this section, we take a much closer look at the phenomenon of increased income inequality.

Why is this discussion important? The main reason is that rising inequality means that much less of the economy's growth is reaching families below the top income tier. In this regard, inequality creates a wedge between overall growth and steadily rising living standards. Imagine the economy as a river, providing the water needed to the various communities along the rivers' banks. Now imagine that one community is able to draw an ever larger share of the river its way, leaving less water for others. Over the past generation or so, the economy has flowed like this river. In some periods, the impact of inequality is more a relative one, in the sense that incomes are rising for most income groups, but are rising much faster at the top of the scale (all the towns are getting more water from the river, but some towns are getting more than others). In other periods, such as the 2000s, the inequality wedge has meant actual declines in real incomes, even as the workforce posted strong productivity gains.

To take one example of this phenomenon, an analysis using the most comprehensive inequality data (the household income series derived by the Congressional Budget Office, discussed below) shows the share of income going to the middle fifth of households fell by 2.5 percentage points between 1979 and 2006. Given the trillions of dollars of growth in national income over this period, this represents a loss of about $11,000 per middle-income household. In other words, had overall incomes grown as they did, but the middle fifth maintained its income share, middle-class families would have been significantly better off.

Other data series in addition to CBO's provide important insights regarding inequality. Census data have the advantage of comprising a long time series, back to the mid-1940s, and offer generally consistent measures of family income throughout the income scale. However, Census income data exclude capital gains—the gains from selling appreciated assets, like a stock—which, given the increased concentration of stock market wealth (see Chapter 5) play an important role in the evolution of inequality. A relatively new series that both goes back even further than the Census data and includes capital gains can be used for looking more closely at income concentration among the very wealthiest families.

We begin this survey of inequality's growth by examining indirect evidence: the historically unprecedented gap between the growth of median family income and that of productivity. **Figure 1G** compares median family income (using Census data) to the trend in productivity. This measure of output per hour is widely considered to be a key determinant of living standards, based on the idea that as an increasingly efficient workforce produces more goods and services per hour of work, families can more readily meet their economic needs and aspirations. However, if those benefits flow largely to the top of the income scale, the potential lift to living standards from faster productivity

FIGURE 1G Productivity and real median family income growth, 1947-2007

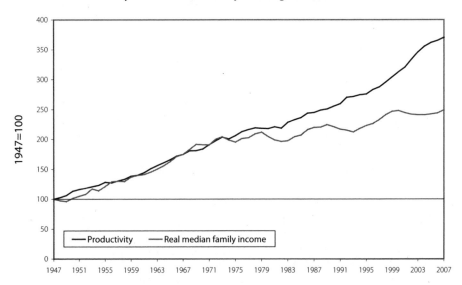

Source: Authors' analysis of U.S. Census Bureau and U.S. Bureau of Labor Statistics data.

FIGURE 1H Real family income growth by quintile, 1947-2007

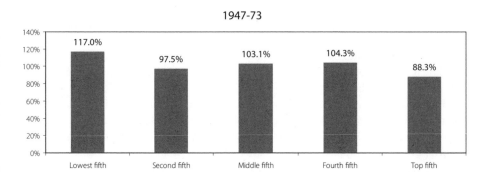

1947-73

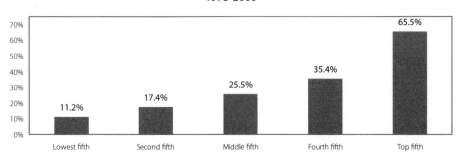

1973-2000

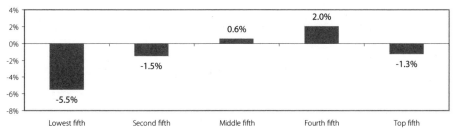

2000-07

Source: Authors' analysis of U.S. Census Bureau data.

growth will elude most families, even while they themselves contribute to the productivity boom. This dynamic was particularly in play in the 2000s.

The figure plots productivity and real median family income growth since 1947. Between 1947 and 1973 or so, the two measures tracked each other, as both doubled. But since 1973, productivity has grown faster than median family income, 80% vs. 22%. The growing gap has two implications. First, it documents that the benefits of growth have increasingly eluded the middle class, and second, it stands as a stark reminder that the connection between faster productivity growth and higher living standards is weaker in an age of inequality.

Figure 1H takes a closer look at inequality over the long term by using Census data to examine income averages for each fifth of families. While this income definition is less complete than others used later (e.g., it excludes realized capital gains, an important income component for inequality research), it is historically consistent and widely cited. The three time periods clearly reveal the contrast between the broadly shared growth of the postwar period and the growing apart since. In the generation following World War II, real income just about doubled for each fifth, though the growth of the lowest income families surpassed that of all others, meaning that inequality was diminished over this period.

The 1973-2000 period is very different, more like a staircase than a picket fence. Real income grew by 11.2% over these years for the poorest families, a rate of 0.4% per

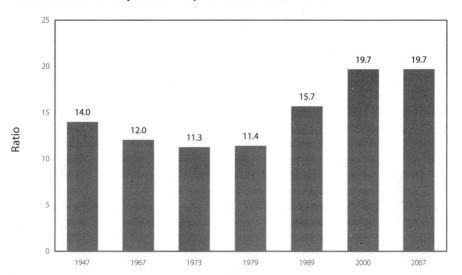

FIGURE 1I Ratio of family income of top 5% to lowest 20%, 1947-2007

Note: The 2000 ratio reflects a change in survey methodology leading to increased inequality.

Source: Authors' analysis of U.S. Census Bureau data.

year. Amazingly, all of that growth occurred in the 1995-2000 period, again underscoring the benefits of full employment for the least well-off. In contrast to the 1947-73
period, how fast a family's income grew in 1973-2000 was a function of their position
in the income scale.

The final panel shows that this inequality pattern persisted in the 2000s. Between
2000 and 2007, there were relatively large income losses for low-income families
(down 5.5%, a trend discussed more in Chapter 6), moderate losses for lower- and
middle-income families, and small gains at the top (the inclusion of realized capital
gains, discussed later, yields much more growth at the top).

The increase in the income gap between upper- and lower-income groups is illustrated
in **Figure 1I**, which shows the ratio of the average incomes of families in the top 5% to
those of the bottom 20% from 1947 to 2007. In 1947 the average income of the top 5% was
14 times that of the average of the bottom 20%; the ratio dropped to 11.4 in 1979. Since
then, the gap has grown consistently over cyclical peaks, hitting 19.7 in 2007.

Table 1.7 breaks down changes in income over time by income fifths. The 20% of
families with the highest incomes claimed 47.3% of all family income in 2007, while
the poorest 20% of families held only 4.1%. Within the top fifth in 2006, the top 5%
received 20.1% of all income, more than that of all the families in the bottom 40% combined (they received 13.8%). In fact, since 2000, the top fifth received just under half of
all income.

TABLE 1.7 Shares of family income going to income fifths and to the top 5%, 1947-2007

Year	Lowest Fifth	Second fifth	Middle fifth	Fourth fifth	Top fifth	Breakdown of top fifth First 15%	Top 5%
1947	5.0%	11.9%	17.0%	23.1%	43.0%	25.5%	17.5%
1973	5.5	11.9	17.5	24.0	41.1	25.6	15.5
1979	5.4	11.6	17.5	24.1	41.4	26.1	15.3
1989	4.6	10.6	16.5	23.7	44.6	26.7	17.9
2000	4.3	9.8	15.4	22.7	47.7	26.6	21.1
2007	4.1	9.7	15.6	23.3	47.3	27.2	20.1
Percentage-point change							
1947-73	0.5	0.0	0.5	0.9	-1.9	0.1	-2.0
1973-79	-0.1	-0.3	0.0	0.1	0.3	0.5	-0.2
1979-89	-0.8	-1.0	-1.0	-0.4	3.2	0.6	2.6
1989-2000	-0.3	-0.8	-1.1	-1.0	3.1	-0.1	3.2
2000-07	-0.2	-0.1	0.2	0.6	0.4	0.6	-1.0

Source: Authors' analysis of U.S. Bureau of the Census data.

TABLE 1.8 Real family income by income group, 1947-2007, upper limit of each group (2007 dollars)

Year	20th percentile	40th percentile	60th percentile	80th percentile	95th percentile
1947	$12,862	$20,755	$28,144	$39,934	$65,545
1973	25,365	41,854	58,397	80,309	125,200
1979	26,247	43,160	61,145	84,195	135,071
1989	25,837	45,207	65,873	96,145	159,779
1995	25,762	44,560	66,175	97,618	167,051
2000	28,897	49,173	73,837	110,017	192,790
2007	27,864	49,510	75,000	112,638	197,216
Annual growth rate					
1947-73	2.6%	2.7%	2.8%	2.7%	2.5%
1973-79	0.6	0.5	0.8	0.8	1.3
1979-89	-0.2	0.5	0.7	1.3	1.7
1989-2000	1.0	0.8	1.0	1.2	1.7
1989-95	0.0	-0.2	0.1	0.3	0.7
1995-2000	2.3	2.0	2.2	2.4	2.9
2000-07	-0.5	0.1	0.2	0.3	0.3

Source: Authors' analysis of U.S. Bureau of the Census data.

The bottom section, which shows the changes in these shares over time, reveals a long-term pattern since the early 1970s of shares shifting up the income scale, with large shifts over the 1980s and 1990s. In fact, since 1973, growing inequality resulted in 7.4% of national income moving from the bottom 80% to the top 20%, with about 80% of that shift (6.0/7.4) going to the top 5%.

Yet another way of viewing the post-1970s surge in income inequality is to compare the "income cutoffs" of families by income group, as in **Table 1.8**. These values represent the income at the top percentile of each fifth and at the 95th percentile. Focusing on this measure both allows an examination of income gains and losses for complete groupings of families (e.g., the bottom 40%) and also facilitates a more nuanced view of inequality's evolution, addressing relationships between the top and the bottom, the bottom and the middle, etc. **Figure 1J** illustrates the divergent fortunes over time of low (20th percentile), middle (median), and top (95th percentile) incomes.

The annualized percent changes in the bottom section of the table and the lines in the figure reveal that, in the mid-1970s, income growth began to diverge. Over the

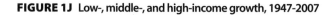

FIGURE 1J Low-, middle-, and high-income growth, 1947-2007

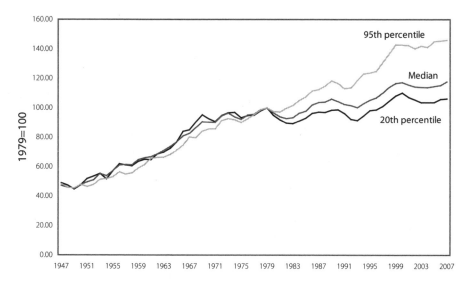

Source: Authors' analysis of U.S. Census Bureau data.

1980s, the higher the income, the faster the growth. In the 1995-2000 period, however, the bottom slightly outpaced the higher percentiles, though families at the 95th percentile continued to pull away from the rest of the pack.

Since 2000, real incomes have fallen at the 20th percentile at a rate of 0.5% per year. The median, as noted elsewhere, was flat in the 2000s, and the higher percentiles rose slightly in these data (e.g., the 95th percentile grew at an annual rate of 0.3%). Yet, as seen in the next section, this relatively small difference in growth rates is largely a function of the omission of realized capital gains in the Census data. Correcting for that shows much faster income growth among the wealthiest families and thus greater inequality in the 2000s.

Using high-quality historical tax data, economists Thomas Piketty and Emmanuel Saez constructed a long-term time-series with useful data on the top end of the income scale, where much of the important inequality dynamics take place. Unlike much of the Census data cited above, the Piketty/Saez data include realized capital gains and thus capture the contribution of this important component of inequality trends. Using this data, **Figure 1K** plots the share of income going to the top 1% of households between 1913 and 2006. Note the sharp increase in the share going to the top percentile in the 1990s: at the 2000 peak, the top 1% held 21.5% of household income, a share exceeded only in the late 1920s, a period of highly unstable economic speculation. When the dot-com bubble burst in late 2000, high-end households experienced sharp capital losses, and the top 1% share fell steeply for a few years.

FIGURE 1K Share of income held by top 1%, 1913-2006

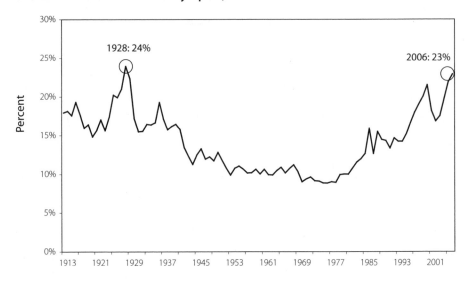

Source: Piketty and Saez (2008).

FIGURE 1L Income share (investment and labor income), top 0.1%, 1916-2005

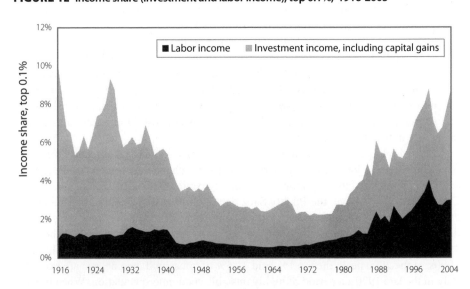

Source: Piketty and Saez (2008).

But the underlying forces generating greater inequality were still much in play, and the inequality trend soon returned. By 2006, income concentration by this measure was higher than in any year since 1913 bar one, 1928.

Figure 1L probes even deeper into the upper reaches of the income scale, examining the income shares and the composition of income of the top 0.1%—the narrow slice representing the top one-thousandth of families. A pattern similar to the last figure is evident here, suggesting that the inequality trajectory of the top percentile is closely linked to that of the very top of that group. But the composition of income among this sliver of rich families is also important and revealing.

Many years ago, inequality was largely a function of investment income, as returns from wealth were a much more important determinant of inequality's growth than was labor income. However, the figure shows that, over time, due to the rising inequality of earnings, labor income also became a major contributor. Thus, both forms of earnings—labor and non-labor—are pushing in the same disequalizing direction.

Another critical insight from the Piketty and Saez data is the integral role that small slivers of wealthy households now play in the evolution of income inequality. Figure 1M shows the income shares going to the bottom 99.5% of households in two years: 1978, a year falling toward the end of a generation of equalizing distributions of income (see Figure 1J), and 2006. Between these years, 12.5% of total income, or about $1 trillion (2006 dollars), was transferred from the bottom 99.5% to the top half-percent.

FIGURE 1M Share of household income, bottom 99.5%

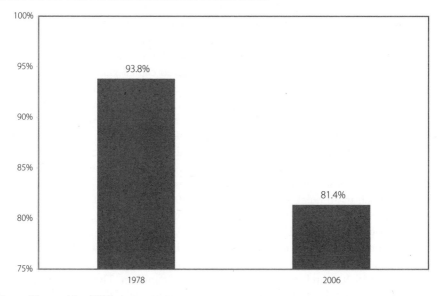

Source: Piketty and Saez (2008).

FIGURE 1N Household income growth by income group, 1979-2005, pre- and post-tax

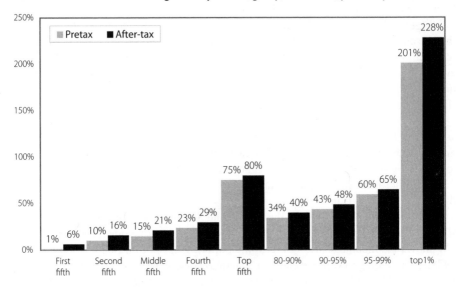

Source: EPI analysis of CBO data.

Narrowing the analysis further reveals that 4.6 percentage points of this transfer—over a third—accrued to the top 0.01%, or the top one in 10,000 families.

While the Pikkety/Saez data provide a long time series, the CBO's household income data series brings a whole different set of advantages to inequality analysis. The time period covered by the data is relatively short, 1979-2005, but the data are very comprehensive in that they include, in addition to realized capital gains, the value of noncash benefits like Medicare, Medicaid, employer-paid health insurance premiums, and food stamps. These data, illustrated in **Figure 1N**, also adjust for family size and provide pre- and post-federal-tax measures. Real income growth over this period was minimal to moderate for most low- and middle-income households. Income grew 1.3% pretax for the poorest households but 6.3% post-tax, the difference due largely to the increase in the refundable earned income tax credit over these years. Middle incomes grew 15% pretax and 21% post-tax, or less than 1% per year over this 26-year period. Income for the top fifth grew much more quickly: 75% pretax and 80% post-tax. But the most dramatic growth occurred at the top of the income scale. Households in the top 1% saw their income triple over these years, 201% pretax and 228% post-tax.

These trends led to stark differences in actual income levels by 2005. In that year, the average after-tax income for households in the bottom fifth was $15,300; in the middle fifth, $50,200; and in the top 1%, just over $1 million. These gaps have led to much greater economic distance between income classes over the years. In 1979, the post-tax income of the top 1% was eight times higher than that of middle-income

TABLE 1.9 Household income shares, 2003-05

Pretax	First fifth	Second fifth	Middle fifth	Fourth fifth	Top fifth	80-90%	90-95%	95-99%	Top 1%
2003	4.2%	9.1%	14.3%	21.0%	52.1%	14.9%	10.2%	12.7%	14.3%
2004	4.1	8.9	13.9	20.4	53.5	14.6	9.9	12.7	16.3
2005	4.0	8.5	13.3	19.8	55.1	14.2	9.8	13.0	18.1
Post-tax									
2003	5.0%	10.3%	15.4%	21.6%	48.8%	14.9%	9.8%	11.9%	12.2%
2004	4.9	10.0	14.9	21.2	50.1	14.6	9.6	11.9	14.0
2005	4.8	9.6	14.4	20.6	51.6	14.2	9.6	12.2	15.6

Source: EPI analysis of CBO data.

families and 23 times higher than that of the lowest fifth. In 2005, those ratios grew to 21 and 70, respectively, a vast increase in the distance between income classes.

Post-tax income grew faster than pretax over this period, suggesting that effective federal tax rates decreased over time ("effective" or "average" tax rates are the ratio of taxes paid to income; if a household with $50,000 pays $10,000 in taxes, the effective rate is 20%). Also, note that the largest difference in growth rates between pre- and post-tax income occurred for the top 1%, a function of regressive tax changes that lowered the tax liabilities of these households more than for lower-income households. We provide more analysis of these tax changes in the next section.

A closer look at the few years at the end of the CBO series demonstrates the way that inequality has developed in recent years. As noted above, in response to a stock market bust and ensuing loss of capital income, inequality contracted for a few years in the early 2000s. But it reversed course in 2003 and started growing quickly in 2004. The data below reveal that, over these three years, the increase in the share of income going to the top of the scale was the largest over the history of the CBO data.

Table 1.9 shows each household fifth's share of income for the latest three years of CBO data; it breaks down the top fifth into subgroups. By 2005, the top fifth held a larger share of both pre- and post-tax income than the bottom 80%. On a pretax basis, in 2005, the top 1%, with 18.1% of total income, held a much larger share of income than the bottom 40% (which held 12.5%).

Figure 1O plots the changes in each income group's share, 2003-05. The first five pairs of bars reveal a shift in income from the bottom 80% to the top fifth. But by breaking down movements within the top fifth, we find small share gains at the 95-99th percentiles and large gains for the top 1%. Together, they amount to about a 4 percentage-point increase for the top 5%, the largest two-year increase over the history of these data. These shifts amount to about $400 billion of pretax income (in 2005 dollars)

FIGURE 1O Change in income shares, pre- and post-tax, 2003-05

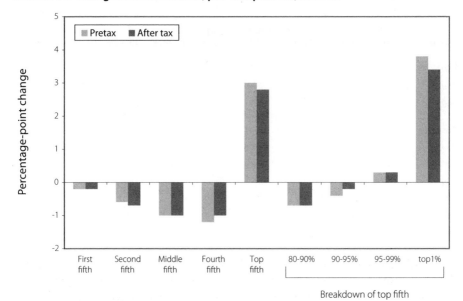

Breakdown of top fifth

Source: EPI analysis of CBO data.

FIGURE 1P Real expenditures by income fifth, 2000-06

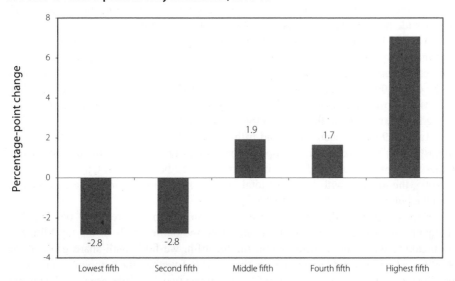

Source: BLS Consumer Expenditure Survey.

over these two years, a loss of $3,660 per household in the bottom 95%. Again, these are the largest income shifts on record over a two-year period.

Some inequality analysts express doubts about measures of income inequality because the incomes of families fluctuate from year to year in response to special circumstances—a layoff, a one-time sale of an asset, and so on. As a result, a family's income may partially reflect transient events and not indicate its economic well-being over the long term. For example, a family experiencing a bad year in terms of income may dip into its savings or may borrow in order to continue consuming at the same level as during a better year. In this view, consumption levels of families provide a better measure of inequality, since families typically gear their consumption to their expected incomes over the long term. On the other hand, many less well-off families may be unable to borrow or save much. In that case, consumption and income inequality would appear much the same. One problem with using consumption data is that the quality is limited. Data from the Bureau of Labor Statistics' consumer expenditure survey, used in many studies, have numerous reliability problems, and, because the survey measures spending, not consumption, it excludes depreciation of assets like cars and homes. However, the quality of the survey data has improved recently, and one study (Attanasio et al. 2006) corrects some of the data problems. The bottom line after these quality adjustments are made is that the trend in consumption inequality is much like that of income.

Figure 1P, which uses recent BLS consumer expenditure data to plot the change in real expenditures in the 2000s, shows a familiar unequal pattern, one that generally tracks income inequality in the 2000s. Expenditures fell about 3% for households in the bottom fifth, were relatively flat in the middle of the income scale, and rose 7% at the top.

The Attanasio et al. data provide a longer-term analysis of consumption expenditures. The line in **Figure 1Q** illustrates the increase from 1986 to 2001 in an inequality measure called the coefficient of variation (a measure of how expenditures are dispersed across the population). The measure increased by 8% over this period, a result in line with similar measures of income inequality.

Recent research has also revealed a high degree of consumption inequality among children relative to adults and elderly persons. **Figure 1R** plots the share of children in each fifth, using the consumption levels of the overall population to set the quintile breakpoints. By this measure, any bar that is greater than 20% shows that children are over-represented in this fifth and vice versa. In each year, children were over-represented in the lowest fifth and under-represented at the top. This means that children consistently had lower levels of relative consumption (i.e., compared to older persons) over these years. Their relative disadvantage increased over the 1980s, as their share in the bottom consumption fifth grew from 26% to 29% before sliding back a bit in the 1990s.

These findings imply that relatively fewer of society's consumption goods and services flowed to children as compared to adults. This is worrisome, given the importance of access to basic necessities for children during their formative years. Further research, not shown here, suggests that much larger consumption inequalities exist for children in single-mother families, who, because of their low incomes, are less able to smooth over periods of disrupted income flows with borrowing or by tapping savings.

FIGURE 1Q Increase in consumption inequality, 1986-2001

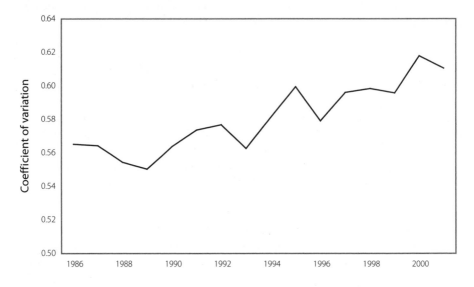

Source: Attanasio et al. (2006).

FIGURE 1R Consumption inequality among children, 1981-2001

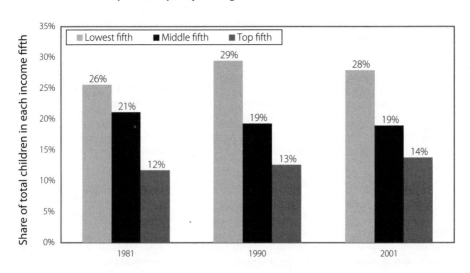

Source: Johnson et al. (2005).

Such families suffer significant income and consumption disadvantages with potentially lasting effects.

The impact of taxes on income and inequality

This section uses the CBO data discussed above to look at the role tax policy has played
in the trends in income and inequality. A more inclusive analysis would include the
impact of state and local taxation, but such distributional data are not available; we do,
however, present some information on state tax trends below.

Table 1.10 presents CBO's estimates of federal effective tax rates (tax payments as
a share of income) at three cyclical peaks—1979, 1989, and 2000—as well as the most
recent year for which CBO produces these data: 2005. The "all" category—the average effective rate for all households—shows that there hasn't been much movement
on average (the lower effective rate for 2005—20.5%—is a function both of recent tax
changes and increases in upper-tier incomes since 2000).

Significant changes have, however, occurred within and between income classes
over these years. Over the 1980s, rates were little changed for the bottom 80%, yet large
cuts occurred at the top of the income scale. Federal taxes paid as a share of income fell
by 3.3 percentage points for the top 10% and 8.1 points for the top 1%.

Federal taxes at the bottom end of the scale fell over the 1990s, largely due to
a significant increase in the earned income tax credit. This result is due to both the
credit being refundable—low-income workers receive the credit even if they have no

TABLE 1.10 Effective federal tax rates for all households, by comprehensive household
income quintile, 1979-2005

Income category	1979	1989	2000	2005
Bottom four-fifths				
First	8.0%	7.9%	6.4%	4.3%
Second	14.3	13.9	13.0	9.9
Third	18.6	17.9	16.6	14.2
Fourth	21.2	20.5	20.5	17.4
Top fifth	27.5%	25.2%	28.0%	25.5%
Top 10%	29.6	26.3	29.6	27.4
Top 5%	31.8	27.2	31.0	28.9
Top 1%	37.0	28.9	33.0	31.2
All	22.2%	21.5%	23.0%	20.5%

Source: Congressional Budget Office (2007).

tax liability—and also the fact that employment among low-wage workers surged in this period.

In short, every income group pays a smaller share of its income in federal taxes today than in years past. This is an important observation that is often ignored in political conversations suggesting that the United States is much more heavily taxed than in the past. While some of this discussion is motivated by state tax changes, it is important to keep this long-term declining trend in federal effective rates in full view during debates over tax policy. We are not arguing here that these *levels* of taxation are too high or too low; that is a complicated discussion involving questions of societal needs on the revenue side of the equation. But the trend has clearly been heading down for some time.

Federal taxes take a variety of forms, some progressive and some regressive, and an examination that looks only at overall effective rates misses the impact of individual federal taxes over time. **Table 1.11** shows the effective tax rate for households at different income levels for the four most important types of federal taxes in 1979, 1989, 2000, and 2005.

The personal income tax is highly progressive, with effective rates rising smoothly with income. As noted, the EITC expansion heightened the progressivity of the income tax by taking the bottom rate from 0% in 1979 to -6.5% in 2005. Thus, while low-income families incurred a zero income tax burden in 1979, they actually received income through the income tax system in 2000 ($65 for every $1,000 of income, on average).

The recent decline in effective income tax rates at the top of the scale is another important dimension of current taxation, one with important implications for the inequality debate. Anti-tax advocates point out that the share of total income taxes paid by top income groups has increased over time. For example, in 2005, the top 1% of households paid 38.8% of all income taxes (up from 36.5% in 2000). But since 2000, the effective tax rate of the income of the top 1% is down almost five percentage points, from 24.2% to 19.4%. Thus, while high-income families are paying a larger share of total federal income taxes, they are doing so with a considerably smaller share of their incomes.

The reason for this outcome is that, as shown above in Table 1.9, most income growth in recent years accrued to those at the top of the scale, households which, despite recent legislated tax changes favorable to them, still have the highest effective rates. Their share of total income taxes paid rose in large part because of their disproportionately large pretax income gains. Moreover, because the recent changes significantly lowered federal income tax liabilities, wealthy families are paying a larger share of a smaller overall tax bill. In fact, the income tax bill of the top 1% fell, on average, by over $50,000 per household from 2000 to 2005.

The payroll tax, which was capped at $102,000 in 2008, is used primarily to finance Social Security and Medicare. All workers pay the payroll tax at the same rate (15.3%, combining the employer and employee's share) from their first dollar of earnings until the point in the year when they reach the cap. With the lowest earners paying the full rate from the first dollar earned and high earners paying no payroll tax on earnings over the cap, the payroll tax is regressive, as borne out by the effective rates in Table 1.11. The rate rises through the bottom, second, middle, and fourth fifths of households,

TABLE 1.11 Effective tax rates for selected federal taxes, 1979-2005

Income category	Personal income tax				Payroll tax				Corporate income tax				Excise tax			
	1979	1989	2000	2005	1979	1989	2000	2005	1979	1989	2000	2005	1979	1989	2000	2005
Bottom four-fifths																
First	0.0%	-1.6%	-4.6%	-6.5%	5.3%	7.1%	8.2%	8.3%	1.1%	0.6%	0.5%	0.4%	1.6%	1.8%	2.3%	2.1%
Second	4.1	2.9	1.5	-1.0	7.7	8.9	9.4	9.2	1.2	0.8	0.6	0.5	1.3	1.2	1.4	1.3
Third	7.5	6.0	5.0	3.0	8.6	9.8	9.6	9.5	1.4	1.1	0.9	0.7	1.1	1.0	1.1	1.0
Fourth	10.1	8.3	8.1	6.0	8.5	10.0	10.4	9.7	1.6	1.2	1.0	1.0	0.9	0.9	0.9	0.8
Top fifth	15.7%	14.6%	17.5%	14.1	5.4%	6.6%	6.3%	6.0%	5.7%	3.5%	3.7%	4.9%	0.7%	0.6%	0.5%	0.5%
Top 10%	17.4	16.3	19.7	16.0	4.2	5.1	5.0	4.8	7.4	4.4	4.4	6.1	0.7	0.5	0.4	0.4
Top 5%	19.0	17.7	21.6	17.6	2.8	3.7	3.8	3.5	9.5	5.3	5.2	7.4	0.6	0.4	0.4	0.3
Top 1%	21.8	19.9	24.2	19.4	0.9	1.4	1.9	1.7	13.8	7.2	6.7	9.9	0.5	0.3	0.2	0.2
All	11.0%	10.2%	11.8%	9.0	6.9%	8.1%	7.9%	7.6%	3.4%	2.3%	2.4%	3.1%	1.0%	0.8%	0.9%	0.8%

Source: Congressional Budget Office (2007).

but falls steeply thereafter. In 2005, for example, households in the middle fifth paid 9.5% of their income in federal payroll taxes, compared to just 1.7% paid by top 1% of households. Comparing rates in 1989 with those in place in 1979 demonstrates that effective rates rose about one percentage point on average as a result of increases in the payroll tax implemented in the 1980s to improve the long-term finances of the Social Security and Medicare systems. But while the payroll tax is itself regressive, the Social Security and Medicare benefits it funds are progressively distributed, offsetting some of the regressive tax effects.

The next set of columns in Table 1.11 displays the effective rates from the corporate income tax, which in this analysis is portioned out to households according to their estimated income from capital. The corporate income tax is progressive, with effective rates rising sharply with income. However, tax changes in the 1980s lowered corporate rates; particularly large drops occurred in effective rates among the groups in the top fifth.

Starting in the latter 1990s, however, the share of household income subject to corporate taxation, such as corporate profits and other income from capital holdings, began to become more concentrated at the top of the scale. For example, in 1995, 79% of corporate tax liabilities were paid by the top fifth of households. By 2005, that share had grown to 88%, the highest share on record going back to 1979. (This accumulation of capital income can also be seen among the top 0.1% in Figure 1L, above.) This accumulation of income taxed by this progressive part of the code has led to higher effective corporate tax rates in the 2000s.

The last set of columns shows effective rates for federal excise taxes (such as those on gasoline, alcohol, and cigarettes). While these taxes claim a small share of income—not more than 1% on average in any year in the table—they tend to be highly regressive because the tax rates do not vary by income level. In 2005, for example, the bottom fifth of households spent about four times more of their income on federal excise taxes than did the top fifth.

The mix of taxes—federal, state, and local—can have an important impact on how the tax burden is shared and thus on after-tax inequality. Federal taxes are more

TABLE 1.12 Federal and state/local revenue as a share of GDP, 1959-2007

Year	Federal	State and local	Total
1959	17.1%	6.8%	23.9%
1969	19.2	8.5	27.7
1979	18.5	8.4	27.0
1989	18.2	9.1	27.3
2000	20.4	9.2	29.6
2007	18.9	9.5	28.4

Source: Authors' analysis of Bureau of Economic Analysis.

progressive than state and local taxes, which tend to raise revenue from more regressive sources, such as sales and property taxes.

Table 1.12 focuses on the changes over time in government revenues as a share of GDP, broken down by federal and state/local sectors. Revenue from all levels of government as a share of GDP remained fairly constant over the 1970s and 1980s, from 27.7% in 1969 to 27.3% in 1989. Over the 1990s, the historically sharp rise in high pre-tax incomes (which face the highest marginal income tax rates) caused this share to rise to 29.6% in 2000, the highest level on record. As discussed earlier, after declining when the dot-com bubble burst, top-level incomes again rose quickly in the 2000s at the same time that legislative changes lowered income and capital

TABLE 1.13 Composition of federal and state/local tax revenue, by progressive and regressive components, 2000 and 2007

	2000	2007
Federal		
Progressive	60.8%	59.1%
Personal income tax	49.8	44.5
Corporate income tax	10.9	14.6
Regressive	38.9%	40.4%
Excise/customs taxes	4.4	3.8
Contributions for social insurance	34.5	36.5
Other*	0.4%	0.5%
State and local		
Progressive	30.1%	29.1%
Personal income tax	26.2	24.3
Corporate income tax	3.9	4.8
Regressive	64.4%	64.1%
Sales	35.0	32.5
Contributions for social insurance	1.2	2.0
Property taxes	28.2	29.6
Other*	5.5%	6.8%

* For federal, this refers to taxes from the rest of the world; for state and local, it refers to other taxes on goods produced or imported.

Source: Authors' analysis of Bureau of Economic Analysis.

tax rates. As a result, federal taxes as a share of GDP dropped from 20.4% of GDP to 18.9%.

Over time, the share of federal taxation to GDP has changed little: it was about the same in 2007 as in 1969. But state and local taxes as a share of GDP have increased more than this, and, because state taxes are more regressive than federal, the rise has negative implications for post-tax inequality. The decline in federal revenue in the 2000s was largely a result of regressive cuts in most forms of federal taxes, including lower marginal rates in the income tax and lower taxes on capital gains, dividend income, and inheritances. **Table 1.13** takes a closer look at this point by breaking federal and state taxes down into progressive (tax liability as a share of income rises with income) and regressive (vice versa) components in two recent years: 2000, the most recent business cycle peak for which we have data, and 2007 (the most recent year for complete data). The top section shows a shift from personal to corporate income taxes, but overall there are few changes between 2000 and 2007 in the distribution of shares between progressive and regressive tax sources.

Federal taxes collect about 60% of their revenue from progressive sources and 40% from regressive sources. State and local taxes, on the other hand, take only about 30% from progressive sources and most of the rest from regressive one. Thus, the share of total taxation has been shifting from federal to state sources, and the latter are much more dependent on regressive revenue sources.

A final table in this section (**Table 1.14**) examines the impact on incomes in 2008 of the changes in federal tax policy introduced by the Bush administration and legislated since 2001. These include lowered marginal income tax rates, lowered taxes on investment and inheritance income, and other smaller changes. Since lower-income families (about the bottom third) pay nothing or little in these forms of taxation, the cuts had little impact on their liability: the federal tax bill of the lowest fifth was essentially unchanged, while that of the second fifth fell by about $400. Middle-income families saw declines in the $1,000 range, but it is not until you get to the highest reaches of the income scale that you see the real impact of these cuts. Cuts for the top 5%—average income of $484,800—were well over $10,000, and for the very richest top 0.1%, with average income over $6 million, the reduction in taxes paid was over $266,000. Note that the effective rate changes are synonymous with tax cuts as a share of income. By 2008, the cuts amounted to about 2% of income for most families, but for the highest-income families they ranged from 3% to 4%.

These regressive changes occurred over a period—the 2000s—when pretax, market-driven outcomes were already trending toward significantly higher levels of inequality. In that sense, changes in the tax code and the composition of taxes have taken an increasingly unequal income distribution and amplified it.

Family income changes by income class

Table 1.15 shifts the analysis to shares of families by constant-dollar income brackets and examines the proportion of families with low, middle, and high incomes. Data such as these are often used to point out that most families are better off in real

TABLE 1.14 Impact of 2001-06 tax cuts on 2008 income

Income class	Average income	Change in: Taxes paid	Change in: Effective rate
Lowest fifth	$8,477	$-26	-0.3
Second fifth	21,597	-397	-1.8
Middle fifth	38,857	-784	-2.0
Fourth fifth	67,869	-1,257	-1.9
Top fifth	213,996	-4,993	-2.3
Top 10%	319,874	-7,846	-2.5
Top 5%	484,800	-13,108	-2.7
Top 1%	1,367,765	-50,495	-3.7
Top 0.5%	2,177,643	-85,881	-3.9
Top 0.1%	6,480,962	-266,151	-4.1

Source: Tax Policy Center.

terms over time because there are fewer families in lower income groups and more in higher ones.

Such movements up the income scale typically occur in any advanced economy experiencing average income growth (though the 2000s were uniquely weak in this regard, as growth bypassed most families). Unless income growth flows exclusively to a very narrow slice of households, as is the case in some undeveloped economies, overall growth will usually lead to improvements of the type shown in Table 1.15. Thus, while it is true there are fewer low-income and more higher-income households over time in the United States, this in and of itself is not a relevant indicator of progress, since we expect most families' average income levels to grow as the economy expands.

Instead, there needs to be a benchmark, a source of comparison, against which to judge the rate at which families are moving upward through the income brackets. Imagine two different periods in which real income on average grows at the same rate. In the first period, every family's income grows at that rate. Over the second period, one characterized by greater inequality, lower-income families experience below-average income growth while high-income families experience above-average growth. In the first period, the lower-income shares will steadily fall and the higher-income shares will increase as families uniformly proceed from lower to higher brackets. But under the other scenario, lower shares will fall less quickly, and the highest-income shares will grow faster.

To explore inequality's impact on the actual shares of families by income class from 1969 to 2006, Table 1.15 includes a measure of inequality, the ratio of family

TABLE 1.15 Family income by income categories, 1969-2006

Year	Income categories					
	Less than $25,000	$25-50,000	$50-75,000	$75-100,000	More than $100,000	Top 5%/ Bottom 20%
1969	21.8%	36.7%	25.4%	9.8%	6.3%	11.1
1979	19.7	29.8	25.5	13.5	11.5	11.4
1989	19.6	26.6	22.4	1 4.3	17.0	15.7
1995	20.0	27.0	21.5	13.7	17.9	18.2
2000	17.1	25.0	20.4	14.8	22.9	19.7
2006	17.6	25.0	19.8	13.5	24.2	21.3
Changes	**Percentage-point changes**					
1969-79	-2.1	-6.9	0.1	3.7	5.2	0.3
1979-89	-0.1	-3.2	-3.1	0.8	5.5	4.3
1989-2000	-2.5	-1.6	-2.0	0.5	5.9	4.0
1995-2000	-2.9	-2.0	-1.1	1.1	5.0	1.5
2000-06	0.5	0.0	-0.6	-1.3	1.3	1.7

Source: Authors' analysis of Census Bureau data.

income in the top 5% to that in the bottom 20%, the same measure used in Figure 1I. The 1970s and the 1980s provide a useful microcosm of the way inequality plays out in these data, because, as can be seen in the bottom section, the ratio grew much larger over the 1980s than it did in the 1970s.

The 1970s saw a 9 percentage-point shift in the population of families with incomes below $50,000 to those with incomes above that level. Most of that shift was to families with incomes above $75,000, with a roughly even split between $75,000-100,000 and $100,000 and up. In the 1980s, however, the pattern was somewhat different, with almost no change in the share in the lowest income category, a smaller growth in the upper middle ($75,000-100,000), and a larger shift to the high end ($100,000 and higher). The difference in these shifts across the decades partly reflects the fact that inequality was a much greater factor in the 1980s than in the 1970s. Over the 1980s the top/bottom ratio grew four times greater; over the 1970s, it was relatively unchanged. The result was that the 1989 low-income share was about the same size as the 1979 share, and the upper-middle share ($75,000-$100,000) grew much less (0.8 points versus 3.7 points). The top-income share, meanwhile, grew slightly faster in the 1980s compared to the 1970s (5.5 points versus 5.2).

Income shares were little changed in the first half of the 1990s, but the latter 1990s was a period of strong growth, especially at the lower end of the income scale. In these five years—1995-2000—the share of low-income (less than $25,000) families fell by almost 3 percentage points, while that of lower-middle families fell by 2.0 points.

This progress stopped short, however, in the 2000s, which saw slower average income growth and greater inequality. Low-income shares changed hardly at all, and the growth that did occur flowed to the top of the scale. Compared to the other periods in the table, the 2000s, at least through 2006, were the only cycle on record in which the share of families with incomes below $50,000 did not fall. Even in the 1980s, when the lowest-income share was stagnant, the second lowest—$25,000-$50,000—fell by over three percentage points; this share was unchanged in the 2000s. The shift toward higher-income classes slowed sharply as well, with the top income group expanding by only 1.3 points.

The above analysis shows that inequality slowed the progress with which average income growth moves families through these income brackets over time. **Table 1.16** uses a simple simulation to underscore that point. It shows the shares of families by income bracket, in this case using 2000 dollars to construct the income brackets (the previous table was based on 2006 shares, which is why the percentages differ). The third column introduces a simulated set of shares, created simply by multiplying family incomes in the 1979 data by the average growth of income between the two years. Thus, these shares partly reflect what the distribution of income across the brackets would have been in 2000 had each family seen its income grow at the average rate instead of at the much more varied rates that actually occurred under the significantly more unequal growth regime. Of course, many other things also changed during these years, including the demographics of the population, and these changes are not accounted for in this simple exercise. But the differences in shares do provide some perspective on how inequality slowed the rate at which families moved up through these brackets.

TABLE 1.16 The impact in inequality on income shares, 1979 and 2000

| | 1979 | 2000 | 2000* | Precentage-point changes | | |
				1979-2000	1979-2000*	Difference
Less than $25,000	25.0%	20.8%	16.1%	-4.2	-8.9	4.7
$25-50,000	34.3	28.4	25.8	-5.9	-8.5	2.5
$50-75,000	24.1	21.1	24.9	-3.0	0.9	-3.9
$75-100,000	9.6	12.8	16.4	3.2	6.8	-3.6
$100-150,000	4.9	10.9	12.0	6.0	7.1	-1.1
$150-200,000	1.7	2.9	2.6	1.2	0.9	0.3
More than $200,000	0.5	3.2	2.2	2.7	1.7	1.0

* Simulated by multiplying 1979 family income data by the average income growth rate between 1979 and 2000.

Source: Authors' analysis of CPS ASEC data.

FIGURE 1S Inequalty and income shares, 1979

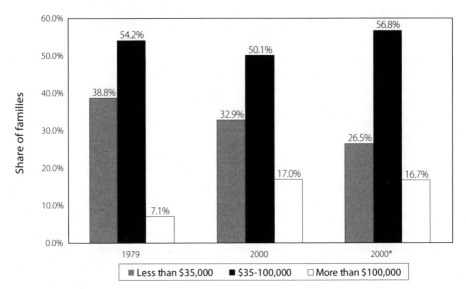

* Simulated by multiplying 1979 family income data by the average income growth rate between 1979 and 2000.

Source: Authors' analysis of CPS ASEC data.

About 10% of families moved out of the less-than-$50,000 range between 1979 and 2000 (see the first column of percentage-point changes), but this share would have been about 17% had income growth been more equal (i.e., had all incomes grown at the average rate). Even the upper-middle group—$75,000-$100,000—would have grown almost four more percentage points than actually occurred had income growth been more broadly shared.

Figure 1S rearranges the brackets from Table 1.16 to illustrate the impact of inequality on the hollowing out of the middle of the income distribution. We have arbitrarily delineated the middle-income group as between $35,000 and $100,000 in 2000 dollars. The second set of bars shows that the size of this group fell by about four percentage points, while the less-than-$35,000 group fell by about 6 points, implying a shift of 10% of families to the above-$100,000 group.

The third set of bars shows that, had incomes grown equally over these years, the low-income group would have diminished in size considerably further than it did, and that most of the difference would have gone to the middle group, which would have expanded by a few points rather than contracted. In other words, the increased disparity of income growth led to a larger share of low-income families and a smaller share of middle-income families than would have otherwise occurred.

In sum, while it is a positive development for families to move from lower to higher real income categories over time, such progress is expected in a growing economy, making this too low a bar against which to meaningfully judge progress. The important question is, how fast have these shares been shifting from lower to higher levels? In this regard, the growth of income inequality becomes an important intervening factor, since it will typically slow the pace of upward progress. Such was the case in certain periods examined above. In fact, had inequality not grown, the share of low-income families would have fallen more quickly and the share of middle-income families would be larger than it is today. Moreover, the most recent period has been uniquely weak by this metric, not even meeting the low-bar test: despite a relatively lengthy economic expansion characterized by fast productivity growth, income shares were virtually unchanged. As with the lack of median income growth, this was the first cycle on record to end without such progress.

Expanding capital incomes

The fortunes of individual families depend heavily on their reliance upon particular sources of income: labor income, capital income, or government assistance. Since most families receive little or no capital income, their economic well-being is determined by their success in the labor market—getting jobs and higher wages. Capital income, however, is a very important source of income to the top 1% and especially the top 0.1% (who receive more than a third of all capital income). Two significant reasons for the unequal growth in family incomes between 1973 and today are (1) a shift toward more capital income (such as rent, dividends, interest payments, and capital gains) and less income earned as wages and salaries; and (2) the substantially increased concentration of capital income among the households in the top 1% of the income distribution.

Table 1.17 projects the sources of income for families in each income group in 2006. These data are from a different source than that used for the earlier analysis of income trends, but they are comparable to the CBO data used to analyze tax trends. The table provides two types of breakdowns of income by income group. One shows how reliant an income group is on a particular source (*sources of income by income type*). The other breakdown shows how concentrated a particular type of income is in particular income groups (*distribution of types of income*). The particular incomes identified are: total wage and salary income; capital income (interest, dividends, and capital gains); business income (income from unincorporated businesses, farms); and other income (primarily government transfers, pensions, and child support).

The families in the bottom four-fifths of the income distribution obtain 70.3% of their income from wages and salaries and have very little business income (just 2.9% of their income) or capital income (4.2% of their income). In fact, the same is true for those families in the 80th to 95th percentiles, who obtain 75% of their income from wages and salaries. The only income groups with a particularly different composition of income are the bottom fifth, which receives a substantial 43.1% of its income from other sources (primarily government transfers) and the top 1%, which receives only 35.3% of its income as wages and salaries but obtains over half of its income from capital and business incomes.

TABLE 1.17 Sources of income by income group and distribution of income types, 2006

Income group	Sources of household income by income type					Distribution of types of income				
	Wage & salary	Business income	Capital income	Other income	Total	Wage & salary	Business income	Capital income	Other income	Total
Bottom four-fifths	70.3%	2.9%	4.2%	22.6%	100.0%	43.7%	16.1%	15.2%	52.4%	40.0%
Bottom	47.0	5.4	4.5	43.1	100.0	1.8	1.9	1.0	6.1	2.5
Second	61.1	3.3	4.4	31.1	100.0	6.1	3.0	2.6	11.5	6.4
Middle	73.1	2.6	3.5	20.8	100.0	12.9	4.1	3.6	13.7	11.4
Fourth	74.6	2.6	4.5	18.4	100.0	22.9	7.1	8.0	21.0	19.8
Top fifth	60.1%	10.8%	15.4%	13.6%	100.0%	56.2%	91.2%	84.2%	47.5%	60.3%
81-90%	76.0	3.6	5.0	15.4	100.0	18.4	7.8	7.1	13.9	15.6
91-95%	75.2	4.9	6.4	13.5	100.0	13.0	7.7	6.4	8.7	11.2
96-99%	62.8	10.9	11.3	15.0	100.0	14.7	23.0	15.4	13.1	15.1
Top 1%	35.3	20.4	33.2	11.1	100.0	10.1	52.6	55.3	11.8	18.4
All	64.5%	7.1%	11.0%	17.3%	100.0%	100.0%	100.0%	100.0%	100.0%	100.0%
Memo										
Top 0.1%	26.7%	19.5%	48.2%	5.6%	100.0%	3.5%	22.8%	36.6%	2.7%	8.4%
Next 0.4%	38.9	23.1	22.9	15.0	100.0	3.7	19.8	12.7	5.3	6.1

Notes:
(A) Calendar year. Current law.
(B) Tax units with negative cash income are excluded from the lowest quintile but are included in the totals.
(C) Includes both filing and non-filing units. Tax units that are dependents of other taxpayers are excluded from the analysis.
(D) Labor income includes taxable wages and salaries, contributions to tax-deferred retirement accounts, and the employer share of payroll taxes for Social Security and Medicare.
(E) Business income includes income or loss reported on Schedules C, E, and F.
(F) Capital income includes taxable and non-taxable interest income, income from dividends, realized capital gains/losses, and imputed corporate tax liability.
(G) Other income includes total Social Security benefits, taxable and non-taxable pension income, taxable distributions from IRAs, unemployment compensation, TANF, worker's compensation, energy assistance, veteran's benefits, SSI, disability income, child support, and alimony received.

Source: Authors' analysis of Urban-Brookings Tax Policy Center Microsimulation Model (version 0305-3A).

The bottom two rows of Table 1.17 present a breakdown of incomes within the upper 0.5%, that of the top 0.1%, and the next 0.4%. The very highest income families, the upper 0.1%, receive nearly half of their income from capital income (48.2%) and another 19.5% from business income: only about a fourth of their income is based on wages and salaries. Table 1.17 also shows the concentration of particular types of incomes. Most important to note is that 84.2% of all capital income is received by the upper fifth, with 55.3% received by the top 1% and 36.6% by the top 0.1% alone. Business income is similarly concentrated at the top.

This income landscape implies that fast growth for capital income will disproportionately benefit the best-off income groups. Those with less access to capital income depend either on wages (the broad middle) or on government transfers (the bottom) as their primary source of income. As a result, any cutback in government cash assistance primarily affects the income prospects of those in the bottom 40% of the income scale, and particularly the bottom fifth. The income prospects of families in the 20th to 99th percentiles, on the other hand, depend primarily on their wages and salaries (which make up at least 60-76% of their income). Thus, understanding changes in the level and distribution of wages (see Chapter 3) is fundamental to understanding changes in the incomes of the broad middle class extending upward to the 95th percentile.

There are two income realms where it is useful to examine the distribution of income between those from work (earnings) and those from wealth (capital incomes). The first is the distribution of *personal* income where one can examine the capital incomes received by households from their wealth holdings. The second is in the business realm, which explores the split of income between that accruing to ownership, primarily profits and interest received by corporations, and the compensation paid to employees.

The shift in the composition of personal income toward greater capital income is shown in **Table 1.18**. In the 1970s, capital income contributed around 14% or 15% of all market-based incomes (personal income less government transfers). By 1989, capital income's share of market-based income had shifted sharply upward to 20.8%, as interest income expanded. This shift toward capital income was slightly reversed by 2000 as interest rates and, therefore, interest income fell. However, dividend income had grown more important by 2000 reflecting the stock market boom. Interest income fell further between 2000 and 2007 as low interest rates, reflecting low inflation, prevailed. However, dividend income expanded further to 7.3% of market-based incomes in 2007 partially offsetting the decline in interest income.

Unfortunately, these data (drawn from the GDP accounts) do not capture realized capital gains as a source of income, and therefore provide only a partial picture of income trends. Adding realized capital gains to the analysis (with data drawn from the Internal Revenue Service shown in the last row) does not affect any conclusions about the 1970s or 1980s, as capital gains were comparably important in 1973, 1979, and in 1989. However, the share of income from capital gains grew to a substantial 7.8% of income in 2000 and remained high in 2007 at 7.6%. Table 1.18 shows that the capital incomes received by households comprised a larger share of all market incomes in recent years (particularly the last 10 years or so) compared to the 1970s or even the end of the 1950s in 1959. Adding realized capital gains to the picture makes this even

TABLE 1.18 Shares of market-based personal income by income type, 1959-2007

Income type	Shares of income					
	1959	**1973**	**1979**	**1989**	**2000**	**2007**
Total capital income	13.3%	13.9%	15.1%	20.8%	19.1%	18.4%
Rent	4.2	2.3	1.2	1.0	1.9	0.6
Dividends	3.3	2.8	2.9	3.6	4.7	7.3
Interest	5.8	8.8	11.0	16.3	12.6	10.6
Total labor income	73.5%	75.6%	75.8%	71.0%	71.8%	72.0%
Wages & salaries	67.9	66.0	63.4	58.6	60.0	58.3
Fringe benefits	5.5	9.5	12.4	12.4	11.8	13.7
Proprietor's income*	13.3%	10.6%	9.1%	8.2%	9.1%	9.6%
Total market-based personal income **	100.0%	100.0%	100.0%	100.0%	100.0%	100.0%
Realized capital gains	n.a.	3.2%	3.5%	3.3%	7.8%	7.6%

* Business and farm owners' income.
** Total of listed income types.
Source: Authors' analysis of NIPA and IRS data.

clearer. If one combines capital gains and other capital income (and rescale the total to reflect capital gains), then one sees that capital income comprised 16.5% of income in 1973 and 25.0% and 24.2%, respectively, in 2000 and 2007. Recall from Table 1.17 that 70% of this additional capital income, roughly 8% of the total, accrues to the upper 5% of households.

This shift away from labor income and toward capital income is unique in the postwar period and is partly responsible for the ongoing growth of inequality since 1979. Since the rich are the primary owners of income-producing property, the fact that the assets they own have commanded an increasing share of total income automatically leads to income growth that is concentrated at the top. Correspondingly, of course, a slightly smaller share of income was paid out as wages and benefits.

It is difficult to interpret changes in proprietor's income (presented in Table 1.18) because it is a mixture of both labor and capital income. That is, the income that an owner of a business (or farmer) receives results from his or her work effort (labor income) and his or her ownership (capital income) of the business or farm. To the extent that the shrinkage of proprietor's income results from a shift of people out of the proprietary sector (e.g., leaving farming) and into wage and salary employment, there will be a corresponding increase in labor's share of income (e.g., as farm income is replaced by wage income). This shift out of proprietor's income thus helps to explain a rising labor share in some periods, such as from 1959 to 1973. However, there has not been a dramatic shift in proprietor's income over the last few decades (it is roughly equivalent in 1973, 1979, and 2007), so it has not been a factor that has shifted the income distribution during that time.

The rise in inequality caused by the shift toward greater capital income is compounded by the growing concentration of capital income among the very highest income groups, particularly the top 1%. This is shown in **Figure 1T** using data from the Congressional Budget Office (which varies somewhat from the data in Table 1.17 and, unfortunately, goes only through 2005). Whereas the top 1% received 34.2% of all capital income in 1979, their share rose to 58.6% by 2000 and rose further to 65.3% in 2005. Thus, the top 1% roughly doubled its share of capital income between 1979 and 2005, an astounding development. Correspondingly, all other income groups, including the remainder of the top 10th (the next 9%), received a much lower share of the economy's capital income in 2005 than in earlier years. For instance, the share of capital income going to the bottom 90% declined from 36.7% in 1979 to just 15.1% in 2005, a roughly 60% reduction in their receipt of capital income.

Table 1.19 examines the split between income from earnings and income from wealth in the business realm. These data show the distribution of income by type of income in the various sectors (incomes generated by the corporate, proprietor, and government sectors). As a first cut, one might take the declining share of labor income

FIGURE 1T Share of capital income received by income groups, 1979-2005

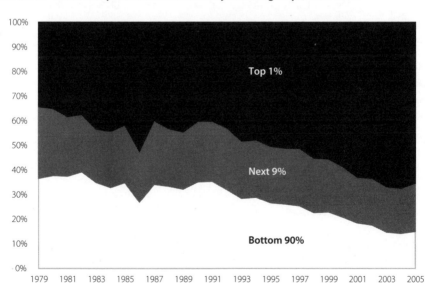

Source: Authors' analysis of CBO data.

TABLE 1.19 Shares of income by type and sector, 1959-2006

Sector	Shares of domestic national income						
	1959	*1969*	*1973*	*1979*	*1989*	*2000*	*2006*
National income, all sectors							
Labor	68.3%	72.3%	72.7%	73.9%	71.7%	72.3%	70.4%
Capital	19.3	18.0	17.2	17.3	20.0	18.6	20.1
Proprietor's profit	12.3	9.7	10.2	8.9	8.3	9.1	9.5
Total	100.0	100.0	100.0	100.0	100.0	100.0	100.0
Corporate and business sector							
Labor	43.8%	47.4%	47.8%	50.4%	47.8%	49.4%	46.1%
Capital	12.8	12.1	11.1	11.0	11.1	10.6	13.1
Total	56.6	59.5	58.9	61.4	58.9	60.0	59.2
Non-corporate sector							
Labor	9.4%	6.4%	5.6%	5.1%	4.7%	5.0%	5.4%
Capital	2.3	2.1	2.5	2.8	3.8	2.9	2.6
Proprietor's profit	12.3	9.7	10.2	8.9	8.3	9.1	9.5
Total	24.0	18.2	18.3	16.7	16.7	17.0	17.5
Government/non-profit sector							
Labor	15.2%	18.5%	19.3%	18.4%	19.2%	17.9%	18.9%
Capital	4.2	3.9	3.6	3.5	5.1	5.1	4.5
Total	19.4	22.4	22.8	21.9	24.3	23.0	23.4
ADDENDUM							
Shares of corporate sector income*							
Labor	77.3%	79.7%	81.2%	82.1%	81.1%	82.3%	77.9%
Capital	22.7	20.3	18.8	17.9	18.9	17.7	22.1
Total	100.0	100.0	100.0	100.0	100.0	100.0	100.0

* Does not include sole proprietorships, partnerships, and other private noncorporate business. The corporate sector, which includes both financial and nonfinancial corporations, accounted for 59% of national income in 2006.

Source: Authors' analysis of NIPA data.

in national income between the 1970s and recent years as evidence of a shift in factor (capital, labor) incomes. For instance, labor's share of national income was 72.7% in 1973 and 73.9% in 1979 but declined to roughly 72.0% in 2000 and to 70.4% in 2006 (the last year of data for all sectors). A closer look at the underlying data, however, suggests a somewhat larger shift away from labor income. First, labor's share of national income rose steadily from 1959 to 1979. One reason for the expanding share of labor income in those years was the steady expansion of the government/nonprofit sector. When the government/nonprofit sector expands, there is a tendency for labor's share of national income to grow because this sector generates mostly labor income and very little capital income. For example, Table 1.19 shows that the growth of the government/nonprofit sector—from 15.2% to 19.2% of national income between 1959 and 1989—necessarily added 4.0 percentage points to labor's share of national income (other things remaining equal). On the other hand, the shrinkage of the government/nonprofit sector over the 1989-2000 period led to a smaller labor share of income. Thus, the growth of the government sector over the 1980s led to an understatement of the decline of labor's share in that decade; in the 1990s, the decline in the government/nonprofit sector had the opposite effect. Thus, when making comparisons of the split between labor and capital income between particular periods, it is critical to take account of changes in the size of the government/non-profit sector. This is also true for changes in the non-corporate sector (farm and non-farm unincorporated businesses): when this sector shrinks, as it did from 1959 to 1979, labor's share of national income grows because labor's share of income in this sector is relatively low (less than a third in 1979).

The clearest way to examine the changes in income shares is to focus on the corporate sector, which accounted for about 60% of national income. Such an analysis is useful because it is not muddied by income shifts among sectors (such as expanding or shrinking government or non-corporate sectors) or the difficulty in defining proprietor's income as either labor or capital income. The division of incomes in the corporate sector is shown in the bottom section of Table 1.19. Labor's share fell from 82.1% in 1979 to 81.1% in 1989, and then to 77.9% in 2006.

More detailed information (including data for 2007) on labor and capital incomes in the corporate sector are presented in **Table 1.20** and in **Figure 1U**, which charts the share of capital income in total corporate income. The reported data are adjusted to account for the rise of "nonqualified exercised stock options" provided to corporate officers that are counted as wages in the national income accounts. This type of income is more akin to capital than labor income and totals a consequential amount in recent years. Drawing on analyses of the Treasury Department and the Congressional Budget Office, we estimate that these options were absent in 1994, grew to be equivalent to about 15% of corporate capital incomes in 2000 (the height of the stock market boom), and fell to a still-considerable amount equivalent to 6% of corporate capital income in the 2004-07 period.

Capital income's share was lower in the 1970s than it had been in the 1960s. By the mid-1990s capital income's share of corporate income surged upward with some erosion in the last years of the recovery ending in 2000 with a greater share, 20.3%, than in 1989. This indicator provides further affirmation that low unemployment strengthened workers' hands in the labor market in the late 1990s, a trend explored in both Chapters 3 and 4. Although the share of capital incomes lost ground in the recession of the early 2000s, it recovered to a very high level at the end of the recovery, averaging 22.3% over the 2004-07 period, which is equivalent to the high capital income shares that prevailed in the 1960s. That is, capital's share of corporate income in the recent recovery was the highest in nearly 40 years.

TABLE 1.20 Corporate sector profit rates and shares, 1959-2007

	Profit rates*		Income shares		
	Pre-tax	After-tax	Profit share**	Labor share	Total
Business cycle peaks					
1959	13.3%	7.3%	22.7%	77.3%	100.0%
1969	13.6	7.9	20.3	79.7	100.0
1973	11.7	7.0	18.8	81.2	100.0
1979	9.6	5.7	17.9	82.1	100.0
1989	10.6	7.4	18.9	81.1	100.0
1995	11.3	7.6	19.9	80.1	100.0
2000	12.1	8.4	20.3	79.7	100.0
2006	13.1	8.8	23.3	76.7	100.0
2007	11.6	7.6	21.9	78.1	100.0

* "Profit" is all capital income. This measure, therefore, reflects the returns to capital per dollar of assets.
** "Profit share" is the ratio of capital income to all corporate income.

Source: Authors' analysis of NIPA and BEA data.

FIGURE 1U Capital shares in the corporate sector, 1959-2007

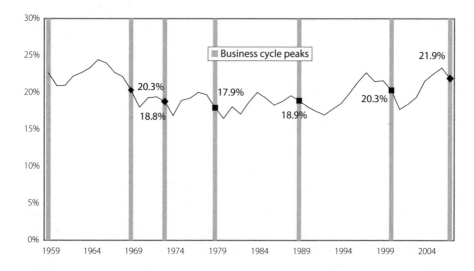

Source: Authors' analysis of NIPA data.

How important is the shift in the shares of labor and capital income? Capital's share in the corporate sector in 2004-07 was 22.3%, 3.1 percentage points above its 19.2% share in the 1976-79 recovery. This corresponds to an erosion in labor's share (wages and benefits) from 80.8% to 77.7%. It would require average hourly compensation to be 4.0% greater (80.8 divided by 77.7, less 1) to return to the previously higher labor share. Thus, the shift toward greater capital income shares can be said to erode compensation growth by 4% since the late 1970s, a non-trivial impact on wage and compensation growth.

Another way to assess changes in capital income's role is to examine changes in the returns to capital (measured as capital income per dollar of assets—the capital stock). This measure takes into account changes in the amount of capital used to produce corporate income and is useful because changes in the capital-output ratio can be responsible for changes in capital's share of income. **Figure 1V** and Table 1.20 show that the amount of before-tax profit received per dollar of assets (i.e., the capital stock) has grown since the 1970s (which had profit rates below that of the 1960s) and seemed to peak in the late 1990s before the downturn in profits around 2000, but recovered to high levels in the later recovery years of 2004 to 2007. This pattern of capital returns affirms the analysis of capital income shares, which showed that income accruing to capital/wealth attained levels in the late 1990s and in the last years of the recent recovery that rivaled the high capital incomes attained in the 1960s. The returns to capital of the 2004-07 period were 18.0% greater than that of the late 1970s recovery. In fact, one might conclude that this

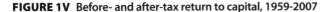

FIGURE 1V Before- and after-tax return to capital, 1959-2007

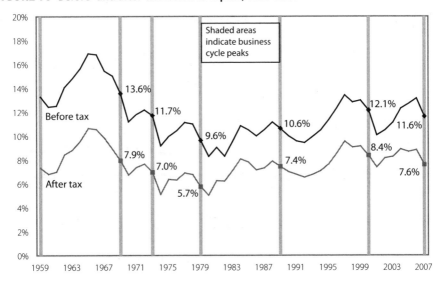

Source: Authors' analysis of NIPA and FRB data.

was the intended consequence of policies adopted in the late 1970s and later years that weakened labor protections and deregulated corporate behavior.

Because of the lowering of taxes on corporate profits, the after-tax return on capital has an even more impressive performance, averaging 9% in the late 1990s recovery (1997-2000) and 8.5% in the last years, 2004-07, of the recent recovery. The after-tax returns to capital in the 2004-07 period were 32% higher than in the late 1970s indicating that tax policy boosted the greater returns to capital given that pre-tax returns were, as discussed above, 18% greater.

Although this analysis incorporates the growth of "exercised nonqualified stock options" by measuring them as capital income rather than wages, it still misses an important part of the picture since the definition of labor's share includes the other elements of CEO pay, all of which are counted as labor income. This analysis thereby overstates the income share going to "workers" and understates "profits," since the bonuses and other stock options given CEOs are more akin to profits than wages. The amount of CEO pay relative to corporate profits has, in fact, grown significantly. Corporate capital income (not inflation-adjusted) grew 175% between 1989 and 2007, but CEO compensation (for the average CEO, not inflation-adjusted) grew 600% in this same period. This suggests that the growth in corporate profits is understated in this analysis because some of the profits are showing up in CEO paychecks and are counted as worker pay. As such, this analysis is not able to assess the magnitude of this bias.

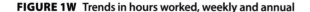

FIGURE 1W Trends in hours worked, weekly and annual

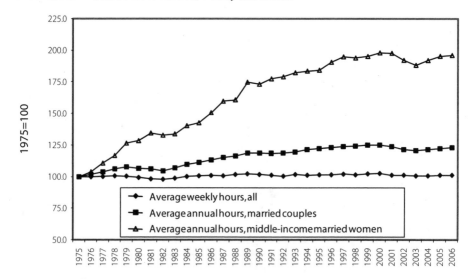

Source: Current Population Survey, Bureau of Labor Statistics.

This growth in profitability has left less room for wage growth. This might be considered the consequence of businesses successfully restraining wage growth as sales and profits grew in recent years, even in years of seemingly low unemployment. If the pre-tax return to capital in the 2004-07 recovery (12.4%) had been at the level of the late 1970s recovery (10.5%), then hourly compensation would have been 4.4% higher in the corporate sector. This was equivalent to an annual transfer of $206 billion from labor to capital (measured for 2004-07 in nominal dollars). This shift in income from labor to capital income is quite large when compared to the size of the loss of wages for the typical worker due to factors such as the shift from manufacturing to services, globalization, the drop in union representation, or any of the other prominent causes of growing wage inequality discussed in Chapter 3.

Family work hours

Much of the discussion in this chapter about recent income trends—those in the 2000s—has emphasized the role of diminished hours of work (see Table 1.1, for example) as the jobless recovery gave way to historically weak job growth over these years. But over the longer term, many working Americans claim to endure significant stress in trying to balance the often countervailing demands of work and family. Many of these families report feeling they are working more hours than their parents did and spending less time with their families. Such a dynamic potentially engenders feelings of stress and guilt that can erode the quality of family life, even as incomes rise.

Yet, it's often noted that the long-term trend in average hours worked per week per worker has changed little over time, a finding that seems to contradict the alleged time squeeze. In fact, as shown by the flat line in **Figure 1W**, the average weekly hours spent in the paid labor market have been unchanged for all workers, bumping up from 38.7 in 1975 to 39.2 in 2006, a small change over a long time period (though 1975 is not a cyclical peak—like 1979—that is when this data series begins; we revert back to peak-to-peak analysis in the tables below).

This trend, however, tells us little about how much families are working, and it is even misleading in that regard. The reason has to do with the entry of more women into the paid labor force. Women are more likely to work part time, and when women increase their share in the labor force, average weekly hours fall despite the fact that more family members are clearly spending more time in paid work.

While more women working may show up as lower weekly average hours, it unequivocally raises the total hours worked by families. That is, consider a married-couple family with one spouse working full-time, around 2,000 hours per year. If the other spouse in that family goes to work for half the year, the family's total hours worked rises to 3,000, but average weekly hours would fall due to the addition of a part-time worker.

The other two lines in Figure 1W convey this information on family work hours. The middle line plots the average annual hours worked, summing across both spouses, from a sample of prime-age families (both spouses 25-54) with children. This line rises fairly steadily through the latter 1990s, up around 25%. The top line in the figure is the growth in the hours of middle-income married women from these families, whose hours doubled since 1975.

   Table 1.21 takes a closer look at the annual hours worked by spouses in these families, with separate sections for married men and women. The section for married men shows relatively little variance. From the second fifth on up, these husbands tend to work more than full time, full year (52 weeks times 40 hours, or 2,080 hours), and thus there is little room for them to expand work hours (this is known as a "ceiling effect," since the variable under analysis—annual hours—is constrained by the available time

TABLE 1.21 Annual hours of work, married men and women, 25-54, with children 1979-2006, by income fifth

Married women	1979	1989	2000	2006	1979-2000	2000-06
Lowest fifth	509	694	750	709	47.4%	-5.5%
Second fifth	741	1,009	1,191	1,122	60.7	-5.7
Middle fifth	892	1,233	1,396	1,383	56.6	-1.0
Fourth fifth	1,103	1,323	1,462	1,475	32.6	0.9
Top fifth	1,069	1,331	1,409	1,415	31.9	0.4
Married men						
Lowest fifth	1,709	1,698	1,797	1,756	5.2%	-2.3%
Second fifth	2,060	2,128	2,121	2,096	3.0	-1.2
Middle fifth	2,143	2,184	2,226	2,220	3.9	-0.3
Fourth fifth	2,192	2,248	2,300	2,259	4.9	-1.8
Top fifth	2,304	2,372	2,394	2,350	3.9	-1.8
Combined						
Lowest fifth	2,218	2,392	2,548	2,465	14.9%	-3.2%
Second fifth	2,801	3,137	3,311	3,218	18.2	-2.8
Middle fifth	3,035	3,417	3,622	3,603	19.4	-0.5
Fourth fifth	3,295	3,571	3,762	3,734	14.2	-0.7
Top fifth	3,372	3,703	3,803	3,765	12.8	-1.0

Addendum: Added wives' hours, 1979-2000

	Added hours	As full-time weeks
Lowest fifth	200	5.0
Second fifth	381	9.5
Middle fifth	491	12.3
Fourth fifth	372	9.3
Top fifth	346	8.6

Source: Authors' analysis of CPS data.

in the day). As emphasized in the first section of this chapter, we again see the decline in hours across income quintiles between 2000 and 2006.

Married women, on the other hand, show marked increases in annual hours worked, particularly over the 1980s, with gains between 30% and 60% between 1979 and 2000. The addendum to the table gives a sense of how much more time these working wives spent in the paid labor market by income fifth. Middle-income wives added the most hours, up 491, the equivalent of over three months of full-time work.

Of course, the increased time that married women are spending in the paid labor market represents a challenge in terms of balancing work and family. It also reflects increased opportunities for women. On the upside, more paid work can mean greater economic independence, and in this sense the greater integration of women into the workforce represents an important advance for both them and society. But the lack of family-friendly policies in the workplace—such as guaranteed paid leave, vacations, or unemployment insurance accessible to those with shorter work histories—and persistent gender wage differentials (see Chapter 3) contribute to the downside of this long-term trend toward more work.

Added work hours by married women meant that their contribution to family income increased over this period. In the light of stagnant or falling men's wages (see Chapter 3), such contributions turned out to be a key factor raising the living standards of these families. The top row of the first section in **Table 1.22** shows the percent change in the real income of prime-age, married-couple families with children, again by income fifth, 1979-2000. Real family income grew for each quintile, from 7.4% at the low end of the income scale, to 24.3% in the middle, to 66.2% at the top fifth. What role did married women's contributions to family income play in these income trends? This is shown by examining family income growth without their earnings. As the second row reveals, family income would have fallen steeply—by almost 10%—in the lowest

TABLE 1.22 Real income growth of prime-age, married-couple families with children, 1979-2006, and married women's contribution

1979-2000	First fifth	Second fifth	Middle fifth	Fourth fifth	Top fifth
Percent change	7.4%	15.7%	24.3%	32.1%	66.2%
Without married women's earnings	-9.8	-1.3	5.3	15.6	53.3
Married women's contributions	17.2	17.0	19.0	16.6	12.9
2000-06					
Percent change	-3.0%	-2.8%	-0.7%	1.7%	2.4%
Without married women's earnings	-6.4	-4.1	-2.6	-0.5	-0.1
Married women's contributions	3.3	1.4	1.9	2.2	2.5

Source: Authors' analysis of CPS ASEC data.

quintile, and would have grown significantly less quickly in each other income fifth. Instead of increasing by 25% from 1979 to 2000, middle-income married-couple families with children would have seen an increase in their average income of only 5.3%.

The difference between the actual and simulated income results yield the percent contribution by married women, shown in the last row. For the bottom 80%, wives' contributions raised family income by about one-fifth. Note that wives' contributions added less—12.9%—to family income at the top of the income scale, a result which suggests that wives' earnings had an equalizing effect on family income growth over this period. That is, in the absence of wives' extra earnings, the income distribution of these families would have been even more unequal than was actually the case (tabulations not shown here suggest wives' contributions reduced the growth of the top fifth/bottom fifth ratio by about a third).

The weak job market of the 2000s led to diminished opportunities for both working husbands and wives, though, as seen in the bottom line of the second panel, married women still made an important contribution, preventing an income decline among the top 40% and dampening it for the bottom 60%. However, as seen in the previous figure and Table 1.21, both married men and women appear to be experiencing some extent of a ceiling effect, where their work hours in the paid job market are topped out given other responsibilities in their lives. The protracted cyclical downturn in the 2000s meant that men's and women's hours fell more than they would have otherwise. But as the middle line in Figure 1W shows, the trend in family work hours flattened well before the 2000s downturn.

This flattening in hours suggests an important structural limitation to future family income growth. The channel by which families raise their incomes by sending more workers into the job market to compensate for falling male wages is growing more narrow. The labor supply margin may offer some income relief for families trying to raise their incomes, but that margin has been largely tapped. The diminishment of this option puts more weight on wage growth as the source of gains from labor income. Of course, if income inequality is rising, it is less likely the hourly wages for middle-income families will rise with productivity, a problem very much present in the 2000s. In an economy where families are hard pressed to get ahead by working more hours, it is ever more important that they are fairly remunerated for the hours they are already putting in.

Conclusion

Family income is a key building block of living standards, and, as the preceding analysis has revealed, many American families have struggled in recent years. The 2000s may prove to be the first business cycle on record where the median family income failed to regain its prior peak. Inequality was temporarily knocked off course by the dot-com bust in late 2000, but it began to grow sharply again in 2003, and by 2006 it stood at the highest level on record since 1928.

The expansion of income accruing to wealth (capital income) and the increasingly concentrated receipt of that income by the very best-off has helped to generate greater income inequality by fueling very fast income growth for the top 1% and the top 0.1%.

Capital income such as interest and dividend income and from realized capital gains (the sale of assets) comprised 16.5% of personal market-based income in 1973 and 25.0% and 24.2%, respectively, in 2000 and 2007. This necessarily generates greater income inequality since most capital income is received by those who are well off.

The growing concentration of capital income among the very highest income groups, particularly the top 1%, has further exacerbated income inequality. Whereas the top 1% received 34.2% of all capital income in 1979, their share rose to 58.6% by 2000 and rose further to 65.3% in 2005. Thus, the top 1% roughly doubled its share of capital income between 1979 and 2005. Correspondingly, the share of capital income going to the bottom 90% declined from 36.7% in 1979 to just 15.1% in 2005.

There has also been a shift from labor to capital income (profits and interest) in the business realm. For instance, the share of income in the corporate sector going to capital income in the recent recovery was the highest in nearly 40 years. The share going to compensation was correspondingly at a low point. The historically high returns to capital are associated with the average worker's compensation being 4.4% lower and the equivalent of transferring $206 billion annually from labor compensation to capital incomes.

Tax policy has not helped. To the contrary, changes since 2000 have cut the tax liabilities of high-income families much more than those of lower-income families, exacerbating market-driven inequalities.

In one recent period—the latter 1990s—income growth was much faster for most families, and especially so for minorities. This trend appears to be closely related to the positive wage impacts from the full employment job market that prevailed over these years, as extremely tight labor markets gave working family members bargaining power they otherwise lacked.

The analysis of recent trends in hours worked by prime-age, married-couple families suggests that such periods of full employment may become increasingly important in terms of income growth. Women in these families have increased their labor supply a great deal over the last 30-plus years, and their extra work in the paid job market has proved to be an important source of family income growth. But their hours have not risen much for a while, and this slowdown appears to be independent of the recent downturn of the business cycle. Thus, in order for working families to get ahead in years to come, the extra labor supply channel may be less accessible, meaning that real wage growth is that much more important.

The importance of wage growth in turn underscores the importance of reducing the growth of inequality in order to reconnect working families to the productivity growth they themselves are creating. Rising inequality has made it harder for families to get ahead, both in an absolute and relative sense. Rising inequality has also had an important impact on economic mobility, a topic we turn to in the next chapter.

CHAPTER 2

Income-class mobility
How much is there?

The previous chapter documented the historically large increase in income inequality in recent years, reaching levels of concentration not seen since the latter 1920s (see Figure 2A). Such analysis essentially takes a snapshot of the distribution of family income at one point in time and compares it to a later date. As the chapter revealed, these pictures present important information about the extent of economic inequality at two points in time. But they say nothing about how individuals themselves have fared over their own lifetimes. For that, one must switch from "snapshots" to "movies." That is the purpose of this chapter.

What do we learn from this "movie" approach compared to the snapshots of Chapter 1? As shown in the previous chapter, over the course of a few generations, real incomes diverged, with the top fifth growing quickly, the middle fifth much less, and the bottom stagnating. These observations provide valuable information about the increasingly skewed distribution of growth, and, for many analysts, generate an image of most families stuck in place while economic growth passes them by. But what if low-income families were catching the growth wave and riding it to the top of the income scale? What if rich families were trading places with middle-class families?

This more mobile scenario paints quite a different picture than one in which families are mired in place. The unequal distribution of growth would perhaps be of less concern if high rates of mobility were offsetting that inequality. If the data showed, for example, that many families were likely to move from the bottom fifth to the top over time, or that children of wealthy families might switch places with middle-class kids when they became adults, then one could conclude that the benefits of growth were more broadly shared than suggested by the findings in Chapter 1.

The evidence reviewed in this chapter, however, does not find this degree of mobility. Of course, some families do move up and down the income scales, but most maintain their relative positions, meaning that relative to other families in their cohort, they remain at or near the income or wealth position in which they started out. For example, one study (Acs and Zimmerman, forthcoming) finds that about 60% of families that start in the bottom fifth are still there a decade later. At the other end of the income scale, 52% of families that start in the top fifth finish there at the end of the decade.

Given its dynamic component, mobility can be a more ambiguous concept than others explored thus far. Simply put, this chapter examines the extent to which your economic position today determines your position tomorrow. If where you start out in the income scale has a strong influence on where you end up, then the rate of economic mobility is low. If, on the other hand, where you start out is largely unrelated to where you end up, then mobility is high. More practically, if researchers look at the characteristics of a child, for example, including her race, parental income, neighborhood, and so on, and can predict with some accuracy what her adult income will be, mobility is low, and visa versa.

This last example invokes the research area of intergenerational mobility—the degree to which a child's position in the economy is determined by that of his or her parents. If class barriers are such that children's economic fate is largely determined by their family's position in the income scale, then the likelihood that, for example, a middle-class child will be a rich adult is diminished.

In fact, this chapter reports significant correlations between parents and their children, implying that income mobility is at least somewhat restricted as one generation's position in the income scale is partially dependent on their parents' position. For example, one recent study finds the correlation between parents and children to be 0.6 (Mazumder 2005). A detailed analysis of the implications of this correlation is provided below, but this finding is significant because it implies that it would take a poor family of four with two children approximately nine to 10 generations—over 200 years—to achieve the income of the middle-income four-person family. Were that correlation only half that size, meaning income differences were half as persistent across generations, it would take four to five generations for the poor family to catch up.

In other words, the extent of income mobility across generations plays a determinant role in the living standards of American families. It is, for example, a key determinant of how many generations a family will be stuck at the low end of the income scale, or snuggly ensconced at the high end. American folklore often emphasizes the rags-to-riches Horatio Alger stories, which suggest that anyone with the gumption and smarts to prevail can pull themselves up by their bootstraps and transverse the income scale in a generation. Reality, however, shows much less mobility.

Still, popular wisdom would suggest that there is probably more mobility in the United States compared with the advanced economies in Europe or Scandinavia. Shouldn't their more extensive social protections and less-freewheeling approach to economic policy dampen the entrepreneurial spark that gives birth to the American rags-to-riches paradigm? To the contrary: one of the most surprising findings of this research is that the opposite is true. Parents' economic positions in these countries are less correlated with their children's later income, meaning there is more intergenerational mobility in many of these European countries than in the United States.

What explains this lack of mobility? Certainly unequal education opportunities and historical discrimination play a role. For example, there are very steep mobility barriers facing African Americans, both in their own chances of moving up, and especially when compared to whites. One study shows that almost two-thirds (63%) of black children who start out in the bottom fourth of the income scale remain there as adults, compared to half that share for white children. Another deeply disturbing study finds that 45% of African American children who start out in middle-income families experience significant downward mobility, ending up in poor families (in the bottom fifth of the income scale) as adults, compared to 16% for whites.

In fact, opportunity itself appears to be unequally distributed, leading to one of the central conclusions of this chapter, one that ties the findings of this chapter to those of the previous one. It is often said that Americans do not object to unequal outcomes, only to unequal opportunities. But what if unequal outcomes themselves lead to diminished opportunities?

If some people are a lot more economically successful than others, either because they work harder, make better choices, or are just plain smarter, so be it. We may, as a society, choose to adjust those outcomes through taxes and transfers, but most would not consider such outcomes unjust. But if success favors those who are not necessarily more meritorious but are instead born wealthier, more connected, more powerful, whiter, male, etc., then this seems like a violation of the basic American value of equal opportunity. If growth flows mostly to those at the top of the scale (i.e., higher inequality), then it is possible that children from these fortunate households will have greater access to quality education relative to children from less well-placed families. If inequality means that some neighborhoods get parks and libraries while others do not, then this too restricts opportunity. If quality health care is more accessible to the haves than the have-nots, then the latter face a mobility barrier born of inequality.

If income concentration leads to a level of political influence that tilts against the have-nots, this too will reduce opportunity and ultimately lower the rate of economic mobility. If, for example, as has occurred in recent federal budgets, opportunity enhancing programs for disadvantaged children, like Head Start or subsidized health care (State Children's Health Insurance Program), are cut in order to maintain high-end tax cuts, then the likelihood that economically disadvantaged children will experience significant mobility is diminished.

While these connections are commonsensical, at this point, research has not generally identified the determinants of mobility in this or other countries. One important exception, however, is higher education. Here, the data do show that children from wealthy families have much greater access to top-tier universities than kids from low-income families, even when controlling for innate skills.

This educational barrier places profound limits on income mobility. Of those adults who grew up in low-income families but managed to earn a college degree, only 16% ended up in the bottom fifth of the income scale as adults. But for those who failed to graduate college, the share that started out and ended up in the bottom fifth was 45%. In other words, among children who grew up in low-income families, those who failed to graduate college were almost three times more likely to still be in the bottom fifth as adults compared to children who completed college.

Switching places...or not: Intragenerational mobility

A central question of mobility research is: How far do families move up or down across the income scale over their life span. Of those families who start out at the bottom, middle, or top of the income scale, what share is still there years later?

Though some research fails to make this adjustment, in answering this question, it is very important to control for the age/income profile, as shown in Table 1.5. That is, one might observe that a young family starting out with $30,000 of annual income has $50,000 a few decades later, and conclude that they are quite upwardly mobile. But what if most of the other families in their age cohort did a lot better, starting out with a similar level of income, but ending up with, say, $80,000? Then, in relative terms, the $30K to $50K family does not look so upwardly mobile.

In order to make these relative comparisons, researchers assign each person to an income fifth at the beginning of the observation period, based on the income distribution at that time. Then, numerous years later, the income cutoffs for the quintiles are re-calculated, and researchers are able to see where these families have ended up. This approach to income mobility examines whether a family becomes better or worse off relative to other families in their age cohort, as opposed to better or worse off in terms of their actual incomes.

If each family's income grew by the same amount (in percentage terms), there would be no change in mobility, that is, no changes in the relative positions of families in the income distribution. If, however, a family that starts out in the bottom fifth experiences faster income growth than other low-income families, then it may move into a higher fifth, that is, this family will experience upward mobility.

Absolute gains in real family income of the type discussed above—the $30K to $50K example—matter too, since higher real incomes enable families to raise their living standards. But inequality researchers have found that relative positions mean a lot to people. Our well-being, along with our sense of accomplishment, is not simply a matter of what we can afford to buy given our income levels. It is also a matter of how we are faring relative to others from our same generation. Research shows that if they pass us by—if we are downwardly mobile relative to others in our cohort—we experience economic stress, even if our buying power is up.

Table 2.1 presents this type of analysis for two 10-year periods: 1984-94 and 1994-2004 (two-year averages are used to control for transitory income fluctuations). The number at the top of the left column ("Lowest") shows that 55.6% of persons who were in the bottom fifth in 1984 were still there 10 years later. Only 3.3% (the top number in the right column labeled "Highest") made the long upward trek from the bottom to the top fifth over these years. Summing the first two cells in the first row, (55.6% plus 24.1%) about 80% of the sample started in the bottom fifth in 1984

TABLE 2.1 Income mobility between quintiles, 1984-94 and 1994-2004 (two-year income averages)

1984 quintile	1994 quintile				
	Lowest	Second	Middle	Fourth	Highest
Lowest	**55.6%**	24.1%	9.8%	7.2%	3.3%
Second	23.0	**33.9**	23.5	14.3	5.2
Middle	10.6	22.8	**28.5**	25.0	13.1
Fourth	3.4	12.9	25.4	**29.2**	29.1
Highest	1.6	5.8	13.6	26.5	**52.6**

1994 quintile	2004 quintile				
	Lowest	Second	Middle	Fourth	Highest
Lowest	**61.0%**	23.3%	9.0%	5.8%	0.9%
Second	23.1	**33.5**	24.6	10.5	8.3
Middle	11.5	23.2	**25.5**	26.2	13.7
Fourth	3.9	12.9	27.9	**30.0**	25.2
Highest	1.3	6.3	12.5	27.7	**52.2**

Source: Acs and Zimmerman (2008).

and ended in the bottom 40% 10 years later. The percent of "stayers" (those who did not move out of the fifth they started out in) are on the diagonal, shown in bold.

Most persons end up close to where they started. In the latter period, for example, of those that started in the fourth fifth in 1994, more than 80% ended up in that same quintile or one quintile higher or lower 10 years later. In both periods, about half stay in the highest fifth.

In fact, and this is an important finding from this work, the rate of mobility was remarkably constant over these two time periods. Comparing the fifths between the two panels, a statistically significant difference occurs in only one case: the share that jumped from the bottom fifth to the top fifth was smaller in the second period compared to the first (i.e., 3.3% down to 0.9%). Comparing overall mobility—the share of persons who made a quintile transition over the decade—is particularly revealing of how static the rate of mobility was between these two periods. In the first period, this share is 60.0%; in the latter period, it is 59.6%.

These data solidly belie any claim that increased mobility has offset rising inequality. Income classes are further apart now than in the past, and families are no more likely to traverse that greater distance.

The data in Table 2.1 come from a longitudinal data set, one that follows families over time, including those families formed by children of the original families in the study. These rich data yield important insights regarding family income mobility, but because they begin to track families in the 1960s, they have a limited time scope. **Figure 2A** takes advantage of data that tracks age cohorts back to the 1940s. Looking back a number of generations, the data show that, while families continue to get ahead as they age, they do so at a diminished rate.

Figure 2A shows the percent growth in real family income for families where the head of the family aged from about 30 to 50 years old (these are "synthetic cohorts," which means they do not track the same people, but they track the same age groups). The fact that each bar shows positive real growth confirms the well-known fact that as families pass through their prime years, their incomes generally rise, primarily due to the higher labor market returns of greater age and experience. Note that this measure is thus an absolute, as opposed to a relative, comparison.

But what is important here is the general decline in the rate at which income grew for these prime-age cohorts over the post-war period. As young families passed through their most important earnings years, their income more than doubled from the mid-1940s through the mid-1960s. For cohorts that started out in the mid-1950s, growth decelerated to 91.8%, still almost doubling. The slowdown continued, however, and the two most recent cohorts, those that passed through their prime earnings years from the mid-1970s through the mid-2000s, experienced the lowest growth rates in the post-World War II period.

FIGURE 2A Real median income growth by cohort, age 30-50, 1947-2006

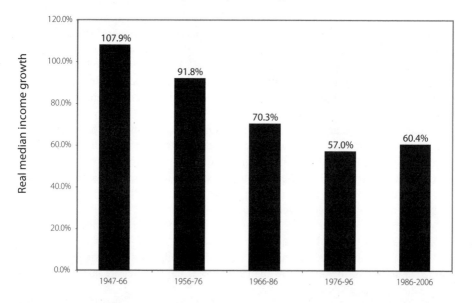

Source: Authors' analysis of Census Bureau data.

These falling growth rates make a real difference in living standards. Had the most recent cohort achieved the 91.8% growth rate of the 1956-76 cohort instead of their actual 60.4% growth rate, then their median income in 2006 would have been about $15,000 higher (about $91,000 instead of $76,000). Recall also from the end of the last chapter that prime-age families are working more in the paid labor market now relative to the labor supply of earlier cohorts. In that sense, today's families are running faster yet gaining less ground.

These mobility and cohort analyses consistently reveal some degree of income mobility and growth in America. By no means does the United States have a totally stagnant, immobile society, where people are stuck in their place in the income scale, decade after decade. But neither are they moving that far from where they start. Most who start at the top and the bottom are there a decade later. Most who start out in the middle-class are still in or near the middle-class a decade later; of those who start out in the middle fifth, about 75% are in one of the middle three-fifths a decade later.

Moreover, the rate of mobility has not changed over time. The data in Table 2.1 cover roughly the last two decades, but the last edition of this book took the analysis back yet another decade (to the 1970s) and showed the same result. This finding is important in the context of the inequality debate. It is true that greater mobility can offset higher inequality. But that is not happening in America. Income classes are further apart than they used to be, and families are no more likely to move across those greater

FIGURE 2B Intergenerational income persistence, sons and daughters, 2000

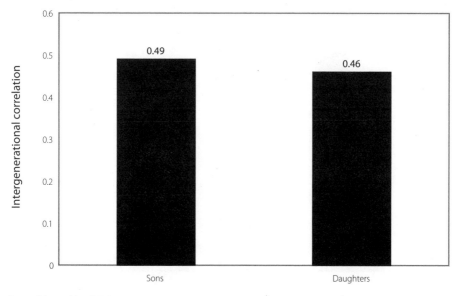

Source: Solon and Lee (2006).

distances. At some point—and America may already be there—excessive levels of in-equality themselves begin to create barriers to opportunity, and thus to mobility.

Intergenerational mobility

While the prior section tracked mobility within generations as they age, this section examines mobility between generations. Below is an investigation of how far the apple falls from the tree, or more prosaically, what is the correlation between the income of parents and their adult children. If one's position in the earnings, income, or wealth distribution is largely a function of birth, then we are left with a more rigid society where even those with prodigious talents will be held back by entrenched class barriers. Conversely, a society with a high level of intergenerational mobility, implying little correlation between parents' position and that of their children, is one with more fluidity between classes.

Economists measure the extent of intergenerational mobility by measuring the cor-relation in income or earnings between parents and their children once they grow up and earn their own incomes. **Figure 2B** shows the correlation between the incomes of parents and that of their sons and daughters. Is this a high, medium, or low level of income persistence? Certainly, a correlation of about half belies any notion of a totally fluid society with no class barriers. Yet, without various benchmarks against which to judge these correlations, it is difficult to know what to make of their magnitude. The rest of the section tries to present such benchmarks.

FIGURE 2C Likelihood that low-income son ends up above various percentiles

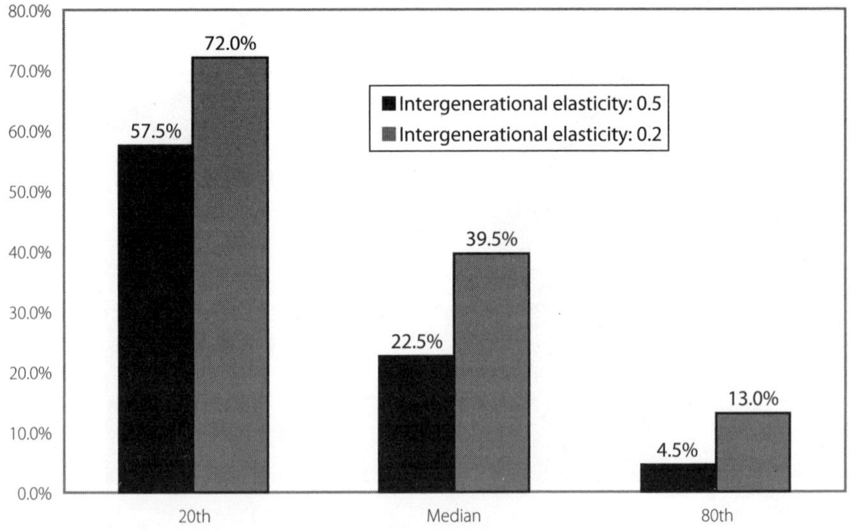

Source: Solon, unpublished.

Figure 2C, based on earnings correlations from mobility expert Gary Solon, shows where sons of low-income (10th percentile) fathers would be expected to end up in the earnings scale, based on their fathers' position. To calculate this expectation, one takes the correlation from Figure 2B, about 0.5, and based on that relationship, determines the likelihood that children from low-income parents end up with middle or high incomes (the technical term for the correlation is the "intergenerational elasticity," or IGE).

The first set of bars in the figure (IGE=0.5) show that while income mobility certainly exists, the apple does not fall far from the tree. Children of low-earning fathers have slightly less than a 60% chance of reaching above the 20th percentile by adulthood, about a 20% chance of surpassing the median, and a very slight chance—4.5%—of ending up above the 80th percentile. Using wage levels income from today's families, a son whose father earns about $17,000 a year has a 5% chance of earning over $60,000 per year.

One way to judge the extent of mobility under these metrics is to ask how the probabilities in Figure 2C would change if, instead of a 0.5 correlation, it was 0.2 (remember, a lower correlation in this work implies greater mobility between generations). With this new assumption, there is a 72.0% chance that the child reaches the 20th percentile, a 39.5% chance they reach the median, and a 13.0% chance they reach at least the 80th percentile. In other words, their chances of being middle- or high-earners are about double under the lower correlation scenario.

FIGURE 2D Intergenerational mobility, 1950-2000

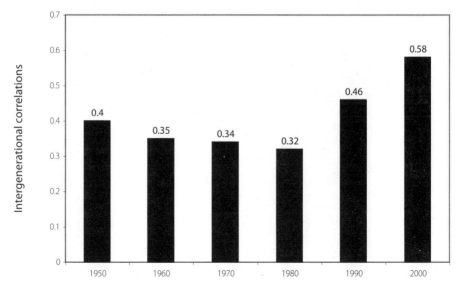

Source: Aaronson and Mazumder (2005).

Has the rate of intergenerational mobility changed over time? As with the 10-year movements by families examined above, there is little evidence that the correlation between children and parents' income has risen over time. Though Solon finds no increase in the trend, another study, using different data and methods, does find larger coefficients and thus less mobility over time.

These results are shown in **Figure 2D**. Since 1950, the rate of mobility initially increased somewhat before declining significantly in recent decades. Note that this trend occurred over the same post-1970s period when cross-sectional inequality was increasing. Thus, instead of faster mobility that might have offset the rise in inequality, the opposite trend occurred.

How do these correlations translate into actual income trends? In 2000, according to income data from the Congressional Budget Office, the average income of the top fifth was 3.9 times that of the bottom fifth. Applying the lower correlation in Figure 2D from 1980 (0.32), it would have taken about six generations to close an income gap that large. But with the diminished mobility implied by the higher correlation—0.58—it would take almost twice as many years, 11 generations, to close an income gap of that magnitude.

Combining intergenerational mobility among all family types masks important differences by race. Recent work by economist Tom Hertz examines the extent of upward and downward mobility of children, by race (Hertz 2006). The analysis focuses on children who started out in families in the bottom fourth of the income scale, and asks what share remained in the bottom fourth, and what share made it all the way to the

FIGURE 2E Income mobility of children, by race

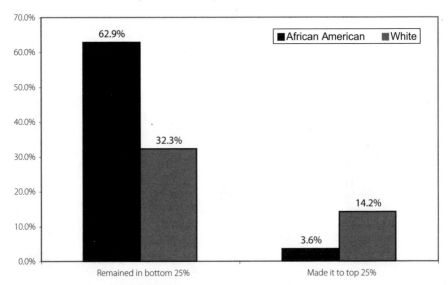

Source: Hertz (2006).

FIGURE 2F Percent of children in bottom fifth as adults, based on parents' income fifth, by race

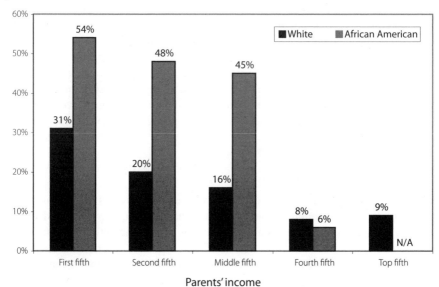

Source: Haskins et al. (2008).

top fourth as adults. Close to two-thirds of African American children who started out in the bottom fourth remain there as adults. For whites, the share remaining in the lowest quartile was half as large at 32.3% (see **Figure 2E**). Conversely, only 3.6% of African American children made it to the top of the income scale as adults, compared to 14.2% of white children. Such results suggest that mobility barriers are steeper for minorities, a finding returned to later in the further discussion of the relationship between parent and children's incomes.

A final look at intergenerational differences shows very significant backsliding by African American children compared to whites. **Figure 2F** examines the share of adults who end up in the bottom fifth of the income scale based on the fifth they started out in as children. That is, the first set of bars shows that about a third of white children and more than half of African American children end up where they started: in the first income fifth. But even when they start in middle-income families, close to half of African American children (45%) slide back to the bottom fifth, compared to 16% of white children.

The finding that significant shares of children, especially African American children, experience downward mobility warrants more careful study. One hypothesis is that middle-class African American children lack the social and societal supports, from informal networks to anti-discrimination rules, to keep them from losing ground. A related hypothesis, explored briefly below, is that in an economy where education returns are much higher now than they were a generation ago, access to higher education is an especially important mobility factor. As shown here, such access is often blocked for lower income children, even those with high cognitive skills. Since minority children are over-represented in low-income families, this barrier is likely in play for them. But Figure 2F shows that even controlling for income, African American children are much more likely to backslide than white children.

Another explanation may be due to differences in wealth across race. As shown in Chapter 5, wealth differentials by race are even larger than income differentials, so even families in the same income fifth are likely have different accesses to wealth. For minorities, this could translate into diminished ability to invest in their children's opportunities, even compared to white families with similar income levels. And this lack of investment/opportunity could explain some portion of the observed downward mobility for African Americans.

International mobility

One of the most interesting areas of mobility research compares the extent of economic mobility across countries. Such comparisons invoke a deeply embedded piece of U.S. social mythology: the Horatio Alger story. This is the notion that due to low class barriers in America, anyone who is willing and able can pull themselves up by their bootstraps and achieve significant upward mobility. Moreover, conventional wisdom holds that since class barriers in the United States are the lowest among the advanced economies, there are many more Mr. Algers in the United States versus Europe or Scandinavia.

The motivating idea behind this set of beliefs is that there is a tradeoff between unregulated markets and mobility. Since the American economic model hews more closely to the fundamentals of market capitalism—lower tax base, fewer regulations, less union coverage, no universal health care, and a much less comprehensive social contract—there should be greater mobility here. Also, the American national image eschews the aristocratic traditions more common in European societies.

The facts, however, show otherwise. There is considerably more mobility in most of the other developed economies of Europe and Scandinavia than in the United States.

How can this be? The answers are not well known, but two hypotheses are possible: First, it appears that the relationship between income inequality and mobility is relevant in this context as well. Since most advanced economies have less income inequality (see Chapter 8), the distance between income classes is smaller, so for a family or child to move from the bottom to the top, for example, over their life cycle is less of a trek. Second, educational outcomes are more highly correlated across generations here than in some other advanced economies.

This first point is shown graphically in **Figure 2G**, which places the hypothetical European income distribution within that of the United States. Because income is far less dispersed in the European Union, the quintile boundaries are closer there than the United States. Here then, is another way in which the higher levels of inequality in the United States dampen the rates of mobility, in this case compared to European and Scandinavian countries.

FIGURE 2G Mobility in the United States vs. European Union

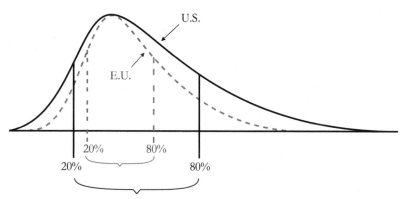

Mobility in the United States is more difficult compared to the E.U.
due to the greater distance between income classes.

Source: Authors' analysis.

Figure 2H shows father/son intergenerational correlations from a variety of countries. Other than the United Kingdom, the income of U.S. sons is most highly correlated with those of their fathers (note, regarding the discussion around Figure 2G, that the United Kingdom also has relatively high levels of income inequality). The relatively low correlations from the Scandinavian countries provide both a stark contradiction to the conventional wisdom and also a good example of the distributional phenomenon shown in the Figure 2G. As shown in Chapter 8, income in these countries is less disbursed. Data in that chapter also reveal far less poverty than in the United States, and this too promotes mobility, as poor families are much less mobile than higher income families (see Table 2.1).

Further evidence of this U.S.–U.K./Scandinavian low-income immobility difference, at least regarding sons, is shown in **Figure 2I**, which reveals: the likelihood that children of fathers in the bottom fifth end up in the bottom 40%, and that these low-income children make it to the top 40%. Two-thirds of the sons of low-income dads in the United States end up in the bottom 40%, compared to about half in the other countries. Conversely, while between 28% and 33% of these low-income children make it to the top 40% in the other countries in the figure, for U.S. sons, it is only 18%.

For daughters (**Figure 2J**), the chance that a daughter remains low-income (bottom 40%) is both lower than that of sons and more similar across countries, implying more mobility for girls than boys. Though research is only beginning to examine these gender differences, one analysis suggests that associative mating plays a role: higher earning women, including those from humbler backgrounds, tend to marry higher earning men, and this weakens the association between their income as adults with that of their family of origin. On the other hand, regarding the likelihood that

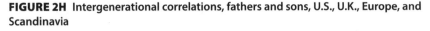

FIGURE 2H Intergenerational correlations, fathers and sons, U.S., U.K., Europe, and Scandinavia

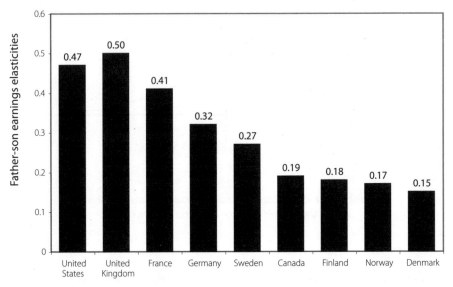

Source: Corak (2006).

daughters of poor fathers make it to the top 40%, the United States does have notably less mobility than other countries.

The next section briefly looks at two of the pathways—wealth and education—that underlie these mobility dynamics, both in the United States and abroad.

Opportunity and mobility

The evidence shown thus far raises the question: what are the determinants of mobility, and how effectively do these factors ensure opportunity for all, regardless of inequities at the starting line?

Two determining mechanisms are education and wealth. Since education is correlated with income, if children of highly educated parents have a better chance of achieving high levels of education themselves, this will lead to greater persistence of income positions—less mobility—across generations. Similarly, one might expect wealth to be correlated across generations, as wealthy parents make bequests to their children. Both factors play a role in the income persistence displayed in much of the evidence shown thus far.

Wealth: **Table 2.2** uses a transition matrix much like that in Table 2.1 to show the extent of wealth mobility between children and their parents over the past few decades.

FIGURE 2I Mobility for sons of low-income fathers

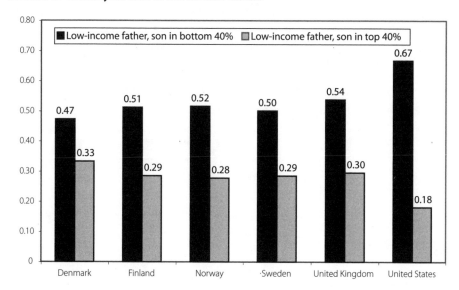

Source: Jantti et al. (2006).

FIGURE 2J Mobility for daughters of low-income fathers

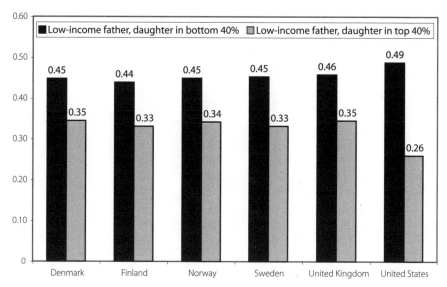

Source: Jantti et al. (2006).

The table shows the percent of children, who by their mid-30s, reached a particular wealth fifth based on their parents' position in the wealth scale.

For example, 36% of those with parents in the bottom wealth quintile ended up there as adults; only 7% ended up in the top wealth fifth. Adding the first two columns of the first row, 65% of children with parents in the least wealthy fifth ended in the bottom 40% of the wealth distribution. Moving to the middle fifth, 25% of the children

TABLE 2.2 Intergenerational wealth, parents to children

Parents' wealth quintile	Child's wealth quintile					
	Lowest	Second	Middle	Fourth	Fifth	Total
Lowest	**36%**	29%	16%	12%	7%	100%
Second	26	**24**	24	15	12	100
Middle	16	21	**25**	24	15	100
Fourth	15	13	20	**26**	26	100
Highest	11	16	14	24	**36**	100

Source: Charles and Hurst (2003).

FIGURE 2K Education correlations: parents and children

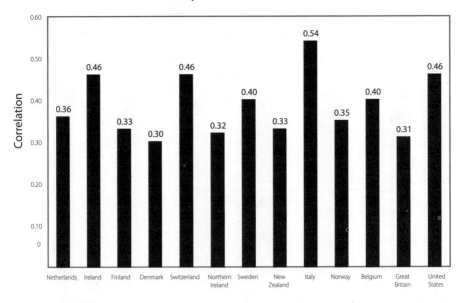

Source: Hertz et al. (2008).

of middle quintile parents stayed in that middle fifth, while 24% moved up one fifth and 21% moved down one fifth. At the top of the wealth scale, 36% of the children of the wealthiest parents were themselves in the top fifth, and 60% stayed in the top 40%.

Education: Education is a critical pathway through which economic mobility occurs. A key issue here is how closely children's educational attainment is related to, or correlated with, that of their parents. Here again, high correlations imply a damaging class barrier that would serve to thwart mobility based on merit. In fact, one of the findings stressed below shows that children from families with low incomes are much less likely to complete college, even controlling for cognitive ability (as measured by test scores). Surely, this provides an example of considerable barriers to opportunities.

One recent study compares the correlation between the education levels of parents and children in a variety of countries (Hertz et al. 2007). These correlations, plotted in **Figure 2K**, show that the educational attainment of children in Italy is most closely linked to that of their parents, compared to the other countries in this survey. The United States, with a correlation of just under half, is tied with a number of countries for the second highest, while relatively low correlations are present for Finland, Sweden, Norway, Denmark, Northern Ireland, and Great Britain. The fact that educational correlations are higher in the United States than in some other countries implies that more education is less likely to lead to greater relative mobility in the United States compared to these other countries.

An interesting corollary to the role of education is the increase in education returns (the wage advantage of more highly educated workers over those with less education) over the last few decades, a development that reinforces the immobility related to intergenerational educational mobility. That is, a child of a parent who went to college has a greater chance of attending college him or herself. Therefore, that child also has a greater chance of benefiting from the higher relative wages earned by college-educated workers today relative to decades earlier. Together, these forces combine to constrain intergenerational income mobility.

Figure 2L shows the significant role played by the large wage advantage of more highly educated workers in the United States relative to other countries (here again, the analysis focuses on the correlation between fathers' income and sons' earnings). The lower part of each bar shows the contribution of education to intergenerational mobility in three countries, the United States, the United Kingdom, and West Germany (Blandon 2004). The rest of the bar is attributable to the myriad other factors that explain intergenerational persistence of earnings. The figure shows that high educational returns in the United States lead to significantly higher levels of earnings immobility here relative to the two other countries in the figure (the other factors are also larger in the United States). In fact, as the last bar shows, were the U.S. educational returns more like those in the United Kingdom and West Germany, the mobility correlation would be 24% lower.

As noted, another relevant issue regarding mobility and education is the quality of education accessible to children from families in different positions in the income scale. **Figure 2M** compares the family income of children in the entering classes at top-tier

FIGURE 2L Intergenerational mobility: role of education

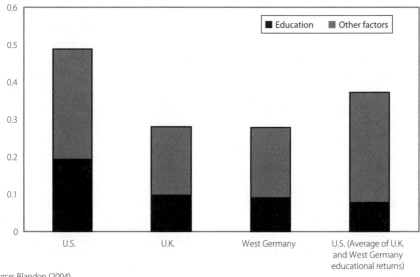

Source: Blandon (2004).

universities versus community colleges. Over 70% of those in the top tier come from families with the highest incomes, while 3% and 6% of the entering class come from the lowest and second lowest income groups, respectively, that is, the bottom 50% of families. At community colleges, however, the distribution is much more uniform.

Still, one might argue that the findings in Figure 2M simply represent a meritocracy at work, as those from high-income families have, perhaps through their privileged positions, acquired the intellectual tools to succeed at the top schools. **Figure 2N** belies this argument. The figure shows that even after controlling for academic ability, higher income children are still more likely to complete college. Each set of bars shows the probability of completing college for children based on income and their math test scores in eighth grade. For example, the first set of bars, for the students with the lowest test scores, shows that 3% of students with both low scores and low incomes completed college, while 30% of low-scoring children from high-income families managed to complete college.

The fact that each set of bars has an upward gradient is evidence against a completely meritocratic system. The pattern implies that at every level of test scores, higher income led to higher completion rates. The first set of bars, for example, shows that even among the highest scoring students in eighth grade, only 29% of those from the low-income families finished college, compared with 74% of those from the wealthiest families. In fact, this 29% share is about identical to the completion rates of low-scoring, high-income students (30%), shown in the third set of bars. In other words, high-scoring, low-income children are no more likely to complete college than low-scoring, wealthy children.

FIGURE 2M Income position of the entering class at top colleges and community colleges

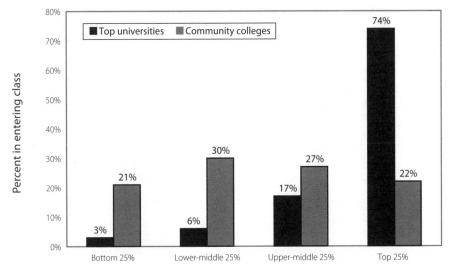

Source: Carnevale and Rosé (2003).

FIGURE 2N College completion by income status and test scores

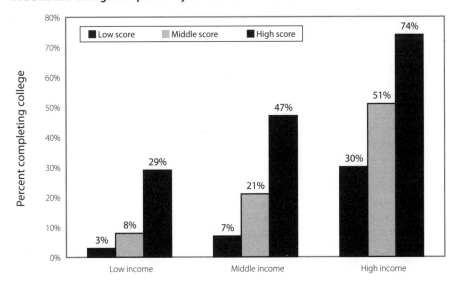

Source: Fox, Connolly, and Snyder (2005).

FIGURE 20 Intergenerational mobility, by college education

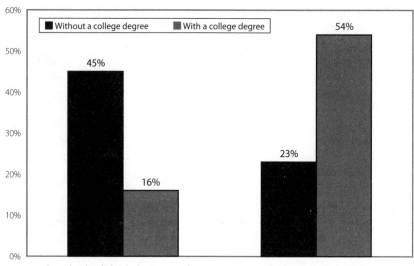

Source: Haskins et al. (2008).

Finally, the barriers to higher education revealed in these last two figures are costly in terms of reduced mobility, as shown in **Figure 20**. This figure returns to inter-generational analysis, but adds college completion to the mix, revealing achievement to be an important mobility booster. The first set of bars shows that among those who lived as children in the lowest income families, college completion was strongly associated with leaving the bottom fifth in adulthood: 16% of those with a college degree remained low-income as adults, compared to 45% without college. Similarly, 54% of high-income children who completed college were high-income adults. But less than half that share—23%—without a college degree managed to maintain their top-fifth status. That is, 77% of the children who grew up in top-fifth families but failed to complete college, fell to lower income classes as adults.

Volatility

This final section takes a brief look at an issue related to income mobility: income volatility. Like the mobility work described thus far, this measure also tracks the same families over time. In this case, however, income volatility tracks the stability of their income defined as the extent of short-term fluctuations around a longer-run average. That is, imagine two families with the same average income over a long period, say 10 years. But in one case, the family's income grew at the same or similar pace each one of those years. In the other case, the family's income was flat one year, grew 10% the next,

FIGURE 2P Cumulative growth in family income volatility since 1973

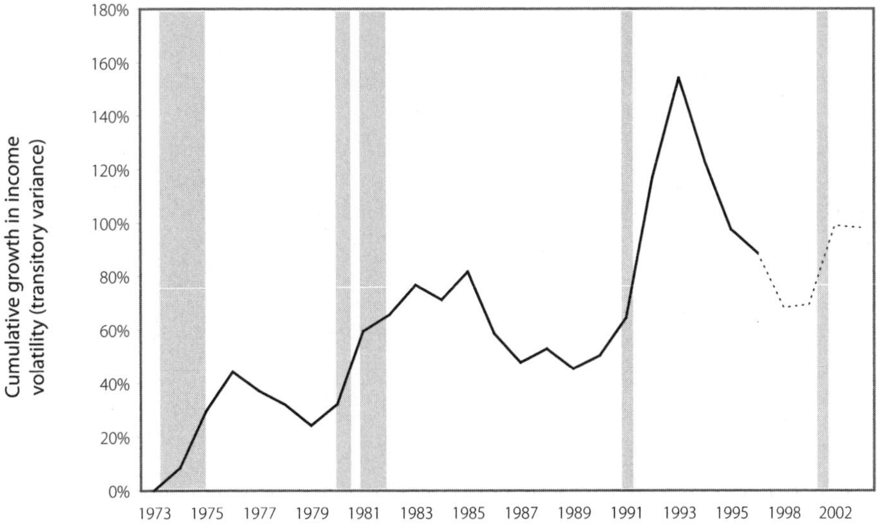

Note: Dotted lines indicate bi-annual survey years.

Source: Hacker and Jacobs (2008).

fell 5% the next, and so on. If one plotted the trajectory of the second family around their mean, it would be a jagged line going under and over the average, whereas for the first family, the line would largely be coincident with the average itself.

The work of various analysts, most notably Jacob Hacker and Peter Gosselin, have found an increase in the variability of income trajectories over the past few decades, that is, more families with the erratic patterns of the second family. **Figure 2P** plots the increase in family income volatility, showing various peaks and valleys around an upward trend since the mid-1970s (Hacker 2008). Volatility appears counter-cyclical: it rises in downturns and falls in recoveries, with a particularly steep decline in the latter 1990s (suggesting that perhaps diminished volatility is an unexplored benefit of full employment). Over the full series, volatility by this measure has doubled.

Figure 2Q focuses on another dimension of volatility: the increased probability of large income losses. The figure reveals that the proportion of working-age individuals experiencing a large drop in their family income (50% or greater) has climbed more steadily—from less than 4% in the early 1970s to nearly 10% in the early 2000s. The likelihood of large income losses rises in recessions, but a structural increase—an underlying increasing trend—is clear in the figure.

Since volatility is a measure of short-term, or transitory income movements, its increase feeds directly into increases in cross-sectional inequality of the type measured in Chapter 1, that is, all else being equal, more short-term instability means more income inequality. But what is the relationship between volatility and mobility?

FIGURE 2Q Prevalence of a 50% or greater drop in family income

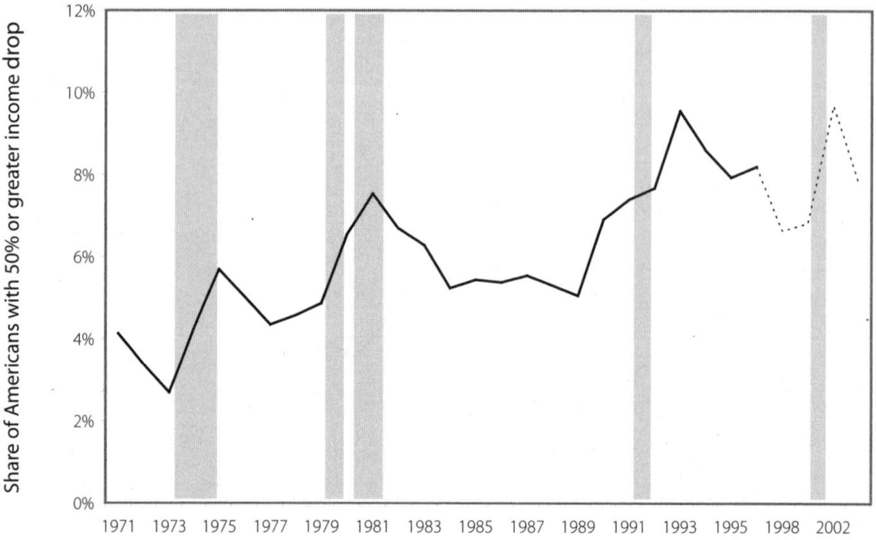

Note: Dotted lines indicate bi-annual survey years.

Source: Hacker and Jacobs (2008).

This is less clear, since mobility is most accurately thought of as a long-term concept. And, in fact, the mobility data fail to show a clear, increasing trend, suggesting little relationship between volatility (which follows an upward trend) and mobility. Of course, it is possible that absent the increase in income instability, mobility might have increased, but this is only conjecture. In fact, higher instability by definition leads to diminished short-run income correlations, but again, the most useful income correlations are taken over longer periods, like those in the intergenerational section above.

What conclusions can be drawn from the increase in short-run volatility? It is widely agreed that the increase in jumps and dips in family income is a source of increased economic insecurity. Families tend to expect and benefit from smooth, predictable income trajectories, However, increased "shocks," even transitory ones, lead to a sense that the economic firmament upon which we stand is shakier than we thought. Thus, the trends Hacker and others demonstrate in their work help to explain the diminished security many families report feeling regarding their own, and their children's, economic fate.

Conclusion

The previous chapter revealed historically high levels of income inequality. For many, this is a troubling development in and of itself, but it is arguably less so if U.S. families are highly mobile, regularly climbing up and down the income ladder even as the ladders' rungs grow further apart. This chapter, however, finds no such acceleration in mobility that might offset the higher inequality observed in Chapter 1. Neither does the chapter find evidence (excepting one study) of diminished mobility. What it does find is considerable and sustained immobility. For example, one recent study finds that about 60% of families that start in the bottom fifth are still there a decade later. At the other end of the income scale, 52% of families start and finish in the top fifth.

Measures of intergenerational mobility find that the incomes of adult children correlate significantly with that of their parents, suggesting that the apple falls not too far from the tree. As a result, low-income kids are very unlikely to become high-income adults. Moreover, this result is amplified by race, as minority children are more closely tied to their income status at birth than white children. In fact, recent research shows considerable backsliding by African American children: 45% who started their lives as children in middle-income families ended up in the lowest income fifth as adults.

These facts suggest the need to scrutinize the condition of a basic American economic value: equality of opportunity. Few expect or desire the economy to deliver equal outcomes, but the concept that roughly the same opportunities should be available to all who have the desire and make the effort to take advantage of them is a deeply held value. Much of the evidence presented in this chapter raises strong doubts about how operative that value is in today's economy.

Perhaps surprisingly, given widespread mythology about sclerotic European economies, international comparisons show greater mobility between generations in Europe than in the United States. Part of the difference has to do with relatively high correlations regarding educational attainment of parents and children here versus Scandinavia, for example. In addition, even controlling for cognitive ability, low-income children in the United States face significant barriers to higher education, a key pathway to upward income mobility.

This last point underscores a central concern raised by these findings: inequality itself may be erecting mobility barriers. As income and wealth become more concentrated in American society, so do access to higher education, to political power, to good neighborhoods with good schools, to decent health care, and ultimately, to opportunity itself. If true, the structure of the economy is actively violating a core American principle: that of fair opportunity for all. The indicators and trends investigated in this chapter warrant scrutiny moving forward. If market forces are failing to provide fair opportunities, and there is ample evidence to support this claim, then policy intervention to reset the balance is essential.

CHAPTER 3

Wages
Historic gap between productivity and compensation during recoveries

Because wages and salaries make up roughly three-fourths of total family income (the proportion is even higher among the broad middle class), wage trends are the driving force behind income growth and income inequality trends. This chapter examines and explains the trends in wage growth and wage inequality during the last few decades up through 2007, with a particular focus on the business cycle from 2000 to 2007. Rising unemployment in 2008 marked the end of that expansion and the beginning of a new business cycle.

The major development in the labor market in recent years has been the stunning disconnect between the possibilities of improved pay and the reality of stunted pay growth, especially in the recent recovery. Productivity grew 11% in the recovery, a faster growth than in any recovery since the 1970s. Yet, hourly compensation for the median worker or for high school or college graduates did not grow at all in the recovery despite historically high productivity growth.

The wage momentum from the late 1990s into the 2000s is important to understand when looking at trends over the just-completed business cycle, the 2000-07 period; all of the wage growth in 2000-07 occurred within the first two years. The poor job creation and increased job shortages during the early 2000s recession and lackluster recovery eventually knocked wage growth down so that prices rose at least as fast. This was the case even in 2007, when the unemployment rate fell to 4.6%. Since 2000, wage growth among the bottom 70% (70th percentile or below) has been modest at 3.0% or less; at the median, growth of 2.6% over the 2000-07 period was just one-third that of the 1995-2000 period. Wage growth among higher-wage workers was also slower in recent years than in the 1995-2000 period. Wage deceleration, then, has been pervasive.

Women are much more likely to earn poverty-level wages than men. In 2007, 31.4% of women earned poverty-level wages or less, significantly more than the share of men (21.8%). The proportion of minority workers earning low wages is substantial—34.0% of black workers and 41.8% of Hispanic workers in 2007. Overall, 26.4% of workers, over one in every four, earned poverty-level wages in 2007.

Momentum in reducing poverty-wage jobs began in the late 1990s, continued until 2002, and then dissipated. There has been no progress, among any racial/ethnic group or among either men or women, in reducing the share of workers with low earnings over the 2002-07 recovery.

Wage inequality has three key elements. One is the gap separating out the "bottom," reflected in the difference between middle-wage (median-wage earners) and low-wage workers. Another is the "top half" gap between high-wage (90th or 95th percentile wage earners) and middle-wage earners. The third element is the gap at the very top, that is, the growth of wages for those in the upper 1% and even the upper 0.1%, including chief executive officers (CEOs). These three elements have had differing historical trajectories. The gap at the bottom grew in the 1980s but has been stable or declining ever since, whereas the "top half" wage gap has persistently grown since the late 1970s. The very highest earners have done considerably better than other workers for at least 30 years, but they have done extraordinarily well over the last 10 years.

Explaining these shifts in wage inequality requires attention to several factors that affect low-, middle-, and high-wage workers differently. The experience of the late 1990s is a reminder of the great extent to which a low unemployment rate benefits workers, especially low-wage earners. Correspondingly, the high levels of unemployment in the early and mid-1980s and in recent years disempowered wage earners and provided the context in which other forces—specifically, a weakening of labor market institutions and globalization—could drive up wage inequality. Significant shifts in labor market policies and institutions, such as the severe drop in the minimum wage and deunionization, can explain one-third of growing wage inequality. Similarly, the increasing globalization of the economy—immigration, trade, and capital mobility—and the employment shift toward lower-paying service industries (such as retail trade) and away from manufacturing can explain, in combination, at least another third of the total growth in wage inequality. Macroeconomic factors also played an important role: high unemployment in the early 1980s greatly increased wage inequality, the low unemployment of the late 1990s reduced it, and the slack labor market of the 2000s refueled it.

The shape of wage inequality shifted in the late 1980s as the gap at the bottom—that is, the 50/10 gap between middle-wage workers at the 50th percentile and low-wage workers at the 10th—began to shrink. However, over the last few years, this wage inequality at the bottom has been growing among both men and women. This reversal is partially the effect of the jobless recovery and the still-remaining shortage of jobs and partially a result of the continued drop in the real value of the minimum wage, at least until 2007. The greatest increase in wage inequality at the bottom occurred among women and corresponded to the fall in the minimum wage over the 1980s, the high unemployment of the early 1980s, and the expansion of low-wage retail jobs. The positive trend in this wage gap over the 1990s owes much to increases in the minimum wage, low unemployment, and the slight, relative contraction in low-paying retail jobs in the late 1990s. The wage gap at the top half—the 90/50 or 95/50 gap between high- and middle-wage earners—continued its steady growth in the 1990s and the 2000s (except the last few years), but at a slightly slower pace than in the 1980s. The continuing influence of globalization, deunionization, and the shift to lower-paying service industries ("industry shifts") can explain the continued growth of wage inequality in the top half.

The top 1% of earners in 2006 had average annual earnings of $576,000 (in 2007 dollars). The top earners' share of earnings was relatively stable from 1947 into the 1970s but nearly doubled from 7.3% in 1979 to 13.6% in 2006 (the latest year of available data). This is the consequence of earnings growth of 144.4% from 1979 to 2006 for the top 1% compared with just 15.6% for the bottom 90%. Those in the upper 0.1% of earners (the top one-thousandth) fared far better, seeing their annual earnings grow 324% since 1979 to reach over $2.2 million in 2006. Consequently, the earnings of the top 0.1% grew to be 77 times the earnings of the bottom 90% in 2006 compared to just 21 times as much in 1979.

The erosion of the extent and quality of employer-provided benefits, most notably pensions and health insurance, is an important aspect of the deterioration in job quality for many workers. Employer-provided health care coverage eroded from 1979 until 1993-94, when it stabilized, and then began falling again after 2000 through 2006 (the latest data): coverage dropped from 69.0% in 1979 to 55.0% in 2006, with a 3.9 percentage-point fall since 2000. Employer-provided pension coverage tended to rise in the 1990s but receded by 2.8 percentage points from 2000 to 2006 to 42.8%, 7.8 percentage points below the level in 1979. Pension plan quality also receded as the share of workers in defined-benefit plans fell from 39% in 1980 to just 18% in 2004. Correspondingly, the share of workers with a defined-contribution plan (and no other plan) rose from 8% to 31%.

Young workers' prospects are a barometer of the strength of the labor market: when the labor market is strong for workers overall, the prospects for young workers are very strong, and when the labor market is weak their prospects are very weak. Wages were stagnant or fell among every entry-level group, both high school and college-educated workers and both men and women, in the period of sluggish wage growth since 2000. For instance, the entry-level hourly wage of a young male high school graduate in 2007 was 18.2% less than that for the equivalent worker in 1979, a drop of $2.62 per hour. Among women, the entry-level high school wage fell 11.2% in this period, with a 6.3% loss since 2000 standing out. Entry-level wages fell among both female and male college graduates from 2000 to 2007, 3.2% among men, and 1.7% among women. This contrasts to the extremely strong wage growth for each of these groups from 1995 to 2000, when wages rose roughly 10% for entry-level high school men and women, and 20.9% for entry-level college men, 11.7% for college women.

Unionized workers earn higher wages than comparable non-union workers and also are 18.3% more likely to have health insurance, 22.5% more likely to have pension coverage, and 3.2% more likely to have paid leave. The erosion of unionization (from 43.1% in 1978 to just 19.2% in 2005) can account for 65% of the 11.1 percentage-point growth of the white-collar/blue-collar wage gap among men over the 1978-2005 period.

The real value of the minimum wage fell steadily in real terms from 2000 until 2007 (when an increase was legislated), thereby causing the earnings of low-wage workers to fall seriously behind those of other workers and contributing to rising wage inequality in this period. Legislated increases through 2009 benefit workers who make important contributions to their family's economic well-being: over half of those benefiting from the most recent increases in the minimum wage work full-time, and another 31% work more than 20 hours weekly. While minorities are disproportionately represented among minimum wage workers, 61% are white. These workers also tend to be women (59% of the total) and are concentrated in the retail and hospitality industries (46% of all minimum wage earners are employed there, compared to just 21% of all workers).

The 1980s, 1990s, and 2000s have been prosperous times for top U.S. executives, especially relative to other wage earners. Over the 1989-2007 period the median CEO's pay rose 106.8%, and average CEO pay rose 167.3%. During that same period a typical worker's wage grew by just 10%, and mostly in the late 1990s. In 1965, U.S. CEOs in major companies earned 24 times more than an average worker; this ratio grew to 298 at the end of the recovery in 2000, fell due to the stock market decline in the early 2000s, and recovered to 275 in 2007. In other words, in 2007 a CEO earned more in one workday (there are 260 in a year) than the typical worker earned all year.

Will the jobs of the future require far more skills and education and necessitate a wholesale upgrading of the educational attainment of the workforce? The jobs of the future will, in fact, require greater education credentials, but not to any large extent. In 2006 the occupational composition of jobs required that 27.7% of the workforce have a college degree or more. This share will rise by just 1 percentage point, to 28.7%, by 2016.

The analysis of wages proceeds as follows. The first half of the chapter documents changes in the various dimensions of the wage structure, that is, changes in average wages and compensation and changes by occupation, gender, wage level, education level, age, and race and ethnicity. These shifts in the various dimensions of wage inequality are then assessed and explained by focusing on particular factors such as unemployment, industry shifts, deunionization, the value of the minimum wage, globalization and immigration, and technology.

Taking stock of the 2000-07 business cycle

Our analyses of income, wages, employment, and the like examine changes between comparable points of business cycles, because it is the underlying movement of the economy, from cyclical peak-to-peak, that is the major force behind changes in income and wages and the standard of living. As discussed in Chapter 1, it is clear, though not officially and technically determined yet, that 2007 was the last year of the recent business cycle that started in 2000-01, when unemployment hit its lowest point (2000), the official downturn occurred (early 2001), and the recovery began (late 2001). Using annual data, as we do for most topics, we measure the recent business cycle from 2000 to 2007, the years of lowest unemployment at the end of the 1990s recovery and at the end of the recovery of the 2000s. It is possible with the data at hand, therefore, to draw conclusions about the performance of the economy in the recent business cycle relative to earlier cycles. The 2000-07 business cycle was the first in the post-World War II period that the median family's income at the end of the recovery was no higher than it was at the start of the downturn: whatever income was lost in the downturn had not been fully "recovered" during the recovery. The data presented in Chapter 1 showed that it was the poor growth in middle-class families' annual earnings (combining those of all the earners in the family) from both slower growth in hourly wages and a fall in their annual work hours that led to the disappointing income results of the recent cycle. It is the task of this section to further explore these trends by examining the hours and wages of individual workers. For individuals and families, not surprisingly, the trends correspond: disappointing hourly wage growth and work hours.

But a traditional analysis of business cycles—looking at wage growth from 1979 to 1989, 1989 to 2000, 2000 to 2007—would mask a surprising element of the wage story, however. Assessing the trends in work hours, wages, and compensation in the 2000-07 period requires an appreciation of the extraordinary characteristics of the 1995-2000 period preceding the current business cycle.

What was so extraordinary? First, productivity gained speed in the mid-1990s and rose 2.5% a year, double the rate of the prior 22 years back to 1973 (see Table 3.2). This shift is important first because productivity growth means that there is a bigger pie to provide rising wages and living standards. Second, this faster rate of productivity growth picked up even more speed during the recent business cycle from 2000 to 2006 (this table ends with 2006 because the annual earning and hours data are available only for this period). In all, over the 1995-2006 period the output of goods and services per hour of work (productivity) grew a remarkable 32.7%; had pay followed, the annual earnings and incomes for most working people would have risen by a third. This is

TABLE 3.1 Median wage and compensation growth and productivity annual growth in recoveries, 1975-2007

	Median		Productivity	Productivity-compensation gap*
	Wage	*Compensation*		
1975-79	0.7%	1.4%	1.4%	0.0%
1983-89	0.4	0.2	1.6	1.3
1992-2000	0.5	0.1	1.8	1.7
2002-07	-0.1	0.0	2.2	2.2

* Productivity growth less the growth of median hourly compensation.

Source: Authors' analysis of BEA (2008), BLS (2008d) and CPS ORG data.

the third extraordinary fact: despite this enormous growth in productivity, wages for the typical worker were about the same in 2006 as in 2000. Pay rose from 1996 to 2001, fueled by the higher productivity and the progressive lowering of unemployment to 4.0% by 2000. Moreover, the wage momentum carried forward through 2001 and into 2002 despite rising unemployment in those years. But that was it; all of the wage growth in the 2000s business cycle occurred within the first two years. The poor job creation, increased unemployment, and diminished job opportunities (see the exploration of the decline in employment rates in Chapter 4) during the early 2000s recession and the lackluster recovery eventually knocked wage growth down so that wages grew only at the pace of inflation—there were no real wage gains in the recovery.

Table 3.1 shows the annual growth rate in the last four recoveries of productivity and of the median worker's hourly wage and hourly compensation. The recent recovery saw no growth in median hourly wages, an inferior performance at least 0.5% slower per year on average than the next worst recovery. Median compensation also was slower than in other recoveries, but the differences were minimal. What makes recent pay growth especially disappointing is that productivity growth in the recent recovery, at 2.2% annually, was the fastest among all the recoveries. This establishes one of the key features of recent economic performance: a large disconnect between growing productivity and pay. As illustrated in the last column of Table 3.1, the gap between productivity growth and the growth of median hourly compensation was 2.2% each year in the recent recovery, larger than in any recovery since the 1970s (when no gap

FIGURE 3A Productivity and median compensation by education, 1995-2007

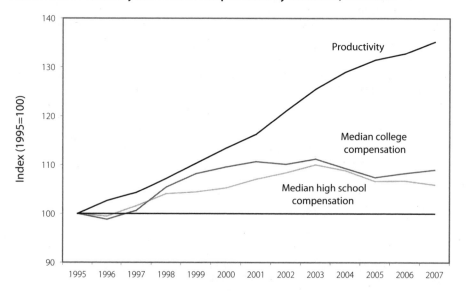

Source: Authors' analysis of BEA (2008), BLS, and CPS ORG data.

existed). Overall, productivity grew 11% in the recovery while median hourly compensation did not grow at all.

The stunning disconnect between the possibilities of improved pay (which could be expected to correspond to productivity growth) and the reality of stunted pay growth is illustrated in **Figure 3A**, which shows the disparity between hourly productivity growth and the growth of hourly compensation (wages and benefits plus payroll taxes) of the median high school graduate and the median college graduate (e.g., those whose highest degree attained is a bachelor's degree). Productivity growth was strong over this entire period, but compensation growth was limited to 1997-2003, and since 2003 neither the typical high school nor college graduate has seen any gains. Therefore, the disconnect between pay and productivity in recent years has encompassed a broad group of the workforce, including those with and without a four year college degree.

With this framework in mind, we now turn to an exploration of the various dimensions of the growth of wages, benefits, and compensation.

Contrasting work hours and hourly wage growth

To understand changes in wage trends, it is important to distinguish between trends in annual, weekly, and hourly wages. Trends in annual wages, for instance, are driven by changes in both hourly wages and the amount of time spent working (weeks worked per year and hours worked per week). Likewise, weekly wage trends reflect changes in hourly pay and weekly hours.

Table 3.2 illustrates the importance of distinguishing between annual, weekly, and hourly wage trends. Over the 2000-06 period (2006 is the latest year of data available in this series), most every indicator saw no growth: annual wages did not grow at all and hourly wages, in inflation-adjusted terms, fell by 0.1% annually. The reason for this disparity was the slight growth in annual hours worked, up 0.1% annually, driven by an increased number of weeks worked a year (despite a shorter workweek). In contrast, the annual wage and salary of the average worker in inflation-adjusted terms grew substantially faster than the average hourly wage in each of the last two decades because of a *rise* in work hours. Specifically, hourly wages grew 0.4% each year over the 1979-89 period and 0.9% over the 1989-2000 period. Yet annual wages grew at 0.8% and 1.3%, reflecting hourly wage growth and the 0.5% growth in annual hours worked in each period.

The most remarkable story in Table 3.2, however, is the sharp acceleration in hourly wage growth (to 1.8%) in the 1995-2000 period, a sharp departure from the measly 0.1% growth of the earlier part of the business cycle from 1989 to 1995 and the slow growth (0.4%) of the prior business cycle of 1979-89. Despite productivity growth in the recent period, 2000-06, that was comparable to that of the late 1990s, wage growth fell off a cliff and became stagnant. With essentially no growth in annual hours worked, annual wage growth in this decade was zero, a disappointing performance the same as that of the stagnant period of the 1970s (which had substantially less productivity growth).

Not surprisingly, trends in family income correspond to the shift from strong annual wage growth in the late 1990s and the falloff thereafter. For instance, the strong pickup

TABLE 3.2 Trends in average wages and average hours, 1967-2006 (2007 dollars)

Year	Productivity per hour (1992=100)	Wage levels			Hours worked		
		Annual wages	Weekly wages	Hourly wages	Annual hours	Weeks per year	Hours per week
1967	65.6	$27,241	$625.45	$15.89	1,716	43.5	39.3
1973	76.3	31,687	729.45	18.90	1,679	43.4	38.6
1979	81.9	31,921	727.96	18.75	1,703	43.8	38.8
1989	94.1	34,735	765.34	19.48	1,783	45.4	39.3
1995	102.0	35,733	777.77	19.56	1,827	45.9	39.8
2000	115.7	40,201	856.31	21.43	1,876	46.9	40.0
2006	135.4	40,180	849.37	21.34	1,883	47.3	39.8
Annual growth rate*							
1967-73	2.5%	2.5%	2.6%	2.9%	-0.4%	0.0%	-0.3%
1973-79	1.2	0.1	0.0	-0.1	0.2	0.2	0.1
1979-89	1.4	0.8	0.5	0.4	0.5	0.3	0.1
1989-2000	1.9	1.3	1.0	0.9	0.5	0.3	0.2
1989-95	1.3	0.5	0.3	0.1	0.4	0.2	0.2
1995-2000	2.5	2.4	1.9	1.8	0.5	0.4	0.1
2000-06	2.6	0.0	-0.1	-0.1	0.1	0.1	-0.1

* Log growth rates.
Source: Authors' analysis of March CPS data and Murphy and Welch (1989).

in wage growth in the late 1990s, along with an even stronger pickup of wage growth at the bottom end of the wage scale (detailed below), is the main factor behind the widespread improvements in family income in the late 1990s, discussed in Chapter 1, and the reductions in poverty, discussed in Chapter 6. Similarly, stagnant annual wages and work hours in recent years have led to the failure of the typical family's income to grow in recent years.

This chapter focuses on the hourly pay levels of the workforce and its sub-groups so that we can distinguish changes in earnings resulting from more (or less) pay rather than more (or less) work. Also, the hourly wage can be said to represent the "true" price of labor (exclusive of benefits, which we analyze separately). Moreover, changes in the distribution of annual earnings have been predominantly driven by changes in the distribution of hourly wages and not by changes in work time. Chapter 4 goes on to address employment, unemployment, underemployment, and other issues related to changes in work time and opportunities.

Contrasting compensation and wage growth

A worker's pay or total compensation is made up of both non-wage payments, referred to as fringe benefits, and wages. Much of the analysis in this chapter focuses on wages because there are no data on workers' hourly compensation, including benefits, which can be analyzed by decile, race, gender, and education. But the available data do allow an examination of overall compensation trends and how they differ from overall wage trends.

Table 3.3 examines the growth of compensation using the only two data series available. We employ the wage and compensation data that are part of the National Income and Product Accounts (NIPA) to track the historical trends from 1948 to 1989. These NIPA data are the Commerce Department's effort to measure the size of the national economy, termed the gross domestic product. Compensation levels exceed wage levels because they include employer payments for health insurance, pensions, and payroll taxes (primarily payments toward Social Security and unemployment insurance). We track more recent trends with data drawn from the Bureau of Labor Statistics' Employer Costs for Employee Compensation (ECEC) survey, which provides the value of wages and employer-provided benefits for each year since 1987. These data vary from those in NIPA because they describe only the private sector (government employment is excluded) and because the definition of "hours worked" is different.

It is important to note that these compensation data are averages covering the entire private sector, including low-paying jobs and executive pay. Since we know that there has been sizable change in wage inequality, we also know that trends in wages or compensation for the "average" worker diverge sharply from (i.e., rise faster than) trends for typical or median workers. Therefore, trends in the compensation data presented in Table 3.3 do not correspond to those experienced by middle-wage or typical workers.

Measured over the long term, benefits have become a more important part of the total compensation package. In 1948 payroll taxes and health and pension programs made up only 5.1% of compensation. By 1989 the share had risen to 18.6%. But the benefits share of compensation has remained flat for the last 20 years: according to the ECEC data the benefit share of compensation was 19.7% in 1987 and 19.4% in 2007, essentially the same. So, the first point is that the growth of compensation has paralleled that of wages over the last 20 or 30 years (note that compensation and wage growth were equivalent in the 1980s). It is still worthwhile tracking each measure of pay separately when possible because they can and have diverged in particular periods (benefits even fell in the late 1990s but then regained ground in recent years). One implication of compensation and wages growing roughly in tandem is that analyses (such as the one below) that focus on wage trends are using an appropriate proxy for compensation, at least on average. However, analyses of wage growth sometimes overstate the corresponding growth of compensation, as in the late 1990s, and sometimes understate compensation growth, as in recent years. If benefits inequality has grown faster than wage inequality, as a few studies have suggested, then our analysis of wage trends understates the growth of compensation inequality.

TABLE 3.3 Growth of average hourly wages, benefits, and compensation, 1948-2007 (2007 dollars)

Year (1st quarter)	Wages and salaries	Benefits*	Total compensation	Benefit share of compensation
Hourly pay (NIPA)*				
1948	$9.69	$0.53	$10.21	5.1%
1989	20.14	4.61	24.75	18.6
Annual percent change				
1948-73	2.6%	7.3%	3.0%	
1973-79	0.2	5.2	1.0	
1979-89	0.8	1.0	0.8	
Hourly pay (ECEC)*				
1987	$19.36	$4.76	$24.12	19.7%
1989	18.99	4.76	23.75	20.0
1995	18.58	4.66	23.24	20.0
2000	19.67	4.31	23.99	18.0
2007	20.88	5.04	25.92	19.4
Annual percent change				
1989-2000	0.3%	-0.9%	0.1%	
1989-95	-0.4	-0.4	-0.4	
1995-2000	1.2	-1.5	0.6	
2000-07	0.9	2.3	1.1	
2002-07	0.4	2.3	0.7	

* Includes payroll taxes, health, pension, and other non-wage benefits.
** Deflated by personal consumption expenditures (PCE) index for all items, except health, which is deflated by PCE medical index.
Source: Authors' analysis of BLS (2008d) and BEA (2008) data.

In the 2000-07 period benefits grew much faster than average wages, 2.3% vs. 0.9%, but since benefits make up only about 20% of compensation the rise in total compensation was just 1.1% a year. A different trend prevailed in the late 1990s, when benefits declined by 1.5% annually while wages rose 1.2%. Hourly compensation, in fact, grew faster in the 2000-07 period than in the late 1990s; thus, while wage growth decelerated there was an acceleration of compensation growth. This comparison is a bit skewed for reasons we have identified above—the momentum of fast pay growth in the late 1990s carried over into the early part of this decade but then disappeared. The trends over the recovery from 2002 to 2007 (after the earlier wage momentum had subsided) illustrated in Table 3.3 affirm this, as wage and compensation growth in that period was just 0.4% and 0.7%, respectively, per year.

The next section returns to a discussion of benefits growth when it examines specific benefits, such as health insurance and pensions.

Wages for production and nonsupervisory workers

We now turn to the pattern of growth or decline in wages for the various segments of the workforce since 1973. There are at least two distinct "wage regimes" over the last 30 years, one from 1973 to 1995 that consisted of stagnant average wage growth and real wage reductions for the vast majority, and one from 1995 to the present that consists of faster real wage growth in the late 1990s followed by slower growth and then declining wages for typical workers in the 2000s. In general, the workers who experienced the greatest fall in real wages in the 1973-95 period were likely to be men, workers who initially had lower wages, workers without a college degree, blue-collar or service workers, or younger workers. In the early 1990s, however, wages also stagnated among male white-collar and college-educated workers. In the late 1990s real wages grew most rapidly among low-wage workers, the very highest-paid workers, and younger workers. The recession of the early 2000s knocked down wage growth, and wages for nearly the entire workforce have failed to grow faster than inflation in the recent recovery. The only groups to see real wage growth in recent years have been the highest-paid workers and those with a degree beyond college.

The data in **Table 3.4** and **Figure 3B** show wage trends for the 80% of the workforce who are either production workers in manufacturing or nonsupervisory workers in other sectors. This category includes factory workers, construction workers, and a wide variety of service-sector workers ranging from restaurant and clerical workers to nurses and teachers; it leaves out higher-paid managers and supervisors. From 2000 to 2007 the hourly wage of production/nonsupervisory workers grew 0.4% per year, though growth was only 0.2% over the 2002-07 recovery. The momentum of the strong wage growth of the late 1990s was offset by the recession, but it took a few years for the recession's impact to be felt; this delay reflects the fact that macroeconomic conditions affect the labor market with a long lag. As we have discussed above, wage growth over the 2000-07 period was substantially less than the 1.4% growth over the 1995-2000 period.

The differences in trends between the early and latter part of the 1989-2000 period are striking: hourly wages fell 0.1% a year from 1989 to 1995 and then grew 1.4% a year from 1995 to 2000, a turnaround of 1.5 percentage points. Over the longer term, from 1979 to 2007, wages are up only slightly, from $16.88 in 1979 to $17.42 in 2007, a growth of just 0.1% per year over nearly 30 years—virtually stagnant—despite some rapid growth in the late 1990s. Figure 3B also tracks the hourly compensation of production/nonsupervisory workers; with the exception of the 1970s, when compensation grew far faster than wages as wages stagnated (see the divergence between the two lines

TABLE 3.4 Hourly and weekly earnings of private production and nonsupervisory workers,* 1947-2007 (2007 dollars)

Year	Real average hourly earnings	Real average weekly earnings
1947	$9.63	$386.55
1967	15.12	573.10
1973	16.88	622.81
1979	16.88	600.81
1982	16.24	563.45
1989	15.82	545.93
1995	15.74	540.53
2000	16.88	579.22
2007	17.42	589.72

Business cycles	Annual growth rate	
1947-67	2.3%	2.0%
1967-73	1.8	1.4
1973-79	0.0	-0.6
1979-89	-0.6	-1.0
1989-2000	0.6	0.5
1989-95	-0.1	-0.2
1995-2000	1.4	1.4
2000-07	0.4	0.3
2002-07	0.2	0.2
1979-2007	0.1	-0.1

* Production and nonsupervisory workers account for more than 80% of wage and salary employment.

Source: Authors' analysis of BLS (2008b) data.

arising in the 1970s), compensation and wage growth show similar trends. That is, the general picture of stagnant pay for typical workers does not change when the focus is compensation rather than wages.

The trend in weekly earnings corresponds closely to that of hourly earnings, with sluggish 0.2% annual growth in the 2002-07 recovery and a much slower growth than in the late 1990s. The fall in weekly hours since 2000 led weekly wages to grow a bit more slowly than hourly wages, 0.3% versus 0.4%. The weekly earnings of production and nonsupervisory workers in 2007 were $589.72 per week (in 2007 dollars), about $10 less than in 1979 and over $30 less than in 1973.

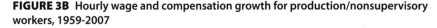

FIGURE 3B Hourly wage and compensation growth for production/nonsupervisory workers, 1959-2007

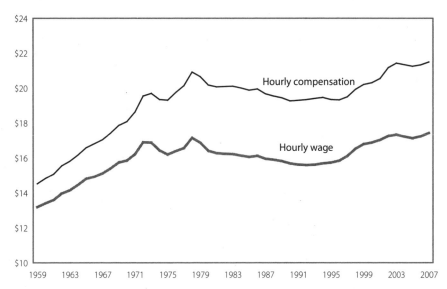

Source: Authors' analysis of BEA (2008) and BLS (2008b) data.

Wage trends by wage level

For any given trend in *average wages*, particular groups of workers will experience different outcomes if wage inequality grows, as it has throughout approximately the last three decades: it grew pervasively in the 1980s, and grew between the top and the middle through most of the 1990s and 2000s. Wage trends can be described by examining groups of workers by occupation, education level, and so on, but doing so omits the impact of changes such as increasing inequality within occupation or education groups. The advantage of an analysis of wage trends by wage level or percentile (the 60th percentile, for instance, is the wage at which a worker earns more than 60% of all earners but less than 40% of all earners) is that it captures all of the changes in the wage structure.

Table 3.5 provides data on wage trends for workers at different percentiles (or levels) in the wage distribution, thus allowing an examination of wage growth for low-, middle-, and high-wage earners. The data are presented for the cyclical peak years 1973, 1979, 1989, 2000, and 2007 as well as for 1995, the point during the 1990s business cycle after which wages grew dramatically.

Wage growth slowed from the 1995-2000 period to the 2000-07 period, though it still remained better than that of the 1979-95 period of relatively stagnant wages. Wages grew strongly across the board from 1995 to 2000, rising at least 7% at every wage level.

TABLE 3.5 Wages for all workers by wage percentile, 1973-2007 (2007 dollars)

Year	Wage by percentile*									
	10	20	30	40	50	60	70	80	90	95
Real hourly wage										
1973	$7.27	$8.78	$10.43	$12.14	$13.91	$15.96	$18.54	$21.20	$26.63	$33.42
1979	7.87	8.97	10.53	12.39	14.02	16.26	19.21	22.39	27.38	33.44
1989	6.72	8.37	10.03	11.99	13.93	16.27	19.37	23.15	29.24	35.94
1995	6.84	8.36	9.99	11.75	13.68	16.19	19.30	23.37	30.20	37.87
2000	7.60	9.35	10.93	12.63	14.74	17.44	20.67	25.12	32.83	41.88
2007	7.79	9.45	11.03	12.94	15.11	17.93	21.29	26.27	35.23	45.52
Percent change in wage										
1973-79	8.2%	2.2%	1.0%	2.1%	0.7%	1.8%	3.6%	5.6%	2.8%	0.1%
1979-89	-14.6	-6.7	-4.7	-3.3	-0.6	0.1	0.8	3.4	6.8	7.5
1989-2000	13.1	11.8	8.9	5.4	5.8	7.1	6.8	8.5	12.3	16.5
1989-95	1.8	-0.1	-0.5	-2.0	-1.8	-0.5	-0.3	0.9	3.3	5.4
1995-2000	11.1	11.9	9.4	7.5	7.7	7.7	7.1	7.5	8.7	10.6
2000-07	2.5	1.0	0.9	2.4	2.6	2.9	3.0	4.6	7.3	8.7
1979-2007	-1.0	5.3	4.7	4.4	7.8	10.3	10.8	17.3	28.7	36.1

* The wage percentiles are the wage at which X% of the wage earners earn less and (100-X)% earn more (eg, 30th percentile = 30% earn less, 70% earn more).

Source: Authors' analysis of CPS ORG data.

Remarkably, the fastest growth was at the two lowest wage levels (10th and 20th), where wage growth was at least 11%. However, workers with the very highest wages, at the 95th percentile, saw almost comparable wage growth of 10.6%. Since 2000, however, wage growth among the bottom 70% (70th percentile or below) has been modest at 3.0% or less; at the median, growth of 2.6% over the 2000-07 period was just one-third that of the 1995-2000 period. Wage growth among higher-wage workers was also slower in recent years than in the 1995-2000 period. Wage deceleration, then, has been pervasive. The deterioration in wage growth is even stronger than Table 3.5 shows because the momentum of the late 1990s carried wage growth into 2002 but was absent in the 2002-07 period (as seen in Table 3.1 earlier).

The deterioration in real wages from 1979 to 1995 was both broad and uneven. Wages were stagnant or fell for the bottom 60% of wage earners over the 1979-95 period and grew modestly for higher-wage workers—over 16 years the growth was just 4.4% at the 80th percentile and 10.3-13.2% at the 90th and 95th percentiles. Starting in the early 1990s low-wage workers experienced wage growth either more than or comparable to that of middle-wage workers, so that the expanding wage gap between the middle and bottom lessened and then stabilized. Increases in the minimum wage in the early and late 1990s and the drop in unemployment in the late 1990s can explain this trend.

This overall picture, however, masks different outcomes for men and women. Among men over the 2000-07 period, wages declined slightly or were relatively stagnant for the bottom 50%, grew 4.0% at the 90th decile, and grew 7.6% for the highest-wage earners (**Table 3.6**). Thus, the wage gap between the top and the middle continued to grow strongly in the 2000-07 period. This trend contrasts with the strong broad-based wage growth of the latter 1990s, when low-wage workers fared better than middle-wage workers. Over the preceding 1979-95 period, the wage declines were substantial, exceeding 10% for the median male worker (Table 3.6 and **Figure 3C**). Between 1979 and 1989, the median male hourly wage fell 7.6%, and low-wage (10th percentile) men lost 11.1%. In the early 1990s, across-the-board wage declines of roughly 3-6% affected the bottom 70% of male earners. Even high-wage men at the 90th percentile, who earned about $31 per hour in 1979, did well only in relative terms, since their wage was only about 6% higher in 1995 than in 1979.

As with the overall trend, the pattern of male wage deterioration shifted between the 1980s and the early 1990s. In the 1980s, wages fell most at the lower levels, while in the 1990s wages eroded in the middle and at the bottom. Thus, the wage gap between middle- and low-wage men was stable in the early 1990s, although the gap between high-wage men (at the 90th percentile and above) and middle- and low-wage men continued to grow.

Over the longer term (1979-2007), the 95th percentile male wage grew faster than any other, at 31.4%, while wages at the middle and lower end fell. The median male wage in 2007, for instance, was still 4.4% below its 1979 level and was essentially the same as in 1973, 34 years earlier, showing that more than a generation of growth bypassed the median male wage earner.

Wages grew more among women than men over the 2000-07 period; they rose from about 2-6% for the 40th to 70th percentiles and about 2% for the lowest-wage

TABLE 3.6 Wages for male workers by wage percentile, 1973-2007 (2007 dollars)

Year	10	20	30	40	50	60	70	80	90	95
					Wage by percentile*					
Real hourly wage										
1973	$8.58	$11.02	$12.99	$14.89	$16.88	$19.13	$21.06	$24.23	$30.86	$37.20
1979	8.66	11.01	13.24	15.41	17.63	20.03	22.46	26.09	31.76	38.09
1989	7.69	9.63	11.83	14.00	16.30	19.18	22.18	26.00	32.57	40.43
1995	7.42	9.37	11.14	13.39	15.70	18.35	21.56	25.78	33.61	42.03
2000	8.26	10.13	12.11	14.35	16.78	19.52	22.98	27.88	37.15	46.51
2007	8.18	10.06	12.10	14.40	16.85	19.79	23.62	29.05	38.65	50.05
Percent change in wage										
1973-79	0.8%	-0.1%	1.9%	3.5%	4.5%	4.7%	6.7%	7.7%	2.9%	2.4%
1979-89	-11.1	-12.5	-10.7	-9.1	-7.6	-4.2	-1.2	-0.4	2.5	6.1
1989-2000	7.4	5.2	2.4	2.5	3.0	1.8	3.6	7.3	14.1	15.0
1989-95	-3.6	-2.8	-5.8	-4.4	-3.7	-4.4	-2.8	-0.8	3.2	4.0
1995-2000	11.5	8.2	8.7	7.2	6.9	6.4	6.6	8.2	10.5	10.7
2000-07	-1.0	-0.7	0.0	0.3	0.4	1.4	2.8	4.2	4.0	7.6
1979-2007	-5.5	-8.6	-8.6	-6.6	-4.4	-1.2	5.1	11.4	21.7	31.4

* The wage percentiles are the wage at which X% of the wage earners earn less and (100-X)% earn more (eg., 30th percentile = 30% earn less, 70% earn more).

Source: Authors' analysis of CPS ORG data.

FIGURE 3C Change in real hourly wages for men by wage percentile, 1973-2007

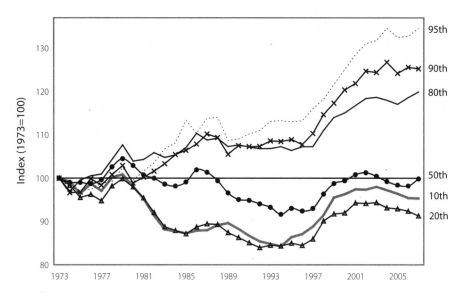

Source: Authors' analysis of CPS ORG data.

women at the 30th percentile and below (**Table 3.7**). The highest-wage women, those at the 95th percentile, enjoyed 9.9% wage growth in this period.

As with men, women's wages rose strongly across the board in the 1995-2000 period. It is remarkable that this wage growth was fairly even among all women, from 8.0% to 10.5%. But the recessionary conditions and weak recovery in recent years knocked down wage growth for most women, as it did for men.

The most persistent wage growth between 1979 and 1995 was among the highest-wage women (Table 3.7 and **Figure 3D**). For instance, wages grew 21.4% for women at the 95th percentile from 1979 to 1989 and another 10.7% over 1989-95. In contrast, low-wage women saw their wages fall in the 1980s; the lowest paid at the 10th percentile experienced a decline of 16.6%. In the early 1990s women's wages at the 40th percentile and above grew more slowly than in the 1980s, with the wages in the middle dropping to a stagnant 1.1% growth over the six years (they grew 7.8% from 1979 to 1989). A positive development of the early 1990s was the fact that wages for 10th percentile women rose, a marked contrast to the sharp decline in the 1980s. As we will discuss below, minimum wage trends—falling in real value in the 1980s and rising in the 1990s—can explain this pattern.

Over the entire 1979-2007 period the wages of the highest-earning women at the 95th percentile grew by 61.4%, substantially greater than the 24.4% wage growth for the median woman over the same period.

TABLE 3.7 Wages for female workers by wage percentile, 1973-2007 (2007 dollars)

Year	\multicolumn{10}{c}{Wage by percentile*}
	10	20	30	40	50	60	70	80	90	95
Real hourly wage										
1973	$6.04	$7.51	$8.45	$9.45	$10.65	$11.99	$13.51	$15.58	$19.26	$22.76
1979	7.50	8.13	8.83	9.85	11.05	12.56	13.99	16.27	20.25	23.94
1989	6.25	7.71	8.92	10.25	11.91	13.61	16.03	19.20	24.11	29.07
1995	6.54	7.80	9.12	10.49	12.05	13.88	16.49	20.15	25.90	32.18
2000	7.22	8.59	9.90	11.47	13.09	15.13	17.92	21.77	28.61	35.14
2007	7.36	8.77	10.10	11.86	13.74	15.97	18.99	23.54	30.98	38.64
Percent change in wage										
1973-79	24.1%	8.2%	4.4%	4.2%	3.7%	4.7%	3.5%	4.5%	5.2%	5.2%
1979-89	-16.6	-5.2	1.0	4.1	7.8	8.4	14.6	18.0	19.0	21.4
1989-2000	15.4	11.5	11.0	11.9	9.9	11.2	11.8	13.4	18.7	20.9
1989-95	4.6	1.2	2.3	2.4	1.1	2.0	2.9	4.9	7.4	10.7
1995-2000	10.4	10.2	8.5	9.3	8.6	9.0	8.7	8.0	10.5	9.2
2000-07	2.0	2.1	2.1	3.5	5.0	5.6	6.0	8.1	8.3	9.9
1979-2007	-1.9	7.8	14.4	20.5	24.4	27.2	35.8	44.6	53.0	61.4

* The wage percentiles are the wage at which X% of the wage earners earn less and (100-X)% earn more (eg. 30th percentile = 30% earn less, 70% earn more).

Source: Authors' analysis of CPS ORG data.

FIGURE 3D Change in real hourly wages for women by wage percentile, 1973-2007

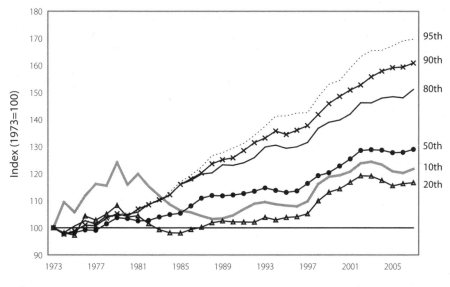

Source: Authors' analysis of CPS ORG data.

Shifts in low-wage jobs

Another useful dimension of the wage structure to analyze is the proportion of workers earning low, or poverty-level, wages. These trends are presented in **Table 3.8** for men and women among all workers and among whites. **Table 3.9** presents corresponding data for blacks and Hispanics. **Figures 3E** and **3F** present these trends by gender and race/ethnicity, respectively. The key indicator in these tables is the proportion of the workforce that earns equal to or less than the "poverty-level wage," the hourly wage that a full-time, year-round worker must earn to sustain a family of four at the official poverty threshold, which was $10.20 in 2007 (in 2007 dollars), equal to two-thirds of the median hourly wage. These tables also show the share of workers earning very low wages, that is, less than or equal to 75% of the poverty-level wage.

Women are much more likely to earn poverty-level wages than men. In 2007, 31.4% of women earned poverty-level wages or less, significantly more than the share of men (21.8%). Overall, 26.4% of workers, over one in every four, earned poverty-level wages in 2007.

The trend in the share of workers earning poverty-level wages corresponds to the story outlined at the start of this chapter: momentum in reducing poverty-wage jobs began in the late 1990s, continued until 2002, then dissipated. There seems to be a spike upward in the share of workers earning poverty-level wages (see Figures 3E and 3F) that may or may not persist: the rising unemployment and real wage losses thereafter

TABLE 3.8 Distribution of employment by wage level, all workers and whites, 1973-2007

| | Share of employment below poverty-level wage (100)* | | | | | |
| | All | | | White | | |
Year	0-75	75-100	Total**	0-75	75-100	Total**
All						
1973	11.7%	18.2%	29.9%	10.3%	17.1%	27.5%
1979	4.9	22.2	27.1	4.5	20.6	25.1
1989	13.9	16.5	30.5	12.3	15.1	27.5
2000	9.8	15.3	25.1	8.0	13.0	21.1
2007	9.4	17.0	26.4	7.9	14.1	21.9
Change						
1979-89	9.0%	-5.7%	3.3%	7.8%	-5.4%	2.4%
1989-2000	-4.1	-1.3	-5.3	-4.3	-2.1	-6.4
2000-07	-0.5	1.7	1.3	-0.2	1.1	0.9
Men						
1973	5.6%	11.9%	17.4%	4.6%	10.3%	14.9%
1979	2.8	12.9	15.7	2.4	11.0	13.4
1989	9.5	13.2	22.7	7.7	11.2	18.9
2000	7.3	12.4	19.6	5.4	9.6	15.0
2007	7.1	14.7	21.8	5.5	11.1	16.6
Change						
1979-89	6.7%	0.3%	7.0%	5.3%	0.2%	5.5%
1989-2000	-2.2	-0.8	-3.0	-2.3	-1.6	-3.9
2000-07	-0.2	2.3	2.1	0.1	1.5	1.6
Women						
1973	20.5%	27.5%	48.0%	18.9%	27.2%	46.1%
1979	7.8	34.4	42.1	7.4	33.2	40.6
1989	19.0	20.3	39.2	17.6	19.5	37.1
2000	12.7	18.4	31.1	10.9	16.7	27.6
2007	11.9	19.5	31.4	10.4	17.2	27.6
Change						
1979-89	11.2%	-14.1%	-2.9%	10.2%	-13.6%	-3.4%
1989-2000	-6.3	-1.8	-8.1	-6.7	-2.9	-9.5
2000-07	-0.7	1.1	0.3	-0.6	0.5	0.0

* The wage ranges are equivalent in 2007 dollars to: $7.65 and below (0-75), $7.65-$10.20 (75-100).
** Combines lowest two categories and represents the share of wage earners earning poverty-level wages.

Source: Authors' analysis of CPS ORG data.

TABLE 3.9 Distribution of employment by wage level, blacks and Hispanics, 1973-2007

| | Share of employment below poverty-level wage (100)* | | | | | |
| | Black | | | Hispanic | | |
Year	0-75	75-100	Total**	0-75	75-100	Total**
All						
1973	20.2%	23.9%	44.1%	16.8%	25.4%	42.3%
1979	7.3	30.2	37.5	6.4	31.5	37.9
1989	19.8	20.9	40.7	21.8	24.4	46.2
2000	12.3	19.5	31.8	17.8	24.9	42.7
2007	11.4	22.6	34.0	15.0	26.8	41.8
Change						
1979-89	12.6%	-9.4%	3.2%	15.4%	-7.1%	8.3%
1989-2000	-7.5	-1.3	-8.9	-4.0	0.5	-3.5
2000-07	-0.9	3.1	2.2	-2.8	1.9	-0.9
Men						
1973	11.8%	20.2%	31.9%	10.6%	21.0%	31.7%
1979	4.9	22.3	27.2	4.3	22.8	27.1
1989	15.5	19.8	35.3	18.1	23.0	41.1
2000	10.0	16.3	26.3	14.5	23.7	38.2
2007	9.8	21.1	30.9	11.6	26.1	37.8
Change						
1979-89	10.6%	-2.5%	8.1%	13.8%	0.1%	14.0%
1989-2000	-5.4	-3.5	-8.9	-3.6	0.7	-2.9
2000-07	-0.2	4.8	4.6	-2.9	2.5	-0.4
Women						
1973	30.1%	28.1%	58.2%	27.6%	33.0%	60.6%
1979	9.8	38.7	48.5	9.6	44.8	54.5
1989	24.0	21.8	45.9	27.2	26.6	53.8
2000	14.3	22.2	36.5	22.6	26.7	49.3
2007	12.7	23.9	36.6	19.9	27.8	47.7
Change						
1979-89	14.2%	-16.9%	-2.7%	17.6%	-18.3%	-0.7%
1989-2000	-9.8	0.4	-9.4	-4.6	0.1	-4.4
2000-07	-1.5	1.7	0.2	-2.7	1.1	-1.6

* The wage ranges are equivalent in 2007 dollars to: $7.65 and below (0-75), $7.65-$10.20 (75-100).
** Combines lowest two categories and represents the share of wage earners earning poverty-level wages.

Source: Authors' analysis of CPS ORG data.

FIGURE 3E Share of workers earning poverty-level wages, by gender, 1973-2007

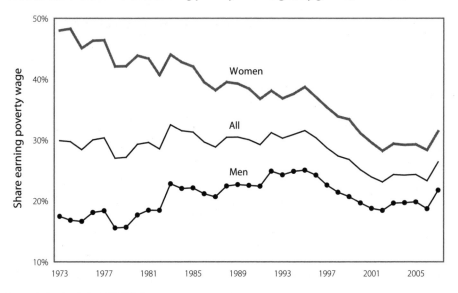

Source: Authors' analysis of CPS ORG data.

FIGURE 3F Share of workers earning poverty-level wages, by race, 1973-2007

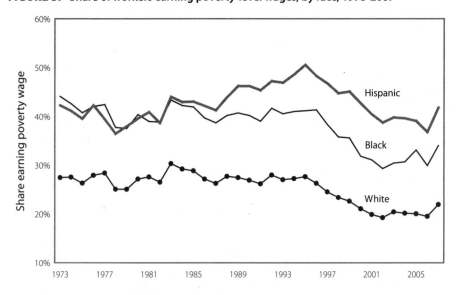

Source: Authors' analysis of CPS ORG data.

may fuel further growth of low earnings. It is clear that there has been no progress in reducing the share of workers with low earnings over the 2002-07 recovery; this is true for all race/ethnic groups and for both genders.

This trend contrasts sharply with the 1989-2000 period, when the share of workers earning poverty-level wages fell from 30.5% to 25.1%, reversing the trend of the 1980s toward more poverty-level jobs. As Figures 3E and 3F show, the erosion of poverty-wage jobs in the 1990s came in the latter part of the decade, which saw falling unemployment and broad-based real wage growth. The turnaround toward more poverty-level jobs after 2002 thus represents a reversal of a seven-year trend.

The share of workers earning at least 25% below the poverty-level wage (labeled "0-75") expanded significantly between 1979 and 1989, from 4.9% to 13.9% of the workforce. This group of very low earners shrank in the 1990s and was stable in the 2000s.

Overall trends in the share of workers earning poverty-level wages are primarily driven by trends among women, since women are disproportionately the ones earning these low wages. The share of women earning poverty-level wages was stable between 2000 and 2007, rising slightly from 31.1% to 31.4%. In the 1989-2000 period, the very bottom of the wage structure shrank as the proportion of women earning poverty-level wages fell from 39.2% to 31.1%: the share earning very low wages also diminished.

The proportion of minority workers earning low wages is substantial—34.0% of black workers and 41.8% of Hispanic workers in 2007. Minority women are even more likely to be low earners—36.6% of black women and 47.7% of Hispanic women in 2007. Figure 3F shows the decline in white workers earning poverty-level wages from 1996 to 2002 and the bump up since then, especially in 2007, ending with 21.9% earning low wages. Among white men over the 2000-07 period the share in low-wage work rose from 15.0% to 16.6%. There was a shift toward lower-paid jobs among whites in the 1979-89 period, driven by the erosion of wages among men, whose share of low-earners rose from 13.4% to 18.9%. The share of earners at very low earnings (25% below the poverty-level wage) grew considerably among white women in the 1980s (from 7.4% to 17.6%), which probably resulted from the eroded minimum wage. This increase was part of a shift downward among low-earners, evidenced by the fact that the share of white women at poverty-level wages actually fell at the same time. The white male and white female wage structures have moved in different directions. Over the longer term, in fact, white women have seen their share of poverty-level earners decline remarkably, from 46.1% in 1973 to 27.6% in 2007. Among white men, however, the long-term trend is toward higher shares of low earners, though white men are far less likely to be low earners than are white women.

Blacks saw the largest growth of low earners over the 2000 to 2007 period (Table 3.9), driven entirely by the growth of low earners among black men from 26.3% to 30.9%. This jump followed the very large reductions of those earning poverty-level wages among both black men and women in the 1989-2000 period (primarily after 1995, as seen in Figure 3F).

Hispanics, unlike other groups, experienced a shrinkage of low-wage work since 2000, though there was a sizable bump up in 2007 (Figure 3F). There were considerably larger reductions in low-earners among Hispanics in the late 1990s (carrying through to 2002). Before the prosperity of the late 1990s there had been a steady climb of low-earnings among Hispanics overall dating back to 1979. While the share of Hispanic women in low-wage work has declined over the long term (down to a still high 47.7% in 2007 from 60.6% in 1973), the share of Hispanic men in low-wage work has risen (up to 37.8% in 2007, from 31.7% in 1973). These trends could be due to a change in the composition of the Hispanic workforce—a larger share of immigrants—or by deterioration in the jobs available, but we are unable to distinguish between the two factors in this analysis. It is noteworthy, though, that immigration does not adequately explain why low-wage work grew among Hispanic men but not among women, since there was substantial immigration among both men and women.

Trends year by year and in other wage groups (multiples of the poverty-level wage) are available at the EPI datazone (www.epi.org/content.cfm/datazone_dznational).

Trends among high earners

Newly available data on the labor earnings of the highest earners allow a long-term look back to nearly the beginning of the last century, though the focus here is the period since 1947, and especially since 1979. The data cover annual earnings because they are drawn from the wage records in the Social Security system.

Figure 3G presents the share of total wage and salary earnings received by the top 1% of earners, a group (see **Table 3.10**) whose average annual earnings were $576,141 in 2006 (in 2007 dollars). The top earners' share of earnings was relatively stable from 1947 into the 1970s but nearly doubled from 7.3% in 1979 to 13.6% in 2006 (the latest year of available data). This is the consequence of earnings growth of 144.4% for the top 1% compared with just 15.6% for the bottom 90%.

It is possible to look at trends for the subgroups among the top 1% of earners over the 1979 to 2004 period and for the topmost sliver (upper 0.1%) from 1979 through to 2006. As the first few columns of Table 3.10 show, the growth of earnings at the very top accrued to the upper tenth of the top 1% of earners (the top 1 of 1,000 earners, who earned 2,223,664 annually in 2006), a group whose share of earnings grew from 1.6% in 1979 to 5.3% in 2006. This corresponds to a 323.4% growth in annual earnings over the 1979-2006 period. In contrast, the bottom half of the upper 1% (the 99.0 to 99.5 percentiles) saw their annual wages grow a fourth as much, but at a still healthy 66.9% pace (from 1979 to 2004, the latest data available for this group). The contrast with the bottom 90% is stark: these earners with roughly $29,000 in 2006) enjoyed 15.6% wage growth over the 1979-2006 period, an increase roughly a tenth that of the upper 1% (**Figure 3H**). These data thus illustrate a characteristic of the inequality we have experienced over the last few decades: the gap between the vast middle of wage earners and the top earners has been growing, but so has the gap between the top and the very top earners, with the upper one-thousandth faring far better than those just below them in the wage hierarchy.

One important component of this fast growth of pay for the highest earners has been the growing gap between the pay of corporate chief executives and that of typical workers. This is explored in a later section.

FIGURE 3G Top 1% share of total wages and salaries, 1947-2006

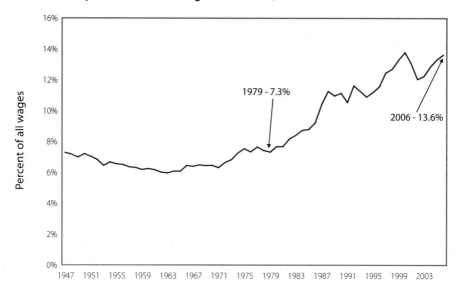

Source: Authors' analysis of Kopczuk, Saez, and Song (2007).

Trends in benefit growth and inequality

The analysis on the preceding pages shows that real wages declined for a wide array of workers over both the 1980s and the early 1990s, rose strongly between 1995 and 2002, then fell flat or declined through 2007. Also, total compensation, the real value of both wages and fringe benefits, grew at the same pace as wages over the 1979-2007 period, though sometimes wages grew faster than compensation (the late 1990s) and sometimes more slowly (e.g., 2000-07). Benefits grew faster than wages during much of that time, but since they make up a small share of compensation (15-20%), their growth did not generate fast compensation growth overall. But fast growth in health care costs and pensions helped benefit growth exceed wage growth after 2000, and total compensation grew. In this section, we examine changes in health and pension coverage for different groups of workers. A more detailed focus on health care benefits and expenses can be found in Chapter 7.

Table 3.11 provides a breakdown of the growth in non-wage compensation, or benefits, using the BLS Employer Costs for Employee Compensation data (the aggregates amounts appeared in Table 3.3). These data, based on a survey of employers, show that total non-wage compensation, including health, pensions, and payroll taxes, were maintained at about $4.75 per hour over the 1987-95 period. Following a 1.5% annual fall in the late 1990s, costs for health and pensions grew in the 2000-07 period, with a net increase of $0.38 per hour from 1995 to 2007. Note, however,

TABLE 3.10 Changes in the distribution and level of wages and salaries, 1979-2006

Wage group	Share of wages			Change in share		Annual wage level ($2007)			Percent change	
	1979	2004	2006	1979-2004	1979-2006	1979	2004	2006	1979-2004	1979-2006
Bottom 90%	**69.8%**	**62.5%**	**61.5%**	**-7.3**	**-8.3**	**$24,990**	**$28,893**	**$28,889**	**15.6%**	**15.6%**
0-20%	3.8	3.3	–	-0.5	–	6,055	6,887	–	13.7	–
20-40%	9.4	8.1	–	-1.3	–	15,090	16,770	–	11.1	–
40-60%	15.6	13.6	–	-2.0	–	25,107	28,380	–	13.0	–
60-80%	24.1	21.4	–	-2.8	–	38,876	44,463	–	14.4	–
80-90%	17.0	16.1	–	-0.9	–	54,658	67,038	–	22.7	–
Top tenth (exc. upper 1%)	**22.8%**	**24.6%**	**24.9%**	**1.8**	**2.0**	**$81,738**	**$113,927**	**$116,742**	**39.4%**	**42.8%**
90-95%	10.8	10.9	10.9	0.1	0.1	69,313	90,633	91,772	30.8	32.4
95-99%	12.1	13.8	14.0	1.7	1.9	97,270	143,044	147,955	47.1	52.1
Upper 1%	**7.3%**	**12.9%**	**13.6%**	**5.6**	**6.3**	**$235,766**	**$535,558**	**$576,141**	**127.2%**	**144.4%**
99.0-99.5%	2.6	3.3	–	0.8	–	165,552	276,309	–	66.9	–
99.5-99.9%	3.1	4.7	–	1.5	–	251,226	484,790	–	93.0	–
99.9-100%	1.6	4.9	5.3	3.3	3.6	524,998	2,034,869	2,223,664	287.6	323.4

Source: Authors' analysis of Kopczuk, Saez, and Song (2007) and Social Security wage data.

FIGURE 3H Annual wage growth, by wage group, 1973-2006

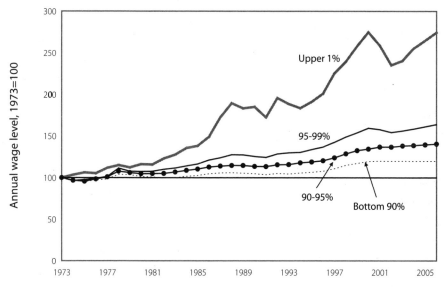

Source: Authors' analysis of CPS ORG data.

that this 8.2% rise in benefit costs occurred at the same time that productivity grew 35.2%.

The data in Table 3.11 show average benefit costs. Given the rapid growth of wage inequality in recent years, it should not be surprising to find a growing inequality of benefits. **Tables 3.12** and **3.13** examine changes in employer-provided health insurance and pension coverage for different demographic groups between 1979 and 2006. The share of workers covered by employer-provided health care plans dropped a steep 13.9 percentage points, from 69.0% in 1979 to 55.0%, in 2006 (Table 3.12). As **Figure 3I** illustrates, health care coverage eroded from 1979 until 1993-94, when it stabilized, and then began falling again after 2000 through 2006 (the latest data). (Indicators of the quality of coverage are examined in Chapter 7).

The 3.9 percentage point erosion of employer-provided health care coverage from 2000 to 2006 was fairly uniform across demographic groups. The erosion of coverage was larger among men (down 5.1 percentage points) then women (down 2.4 percentage points) but declined comparably among whites, blacks, and Hispanics. Coverage eroded for both high school graduates (5.0 percentage points) but also among college graduates (3.7 percentage points). Health coverage declined for every wage group, with the top 40% losing as much ground as the bottom fifth (though clearly the top earners had much more ground to lose).

Over the longer period from 1979 to 2006, health care coverage has declined twice as much among men (down 17.3 percentage points) than among women (down

TABLE 3.11 Growth of specific fringe benefits, 1987-2007 (2007 dollars)

| Year* | Voluntary benefits | | | Payroll taxes | Total benefits and non-wage compensation |
	Pension	Health**	Subtotal		
Hourly pay					
1987	$0.84	$1.95	$2.79	$1.97	$4.76
1989	0.68	2.03	2.71	2.05	4.76
1995	0.70	1.83	2.52	2.13	4.66
2000	0.71	1.60	2.31	2.00	4.31
2007	0.87	1.97	2.84	2.20	5.04
Annual dollar change					
1989-2000	$0.00	-$0.04	-$0.04	$0.00	-$0.04
1989-95	0.00	-0.03	-0.03	0.01	-0.02
1995-2000	0.00	-0.05	-0.04	-0.03	-0.07
2000-07	0.02	0.05	0.08	0.03	0.10
Annual percent change					
1989-2000	0.4%	-2.1%	-1.4%	-0.2%	-0.9%
1989-95	0.5	-1.7	-1.1	0.6	-0.4
1995-2000	0.3	-2.6	-1.8	-1.3	-1.5
2000-07	3.0	3.0	3.0	1.3	2.3

* Data are for March.
** Deflated by medical care price index.

Source: Authors' analysis of BLS (2008d) data.

8.2 percentage points), and equally among whites and blacks (10.7 percentage points); Hispanics, though, suffered by far the largest drop—23.1 percentage points. The pattern in the erosion of health insurance coverage by wage level shows a growth in inequality in the 1980s, with greater erosion the lower the wage. The 1990s, however, saw modest extensions of coverage for the bottom 20%, while erosion continued for middle- and high-wage workers. Coverage eroded for all wage groups in 2000-06, and over the longer period, 1979-2006, health insurance coverage declined sizably and comparably across the wage spectrum. Along education lines, however, there is evidence of growing inequality: employer-provided health insurance coverage fell 18.4 percentage points among high school graduates but by a smaller but still sizeable 12.1 percentage points among college graduates.

Employer-provided pension plan coverage (Table 3.13) eroded by 5.5 percentage points from 2000 to 2006, a sharp break from the 1990s, when pension coverage grew

TABLE 3.12 Change in private sector employer-provided health insurance coverage, 1979-2006

	Health insurance coverage (%)					Percentage-point change			
Group*	1979	1989	1995	2000	2006	1979-89	1989-2000	2000-06	1979-2006
All workers	69.0%	61.5%	58.5%	58.9%	55.0%	-7.4	-2.7	-3.9	-13.9
Gender									
Men	75.4%	66.8%	62.6%	63.2%	58.1%	-8.7	-3.6	-5.1	-17.3
Women	59.4	54.9	53.3	53.6	51.2	-4.5	-1.3	-2.4	-8.2
Race									
White	70.3%	64.0%	61.7%	62.7%	59.6%	-6.3	-1.2	-3.2	-10.7
Black	63.1	56.3	53.0	55.4	52.4	-6.8	-0.9	-3.0	-10.7
Hispanic	60.4	46.0	42.1	41.8	37.3	-14.3	-4.3	-4.5	-23.1
Education									
High school	69.6%	61.2%	56.3%	56.2%	51.2%	-8.4	-5.0	-5.0	-18.4
College	79.6	75.0	72.1	71.3	67.5	-4.6	-3.8	-3.7	-12.1
Wage fifth									
Lowest	37.9%	26.4%	26.0%	27.4%	24.0%	-11.5	1.0	-3.4	-13.9
Second	60.5	51.7	49.5	50.9	44.7	-8.8	-0.8	-6.3	-15.8
Middle	74.7	67.5	62.9	63.9	61.2	-7.2	-3.6	-2.7	-13.6
Fourth	83.5	78.0	74.0	73.7	69.2	-5.5	-4.3	-4.5	-14.3
Top	89.5	84.7	81.5	79.9	76.9	-4.7	-4.8	-3.0	-12.6

* Private sector, wage and salary workers age 18-64, who worked at least 20 hours per week and 26 weeks per year.

Source: Authors' analysis of March CPS data.

across the board (likely due to the increase in defined-contribution plans; see below). In 2000 almost half the workforce (48.3%) had an employer-provided pension plan, almost as much as in 1979. The recent erosion, however, lowered pension coverage to just 42.8%. The erosion in recent years was widespread, occurring among both high school and college graduates and at every wage level. In fact, the groups with the highest coverage have tended to lose the most ground in recent years (again, they had more to lose). Large groups in the workforce now have very little pension coverage. Only 37.1% of high school graduates and just 30.2% of wage earners in the second (not lowest) fifth had coverage. Less than a fourth of Hispanic workers and only 37.5% of black workers enjoyed employer-provided pension coverage in 2006. The

TABLE 3.13 Change in private sector employer-provided pension coverage, 1979-2006

Group*	Pension coverage (%)					Percentage-point change			
	1979	1989	1995	2000	2006	1979-89	1989-2000	2000-06	1979-2006
All workers	50.6%	43.7%	45.8%	48.3%	42.8%	-7.0	4.6	-5.5	-7.8
Gender									
Men	56.9%	46.9%	48.6%	50.3%	43.8%	-10.1	3.4	-6.4	-13.1
Women	41.3	39.6	42.5	45.8	41.5	-1.7	6.2	-4.3	0.2
Race									
White	52.2%	46.1%	49.5%	53.7%	48.5%	-6.1	7.6	-5.2	-3.7
Black	45.8	40.7	42.6	41.3	37.5	-5.1	0.7	-3.8	-8.3
Hispanic	38.2	26.3	24.7	27.5	22.6	-11.9	1.2	-4.8	-15.5
Education									
High school	51.2%	42.9%	43.2%	43.8%	37.1%	-8.3	0.9	-6.7	-14.1
College	61.0	55.4	58.8	63.7	57.0	-5.6	8.3	-6.6	-3.9
Wage fifth									
Lowest	18.4%	12.7%	13.7%	16.3%	14.4%	-5.7	3.6	-1.9%	-4.0
Second	36.8	29.0	32.0	35.8	30.2	-7.7	6.8	-5.7	-6.6
Middle	52.3	44.5	47.0	50.9	44.2	-7.8	6.4	-6.6	-8.1
Fourth	68.4	60.0	63.2	64.8	57.8	-8.3	4.8	-7.1	-10.6
Top	78.5	72.8	74.8	74.8	68.2	-5.8	2.1	-6.6	-10.3

* Private sector, wage and salary workers age 18-64, who worked at least 20 hours per week and 26 weeks per year.

Source: Authors' analysis of March CPS data.

coverage among men and women was comparably low in 2006, though men had much higher coverage than women back in 1979 or even in 1989. This is one area where we are seeing less inequality: coverage among men has declined precipitously since 1979, while women's coverage has returned to its 1980s level after falling in recent years.

Over the long period from 1979 to 2006 pension coverage declined overall by 7.8 percentage points. The pattern by wage level shows coverage dropping relatively evenly across wage groups in the 1980s and rising across the board in the 1990s, with coverage expanding the most in the middle. Coverage declined across each wage fifth during the 1980s, between 2000 and 2006, and over the entire 1979-2006 period. Lower-wage workers now are very unlikely to have jobs with employer-provided pension plans

FIGURE 3I Private-sector employer-provided health insurance coverage, 1979-2006

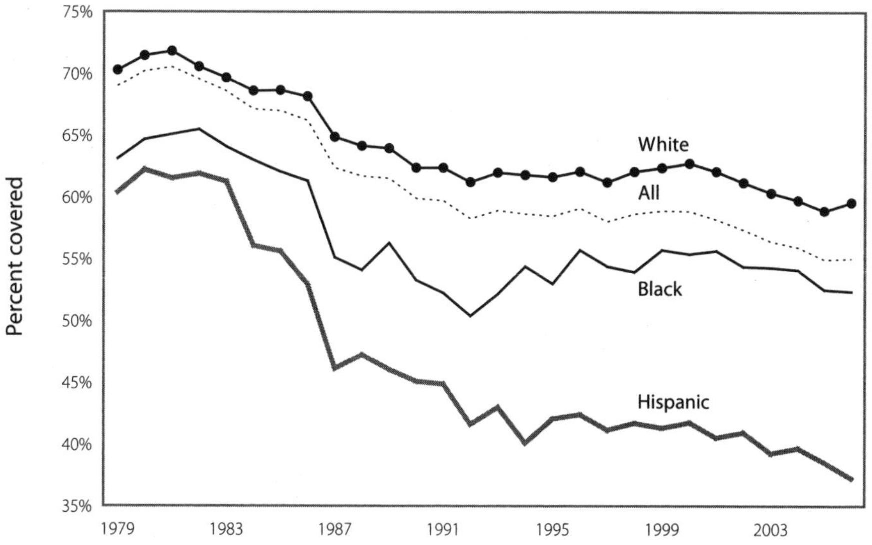

Source: Authors' analysis of March CPS data.

(14.4% were covered in 2006), and less than half of middle-wage workers have pension coverage. It should be noted that there was little coverage for low-wage workers to lose—just 18.4% for the lowest fifth and 36.8% for the second-lowest fifth in 1979. In 2006, the highest-wage workers were 4.7 times as likely to have pension coverage as the lowest-wage workers (68.2% versus 14.4%). Changes in pension coverage by education show a growing inequality: over the 1979-2006 period pension coverage fell 14.1 percentage points among high school graduates but 3.9 percentage points among college graduates.

The widening coverage of employer-provided pension plans in the 1990s was most likely due to the expansion of 401(k) and other defined-contribution pension plans. These plans differ from defined-benefit plans, which are generally considered the best plans from a workers' perspective because they guarantee a fixed payment in retirement based on pre-retirement wages and years of service regardless of stock market performance. Yet, as shown in **Figure 3J**, a much larger share of workers are now covered by defined-contribution plans, in which employers make contributions (to which employees often can add) each year. With this type of plan, a worker's retirement income depends on his or her success in investing these funds, and investment risks are borne by the employee rather than the employer. Therefore, the shift from traditional defined-benefit plans to defined-contribution plans represents an erosion of pension quality. Chapter 5 provides further discussion of pensions and retirement assets and income.

FIGURE 3J Share of pension participants in defined-contribution and defined-benefit plans, 1980-2004

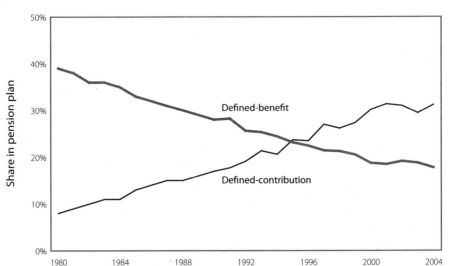

Source: Authors' analysis of Center for Retirement Research.

Dimensions of wage inequality

In this section we shift the discussion from a descriptive presentation of wage and benefit trends overall and for sub-groups to an examination of explanations for the pattern of recent wage growth. It is important to understand the average performance of wage growth and why particular groups fared well or poorly compared to others.

The data presented up to this point have shown the stagnation of wages and overall compensation between 1973 and 1995 and the strong wage growth in the late 1990s that carried into the 2000s but waned after 2002.

Table 3.14 presents indicators of a variety of dimensions (excluding race and gender differentials, discussed below) of the wage structure that have grown more unequal over the 1973-2007 period. Any explanation of growing wage inequality must be able to explain the movement of these indicators. (These inequality indicators are computed from our analysis of the Current Population Survey (CPS) outgoing rotation group (ORG) data series. These trends, however, parallel those in the other major wage data series, the March CPS.)

The top section of Table 3.14 shows the trends, by gender, in the 90/10 wage differential and its two components, the 90/50 and 50/10 wage differential (whose annual values are shown in **Figures 3K** and **3L**), over the 1973-2007 period. These differentials reflect the growth in overall wage inequality and reflect the wage decile levels presented in Tables 3.6 and 3.7. The 90/10 wage gap, for instance, shows the degree to which 90th percentile workers—"high-wage" workers who earn more than 90% but less than 10% of the workforce—fared better than "low-wage" workers, who earn at the 10th percentile. The 90/50 wage gap shows how high earners fared relative to middle earners, and the 50/10 wage gap shows how middle earners fared relative to low earners.

Wage inequalities have been growing continuously since 1979, although the pattern differs across time periods. For instance, among both men and women the shape of growing inequality differed in the 1980s (through about 1987-88) and thereafter. Over the 1979-89 period (as we saw above in the analysis of wage deciles in Tables 3.5 through 3.7), there was a dramatic across-the-board widening of the wage structure, with the top pulling away from the middle and the middle pulling away from the bottom. In the late 1980s, however, the wage inequality in the bottom half of the wage structure, as reflected in the 50/10 differential, began shrinking among men but has been relatively stable among women. On the other hand, the 90/50 differential continued to widen in the 1980s and 1990s and 2000s, except for the last few years. This widening of the wage gap at the top is even stronger in the 95/50 differential, shown **Figure 3M**. (The 95th percentile is the highest wage we judge can be tracked in these data with technical precision. The Social Security data on annual earnings presented in Table 3.10 show a widening inequality among the very top earners). These disparate trends between high- versus middle-wage growth and middle- versus low-wage growth should motivate explanations that focus on how causal factors affect particular portions of the wage structure—top, middle, or bottom—rather than on how causal factors affect inequality generally. This break in trend in the late 1980s (when inequality in the bottom half stopped expanding and started falling among men) also raises the possibility of a differing mix of factors raising inequality in the 1980s and thereafter, or a shifting over time in the type of impact of a factor, such as technology or globalization (we will visit this issue when we examine both trade and technology's impact).

The trends in recent years, 2000-07, may signal a return to the 1980s pattern of an across-the-board widening of wage inequality. The 50/10 wage gap started growing again among women after 1999, a movement that corresponds to the earlier pattern— rising inequality at the top and the bottom of the wage distribution. However, among men inequality declined at the bottom (50/10 ratio) in the early part of this decade then bumped up in the last few years. At the top, the wage gap (95/50 or 90/50) spiked upward sharply among men but then flattened in 2004, and it grew moderately among women (especially the 95/50 ratio), except in the last two years. Overall wage inequality, measured by the 90/10 ratio, grew among men and women over the 2000-07 period at about the same pace (per year) as in the 1990s for men and at an even greater pace than in the 1990s among women.

Among women, the wage inequality trends across time periods correspond to those of men. The 90/10 ratio dropped significantly between 1973 and the late 1970s, primarily because of the strong equalization in the 50/10 wage gap. In the 1980s, however, the 50/10 wage gap grew tremendously (up 21.9 percentage points), reversing the 1970s compression and increasing the gap another 8 percentage points over 1973. One conclusion that can be reached about women's wage inequality is that it has been driven

TABLE 3.14 Dimensions of wage inequality, 1973-2007

	Wage gap*						Percentage-point change			
	1973	1979	1989	1995	2000	2007	1973-79	1979-89	1989-2000	2000-07
Total wage inquality										
90/10										
Men	128.0%	130.0%	144.3%	151.1%	150.3%	155.3%	2.0	14.3	6.0	5.0
Women	115.9	103.2	134.9	137.6	137.7	143.7	-12.7	31.8	2.8	6.0
90/50										
Men	60.3%	58.8%	69.2%	76.1%	79.5%	83.0%	-1.5	10.4	10.2	3.6
Women	59.2	60.6	70.5	76.5	78.2	81.3	1.4	9.9	7.7	3.1
50/10										
Men	67.6%	71.1%	75.1%	75.0%	70.8%	72.3%	3.5	3.9	-4.2	1.4
Women	56.7	42.5	64.4	61.1	59.5	62.4	-14.2	21.9	-4.9	2.9
Between group inequality**										
College/high school (H.S.)										
Men	25.3%	20.1%	33.9%	37.1%	42.0%	44.1%	-5.2	13.9	8.1	2.1
Women	37.7	26.5	41.0	46.7	47.9	48.5	-11.2	14.5	6.9	0.6
H.S./Less than H.S.										
Men	22.3%	22.0%	22.1%	26.5%	26.0%	25.2%	-0.3	0.1	3.9	-0.7
Women	26.2	21.3	26.4	29.8	29.5	27.7	-4.9	5.1	3.0	-1.7

Experience***										
Middle/young										
Men	22.0%	21.5%	25.7%	27.0%	22.9%	24.3%	-0.5	4.1	-2.8	1.4
Women	8.0	9.5	17.8	21.8	18.4	20.9	1.5	8.3	0.6	2.5
Old/middle										
Men	3.4%	8.2%	12.4%	12.7%	8.8%	9.5%	4.7	4.3	-3.6	0.7
Women	-2.0	0.4	2.1	5.4	4.6	8.4	2.4	1.7	2.5	3.7
Within group inequality****										
Men	42.3%	42.8%	46.7%	47.8%	48.1%	50.1%	1.4	9.0	3.0	5.0
Women	41.8	40.2	44.7	46.7	45.8	48.4	-3.8	11.4	2.4	3.8

*   Log wage differental.
**   Differentials based on a simple human capital regression of log wages on four education categorical variables, age as a quartic, race, marital status, region, and ethnicity (Hispanic).
***   Age differentials between 25- and 35-year-olds and 35- and 50-year-olds.
**** Mean square error from same regressions used to estimate experience and education differentials. Changes measured as percent change.

Source: Authors' analysis of CPS ORG data.

FIGURE 3K Men's wage inequality, 1973-2007

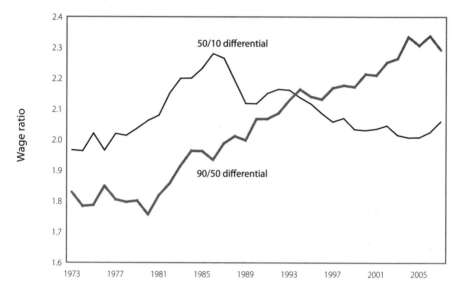

Source: Authors' analysis of CPS ORG data.

FIGURE 3L Women's wage inequality, 1973-2007

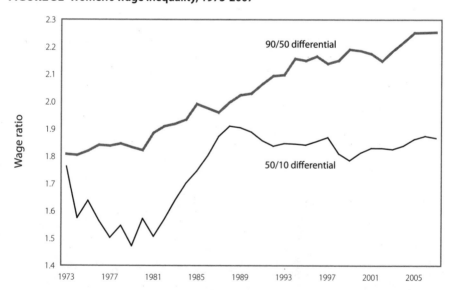

Source: Authors' analysis of CPS ORG data.

FIGURE 3M 95/50 percentile wage inequality, 1973-2007

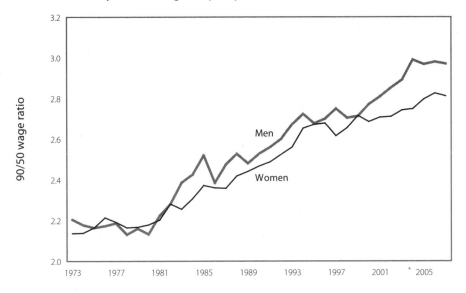

Source: Authors' analysis of CPS ORG data.

much more by what happened at the bottom—the 10th percentile—than was the change for men. This is likely due to the importance of the legal minimum wage to low-wage women, as we will discuss in a later section. Among women, the growth of the 90/50 differential was comparable to that of men in the 1980s but somewhat less in the 1990s. As with men, the 50/10 wage gap declined in the 1990s (Figure 3L shows the drop starting in about 1987). As mentioned above, the wage gap at the bottom among women started rising again after 1999.

The 95/50 wage gap among women has followed approximately the same track as for men (Figure 3M). Wage inequality between the very top earners and those in the middle has been growing strongly, and steadily, since about 1980, confirming the continuous widening of wages at the top over the last two decades. The only exception is the flattening of the 95/50 gap among men and women in the last few years.

Analysts decompose, or break down, growing wage inequality into two types of inequality—"between group" and "within group." The former is illustrated in Table 3.14 in two ways: the growing wage differentials between groups of workers defined by their *education* levels and by their labor market *experience*. The most frequently discussed differential is the "college wage premium"—the wage gap between college and high school graduates. In this analysis the premiums discussed, such as the college premium, are "regression-adjusted": this means that the impact of other factors such as experience, marital status, race, ethnicity, and region of residence are controlled for. Thus, the education premium presented here will differ from one computed by simply dividing the college wage by the high school wage (because the calculation here takes account, for instance, of the differing age and racial distribution of each group). The college wage premium fell in the 1970s among both men and women but exploded in the 1980s, growing about 14 percentage points for each. Growth then slowed after 1989. The pattern of growth of this key education differential in the 1990s, however, differed between men and women (see **Figure 3N**). Among men the education premium grew only modestly in the early 1990s—year-by-year trends (discussed below) show it to be relatively flat between 1987 and 1996—but it grew strongly thereafter. Thus, the 1990s growth in the male education premium primarily occurred in the last few years of that period. Among women, however, the college wage premium grew steadily but modestly in the early 1990s and then evened out starting around 1995. The college wage premium was flat among women in the 2000 to 2007 period and grew modestly among men.

Table 3.14 also presents the trends in another education differential—between those completing high school and those without high school degrees. This differential would be expected to affect the wage distribution in the bottom half, as about 10% of the workforce has less than a high school education, and high school graduates make up about a third of the workforce (see discussion of Tables 3.15 through 3.17). In 2007 as in 1973, those with a high school degree earned between 22% and 28% more than those without a degree, remarkably stable relative to the college premium. One reason for the stability of this differential is that, even as having a high school degree was becoming

FIGURE 3N College/high school wage premium, 1973-2007

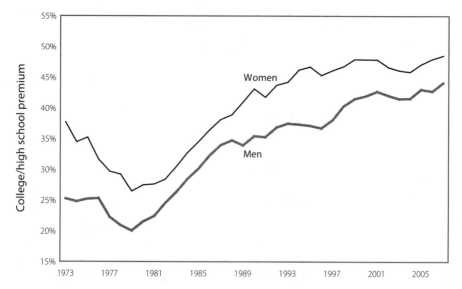

Source: Authors' analysis of CPS ORG data.

more valuable, the share of workers without a high school degree dramatically declined. It may also be the case that growth of the "high school wage" was diminished because a larger share of those completing high school (which is our measure here) have done so with an equivalency degree rather than a traditional diploma. Nevertheless, since this wage differential has been fairly stable among men over the last 30 years, one can conclude that education differentials have not been a driving force behind the changes in the 50/10 wage gap (which grew in the 1980s and declined thereafter). Among women, the wage gap between middle- and low-wage workers is far higher in 2007 than in 1973, yet the high school/less than high school differential is roughly the same. This suggests that changing wage differentials at the bottom among women are only weakly, at best, related to changing education differentials.

Experience, or age, is another way of categorizing "skill." The growth of experience differentials reflects the wage gap between older and middle-aged and younger workers. Among men, at least since 1979, there has not been any sizable increase in experience differentials. Among women, however, experience differentials have grown between older and middle-aged women and between middle-aged and younger women. Most of the growth of the latter differential developed in the 1980s, consistent with the rapid decline in value of the minimum wage (which would affect younger women heavily). The wage gap between older and middle-aged women workers grew over the 1973-95 period and then again in the 2000-07 period.

Within-group wage inequality—wage dispersion among workers with comparable education and experience—has been a major dimension of growing wage inequality. Unfortunately, most discussions of wage inequality focus exclusively on the between-group dimensions discussed above, even though within-group wage inequality is by far the most important dimension of wage inequality's growth. The growth of within-group wage inequality is presented in the last section of Table 3.14, with changes measured in percent. These data show that within-group inequality grew slightly among men in the 1970s and 1990s but grew strongly in the 1980s (9.0%) and the 2000s (5.0%). Among women, within-group inequality fell in the 1970s, grew by 11.4% in the 1980s, followed by a modest 2.4% in the 1990s and a bit more rapid growth in recent years. Within-group inequality is explored further in Tables 3.20 and 3.21.

The measure of within-group wage inequality in Table 3.14 is a "summary measure" describing changes across the entire wage distribution. Unfortunately, such a measure does not help us understand changes in particular measures of wage inequality, such as the 90/50 and 50/10 differentials presented in the top portion of the table. This shortcoming is particularly troublesome for an analysis of the period after the late 1980s, in which inequalities were expanding at the top (i.e., the 90/50 differential) but shrinking or stable at the bottom (i.e., the 50/10). A summary measure of inequality by definition reflects the net effect of the two disparate shifts in wage inequality since the late 1980s, and probably as a result the change in within-group wage inequality from 1989 to 2007 appears small.

Since changes in within-group wage inequality have been a significant factor in various periods, it is important to be able to explain and interpret these trends. In a later section, we show that over half of the growth of wage inequality since 1979 has been from growing within-group inequality. Unfortunately, the interpretation of growing wage inequality among workers with similar "human capital" has not been the subject of much research. Some analysts suggest it reflects growing premiums for skills that are not captured by traditional human capital measures available in government surveys. Others suggest that changing "wage norms," employer practices, and institutions are responsible.

We now turn to a more detailed examination of between-group wage differentials such as education, experience, and race/ethnicity, as well as an examination of within-group wage inequality.

Productivity and the compensation/productivity gap

Productivity growth, which is the growth of the output of goods and services per hour worked, provides the basis for the growth of living standards. However, for the vast majority productivity growth actually provides only the *potential* for rising living standards: recent history, especially since 2000, has shown that wages, compensation, and income growth for the typical worker or family have lagged tremendously behind the nation's fast productivity growth. In contrast, between 1995 and 2000 wage growth accelerated along with productivity growth. It seems important, therefore, to understand why productivity growth was better shared in the late 1990s than in the years since.

The relationship between hourly productivity and hourly compensation growth is portrayed in **Figure 3O**, which shows the growth of each relative to 1973 (i.e., each is indexed so that 1973 equals 100). As the figure illustrates, productivity grew 83% from 1973 to 2007, enough to generate large advances in living standards and wages if productivity gains were broadly shared. As Figure 3A showed at the start of this chapter, the largest differences between productivity and wages or compensation have prevailed in the 2000-07 period.

There are two important gaps displayed in Figure 3O. First, the growth in average compensation—which includes the pay of CEOs and day laborers alike—lagged behind productivity growth, 83% versus 49%. Second, median hourly compensation grew far less than average compensation, reflecting growing wage and benefit inequality. Thus, there have been two wedges between the typical or median worker's compensation and overall productivity growth: one is that workers, on average, have not seen their pay keep up with productivity (partly reflecting the shift from wage to capital income described in Chapter 1), and the other is that median workers have not enjoyed growth in compensation as fast as that of higher-wage workers, especially the very highest paid (as seen in an earlier section). This wedge reflects growing wage and benefit inequality.

There are several possible interpretations of the gap between average compensation and productivity. A benign explanation is that prices for national output have grown more slowly than prices for consumer purchases. Therefore, the same growth in nominal, or current dollar, wages and output yields faster growth in real (inflation-adjusted) output (which is adjusted for changes in the prices of investment goods, exports, and consumer purchases) than in real wages (which is adjusted for changes in consumer purchases only). That is, workers have suffered worsening "terms of

FIGURE 30 Productivity and hourly compensation growth, 1973-2007

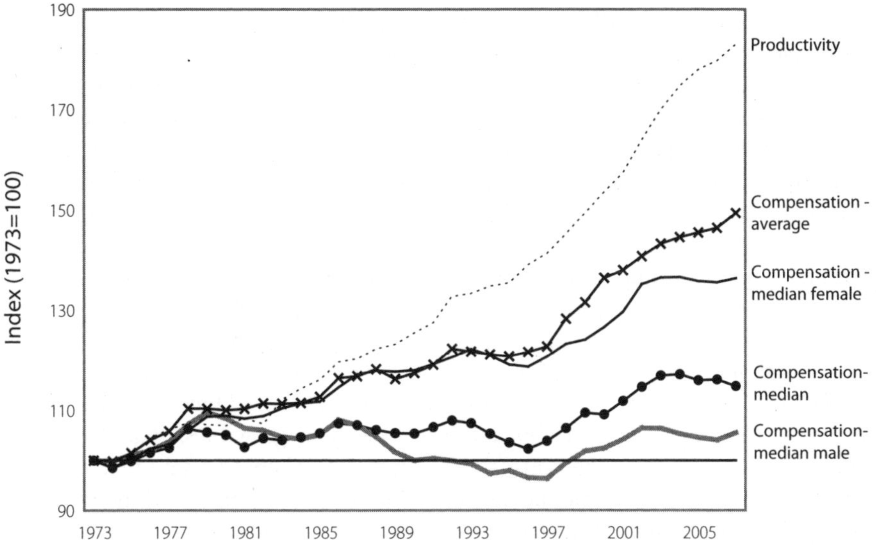

Source: Authors' analysis of CPS ORG and BEA (2008) data.

trade," in which the prices of things they buy (i.e., consumer goods) have risen faster than the items they produce (consumer goods but also capital goods). Thus, if workers consumed microprocessors and machine tools as well as groceries, their real wage growth would have been better and in line with productivity growth.

This terms-of-trade scenario is, at best, a description rather than an explanation of the divergence of pay and productivity. A growing gap between output and consumer prices has not been a persistent characteristic of the U.S. economy or other economies, and the emergence of this gap requires an exploration of what economic forces are driving it. Once the causes of the price gap are known (not simply accounted for), it can be interpreted and not simply used as a way to dismiss the gap between productivity and compensation growth. In the meantime, there are two ways to look at the divergence of compensation and productivity growth created by the terms-of-trade shift of prices. One is to note that, regardless of cause, the implication is that the "average" worker is not benefiting fully from productivity growth. Another is to note that the price divergence reflects both a shift in income from labor to capital and differences between output and consumer prices.

A detailed look at the data provides a gauge of the relative contribution of the two components of the productivity-compensation gap, the price divergence just discussed and the shift in "factor incomes" (a growth in capital's profits at the expense of labor's compensation). The annual gap between productivity and average hourly compensation over the 1979-2007 period was 0.8%, of which divergent price trends (gross domestic product or "output prices" versus consumer prices) could explain roughly 41%. This time period, however, includes some different dynamics in particular sub-periods, particularly over the last 10 years. From 1995 to 2000 productivity grew just slightly faster than real hourly compensation, 2.5% versus 2.4% annually. In this period the divergence between output price inflation and consumer inflation more than explains the divergence, indicating that in this boom period compensation growth exceeded the growth of profitability. However, in the most recent business cycle from 2000 to 2007, productivity grew about twice as fast as real hourly compensation, 2.5% versus 1.3%, reflecting a productivity-compensation gap growing 1.2% each year. In this period, price divergence can explain less than 10% of the growth of the productivity-compensation gap, suggesting that the rapidly widening gap in recent years reflects a giant-scale shift from wages to profits. Over the entire period from 1979 to 2007 roughly 42% of the growth in the productivity-compensation gap can be explained by the relatively faster inflation in consumer purchases than in the inflation of overall output.

The issue of whether the growth in rates of profit (defined broadly as profits and interest per dollar of assets) has meant that wages have grown less than they would have otherwise was examined directly in Chapter 1. There, we saw that the share of capital income in the corporate sector has grown significantly, and the trend was driven by a comparably large increase in "profitability," or the return to capital per dollar of plant and equipment. For instance, the share of income in the corporate sector going to capital income in the recent recovery was the highest in nearly 40 years. The share going to compensation was correspondingly at a low point. The historically high returns to capital in the recent recovery (relative to the late 1970s recovery) are associated with the average worker's compensation being 4.4% lower and the equivalent of transferring $206 billion annually from labor compensation to capital incomes. The shift that has occurred in income from labor to capital has been large when compared to the size of the loss of wages for the typical worker due to factors such as the shift to services, globalization, the drop in union representation, or any of the other prominent causes of growing wage inequality discussed in this chapter.

Rising education/wage differentials

Changes in the economic returns to education affect the structure of wages by changing the wage gaps between different educational groups. The growth in "education/wage differentials" or "premiums" has led to greater wage inequality since 1979 but to a different degree in each decade (see Table 3.14 and Figure 3N). The rise of the college premium helps to explain the relatively faster wage growth among high-wage workers. This section examines wage trends among workers at different levels of education and begins the discussion, carried on through the remainder of the chapter, of the causes of rising education/wage differentials and of overall wage inequality.

Table 3.15 presents the wage trends and employment shares (percentage of the workforce) for workers at various education levels over the 1973-2007 period. It is common to point out that the wages of "more-educated" workers have grown faster than the wages of "less-educated" workers since 1979, with the real wages of less-educated workers falling sharply (or rising more slowly in the 1995-2000 period). This pattern of wage growth is frequently described in terms of a rising differential, or premium, between the wages of the college-educated and high-school-educated workforces (as shown earlier in Table 3.14).

The frequent categorizing of workers as either "less educated" (those who are faring relatively poorly) or "more educated" (those faring relatively better) is potentially misleading. As we will show shortly, in some periods the better-educated workers do not fare so well. Moreover, the group labeled "less educated" actually comprises about 70-75% of the workforce during most of this period and has skills and education

TABLE 3.15 Real hourly wage for all by education, 1973-2007 (2007 dollars)

Year	Less than high school	High school	Some college	College	Advanced degree
Hourly wage					
1973	$13.45	$15.41	$16.60	$22.48	$27.17
1979	13.69	15.36	16.42	21.53	26.29
1989	11.70	14.25	16.01	22.45	28.94
1995	10.59	14.00	15.66	23.23	30.65
2000	11.00	14.81	16.83	25.86	32.69
2007	11.38	15.01	16.94	26.51	33.57
Annual percent change					
1973-79	0.3%	-0.1%	-0.2%	-0.7%	-0.5%
1979-89	-1.6	-0.7	-0.3	0.4	1.0
1989-2000	-0.6	0.3	0.5	1.3	1.1
1989-95	-1.6	-0.3	-0.4	0.6	1.0
1995-2000	0.8	1.1	1.5	2.2	1.3
2000-07	0.5	0.2	0.1	0.4	0.4
2002-07	0.1	-0.3	-0.3	0.1	-0.1
Share of employment					
1973	28.5%	38.3%	18.5%	10.1%	4.5%
1979	20.1	38.5	22.8	12.7	6.0
1989	13.7	36.9	26.0	15.6	7.9
2000	11.1	31.8	29.6	18.8	8.8
2007	9.8	29.6	29.6	20.9	10.1

Source: Authors' analysis of CPS ORG data.

that exceed those of most workers in the world. Less than 10% of the U.S. workforce age 18-64 is lacking a high school or equivalent degree. Last, it is notable that the "college-educated" group consists of two groups: one with just four years of college, and another more-educated ("advanced degree") group; the wage trends for these two groups have frequently diverged so it makes sense to examine them separately.

In the current cycle from 2000 to 2007 wages grew far more slowly for every education group compared to their wage growth in the late 1990s. The contrast is even starker when one looks at the wage growth during the 2002-07 recovery after the wage momentum from the late 1990s had subsided and the jobless recovery took hold. During the recovery, as seen in Table 3.17, wages failed to grow at all for any education group; those in the middle (high school and some college) saw their real wages decline. These are disappointing outcomes for a period with fast productivity growth.

Over the entire 1979-2007 period the simple story is that the greater the education level of the group, the more wages rose. This trend played out differently in various time periods. From 1979 to 1995 the wages of those with less than a college degree actually declined while those of college-educated workers rose modestly (Table 3.15). Between 1995 and 2000 (up until 2002 actually) real wages grew for all educational groups while, as just discussed, after 2002 wages failed to grow for those with a high school education or above. One interesting pattern to note is that those with advanced degrees (master's degrees, professional degrees in law, medicine, and so on) sometimes saw their wages grow faster than those with just a college degree (1979-89, 1989-95) but sometimes saw lower wage growth (1995-2000) and sometimes comparable growth (2000-07).

The increased wage differential between college-educated and other workers is frequently ascribed to a relative increase in employer demand for workers with greater skills and education. This interpretation follows from the fact that the wages of college-educated workers increased relative to others despite an increase in their relative supply, from 12.7% of the workforce in 1979 to 20.9% in 2007. That is, given the increased relative supply of college-educated workers which, all else equal, would be expected to reduce the college wage, the fact that the relative wage of college graduates went up implies a strong growth in employer demand for more-educated workers, presumably reflecting technological and other workplace trends.

Yet an increased relative demand for educated workers is only a partial explanation, especially if it is credited to a benign process of technology or other factors leading to a higher value for education and thus bidding up the wages of more-educated workers. Note, for instance, that the primary reason for an increased wage gap between college-educated and other workers is the precipitous decline of wages among the non-college-educated workforce in the 1979-95 period and not any strong growth in the college wage (it was rising a modest 0.5% annually in this time period). Moreover, as discussed below, there are many important factors that may not reflect changes in the relative demand for skill; these might include high unemployment, the shift to low-wage industries, deunionization, a falling minimum wage, and import competition that can also lead to a logical change has not been the driving force behind growing wage inequality.

Tables 3.16 and **3.17** present trends in wage and employment shares for each education group for men and women. Among men, wage growth in the most recent 2000-07 period has been stagnant or slow, especially compared to the fast wage growth for each education group in the late 1990s. Wages for those with less than a college degree were stagnant or falling during the recovery years from 2002 to 2007 and wage growth was minimal for those with a college degree or more. As noted, the exceptionally strong wage growth in the late 1990s stands apart from the long-term trend over the 26 years from 1979 to 1995, when wages fell strongly among non-college-educated men. The decline was sizable even among men with "some college"—8.4% from 1979 to 1995. The wage of the average high-school-educated male fell more, 14.6%, from 1979 to 1995, while the wages of those without a high school degree fell 26.2%. By contrast, the wages of male college graduates rose, but more modestly than commonly thought—just 2.3% from 1979 to 1989 and an additional 1.5% over the 1989-95 period. Year-by-year data show that male college wages in the 1979-95 period peaked in 1987.

Over the entire 1979-2007 period the pattern of growing wages for college-educated males (almost entirely due to the 1995-2000 period) and declining or stagnant wages for non-college-educated males meant a rise in the relative wage, or wage premium, for male college graduates. As shown in Table 3.14, the estimated college/high school wage premium (where experience, race, and other characteristics are controlled for) grew from 20.1% in 1979 to 33.9% in 1989 and to 44.1% by 2007. As Figure 3N shows, however, there was a flattening of the male college/high school premium over the 1988-96 period, particularly in the early 1990s. Since there has not been an acceleration of the supply of college-educated men (as shown in a later section), this slower wage growth implies, within a conventional demand-supply framework, that growth in the relative demand for college workers slowed in that period. From 1996 to 2000, however, this key education differential among men jumped again, followed by a decline and modest recovery by 2007. Thus, the growth in the male college wage premium has been relatively modest after 1988 with the exception of the late 1990s.

As we have seen in our earlier examinations of the wage structure, women's wages have grown faster than men's in nearly every category (deciles, shrinkage of poverty-level wages, etc). However, the same general pattern of relative wages—that is, who does better—prevails among women as among men (Table 3.17). From 2000 to 2007, wage growth among women of all education groups rose modestly, with not much difference across education groups. Wages rose 0.3% annually for those with a high school, some college, and a college education and a bit faster for those without a high school degree and those with an advanced degree. In the recovery from 2002 to 2007 the wage growth among women was as disappointing as it was among men, with those with a high school degree or more seeing no wage growth or declining wages. In the late 1990s wages grew much more strongly among women in every education group, with the familiar pattern of the greatest growth among college graduates (even greater than those with advanced degrees). In the 1979-89 and 1989-95 periods wages were stagnant among high-school-educated women but fell significantly among those without a high school degree (11.9% overall). Women with some college saw significant wage gains in the 1980s (unlike their male counterparts), but not in the early

TABLE 3.16 Real hourly wage for men by education, 1973-2007 (2007 dollars)

Year	Less than high school	High school	Some college	College	Advanced degree
Hourly wage					
1973	$15.72	$18.64	$19.05	$25.71	$28.56
1979	15.79	18.51	19.25	25.16	28.63
1989	13.26	16.55	18.25	25.74	32.01
1995	11.66	15.80	17.63	26.13	33.99
2000	1 2.08	16.72	19.06	29.35	36.67
2007	12.32	16.68	18.95	30.36	38.10
Annual percent change					
1973-79	0.1%	-0.1%	0.2%	-0.4%	0.0%
1979-89	-1.7	-1.1	-0.5	0.2	1.1
1989-2000	-0.8	0.1	0.4	1.2	1.2
1989-95	-2.1	-0.8	-0.6	0.2	1.0
1995-2000	0.7	1.1	1.6	2.4	1.5
2000-07	0.3	0.0	-0.1	0.5	0.5
2002-07	0.1	-0.4	-0.3	0.2	0.1
Share of employment					
1973	30.6%	34.4%	19.2%	10.3%	5.4%
1979	22.3	35.0	22.4	13.2	7.1
1989	15.9	35.2	24.4	15.7	8.8
2000	13.1	32.0	27.5	18.4	9.1
2007	12.0	31.1·	27.3	19.9	9.8

Source: Authors' analysis of CPS ORG data.

1990s. College-educated women saw strong wage growth throughout the 1979-95 period (22.7% overall), faring by far the best among all gender-education categories. This pattern of wage growth resulted in growth of the college/high school wage differential comparable to that of men (Table 3.14), from 26.5% in 1979 to 41.0% in 1989 and to 46.7% in 1995 (the increase up to 1995 being higher than among men). However, the college wage premium among women has barely budged over the last 10 years, rising only to 48.5 by 2007. Thus, the education/wage gap grew more among women than among men in the 1979-95 period and then stagnated thereafter, while it rose somewhat among men. The relative losers among women—the

TABLE 3.17 Real hourly wage for women by education, 1973-2007 (2007 dollars)

Year	Less than high school	High school	Some college	College	Advanced degree
Hourly wage					
1973	$9.48	$11.73	$12.68	$17.56	$23.26
1979	10.14	12.02	12.91	16.34	20.93
1989	9.20	11.90	13.79	18.66	24.32
1995	8.88	12.03	13.78	20.05	26.39
2000	9.27	12.70	14.73	22.19	27.99
2007	9.72	13.00	15.09	22.72	28.93
Annual percent change					
1973-79	1.1%	0.4%	0.3%	-1.2%	-1.7%
1979-89	-1.0	-0.1	0.7	1.3	1.5
1989-2000	0.1	0.6	0.6	1.6	1.3
1989-95	-0.6	0.2	0.0	1.2	1.4
1995-2000	0.9	1.1	1.3	2.1	1.2
2000-07	0.7	0.3	0.3	0.3	0.5
2002-07	0.3	-0.4	-0.2	0.0	0.0
Share of employment					
1973	25.6%	44.0%	17.5%	9.9%	3.1%
1979	17.2	43.0	23.4	12.0	4.4
1989	11.2	38.8	27.8	15.4	6.8
2000	8.9	31.7	31.9	19.2	8.4
2007	7.4	28.0	32.2	22.0	10.4

Source: Authors' analysis of CPS ORG data.

non-college-educated—saw relatively stagnant wages, whereas among men the wages of those same groups fell.

Even though the wages of college-educated women have grown rapidly since 1979, a female college graduate in 2007 still earned $7.64, or 25%, less than a male college graduate in 2007.

Table 3.18 shows a breakdown of employment in 2007 by the highest degree attained and by gender and immigrant/native status. Some 31.0% of the workforce had at least a four-year college degree (20.9% have a college degree only and 10.1% also have a graduate or professional degree). Correspondingly, 69.0% of the workforce has less than a college degree, with 9.8% never completing high school; 29.6% completing high school or obtaining a GED; another 19.8% attending college but earning no degree beyond high school; and 9.8% holding associate degrees. These data reinforce the earlier discussion that the poor wage performance experienced by the "less educated" (frequently defined by economists as those without a college degree) between 1979 and 1995 and then from 2000 to 2007 affected a very large share of the workforce. This is important to note because the language used in public discussion asserts that the "less-educated" have done poorly, leaving the impression that they are a small part of the population. But "less-educated" implicitly corresponds to those without a four-year college degree, and their share of the workforce, at 69.0%, is huge today and was even larger over the last 30 years.

It is also interesting to note that the group of workers with more than a high school degree but less than a four-year college degree now make up a group equivalent in size (29.6%) to groups of high school graduates (29.6%) and bachelor's degree holders (31.0%). Among women, those with some college or an associate's degree (32.2 %) now exceed those holding at most a high school degree (28.0%).

The educational attainment of the workforce differs by immigration status. The likelihood of having at least a college degree is about the same for both foreign- and

TABLE 3.18 Educational attainment of employed, 2007

	Percent of employment				
Highest degree attained	Men	Women	All	Natives only	Immigrants only
Less than high school	12.0%	7.4%	9.8%	6.1%	29.1%
High school/GED	31.1	28.0	29.6	30.5	25.1
Some college	18.7	21.1	19.8	21.5	11.3
Assoc. college	8.6	11.1	9.8	10.5	5.9
College B.A.	19.9	22.0	20.9	21.5	17.6
Advanced degree*	9.8	10.4	10.1	9.9	11.1
Total	**100.0**	**100.0**	**100.0**	**100.0**	**100.0**
Memo					
High school or less	43.1%	35.4%	39.4%	36.6%	54.2%
Less than B.A. degree	70.4	67.6	69.0	68.6	71.3
College B.A. or more	29.6	32.4	31.0	31.4	28.7
Advanced degree*	9.8	10.4	10.1	9.9	11.1

* Includes law degrees, Ph.D.s, M.B.A.s, and similar degrees.
Source: Authors' analysis of CPS ORG data.

native-born workers. Immigrants are more likely to have advanced degrees (11.1% versus 9.9%), but fewer have just college degrees (17.6% versus 21.5%). The starkest difference between immigrant and native-born workers is that immigrants are far more likely to lack a high school education (29.1%) than is the case among natives (6.1%).

Young workers' wages

Young workers' prospects are an apt barometer of the strength of the labor market. When the labor market is strong for workers the prospects for young workers are very strong, and when the labor market is weak their prospects are very weak. The recent period affirms this general finding, as the wages of entry-level workers have fared poorly in recent years. This happened as well over the 1973-1995 period, when the most dramatic erosion of wages was among young workers. Also consistent with this volatility of young workers' wages is that young workers also experienced the fastest wage growth over the 1995-2000 period of booming wages.

Table 3.19 presents trends in wages for entry-level (one to seven years of experience) high school and college graduates by gender. It is interesting to note that in the recent period of disappointing wage growth, wages actually fell or were stagnant among every entry-level group, both high school and college workers and both men and women. This contrasts to the extremely strong wage growth for each of these groups from 1995 to 2000, when wages rose roughly 10% for entry-level high school men and women and 20.9% for entry-level college men, 11.7% for college women. This change illustrates the vast swing in wages for entry-level workers between a period of strong wages and stagnant wages.

The generally poor wage performance of non-college-educated workers has been magnified among young entry-level workers (**Figure 3P**). Since the wages of both younger and non-college-educated workers fell most rapidly in the 1979-95 period and fared poorly from 2000 to 2007, it should not be surprising that entry-level wages for men and women high school graduates in 2007 were still below their levels of 1979 or 1973. For instance, the entry-level hourly wage of a young male high school graduate in 2007 was 18.2% less than that for the equivalent worker in 1979, a drop of $2.62 per hour. Among women, the entry-level high school wage fell 11.2% in this period, with a 6.3% loss since 2000 standing out. Entry-level wages for high school graduates grew rapidly, over 9%, between 1995 and 2000 for both men and women, and this growth ameliorated the long-term decline in their wages. Note that wages in entry-level jobs held by high-school-educated women are still far less than those for their male counterparts, and the gap widened in the 2000s (though it is not as wide as in the 1970s).

Entry-level wages fell among both female and male college graduates from 2000 to 2007, 3.2% among men and 1.7% among women (**Figure 3Q**). This follows the sole period of rising wages for entry-level male college graduates, up 20.9% from 1995 to 2000. In the prior 16 years, from 1979 to 1995, the male entry-level college wage fell about a dollar. Thus, the period of falling wages in the 2000s does not stand as the exception to the rule: it is the wage boom in the late 1990s that seems exceptional.

TABLE 3.19 Hourly wages of entry-level and experienced workers by education, 1973-2007 (2007 dollars)

Education/experience	Hourly wage						Percent change				
	1973	1979	1989	1995	2000	2007	1973-79	1979-89	1989-2000	1995-2000	2000-07
High school											
Men											
Entry*	$14.34	$14.41	$11.61	$10.78	$11.79	$11.79	0.5%	-19.5%	1.5%	9.3%	0.0%
34-40	20.49	20.63	17.95	17.22	17.92	17.96	0.7	-13.0	-0.1	4.1	0.2
49-55	21.59	22.01	20.24	19.45	19.25	19.33	1.9	-8.0	-4.9	-1.0	0.4
Women											
Entry*	$10.50	$10.65	$9.50	$9.18	$10.08	$9.45	1.4%	-10.8%	6.1%	9.8%	-6.3%
34-40	12.05	12.44	12.45	12.60	13.36	13.53	3.2	0.0	7.3	6.1	1.3
49-55	12.56	12.80	13.10	13.21	14.05	14.59	1.9	2.3	7.3	6.3	3.9
College											
Men											
Entry**	$19.02	$19.00	$19.42	$18.01	$21.78	$21.09	-0.1%	2.2%	12.2%	20.9%	-3.2%
38-44	30.69	29.52	28.73	29.45	32.62	34.35	-3.8	-2.7	13.5	10.8	5.3
53-59	31.63	32.72	32.31	32.65	33.60	33.76	3.5	-1.3	4.0	2.9	0.5
Women											
Entry**	$15.94	$15.03	$16.91	$16.55	$18.49	$18.17	-5.7%	12.5%	9.4%	11.7%	-1.7%
38-44	19.01	17.22	19.52	22.01	24.03	25.08	-9.4	13.4	23.1	9.2	4.4
53-59	18.14	17.43	18.95	22.20	23.18	25.02	-3.9	8.8	22.3	4.4	7.9

* Entry-level wage measured as wage of those from 19 to 25 years of age.
** Entry-level wage measured as wage of those from 23 to 29 years of age.

Source: Authors' analysis of CPS ORG data.

FIGURE 3P Entry-level wages of male and female high school graduates, 1973-2007

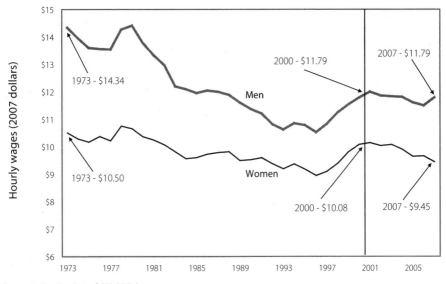

Source: Authors' analysis of CPS ORG data.

FIGURE 3Q Entry-level wages of male and female college graduates, 1973-2007

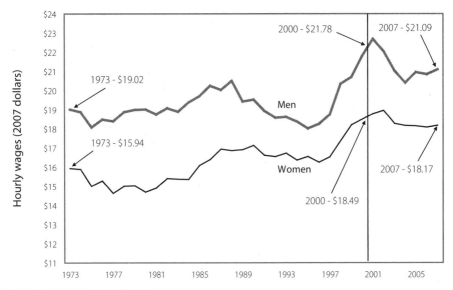

Source: Authors' analysis of CPS ORG data.

Women college graduates' wages have grown more strongly than the wages among any other group of women, and this strength is reflected in the long-term trend among entry-level women college graduates; their wages grew 20.9%, or $3.14, from 1979 to 2007. In this light, the 1.7% erosion of wages among entry-level women college graduates in the 2000-07 period stands out. In the most recent business cycle, the better-educated workers with the newest skills (young college graduates) did not fare well at all as the wages they could earn fell even as productivity soared.

The erosion of job quality for young workers can also be seen in the lower likeli-hood of their receiving employer-provided health insurance or pensions. **Figures 3R** and **3S** show the rate of employer-provided health insurance and pension coverage in entry-level jobs for high school and college graduates. Employer-provided health in-surance among recent high school graduates fell by roughly half, from 63.3% to 32.1%, between 1979 and 2006 (the latest data). Pension coverage fell over this period as well, from an already low 36.0% in 1979 to an even lower 18.2% in 2006.

Health insurance coverage also fell among recent college graduates, but not as drastically as among recent high school graduates. The share covered was 77.7% in 1979 and 64.7% in 2006, with much of the decline resulting from the roughly six per-centage point drop after 2000. Pension coverage among young college graduates follows the overall pattern discussed in an earlier section. It fell between 1979 and the late 1980s and then regained its earlier level by 1998. However, this group's pension

FIGURE 3R Health and pension benefit coverage for recent high school graduates, 1979-2006

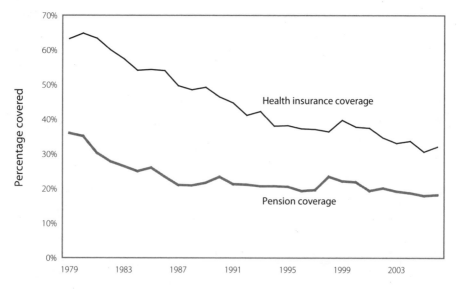

Source: Authors' analysis of March CPS data.

coverage fell over the 2000-06 period by 8.5 percentage points, from 54.6% to 46.1%. This sharp reduction in both health and pension benefits for young college graduates over the last few years indicates a substantial job quality problem even for those with the highest educational attainment.

The growth of within-group wage inequality

The data presented so far illustrate the various dimensions of wage inequality. The "between-group" inequality for workers by both education and experience (or age) can be characterized as a growth in differentials in education and experience, which are sometimes labeled as an increase in the "returns to education and experience" or as a shift in the rewards or price of "skill." We now examine in greater depth the growth of "within-group" wage inequality, the inequality among workers with similar education and experience.

This growth in within-group wage inequality was shown earlier in Table 3.14. The analysis in **Table 3.20** illustrates the growth of this type of inequality by presenting wage trends of high-, middle-, and low-wage workers among high school and college graduates. In other words, the data track the wages of 90th, 50th (median), and 10th percentile high-school-educated and college-educated workers by gender and show a growing wage gap among college graduates and high school graduates.

FIGURE 3S Health and pension benefit coverage for recent college graduates, 1979-2006

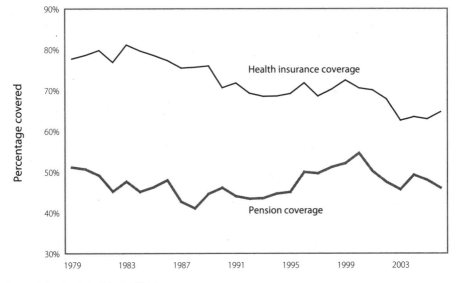

Source: Authors' analysis of March CPS data.

TABLE 3.20 Hourly wages by decile within education groups, 1973-2007 (2007 dollars)

Education/ gender decile	Hourly wage						Percent change				
	1973	1979	1989	1995	2000	2007	1973-79	1979-89	1989-2000	1995-2000	2000-07
High school											
Men											
Low*	$9.52	$9.02	$7.76	$7.53	$8.23	$8.02	-5.2%	-14.0%	6.1%	-11.1%	-2.6%
Median	17.17	17.21	15.06	13.89	14.62	14.60	0.2	-12.5	-2.9	-15.2	-0.2
High	28.04	28.08	26.55	25.55	26.78	27.33	0.1	-5.4	0.8	-2.7	2.1
Women											
Low	$6.45	$7.53	$6.16	$6.43	$7.05	$7.01	16.7%	-18.2%	14.4%	-6.9%	-0.5%
Median	10.65	10.65	10.65	10.50	11.23	11.24	0.0	0.0	5.5	5.5	0.0
High	17.63	18.18	19.19	19.39	20.16	20.23	3.1	5.5	5.0	11.3	0.4
College											
Men											
Low	$11.76	$11.64	$11.00	$10.52	$12.00	$11.57	-1.0%	-5.5%	9.1%	-0.6%	-3.6%
Median	22.07	21.94	22.80	22.52	24.81	24.88	-0.6	3.9	8.8	13.4	0.3
High	41.15	40.31	41.34	43.99	48.11	52.22	-2.0	2.5	16.4	29.5	8.6
Women											
Low	$9.04	$8.36	$8.67	$8.85	$9.81	$9.95	-7.5%	3.7%	13.1%	18.9%	1.4%
Median	15.62	14.52	16.76	17.83	19.30	19.24	-7.0	15.4	15.1	32.5	-0.3
High	24.67	24.68	29.19	33.08	37.00	38.45	0.0	18.3	26.7	55.8	3.9

* Low, median, and high earners refer to, respectively, the 10th, 50th, and 90th percentile wage.

Source: Authors' analysis of CPS ORG data.

Because of rising within-group inequality, the wage growth of the median or "typical" worker within each group has been less than that of the average worker. For instance, the median wage of the male high school graduate fell 14.9% over the 1973-2007 period, compared to a 10.5% drop in the average wage (Table 3.16). Similarly, the wage growth of male college graduates in the 1973-2007 period was 18.1% at the average (Table 3.16) but only 12.7% at the median (Table 3.20).

Table 3.20 shows that, while the high (90th percentile) wage among female college graduates grew 55.8% from 1995 to 2000, the low (10th percentile) wage in this group rose just 18.9%, a 36.9 percentage-point disparity. Similarly, wage trends at the top of the college male wage ladder (29.5% growth) and the bottom (a 0.6% decline) diverged dramatically over the 1995-2000 period.

The question remains, however, as to how much the growth in overall wage inequality in particular time periods has been driven by changes in between-group versus within-group wage inequality. It would also be useful to know the role of the growth of between- and within-group inequality on growing wage inequality at the top (the 90/50 differential) versus the bottom (the 50/10 differential), but measurement techniques for answering this question are not readily available.

Table 3.21 presents the trends in overall wage inequality, as measured by the standard deviation of log hourly wages, and the trends in within-group wage inequality. These measures allow an examination of how much of the change in overall wage inequality in particular periods was due to changes in within-group wage inequality and between-group wage inequality (primarily changes in the differentials for education and experience).

The data in Table 3.21 indicate that roughly 60% of the growth of wage inequality since 1979 (or 1973) has been driven by the growth of within-group wage inequality. Among women, for instance, overall wage inequality grew 0.140 over the 1979-2007 period, of which 0.082 was due to growth of within-group inequality. Similarly, 0.073 of the 0.114 increase in overall male wage inequality over the 1979-2007 period was due to growing within-group inequality.

The growth of wage inequality in the 2000-07 period is a departure from the prior five years of the late 1990s wage boom, when wage inequality was stable. For men, this shift to a renewed growth of wage inequality is mostly due to a renewed growth of within-group wage inequality (up 0.020 among men compared to a between-group change of just 0.005). The same pattern holds among women, with renewed growth of wage inequality in the 2000-07 period due to growing within-group inequality rather than rising age or education differentials. Note that wage inequality grew more among both men and women in the recent business cycle than over the prior one from 1989 to 2000.

Table 3.21 makes clear that any explanation of growing wage inequality must go beyond explaining changes in skill, education, experience, or other wage differentials and be able to explain growing inequalities within each of these categories.

Wage growth by race and ethnicity

Race and ethnicity have long played an important role in shaping employment opportunities and labor market outcomes, and **Table 3.22** examines changes in those dimen-

TABLE 3.21 Decomposition of total and within-group wage inequality, 1973-2007

	Women				Men			
Year	Overall wage inequality* (1)	Between-group inequality** (2)	Within-group inequality*** (3)	Contribution of within-group inequality (3)/(1)	Overall wage inequality* (1)	Between-group inequality** (2)	Within-group inequality*** (3)	Contribution of within-group inequality (3)/(1)
1973	0.478	0.061	0.418	0.873	0.506	0.083	0.423	0.836
1979	0.446	0.044	0.402	0.901	0.506	0.078	0.428	0.847
1989	0.529	0.082	0.447	0.845	0.579	0.112	0.467	0.807
1995	0.562	0.095	0.467	0.831	0.595	0.118	0.478	0.802
2000	0.552	0.094	0.458	0.829	0.595	0.114	0.481	0.808
2007	0.586	0.102	0.484	0.827	0.620	0.119	0.501	0.808
Change								
1973-79	-0.033	-0.017	-0.016	49.1%	0.000	-0.005	0.006	n.a.****
1979-89	0.083	0.038	0.046	54.7	0.073	0.034	0.038	52.8%
1989-2000	0.023	0.012	0.011	46.6	0.016	0.002	0.014	86.3
2000-07	0.033	0.007	0.026	78.0	0.025	0.005	0.020	80.9
1979-2007	0.140	0.057	0.082	58.9	0.114	0.041	0.073	63.8
1973-2007	0.107	0.041	0.066	62.0	0.115	0.036	0.079	68.6

*   Measured as standard deviation of log wages.
**   Reflects changes in education, experience, race/ethnicity, marital status, and regional differentials.
***   Measured as mean square error from a standard (log) wage regression.
****   Not applicable because denominator is zero or too small.

Source: Authors' analysis of CPS ORG data.

sions of the wage structure. Wage trends are presented by gender for two indicators of the middle of the wage structure (the median wage and the high school wage) for four populations: white, black, Hispanic, and Asian. (A finer breakdown of groups, for example, sub-populations of Hispanics, is not possible because of sample size limitations; for the same reason, the trends for the 1980s are not available. Also, note that our definitions of race/ethnicity categories exclude Hispanics from the white, black, and Asian groups.)

TABLE 3.22 Hourly wage growth by gender, race/ethnicity, 1989-2007

Demographic group	Hourly wage				Percent change	
	1989	1995	2000	2007	1989-2000	2000-07
Men						
Median						
White	$17.52	$16.86	$18.35	$18.75	4.7%	2.2%
Black	12.68	12.32	13.42	13.47	5.8	0.4
Hispanic	11.79	10.74	11.77	12.20	-0.1	3.6
Asian	16.37	16.23	18.24	20.73	11.4	13.6
High school*						
White	$17.21	$16.52	$17.69	$17.73	2.8%	0.2%
Black	13.75	13.22	14.16	13.76	3.0	-2.8
Hispanic	14.26	13.63	14.14	14.81	-0.8	4.8
Asian	15.05	14.70	15.64	15.94	3.9	1.9
Women						
Median						
White	$12.27	$12.57	$13.76	$14.71	12.1%	6.9%
Black	10.93	10.81	12.03	12.23	10.0	1.7
Hispanic	9.75	9.56	10.17	10.74	4.2	5.6
Asian	12.70	12.93	14.67	15.73	15.5	7.3
High school*						
White	$12.08	$12.28	$13.00	$13.45	7.6%	3.5%
Black	11.15	11.09	11.94	12.28	7.1	2.8
Hispanic	11.21	11.30	11.75	11.96	4.8	1.8
Asian	11.50	11.63	12.51	12.15	8.7	-2.8

* Average wage.

Source: Authors' analysis of CPS ORG data.

Over the recent 2000-07 period the male median wage was relatively stagnant for whites, Hispanics, and blacks. The 13.6% rise among Asian men is a standout exception. The wage trends among male high school graduates tell a similar story of stagnant wages for each race/ethnic group in recent years, including Asians (the Asian male high school wage is far below the median wage so, unlike other groups, reflects a different work group). The male high school wage fared poorly among each race/ethnic group over the 1989 to 2000 period despite strong wage growth in the late 1990s.

Wage growth among women was stronger than that for men in recent years, at least as measured by median wages. White and Asian women fared best with, respectively, 6.9% and 7.3% growth. The slight 1.7% growth of the median black woman's wage stands out as the worst performance. In contrast, the median wage for black, Asian, and white women grew significantly in the 1989-2000 period, all due to the wage boom of the late 1990s. Hispanic women's wages grew the least in this earlier period. The wage trend among women high school graduates differs from that of the median wage, especially among Asian woman, whose median wage rose 7.3% but whose high school wage fell 2.8%. Among white, black, and Hispanic women the high school wage rose less than the median wage, though the difference was slight among black women.

The gender wage gap

As discussed in several earlier sections, women's wages have generally fared better than men's over the last few decades. For instance, in 1973 the ratio of the median woman's wage to the male median wage was 63.1%, but by 2007 it had risen to 81.5% (see **Table 3.23**). The rapid closing of the gender gap occurred primarily between 1979 and 1995, mostly as the result of a steady fall in the male median wage during the 1980s and but also because of a modest growth of the female median wage. The gender wage gap closed further after 2000 as the median male hourly wage grew a modest $0.07 and the corresponding female wage grew $0.66.

TABLE 3.23 The gender wage ratio, 1973-2007

	Median		Ratio
	Women	*Men*	*Women/Men*
1973	$10.65	$16.88	63.1%
1979	11.05	17.63	62.7
1989	11.91	16.30	73.1
1995	12.05	15.70	76.7
2000	13.09	16.78	78.0
2007	13.74	16.85	81.5

Source: Authors' analysis of CPS ORG data.

Another important dimension to examine is how the gender wage gap has changed for the various cohorts of workers over the postwar period and by age within each cohort. **Figure 3T** shows the gender wage gap at particular ages for several birth cohorts (such as those born between 1946 and 1955 or between 1956 and 1965). It is clear that in each cohort the wage gap rises from when workers enter the workforce in their 20s to the late 30s or age 40. For instance, for those born between 1956 and 1965 the gender wage gap was about 21% when they were in their late 20s but rose to 29% by their late 30s. Perhaps most important, the wage gap has lessened over time as the gap is less for each succeeding cohort (since each successive cohort's line is lower than that of the preceding cohort). For example, women born between 1936 and 1945 were paid 58% less per hour worked than men when they were in their late 30s; for women born 20 years later the gender wage gap was just half that large, 29%.

Research shows that shifts in skills, educational attainment, the gender composition of work, reductions in discrimination, changing social norms, and other factors have contributed to the closing of the gender gap.

Unemployment and wage growth

One category of factors shaping wage growth can be labeled macroeconomic. These factors reflect the overall health of the economy and determine whether it is producing less than it has the capacity to do, as indicated by high unemployment and

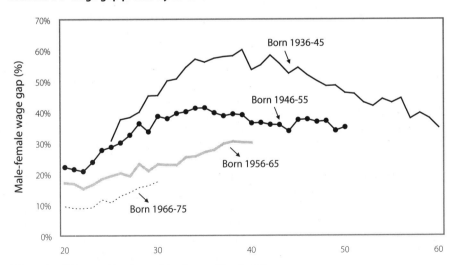

FIGURE 3T Wage gap profile by cohort*

* Percent by which women's hourly wage is less than men's hourly wage.

Source: Authors' analysis of Moore and Shierholz (2007).

excess production capacity. Generally, slack in the economy is driven by monetary policy (the growth of the money supply, interest rates), fiscal policy (the size of the government surplus/deficit, with increasing deficits adding to demand and thereby lessening slack), and the U.S. international position (trade deficits, the flow of investment dollars abroad or from abroad to the United States). Factors that affect growth include those that limit or generate slack but also those that shape productive potential, such as public and private investment, technological change, workforce skills, and work organization (how factors of production are combined).

Macroeconomic conditions greatly affect wage growth and wage inequality and are too often overlooked in explanations of rising wage and income inequality. The issue of productivity and wage growth was discussed in an earlier section, so here this section focuses on other macroeconomic factors, particularly the extent of unemployment and underemployment (trends in these factors are explored in detail in Chapter 4). The burdens of an underperforming economy and high employment are not equally shared; lower- and middle-income families are more likely to experience unemployment, underemployment, and slower wage growth because of a weak economy. For many years, until recently, white-collar workers and high-wage workers were relatively unaffected by unemployment and recessions. Not surprisingly, therefore, high unemployment is a factor that widens wage and income inequality.

There are a number of mechanisms through which high unemployment affects wages and, especially, affects them differently for different groups of workers. The wages of groups that have lower wages, less education or skill, and less power in the labor market are generally more adversely affected by high unemployment and underemployment. In other words, those already disadvantaged in the labor market become even more disadvantaged in a recession or in a weak economy. Conversely, as unemployment falls in a recovery and stays low, the greatest benefit accrues to those with the least power in the labor market—non-college-educated, blue-collar, minority, and low-wage workers.

How does this happen? First, these groups experience the greatest employment decline in a downturn and the greatest employment growth in a recovery. This greater-than-average gain in employment reflects higher demand for these workers and consequently provides them with a greater increase in leverage with employers, a position that generates higher wages. Second, as unemployment drops, more opportunities arise for upward mobility for these workers, as they switch jobs either to a new employer or within the same firm. Third, unions are able to bargain higher wages when unemployment is low. Fourth, macroeconomic conditions and institutional and structural factors interact in important ways. For instance, the early 1980s saw a surge of imports and a growing trade deficit, a decline in manufacturing, a weakening of unions, and a large erosion of the minimum wage that coincided with (and in some cases partly caused, as was the case with the trade and manufacturing problems) the rising unemployment at that time. The impact of these microeconomic factors on wage inequality was surely greater because they occurred at a time of high unemployment. So, for example, the impact of trade on wages (discussed below) was greater because the recession had already induced a scarcity of good jobs. It should not be surprising that the most radical restructuring of wages (a tremendous growth in wage inequities) and the substantial real wage reductions for non-college-educated workers occurred during the period of very high unemployment from 1979 to 1985.

The impact of rising and falling unemployment can be illustrated by examining the effect on wages of increases in unemployment in the 1979-85 period and decreases in unemployment in the 1995-2000 period, as shown in **Table 3.24**. These estimates focus on the effect of unemployment trends on the 10th, 50th, and 90th percentile wages and the 90/50 and 50/10 wage ratios for each gender.

Figure 3U shows the course of unemployment in these two periods—the sharp rise in unemployment in the early 1980s and the persistent drop in unemployment to roughly 4% in the late 1990s. During the 1980s recession wage inequality rose sharply, both at the top (the 90/50 ratio) and the bottom (the 50/10 ratio), with low-wage women being most adversely affected. Correspondingly, during the 1995-2000 boom the 50/10 wage ratios became smaller among both men and women while the 90/50 ratio among women continued to grow.

TABLE 3.24 Impact of rising and falling unemployment on wage levels and wage ratios, 1979-2000

	1979-85		1995-2000	
	Men	*Women*	*Men*	*Women*
Actual changes				
Unemployment rate	1.9%	-1.7%	0.6%	-1.5%
50/10 (log)	9.6	17.0	-3.9	-1.8
90/50 (log)	8.7	8.0	3.8	1.1
Simulated effect of change in unemployment on:				
Hourly wages				
10th percentile	-15.2%	-17.2%	10.2%	7.0%
50th percentile	-9.4	-8.0	4.1	2.3
90th percentile	-8.9	-8.3	3.1	3.7
Wage ratios (log)				
50/10	6.6	10.5	-5.7	-4.5
90/50	0.6	-0.3	-0.9	1.4
Unemployment contribution to change				
50/10 (log)	68.0%	62.0%	145.0%	257.0%
90/50 (log)	6.0	-4.0	-25.0	131.0

Source: Authors' analysis of CPS ORG and BLS (2008c) data.

How much of these shifts in wage inequality were due to unemployment trends? Table 3.24 presents the results of simulations that estimate the effect of unemployment trends during the 1979-85 and 1995-2000 periods on the wages in the final year of each period—1985 and 2000, respectively. For instance, the early 1980s recession lowered the wages (relative to what they otherwise would have been) of workers at the 10th percentile in 1985 by 15.2% among men and 17.2% among women. The drop in un-employment in the 1995-2000 period raised wages for low-wage (10th percentile) men and women by 10.2% and 7.0%, respectively. Unemployment had a sizable but lesser effect on the wages of middle- and high-wage workers, but it affected each of them to the same extent—about an 8-9% reduction in the 1980s and a 3-4% improvement in the late 1990s. Thus, unemployment did not greatly affect the 90/50 wage ratio, which grew overall in both periods. However, the large impact of unemployment on the wages at the bottom led to large changes in the 50/10 wage ratio—a roughly 5 percentage-point reduction in the late 1990s and a 6.6 percentage-point increase for men and a 10.5 percentage-point increase for women in the early 1980s. Consequently, the higher unemployment in the early 1980s can account for over 60% of the growth in the 50/10 wage ratio in that period, while lower unemployment can account for more than all of the diminution of wage inequality in the bottom half in the late 1990s. In the latter period, then, unemployment likely offset other factors (such as immigration, trade, and so on, as discussed below) that otherwise would have generated growth in wage inequality.

The higher unemployment and overall labor slack in the early 2000s (documented in Chapter 4 in terms of reduced employment-to-population rates) took their toll on

FIGURE 3U Unemployment, 1973-2007

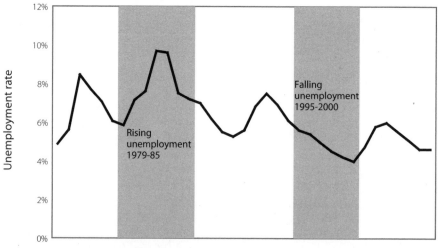

Source: Authors' analysis of BLS (2008c) data.

wage growth and exacerbated wage inequality. We have already seen how the wage momentum from the late 1990s (due, in great measure, from persistently falling unemployment) carried through the early years of the 2000s but eventually wilted in the face of a jobless recovery and higher unemployment. Moreover, the nudging up of the 50/10 wage gap is consistent with labor market slack causing or facilitating greater wage gaps in the bottom half in recent years.

The shift to low-paying industries

One factor that contributes to growing inequality and lower pay, especially for non-college-educated workers, is a changing mix of industries in the economy. Such changes include the continued shift from goods-producing to service-producing industries and at times to lower-paying service industries. The shift in the industry mix of employment matters because some industries pay more than others for workers of comparable skill.

These industry employment shifts result from trade deficits and deindustrialization as well as from differential patterns of productivity growth across industries. (Industries facing the same growth in demand for their goods and services will generate more jobs the slower their productivity growth.) This section examines the significant erosion of wages and compensation for workers resulting from the employment shift to low-paying industries since the early 1980s.

Despite a common perception, this industry-shift effect is not the simple consequence of some natural evolution from an agricultural to a manufacturing to a service economy. For one thing, a significant part of the shrinkage of manufacturing is trade-related. More important, industry shifts would not provide a downward pressure on wages if service-sector wages were more closely aligned with manufacturing wages, as is the case in other countries. Moreover, since health coverage, vacations, and pensions in this country are related to the specific job or sector in which a worker is employed, the industry distribution of employment matters more in the United States than in other countries. An alternative institutional arrangement found in other advanced countries sets health, pensions, vacation, and other benefits through legislation in a universal manner regardless of sector or firm. Therefore, the downward pressure of industry shifts on pay can be said, in part, to be the consequence of the absence of institutional structures that lessen inter-industry pay differences.

Trends in employment growth by major industry sector through 2007 and the annual compensation and "college intensity" (the share of workers with a college degree) for each sector as of 2005 are presented in **Table 3.25**. Over the 2000-07 period payroll employment rose by 5,841,000 (the sluggish job growth is explored in detail in Chapter 4). Many jobs were lost in this period in the highest-paying sectors, including manufacturing (down 3,380,000) and especially durable manufacturing (down 2,061,000), with jobs also lost in other highly paid industries, such as information, that had grown rapidly in the 1989-2000 period. Thus, industry shifts in the current business cycle have put downward pressure on compensation. Table 3.25 also shows the longer-term shifts in employment, including the more than 50 million jobs created

TABLE 3.25 Employment growth by sector, 1979-2007

Industry sector	Employment shares				Change 1979-2007		Change 2000-07		Hourly compensation 2005	Percent college graduates 2005
	1979	1989	2000	2007	Shares	Level*	Shares	Level*		
Goods producing	27.8%	22.3%	18.7%	16.1%	-11.6	-2,776	-2.6	-2,428	$29.37	18.6%
Mining	1.1	0.7	0.5	0.5	-0.6	-285	0.1	124	37.07	15.6
Construction	5.1	4.9	5.2	5.5	0.5	3,053	0.4	828	28.48	9.6
Manufacturing	21.6	16.7	13.1	10.1	-11.5	-5,543	-3.0	-3,380	29.47	23.3
Durable goods	13.6	10.2	8.3	6.4	-7.2	-3,404	-1.8	-2,061	30.98	24.6
Nondurable goods	8.0	6.5	4.8	3.7	-4.3	-2,139	-1.2	-1,319	26.96	21.2
Service producing	72.2%	77.7%	81.3%	83.9%	11.6	50,470	2.6	8,269	$23.58	32.0%
Trans., utilities	4.0	3.8	3.8	3.7	-0.3	1,452	-0.1	77	20.48	16.9
Wholesale trade	5.0	4.9	4.5	4.4	-0.6	1,543	-0.1	95	27.44	25.5
Retail trade	11.3	12.1	11.6	11.3	-0.1	5,310	-0.3	211	15.23	15.9
Information	2.6	2.4	2.8	2.2	-0.4	654	-0.6	-601	36.38	42.4
Fin, ins, real est	5.4	6.1	5.8	6.0	0.7	3,466	0.2	622	32.80	39.4
Services	26.0	31.8	37.0	40.1	14.2	31,909	3.1	6,451	22.86	37.0
Government	17.9%	16.6%	15.8%	16.1%	-1.7	6,136	0.4	1,414	n.a.	49.9%
Federal	3.2	2.9	2.2	2.0	-1.2	-167	-0.2	-138	n.a.	40.3
State and local	14.6	13.7	13.6	14.2	-0.5	6,303	0.6	1,552	$36.55	51.2
Total	100.0%	100.0%	100.0%	100.0%	--	47,695	--	5,841	$26.60	29.6%

* In thousands.

Source: Authors' analysis of BLS (2008b, 2008d), BEA (2008), and CPS ORG data.

in the service-producing industries since 1979 and the 3 million jobs lost in the goods producing sector.

The extent of adverse industry shifts in the past is best examined in an analysis of changes in the shares of the workforce in various sectors (**Table 3.26**). When industries with above (or below) average pay levels expand employment share, they raise (or lower) the average pay. The 1979-89 period saw significant downward pressure on pay due to industry shifts: the share of the workforce in low-paying services and in retail trade was 6.4 percentage points higher in 1989 than in 1979. The parallel trend was the roughly 7 percentage-point drop in the share of the workforce in high-paying industries such as manufacturing, construction, mining, government, transportation, and utilities.

The data in Table 3.26 illustrate the less adverse shifts in industry employment in the 2000s relative to either the1990s or the 1980s. Specifically, it shows the annual wages and compensation of the expanding and contracting industries in each business cycle since 1979. The wages and compensation of "expanding" industries, for instance, reflect the pay levels of each industry that experienced a rise in the share of total employment, weighted by the extent of the expansion in employment shares. These calculations show that expanding industries in the 2000s have paid annual compensation of $55,300, or 15% less than contracting industries, which paid $65,100. The consequence of employment expanding in lower-paid industries in the 2000-07 period has been to depress compensation and wage growth by 0.1% each year. Thus, industry shifts in recent years have been less adverse than in the 1979-89 period, when the impact was to reduce compensation growth by 0.3% annually. This reduced impact is due to a lower pay gap between expanding and contracting industries in the 2000s than in the 1980s

TABLE 3.26 Annual pay of expanding and contracting industries, 1979-2007

	Industries		Difference		Annual
Annual pay	*Contracting*	*Expanding*	*Dollars*	*Percent*	impact
Compensation (000)					
2000-07	$65.1	$55.3	-$9.8	-15.0%	-0.1%
1989-2000	53.3	41.6	-11.7	-21.9	-0.2
1979-89	54.3	37.2	-17.1	-31.4	-0.3
Wages and salaries (000)					
2000-07	$53.9	$47.6	-$6.3	-11.7%	-0.1%
1989-2000	44.1	35.7	-8.4	-19.0	-0.1
1979-89	44.3	34.1	-10.2	-23.0	-0.2

Source: Authors' analysis of BLS (2008b) and BEA (2008) for roughly 60 industries in each time period.

and to a diminished shift from one to the other in recent years. This analysis also shows that industry employment shifts have been consequential; they lowered compensation by 5.3% over the 1979 to 2007 period (based on the annual impact times the number of years in each period).

Trade and wages

The process of globalization since the 1980s has been an important factor in both slowing the growth rate of average wages and reducing the wage levels of workers with less than a college degree. In more recent years trade and globalization have begun to affect white-collar and college-educated workers to a great extent as well. The increase in international trade and investment flows affects wages through several channels. First, increases in imports of finished manufactured goods, especially from countries where workers earn only a fraction of what U.S. workers earn, reduces manufacturing employment in the United States. While increases in exports create employment opportunities for some domestic workers, imports mean job losses for many others. Large, chronic trade deficits over the last nearly three decades suggest that the jobs lost to import competition have outnumbered the jobs gained from increasing exports. Given that export industries tend to be less labor intensive than import-competing industries, even growth in "balanced trade" (where exports and imports both increase by the same dollar amount) would lead to a decline in manufacturing jobs.

Second, imports of intermediate manufactured goods (used as inputs in the production of final goods) also help to lower domestic manufacturing employment, especially for production workers and others with less than a college education. The expansion of export platforms in low-wage countries has induced many U.S. manufacturing firms to purchase part of their production processes from low-wage countries. Since firms generally find it most profitable to purchase the most labor-intensive processes, the increase in intermediate inputs from abroad has hit non-college-educated production workers hardest.

Third, low-wages competition and greater world capacity for producing manufactured goods can lower the prices of many international goods. Since workers' pay is tied to the value of the goods they produce, lower prices from international competition, despite possible lower inflation, can lead to a reduction in the earnings of U.S. workers, even if imports themselves do not increase.

Fourth, in many cases the mere threat of direct foreign competition or of the relocation of part or all of a production facility can lead workers to grant wage concessions to their employers. This is referred to as the "threat effect."

Fifth, the large increases in direct investment flows (i.e., plant and equipment) to other countries have meant reduced investment in the domestic manufacturing base and significant growth in the foreign manufacturing capacity capable of competing directly with U.S.-based manufacturers.

Sixth, the effects of globalization go beyond those workers exposed directly to foreign competition. As trade drives workers out of manufacturing and into lower-paying service jobs, not only do their own wages fall, but the new supply of workers to the service or other sectors (from displaced workers plus young workers not able to find manufacturing jobs) helps to lower the wages of similarly skilled workers already employed in service jobs. That is, globalization's impact is not just on those who are directly displaced by trade or face international competition but also on those workers with similar skills throughout the economy.

Last, trade in services has gained prominence in recent years as call center operations, computer programming, doctor support services (reading X-rays, for instance), research and development, and other white-collar services have been transferred (or purchased) abroad, sometimes to countries with far lower wages than those in the United States, most notably India and China. Less is known about this recent phenomenon, sometimes called "offshoring," but it seems to be a mechanism through which globalization is now adversely affecting white-collar jobs and wages (and will increasingly continue to do so). Not only are jobs directly displaced, but also the wage growth of still-employed white-collar workers threatened by offshoring is constrained.

This section briefly examines the role of international trade and investment in recent changes in the U.S. wage structure. Since even the preceding list of channels through which globalization affects wages is not complete and not fully able to be quantified, this analysis *understates* the impact of globalization on wages in the 1980s, 1990s, and the 2000s.

Figure 3V presents the trends in the imports and exports of goods as well as the size of the trade deficit in goods relative to GDP over the postwar period. Trade was balanced for the most part from 1947 through the end of the 1970s. A large deficit emerged in the mid-1980s as exports fell and imports continued to grow. Exports recovered after the fall-off in the dollar's value in the late 1980s and helped to close the deficit by the early 1990s. The goods trade imbalance spiked in the mid-1980s, rising to 3.3% of GDP (up 2.3% of GDP), then fell to the 1.5% of GDP range in the early 1990s before rising rapidly in the late 1990s to 4.7% of GDP in 2000. The pace quickened between 2000 and 2007, however, as the imbalance grew to over 6.0% of GDP in the 2005-07 period.

An important characteristic of globalization has been the rising importance of trade with lower-wage developing countries, especially since the end of the 1980s. This development is illustrated in **Figure 3W** by the growth in the share of manufacturing imports originating in developing countries (measured as a share of GDP). In 1979, imports from low-wage countries represented only 1.6% of GDP and, despite a rapid rise in imports in the 1980s, they reached only 2.6% of GDP in 1989. By 2000, however, imports from low-wage countries had doubled their importance, achieving 5.1% of GDP, and grew even further to 6.2% of GDP by 2006 when they made up more than half of all manufacturing imports. We can see that industries subject to foreign competition have seen a growth of such competition over the last 30 years, and this competition increasingly comes from lower-wage countries.

We further explore the changes in the composition of trade by examining the relative (to the United States) productivity levels of nations to which the United States exported and from which it received imports since the early 1970s. A nation's productivity level is an indicator of its wage level and its level of development, so a lower relative

FIGURE 3V Imports, exports, and trade balance as percent of U.S. GDP

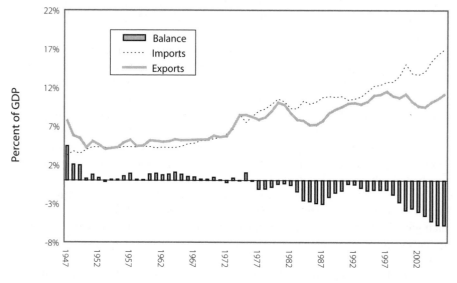

Source: Bivens (2008).

FIGURE 3W Manufacturing imports as a share of U.S. GDP

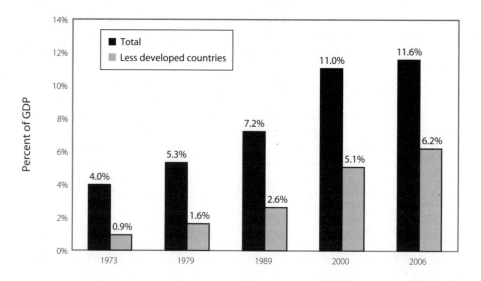

Source: Bivens (2008).

productivity level of our import partners indicates increased competition from developing, lower-wage countries. As **Figure 3X** shows, U.S. export and import trading partners had equivalent productivity levels in 1973, at roughly 57% of the productivity of the United States, and this parity prevailed up until 1989. However, by 2000 the productivity levels of U.S. import trading partners had fallen, a shift that continued to 2005. In contrast, the productivity levels of U.S. export partners in 2005 remained at roughly the same level as over the prior 30 years.

The growth in the trade deficit and increased global competition from lower-wage countries can, and would be expected to, adversely affect the wages of non-college-educated workers relative to others. In fact, any potential gains from trade would be created precisely through such a mechanism—a redeployment of workers and capital into more highly skilled or capital-intensive industries, a movement that lessens the need for non-college-educated workers.

We now turn to an examination of the types of jobs that were lost as trade competition and the trade deficit grew and as job losses in import-sensitive industries exceeded job gains in export industries. In periods of low unemployment, it may be the case that a trade deficit does not cause actual job loss because workers displaced by rising imports have found employment in non-traded sectors such as services. Nevertheless, even with low unemployment a trade deficit will affect the composition of jobs (less manufacturing, more services), thereby affecting wage inequality. In this light, **Table 3.27** indicates how trade flows affect the composition of employment by education level by separately

FIGURE 3X Relative productivity of U.S. trading partners

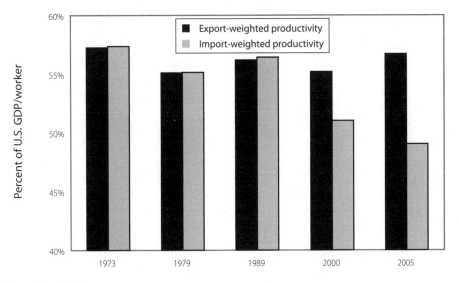

Source: Bivens (2008).

indicating the impact on those with a college degree or more (B.A. or more) and those without a four-year college degree (less than B.A.). This analysis relies on information on the types of jobs in each industry and the changes in imports and exports by industry. By using an input-output model, the analysis can examine how jobs across the economy are affected, including jobs that feed into other industries (e.g., showing how steel workers are affected by fewer car sales).

To examine the historical shifts of the effect of globalization, it is worthwhile to first examine the 1980s, a period where large trade imbalances and job-related losses became important and very visible to the public. In 1979 imports and exports were comparable, as were the jobs created by exports (3.1 million) and lost to imports (3.4 million). Translated into jobs by education level we can see that manufacturing trade in 1979 cost 335,000 "less than B.A." jobs while generating 66,000 "B.A. or more" jobs. After imports grew faster than exports in the 1980s, trade cost about 2 million jobs in 1989, with most of the job erosion (about 1.9 million) among jobs not requiring a college degree. In 1989, this job loss for non-college-educated workers was equivalent to a 2.3% loss in their employment, or a 1.8% loss relative to the employment loss of college graduates (0.5%). Therefore, trade disproportionately affected the non-college-educated workforce. Consequently, non-college-educated and middle- and lower-wage workers disproportionately bore the costs and pressures of trade deficits and global competition in the 1980s.

Interestingly, trade-related job losses were more evenly spread across education levels in the 1990s. Trade flows in the 1990s led to a loss of non-college jobs equivalent to 3.8% of their total by 2000, a 1.5 percentage-point increase over the 2.3% loss in 1989. This is roughly the same increased loss as among the "college jobs," which rose from 0.5% in 1989 to 2.1% in 2000. By 2005 the trade-imposed job losses among jobs not requiring a college degree totaled more than 4.3 million, or 4.6% of their total. Job loss among "college jobs" had grown to nearly a million in 2005, or 2.5% of their total. Nevertheless, the impact of trade on non-college jobs was nearly double that on jobs requiring a college degree in 2005, so that the employment of those without a college degree fell 2.1% relative to those with a college degree. Thus, the pattern of job erosion due to trade depressed opportunities for non-college-educated workers relative to those with more education. The last column in Table 3.27 shows the changes over the post-1979 period: a loss of 4 million non-college jobs and an erosion of relative employment of 1.3%. This analysis probably overstates the adverse trade impact on the higher wage and education groups because one of its underlying assumptions is that when an industry loses jobs, it does so proportionately across types of jobs (e.g., a 10% loss of jobs means 10% fewer jobs in each category within the industry). In other words, since the response to lost export opportunities or displacements from greater imports has almost surely fallen disproportionately on the non-college-educated workforce of each industry (rather than the white-collar or technical workers), this analysis understates the degree to which trade and globalization affect non-college-educated workers relative to those with college degrees.

The data presented so far suggest that trade, particularly with low-wage developing countries, accelerated the long-term decline in manufacturing and related employment.

TABLE 3.27 Effect of trade on composition of employment by education level, 1979-2005

	1979	1989	2000	2005	Change 1979-2005
Trade ($ millions)					
Imports	$112,235	$379,426	$1,012,856	$1,288,223	$1,175,988
Exports	116,585	272,167	625,892	685,077	568,492
Net trade (exports minus imports)	4,350	-107,259	-386,964	-603,146	-607,496
Trade-related employment (000s)					
Imports	3,412	5,623	10,910	9,936	6,525
Exports	3,142	3,615	6,564	4,597	1,455
Net trade (exports minus imports)	-269	-2,008	-4,346	-5,339	-5,070
Education intensity of trade (% jobs)					
Imports					
Less than B.A.	89.8%	85.6%	79.0%	77.8%	-12.0%
B.A. or more	10.2	14.4	21.0	22.2	12.0
Exports					
Less than B.A.	86.8%	80.9%	76.6%	73.5%	-13.3%
B.A. or more	13.2	19.1	23.4	26.5	13.3
Net trade (exports minus imports) employment impact on:					
Employment level (000s)					
Less than B.A.	-335	-1,891	-3,590	-4,354	-4,019
B.A. or more	66	-117	-757	-985	-1,051
Total	-269	-2,008	-4,346	-5,339	-5,070
Relative employment (change as % of group employment):					
Less than B.A.	-0.5%	-2.3%	-3.8%	-4.6%	-4.2%
B.A. or more	0.4	-0.5	-2.1	-2.5	-2.9
Relative change	-0.8	-1.8	-1.7	-2.1	-1.3

Source: Bivens (2008).

The data also suggest that the fall in employment opportunities was especially severe for non-college-educated manufacturing production workers. Since millions of trade-displaced workers sought jobs in non-manufacturing sectors, trade also worked

to depress the wages of comparable workers employed outside manufacturing. The r
sesult has been to weaken the wages of middle- and low-wage workers relative to those
of high-earning workers.

It is difficult to quantify the other channels, discussed at the beginning of this
section, through which the increase in international trade and investment flows affects
wages—channels such as the threat effect of imports and plant relocation on U.S.
manufacturing wages and the reality of large-scale international direct investment
flows. Nevertheless, these effects are likely to be as large as or larger than those that are
more readily quantifiable.

To gauge the impact of globalization on wages and wage inequality, particularly
the rising competition from lower-wage nations, we examine the results of a "computable general equilibrium" model developed by economist Paul Krugman in the mid-
1990s. What drives this model's estimates of the impact of trade on wage inequality is
the share of trade coming from low-wage developing countries. The model answers two
questions: how much would global prices (both of products and labor) have to change
in order make goods from less-developed countries unprofitable to send to the U.S.
market, and how much would U.S. wages change in response? In other words, what
would U.S. wages (and domestic product prices) be but for the opportunity to trade with
less-developed countries? The larger the real-world share of trade with less-developed
countries in any given year, the larger the hypothetical change in prices and wages
needed to zero it out and the larger trade's impact on American wages.

In 1979, when such trade made up just 1.8% of GDP, the model shows a modest
2.7% deterioration of the wages of those without a college degree relative to those with
a college degree (**Table 3.28**). In 1995 when trade with low-wage nations had risen to
3.6% of GDP, the relative impact was correspondingly higher at 5.6%. However, as the
column showing the changes across the 1979 to 1995 time period shows, the greater
impact of trade (2.9 percentage points) was equivalent to 16.7% of the 17.2 percentage-
point rise of the college/high school wage premium in this period. By 2005 the trade
share from low-wage countries had risen to 5.6% of GDP, more than double the share
in 1989. The wage impact of this increased trade from low-wage countries was 8.8%
in 2005, 3.2 percentage points higher than in 1995. Because the college premium rose
only modestly in this period, from 46.1% in 1995 to 48.7% in 2005, the increased
impact of trade on relative wages (3.2 percentage points) was larger than the corresponding growth of the college/high school premium, a widely used measure of wage
inequality. Thus, increased competition from low-wage countries has been a strong disequalizing factor since 1995. Over the entire 1979-2005 period, trade from low-wage
nations caused a 6.1 percentage point rise in relative wages between high school and
college-educated workers and accounted for 30.7% of the total rise of the college/high
school wage premium.

In the early 2000s globalization's adverse impacts seemed to be moving upscale,
affecting so-called knowledge workers such as computer programmers, scientists, and
doctors as work previously done in the United States was located in or relocated to other
countries. This phenomenon of offshoring high-tech, white-collar work is noteworthy
because the workers affected, especially computer-related professionals, are frequently

TABLE 3.28 Estimated relative wage impact of trade based on Krugman CGE model*

							Percentage-point change		
	1973	1979	1989	1995	2000	2005	1979-95	1995-2005	1979-2005
Less developed country trade (% GDP)	1.0%	1.8%	2.5%	3.6%	4.6%	5.6%	1.8%	2.0%	3.8%
Relative wage impact	1.6	2.7	4.0	5.6	7.3	8.8	2.9	3.2	6.1
College wage premium	36.9	28.9	41.5	46.1	48.2	48.7	17.2	2.6	19.8
Trade share of premium	4.3	9.5	9.5	12.1	15.0	18.1	16.7	123.7	30.7

* CGE is a computable general equilibrium model.

Source: Bivens' (2008) re-analysis of Krugman (1995).

discussed as the winners in the globalization process. If the jobs of such highly educated workers are now at risk in the global economy, it makes one wonder which jobs cannot be moved offshore. Two factors seem to have made offshoring of white-collar work a potentially significant phenomenon. One is that technology, particularly fast Internet and other communications technology, makes coordination and transmission of work worldwide much easier. A second factor is what could be called a "supply shock" arising from the availability of millions of highly educated workers in places such as China, India, Eastern Europe, Russia, and elsewhere who are willing to do the work for a lower wage than U.S. workers.

Hard data that could inform us of the extent of offshoring and how much more to expect in the future are not available because our data systems are not well suited to measuring trade in services (including that which is transferred over the Internet) as opposed to goods. Even if the current level of offshoring is modest, the high public profile of this practice and the statements from firms of their intentions to intensify their offshoring is sufficient to depress wage expectations in the relevant labor markets.

Outsourcing has also emerged as a concern for many workers at a time when the labor market for college-educated workers, especially new college graduates, has not been robust. As discussed above, wages for entry-level college graduates have declined since 2000, and the ability of new graduates to receive employer-provided benefits has diminished as well. The review of unemployment and employment trends in Chapter 4 shows that the college graduate unemployment rate increased more in this recession than in earlier ones and that the employment rates of college graduates declined in recent years, a highly unusual development. **Table 3.29** uses an analysis of which detailed occupations are most offshorable to characterize the education and skill requirements of the particular jobs that are most offshorable. Each occupation was rated as highly offshorable, offshorable, highly non-offshorable, or non-offshorable.

Given these ratings and information about the total employment and the education and skill requirements of each occupation, it is possible to determine the amount of employment that falls into each category and the characteristics of jobs in each. "Offshorable" or "highly offshorable" in this context denotes, based on the nature of the job, whether

TABLE 3.29 Characteristics of offshorable jobs

	Category 1	Category 2	Category 3	Category 4	
	Highly offshorable	*Offshorable*	*Non-offshorable*	*Highly non-offshorable*	*All*
Total					
Levels	9,517,000	22,116,667	9,525,167	104,976,167	146,135,001
Shares	6.5%	15.1%	6.5%	71.8%	100.0%
Annual salary	$36,246	$42,775	$33,116	$33,020	$34,713
Education and percents					
High school or less	28.5%	42.4%	41.4%	45.2%	43.5%
Some college	37.8	27.0	35.6	27.7	28.8
College or higher	33.8	30.6	23.0	27.1	27.8
Total	100.0	100.0	100.0	100.0	100.0
Education and training					
Short-term on-the-job training	19.8%	18.8%	49.7%	39.0%	35.4%
Moderate-term on-the-job training	40.8	32.6	17.3	15.4	19.8
Long-term on-the-job training	0.8	6.4	3.1	8.8	7.5
Work experience in a related occupation	0.0	6.0	7.3	8.6	7.6
Postsecondary vocational award	4.1	0.5	2.6	6.8	5.4
Associate degree	8.7	5.5	4.8	3.3	4.1
Bachelor's degree	24.0	14.9	6.1	10.4	11.7
Bachelor's or higher degree, plus work experience	0.2	13.1	9.1	2.6	4.4
Master's degree	1.1	0.0	0.0	1.9	1.5
Doctoral degree	0.6	0.4	0.0	1.7	1.3
First professional degree	0.0	1.7	0.0	1.4	1.3
Total	100.0	100.0	100.0	100.0	100.0

Source: Bernstein, Lin, and Mishel (2007) analysis of Blinder (2007) and BLS Occupational Employment Statistics.

the work is *potentially* offshorable and only a fraction of such jobs will actually be offshored. Nevertheless, just the potential for being offshored will likely suppress wage growth in these occupations.

This analysis shows that 6.5% of employment is highly offshorable and another 15.1% is offshorable, translating into about 31.6 million of today's jobs that are vulnerable to future offshoring. This group of vulnerable occupations is more than three times the employment of the manufacturing sector. More of the highly offshorable occupations require at least a college degree (33.8% of the jobs) than the jobs that are in either of the non-offshorable categories (23.0% or 27.1%). Likewise, the jobs most vulnerable to being offshored are more likely to require some college, indicating that they are middle-wage jobs. Offshorable occupations have somewhat more education requirements than the average in the economy (i.e., 30.6% require a college degree or more versus 27.8% economy-wide).

It is interesting to note that occupations vulnerable to offshoring pay more than other occupations. For instance, the annual wages in the highly offshorable and offshorable occupations are, respectively, $36,246 and $42,775, far higher than the roughly $33,000 of pay in non-offshorable occupations. **Figure 3Y** shows the wage premium in offshorable jobs, the percent more that such jobs pay than comparably skilled jobs that are not offshorable. Overall, offshorable occupations pay 10.8% more; among jobs requiring at least a college degree the offshorable jobs pay 13.9% more. This analysis seems to confirm fears that offshoring threatens some of the best U.S. jobs, both in terms of their pay and the education required to obtain the jobs.

That offshorable jobs are highly paid and require above average education credentials tells us that globalization will be asserting greater downward pressure on the wages of these vulnerable jobs and jobs like them throughout the economy. It does not follow, however, that globalization will be more of a burden to the more highly educated and better-paid workforce: globalization will be increasingly evident in greater import flows and international competition in a wide variety of industries and occupations that have already experienced competition from producers in low-wage countries—an impact, as we have seen, that has disproportionately fallen on the non-college-educated workforce. Though white-collar workers have started to face more international competition, it may be a while before they face as much as do typical blue-collar workers.

Another aspect of globalization is immigration. The percentage of the labor force that are immigrants declined in the United States over the first half of the last century but began to grow in the 1970s and then grew faster in the 1980s, as seen in **Table 3.30** (which shows the immigrant share of the workforce from 1940 to 2007 for all immigrants and for those from Mexico, the largest single source country). These data indicate that the growth in the number of immigrant workers, relative to the growth in the native labor force, has doubled in each decade starting in 1970: the immigrant share grew 1.3 percentage points in the 1970s, followed by 2.3 percentage points in the 1980s and 4.4 percentage points in the 1990s. The immigrant share continued to grow between 2000 and 2007 but at a somewhat slower annual rate than in the 1990s. By 2007 immigrants comprised nearly 16% of the workforce, triple the share in 1970. Immigration

FIGURE 3Y Wage premium of offshorable jobs

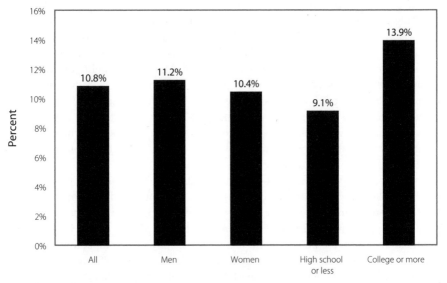

Source: Bernstein, Lin, and Mishel (2007) analysis of Blinder (2007) and BLS Occupational Employment Statistics.

from Mexico contributed almost half (44%) of the growth in immigrants as a share of the workforce, with a greater role among men.

A rise in immigration increases the available labor supply in the United States and thus tends to reduce wages if all else is constant (which it rarely is). If one workforce group—say, those without a high school degree—experiences the largest growth in immigration, then that group will have wage growth inferior to (or real wage declines greater than) that of other less-affected groups. Since the largest share of immigrants is found among those without a high school degree, it would be that group of native workers most affected by immigration. (Recall from Table 3.18 that 6.1% of the native-born workforce had less than a high school education, compared with 29.1% of immigrant workers.) A particular concern is whether new immigrants adversely affect the relative employment and wages of other disadvantaged populations (e.g., the less-educated portion of the black workforce, native Hispanics, and Hispanics who immigrated some time ago) where a disproportionate share of workers lack a high school degree. The impact of immigrants on native born workers' relative wages could also be felt by those with high school degrees or above to the extent they compete for jobs in the same occupations and industries.

The offsetting factor is that immigrants may also be "complements" rather than "substitutes" to native born workers such that immigrant workers facilitate the employment of other workers (presumably more skilled workers) or raise the effectiveness of capital investments (thereby raising productivity). There may also be situations in

TABLE 3.30 Share of Mexican and other immigrants in workforce, 1940-2007

Year	Share of workforce (decennial Census)*							Share of workforce (CPS)		Change		
	1940	1950	1960	1970	1980	1990	2000	2000	2007	1980-90	1990-2000	2000-07
Total												
All immigrants	9.8%	7.3%	6.0%	5.2%	6.5%	8.8%	13.2%	13.4%	15.8%	2.3	4.4	2.4
Mexican immigrants	0.3	0.4	0.4	0.4	1.1	2.0	4.0	3.9	5.1	0.9	2.0	1.2
Other immigrants	9.5	6.9	5.6	4.8	5.4	6.8	9.2	9.6	10.7	1.4	2.4	1.2
Male												
All immigrants	10.9%	7.8%	6.1%	5.0%	6.4%	9.4%	14.5%	15.0%	17.9%	3.0	5.1	2.8
Mexican immigrants	0.4	0.4	0.4	0.5	1.3	2.5	5.1	5.0	6.7	1.2	2.6	1.6
Other immigrants	10.5	7.4	5.7	4.5	5.1	6.9	9.4	10.0	11.2	1.8	2.5	1.2
Female												
All immigrants	6.9%	6.0%	5.9%	5.4%	6.5%	8.2%	11.7%	11.6%	13.5%	1.7	3.5	1.9
Mexican immigrants	0.2	0.2	0.3	0.3	0.9	1.4	2.8	2.5	3.3	0.5	1.4	0.8
Other immigrants	6.7	5.8	5.6	5.1	5.6	6.8	8.9	9.1	10.2	1.2	2.1	1.1

* Population age 18-64.

Source: Borjas and Katz (2005) and authors' analysis of BLS data.

which immigrants are working in somewhat distinct markets. Last, the increased supply of immigrant workers could in some circumstances be offset by a rapid growth in demand for those particular types of workers. Unfortunately, economic analyses have not been able to clearly identify the impact of increased immigration on the absolute wages and employment of other workers. However, a consensus exists that immigration heavily weighted toward those lacking a high school degree or with just a high school degree will increase wage inequality (it may not force wages for the "less-educated" to fall, but it will lead them to rise less than for workers with more education).

Table 3.31 shows that a majority of Mexican immigrants, 59.7% of men and 51.6% of women, do not have a high school education. Among non-Mexican immigrants the share without a high school degree (13.0% of women and 16.6% of men) is larger than among native workers (6.1% overall). Thus, immigration disproportionately adds to the supply of "less than high school" or "dropout" workers relative to other education levels.

At the other end of the education spectrum, Table 3.18 showed a greater share of immigrants than native workers with advanced degrees, 11.1% vs. 9.9%, and a not dissimilar share of those with just a college degree, 17.6% versus 21.5%. Therefore, the impact of growing immigration has been broadly felt, including among those with college or advanced degrees. These numbers suggest that immigrants compete dispro-portionately with the least-educated U.S. workers and therefore may have generated pressure to lower wages for those without a high school degree, particularly since the end of the 1970s. On the other hand, immigration has probably not been associated with growing wage inequality between high- and middle-wage earners and may have lessened the growth in inequality. This might be the case because immigration has added more workers relative to native workers in the college and advanced degree categories than it has added among the high school educated or among those with some college or an associate's degree.

As noted, the degree to which immigration adversely affects the wages of par-ticular groups of workers, if at all, is a matter of some dispute among economists. Given the expected downward pressure on the wages of low-wage workers from in-creased immigration, it is surprising that, while there was faster immigration in the 1990s, the wages at the bottom did better in the 1990s than in the 1980s and that, correspondingly, the 50/10 wage gap has been stable or declining since the late 1980s. However, two sets of increases in the minimum wage and many years of persistent low unemployment in the late 1990s may have offset the impact of immigration. The early 2000s, a period of considerable labor market slack and no increase in the mini-mum wage, had no offsets to the impact of immigration. During this period the 50/10 wage gap stopped its strong descent and instead grew slightly among women and fell more slowly among men (see Table 3.14). Immigration may have asserted an adverse relative impact under these conditions.

The union dimension

The percentage of the workforce represented by unions was stable in the 1970s but fell rapidly in the 1980s and continued to fall in the 1990s and the early 2000s, as

TABLE 3.31 Percent distribution of educational attainment of immigrants, 1940-2007

	Decennial Census							CPS	
	1940	*1950*	*1960*	*1970*	*1980*	*1990*	*2000*	*2000*	*2007*
Male workers									
Mexican immigrants									
High school dropouts	94.6%	91.2%	88.3%	82.6%	77.2%	70.4%	63.0%	64.6%	59.7%
High school graduates	3.0	6.7	6.7	11.7	14.3	19.0	25.1	22.2	26.8
Some college	1.0	1.5	2.7	3.6	5.7	7.8	8.5	9.3	8.7
College graduates	1.4	0.6	2.4	2.2	2.9	2.8	3.4	3.8	4.8
Non-Mexican immigrants									
High school dropouts	84.4%	76.4%	64.5%	45.5%	30.2%	21.0%	17.0%	18.5%	16.6%
High school graduates	9.2	14.5	16.8	23.9	26.7	26.0	25.8	24.6	24.4
Some college	2.8	4.0	8.3	11.7	15.2	21.3	20.9	19.7	18.7
College graduates	3.7	5.1	10.4	18.9	27.9	31.7	36.3	37.3	40.3
Female workers									
Mexican immigrants									
High school dropouts	84.5%	82.4%	83.9%	77.3%	72.9%	64.7%	57.0%	57.3%	51.6%
High school graduates	12.5	10.3	11.4	16.9	17.7	21.9	26.6	24.0	27.2
Some college	2.1	4.4	2.7	4.5	7.0	10.5	11.8	13.4	13.9
College graduates	0.9	2.9	2.0	1.4	2.4	3.0	4.5	5.2	7.3
Non-Mexican immigrants									
High school dropouts	79.2%	68.5%	59.3%	43.9%	30.1%	20.0%	15.5%	16.6%	13.0%
High school graduates	15.8	22.3	25.5	33.7	35.2	31.1	27.6	27.1	25.7
Some college	2.8	5.0	9.6	12.6	16.8	24.0	24.4	22.6	22.6
College graduates	2.2	4.2	5.7	9.9	17.9	24.9	32.6	33.7	38.8

Source: Borjas and Katz (2005) and authors' analysis of BLS data.

shown in **Figure 3Z**. This falling rate of unionization has lowered wages, not only because some workers no longer receive the higher union wage, but also because there is less pressure on non-union employers to raise wages (a "spill over" or "threat effect" of unionism). The possibility that union bargaining power has weakened adds a qualitative shift to the quantitative decline. This erosion of bargaining power is partially related to a harsher economic context for unions because of trade pressures, the shift to services, and ongoing technological change. However, analysts have also pointed to other factors, such as employer militancy and changes in the application

FIGURE 3Z Union coverage rate in the United States, 1973-2007

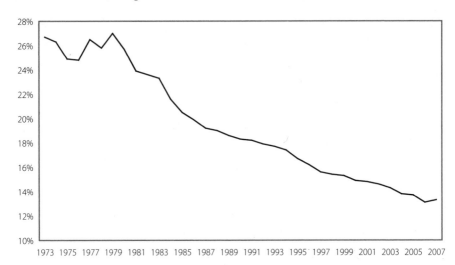

Source: Hirsch and Macpherson (2003) and authors' analysis of BLS data.

and administration of labor law that have helped to weaken unions and their ability to raise wages.

Table 3.32 presents estimates of the union wage premium computed to reflect differences in hourly wages between union and non-union workers who are otherwise comparable in experience, education, region, industry, occupation, and marital status. The union premium is presented as the extra dollars per hour and the percentage higher wage earned by those covered by a collective bargaining contract. This methodology yields a union premium of 14.1% overall—17.1% for men and 10.7% for women.

Sizable differences exist in union wage premiums across demographic groups, with blacks and Hispanics having union premiums of 18.3% and 21.9%, respectively, far higher than the 12.4% union premium for whites. Consequently, unions raise the wages of minorities more than of whites (the wage effect of unionism on a group is calculated as the unionism rate times the union premium), helping to close racial/ethnic wage gaps. Hispanic and black men tend to reap the greatest wage advantage from unionism, though minority women have substantially higher union premiums than their white counterparts enjoy. Unionized Asians have a wage premium somewhat higher than that of whites, with Asian men obtaining a premium on par with that of other minority men.

Unionized immigrant workers obtain a premium comparable to other workers, whether they have immigrated relatively recently (within 10 years) or further back in time.

Table 3.33 provides information on the union premium for various non-wage dimensions of compensation related to health insurance, pensions, and paid time off. The first two columns present the characteristics of compensation in union and non-union settings. The difference between the union and non-union compensation packages are presented in two ways, unadjusted (simply the difference between the first two columns)

TABLE 3.32 Union wage premium by demographic group, 2007

Demographic group	Percent union*	Union premium**	
		Dollars	*Percent*
Total	13.3%	$1.50	14.1%
Men	14.1	2.22	17.1
Women	12.4	1.06	10.7
Whites	13.5%	$1.19	12.4%
Men	14.6	1.86	15.0
Women	12.3	0.81	9.1
Blacks	15.8%	$2.44	18.3%
Men	17.3	3.29	22.7
Women	14.5	1.82	14.5
Hispanics	10.8%	$3.07	21.9%
Men	10.8	3.53	23.4
Women	10.7	2.38	18.7
Asians	11.9%	$2.51	17.4%
Men	10.9	3.75	23.2
Women	13.0	1.69	12.6
New immigrants (less than 10 years)			
Men	--	$2.05	16.5%
Women	--	2.29	16.2
Other immigrants (more than 10 years)			
Men	--	$2.10	16.4%
Women	--	0.98	10.3

* Union member or covered by a collective bargaining agreement.
** Regression-adjusted union premium advantage controlling for experience, education, region, industry, occupation, and marital status.

Source: Authors' analysis of CPS ORG data.

and adjusted (for differences in characteristics other than union status such as industry, occupation, and establishment size). The last column presents the union premium, the percentage difference between union and non-union compensation, calculated using the "adjusted" difference.

These data show that a union premium exists in every dimension of the compensation package. Unionized workers are 28.2% more likely to be covered by employer-provided health insurance. Unionized employers also provide better health insurance, paying an 11.1% higher share of single-worker coverage and a 15.6% higher share of family coverage. Moreover, deductibles are $54, or 18.0%, less for union workers. Finally, union workers are 24.4% more likely to receive health insurance coverage in their retirement.

Similarly, 71.9% of union workers have employer-provided pensions, compared to only 43.8% of non-union workers. Thus, union workers are 53.9% more likely to

TABLE 3.33 Union premiums for health, retirement, and paid leave

Benefit	Union	Nonunion	Difference Unadjusted	Adjusted*	Union premium
Health insurance					
Percent covered	83.5%	62.0%	21.5%	17.5%	28.2%
Employer share (%)					
Single	88.3%	81.8%	6.5%	9.1%	11.1%
Family	76.3	64.9	11.4	10.1	15.6
Deductible ($)	$200	$300	-$100	-$54	-18.0
Retiree health coverage	76.6	59.8	16.7	14.6	24.4
Pension					
Percent covered	71.9%	43.8%	28.1%	23.6%	53.9%
Employer costs (per hour)					
Defined benefit	--	--	--	$0.39	36.1%
Defined contribution	--	--	--	-0.11	-17.7
Time off					
Vacation weeks	2.98	2.35	0.63	--	26.6%
Paid holiday/vacation (hours)	--	--	--	22.2	14.3

* Adjusted for establishment size, occupation, industry, and other factors.

Source: Buchmueller, DiNardo, and Valletta (2001) and Mishel and Walters (2003).

have pension coverage. Union employers spend 36.1% more on defined-benefit plans but 17.7% less on defined-contribution plans. As defined-benefit plans are preferable, as discussed earlier, these data indicate that union workers are more likely to have the better form of pension plans.

Union workers also get more paid time off. Their three weeks of vacation amount to about three days (0.63 weeks) more than non-union workers receive. Including both vacations and holidays, union workers enjoy 14.3% more paid time off.

Table 3.34 provides a more refined analysis of the union wage premium by comparing the employer costs in unionized settings to non-union settings in comparable occupations and establishments (factories or offices). Specifically, the estimated union premium controls for the sector (public or private) in which the establishment is located, the establishment's size, full-time or part-time status of its employees, and its detailed industry and region. Unionized workers are 18.3% more likely to have health insurance, 22.5% more likely to have pension coverage, and 3.2% more likely to have paid leave. Unionized employers pay more for these benefits because the benefits they provide are better than those offered by non-union employers and because unionized employers are more likely to provide these benefits. For instance, unionized employers pay 77.4% more in health insurance costs per hour, 24.7% more because of the greater incidence and 52.7% because of the better benefit.

This analysis also shows that unionized employers pay 56.0% more per hour for pension plans, 28.4% from a greater incidence of providing pensions, and 27.7% from providing better pensions. Similarly, unionized workers have 11.4% greater costs for their paid leave, mostly because of the more extensive paid leave (the 8.0% "better benefit" effect).

The effect of the erosion of unionization on the wages of a segment of the workforce depends on the degree to which deunionization has taken place and the degree to which the union wage premium among that segment of the workforce has declined. **Table 3.35** shows both the degree to which unionization and the union wage premium have declined by occupation and education level over the 1978-2005 period (1979 data were not available). These data, which are for men only, are used to calculate the effect of weakened unions (less representation and a weaker wage effect) over the period on the wages of particular groups and the effect of deunionization on occupation and education/wage differentials.

Union representation fell dramatically among blue-collar and high-school-educated male workers from 1978 to 2005. Among the high-school-graduate workforce, unionization fell from 37.9% in 1978 to 19.0% in 2005, or by about half. This decline obviously weakened the effect of unions on the wages of both union and non-union high-school-educated workers. Because unionized high school graduates earned about 17% more than equivalent non-union workers (a premium that declined from roughly 22% in 1978, not shown in table), unionization raised the wage of the average high school graduate by 8.2% in 1978 (the "union effect"). Unions had a 0.9% impact on male college graduate wages in 1978, meaning that unions had the net effect of narrowing the college/high school gap by 7.3 percentage points in that year. The decline in union representation from 1978 to 2005, however, reduced the union effect

TABLE 3.34 Union impact on paid leave, pension, and health benefits

Benefit	Paid leave	Pension and retirement	Health insurance
Union impact on benefit incidence	3.2%	22.5%	18.3%
Union impact on benefit cost per hour			
Total impact	11.4%	56.0%	77.4%
From greater incidence	3.4	28.4	24.7
From better benefit	8.0	27.7	52.7

Source: Pierce (1999) and Mishel and Walters (2003).

for high school male workers to just 3.3% in 2005 while hardly affecting college graduates. Thus, unions closed the college/high school wage gap by only 2.8 percentage points in 2005. The lessened ability of unions to narrow this wage gap (from a 7.3% to a 2.8% narrowing effect) contributed to a 4.4 percentage-point rise in the college/high school wage differential from 1978 to 2005, an amount equal to 20.1% of the total rise in this wage gap. In other words, deunionization can explain a fifth of the growth in the college/high school wage gap among men between 1978 and 2005.

The weakening of unionism's wage impact had an even larger effect on blue-collar workers and on the wage gap between blue-collar and white-collar workers. The 43.1% unionization rate among blue-collar workers in 1978 and their 26.6% union wage premium boosted blue-collar wages by 11.5%, thereby closing the blue-collar/white-collar wage gap by 11.3 percentage points in that year. The union impact on this differential declined as unionization and the union wage premium declined, such that unionism reduced the blue-collar/white-collar differential by 4.1 rather than 11.3 percentage points in 2005, a 7.2 percentage-point weakening. This lessened effect of unionism can account for 65% of the 11.1 percentage-point growth of the blue-collar/white-collar wage gap over the 1978-2005 period. It was primarily driven by the enormous decline of unionism among blue-collar men, from 43.1% in 1978 to just 19.2% in 2005. In that nearly 30-year period unionism among blue-collar workers lost much of its ability to set wage patterns.

Unions reduce wage inequalities because they raise wages more at the bottom and in the middle of the wage scale than at the top. Lower-wage, middle-wage, blue-collar, and high-school-educated workers are also more likely than high-wage, white-collar, and college-educated workers to be represented by unions. These two factors—the greater union representation and the larger union wage impact for low- and mid-wage workers—are key to unionization's role in reducing wage inequalities.

The larger union wage premium for those with low wages, in lower-paid occupations, and with less education is shown in **Table 3.36**. For instance, the union wage

TABLE 3.35 Effect of declining union power on male wage differentials, 1978-2005

A. Effect of union decline on wages

	Percent union				Union effect*			
	1978	1989	2000	2005	1978	1989	2000	2005
By occupation								
White collar	14.7%	12.1%	11.2%	10.7%	0.2%	0.0%	-0.2%	-0.2%
Blue collar	43.1	28.9	23.1	19.2	11.5	6.7	4.3	3.8
Difference	-28.4	-16.7	-11.9	-8.5	-11.3	-6.8	-4.5	-4.1
By education								
College	14.3%	11.9%	13.1%	11.0%	0.9%	0.5%	0.9%	0.4%
High school	37.9	25.5	20.4	19.0	8.2	5.5	3.1	3.3
Difference	-23.6	-13.6	-7.4	-8.0	-7.3	-5.0	-2.3	-2.8

B. Contribution of union decline on wage differentials

	Change in wage differential**				Change in union effect				Deunionization contribution			
	1978-89	1989-2000	2000-05	1978-2005	1978-89	1989-2000	2000-05	1978-2005	1978-89	1989-2000	2000-05	1978-2005
White collar/blue collar	5.0%	4.2%	1.9%	11.1%	-4.6%	-2.3%	-0.5%	-7.3%	-90.5%	-54.3%	-23.5%	-65.3%
College/high school	13.0	8.1	1.1	22.1	-2.3	-2.7	0.6	-4.4	-17.8	-33.5	53.6	-20.1

* Premium estimated with simple human capital model plus industry and occupational controls. Union effect is premium times union coverage.
** Estimated with a simple human capital model.

Source: Freeman (1991) and authors' analysis of CPS ORG data.

premium for blue-collar workers in 1997, 23.3%, was far larger than the 2.2% union wage premium for white-collar workers. Likewise, the 1997 union wage premium for high school graduates, 20.8%, was much higher than the 5.1% premium for college graduates. The union wage premium for those with a high school degree or less, at 35.5%, is significantly greater than the 24.5% premium for all workers.

Table 3.36 presents a comprehensive picture of the impact of unions on wage inequality by drawing on the estimated union wage premiums for the different fifths of the wage distribution. The table presents the results of three different studies, and each demonstrates that the union premium is higher among lower-wage workers than among the highest-wage workers. This wage premium can be seen in the line that shows the percent by which the premium of the bottom 40% exceeds that of the top 40% of earners; the results range from 140% to 223%. These numbers illustrate that unions generate a less unequal distribution of wages in the unionized sector by being able to raise the wages of low- and middle-wage workers more than those of higher-wage workers. That is, lower-wage workers benefit more than higher-wage workers from coverage by a collective bargaining agreement. The countervailing factor, however, is that unionization rates are lower for low-wage workers than other workers.

There are several ways that unionization's impact on wages goes beyond the workers covered by collective bargaining agreements and extends to non-union wages and labor practices. For example, in industries and occupations in which a strong core of workplaces are unionized, non-union employers will frequently meet union standards or at least improve their compensation and labor practices beyond what they would have provided in the absence of a union presence. As noted above, this dynamic is sometimes called the union threat effect, the degree to which non-union workers get paid more because their employers are trying to forestall unionization.

A more general mechanism (without any specific "threat") through which unions have affected non-union pay and practices is the institution of norms and established practices that become more generalized throughout the economy, thereby improving pay and working conditions for the entire workforce. These norms and practices have particularly benefited the 70% of workers who are not college educated. Many fringe benefits, such as pensions and health insurance, were first provided in the union sector and then became more generalized. Union grievance procedures, which provide due process in the workplace, have been adapted to many non-union workplaces. Union wage-setting, which has gained exposure through media coverage, has frequently established standards for what workers expect from their employers. Until the mid-1980s, in fact, many sectors of the economy followed the patterns set in collective bargaining agreements. As unions have weakened, especially in the manufacturing sector, their ability to set broader patterns has diminished. However, unions remain a source of innovation in work practices (e.g., training, worker participation) and in benefits (e.g., child care, work-time flexibility, sick leave).

The impact of unions on wage dynamics and the overall wage structure is not easily measurable. The only dimension that has been subject to quantification is the threat effect. The union effect on total non-union wages is nearly comparable to the effect of unions on total union wages. **Table 3.37** illustrates the union impact on union, non-

TABLE 3.36 Union wage premium for subgroups

Benefit	Union wage premiums	Percent union
Occupation		
White collar (1997)	2.2%	11.6%
Blue collar (1997)	23.3	20.8
Education		
College (1997)	5.1%	10.4%
High school (1997)	20.8	23.6
All (1992, 1993, 1996)	24.5	n.a.
High school or less	35.5	n.a.

| Wage distribution (1989) | Wage premium estimates | | | Percent union |
	1	2	3	
Lowest fifth	17.2%	20.6%	24.2%	4.9%
Second fifth	21.8	16.8	34.6	8.9
Middle fifth	20.6	13.7	30.8	14.0
Fourth fifth	15.5	10.7	24.5	20.3
Top fifth	12.4	6.1	6.1	19.1
Average effect	19.0%	11.9%	n.a.	--
Percent bottom 40% to top 40%	140	223	193%	35%

Source: Mishel and Walters (2003), Gunderson (2003), Gittleman and Pierce (2007), Schmitt (2008), and Card, Lemieux and Riddle (2002).

union, and average wages among workers with a high school education. Assuming that unions have raised the wages of union workers by 20%, the average high school wage would be raised by 5.0% (25% of 20%). The total effect of unions on the average high school wage in this example is an 8.8% wage increase, 3.8 percentage points of which are due to the higher wages earned by non-union workers and 5.0 percentage points to the union wage premium enjoyed by unionized workers.

Two conclusions can be reached based on these studies. First, unions have a positive impact on the wages of non-union workers in industries and markets in which unions have a strong presence. Second, because the non-union sector is large, the union effect on the overall aggregate wage comes almost as much from the impact of unions on non-union workers as on union workers.

TABLE 3.37 Impact of unions on average wages of high school graduates

	Share of workforce	Union wage impact	Union contribution to higher average wage
Nonunion	75.0%	5.0%	3.8%
Union	25.0	20.0	5.0
Total	100.0	8.8	8.8

Source: Mishel and Walters (2003).

The decline of union coverage and power affects men more than women and adversely affects middle-wage men more than lower-wage men. Consequently, de-unionization has its greatest impact on the growth of the 90/50 wage gap among men. In this light, it is not surprising that the period of rapid decline of union coverage from 1979 to 1984 (during a deep recession, and at a time when the manufacturing sector was battered by the trade deficit) was also one where the male 90/50 wage gap grew the most. Recall from Table 3.35 that male blue-collar unionization fell from 43.1% in 1978 to just 28.9% in 1989, contributing to the rapid growth of male wage inequality in

FIGURE 3AA Real value of the minimum wage, 1960-2009

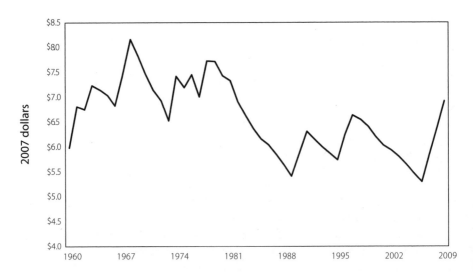

Source: Authors' analysis of Shapiro (1987).

the 1980s. The decline of unionization in the 1990s and 2000s put continued downward pressure on middle-wage men and contributed to the continued growth of the 90/50 wage gap between middle- and high-wage men.

The minimum wage dimension

Legislated increases in the federal minimum wage in both 2007 and 2008 boosted it from $5.15 in 2006 to $7.25 in 2009, its highest level in real terms since 1981 but still, after a 41% increase, 6.8% less than its peak value in the late 1960s (**Figure 3AA**). The decline in the minimum wage's value was particularly steep and steady between 1979 and 1989, when inflation whittled it down from $7.72 to $5.41 (in 2007 dollars), a fall of 29.9% (**Table 3.38**). The legislated increases in the minimum wage in 1990 and 1991 and again in 1996 and 1997 raised the value of the minimum wage over the 1989-2000 period by 14.6%. The value grew another 11.6% in 2000-09.

A more appropriate way to assess the level of the current minimum wage in historical terms is to examine the ratio of the minimum wage to the average workers' wage (as measured by the average hourly earnings of production/nonsupervisory workers), as shown in **Figure 3AB**. In 2007, the minimum wage was worth just 34% of what an average worker earned per hour, not far above its lowest point, in 2006, in 40 years. This ratio will rise in the next few years but still remain historically low. In contrast, the ratio of the minimum wage to the average wage was about 50% in the late 1960s, about 45% in the mid-1970s, and about 40% in the early 1990s. This analysis shows that the earnings of low-wage workers have fallen seriously behind those of other workers, and the decline in the minimum wage is a causal factor in rising wage inequality.

It has been argued that the minimum wage primarily affects teenagers and others with no family responsibilities. To address this criticism, **Table 3.39** examines the demographic composition of the workforce that will benefit from the increase in the minimum wage to $7.25 in 2009. An analysis of only those earning between the old and the new minimum wage would be too narrow, since a higher minimum wage affects workers who earn more than but close to the minimum; they will receive increases when the minimum wage rises. For these reasons, Table 3.39 also includes other low-wage workers who would gain from the "spillover effect" of a higher minimum wage. The table presents information on these workers in the column labeled "indirectly affected," a group totaling 7.2 million workers or 5.5% of the workforce. Therefore, the change in the minimum wage to $7.25 would affect a substantial group, 12.5 million workers or 9.6% of the workforce.

The impact of the current increases in the federal minimum wage is diminished somewhat compared to earlier increases because a substantial number of states have raised their own minimum wage levels in recent years, reducing the number of workers affected by the federal change. **Figure 3AC** contrasts the value of the federal minimum wage with the share of the workforce covered by legislated state minimum wages that exceed the federal level. Since 2005 at least half the nation's workforce has been covered by a state minimum wage exceeding the federal level; about 60% of the workforce was unaffected by the higher federal level in 2008.

TABLE 3.38 Value of the minimum wage, 1960-2009

Year	Minimum wage	
	Current $	2007 $
1960	$1.00	$5.98
1967	1.40	7.43
1973	1.60	6.52
1979	2.90	7.72
1989	3.35	5.41
1990	3.80	5.84
1991	4.25	6.31
1996	4.75	6.25
1997	5.15	6.63
2000	5.15	6.20
2007	5.85	5.85
2008	6.55	6.37
2009	7.25	6.92
Period averages		
1960s	$1.29	$7.12
1970s	2.07	7.26
1980s	3.33	6.38
1990s	4.53	6.18
2000s (through 2009)	5.57	5.95
Percent change		
1979-89	--	-29.9%
1989-2000	--	14.6
2000-09	--	11.6
1967-2009	--	-6.8

Source: Authors' analysis of Shapiro (1987).

Of the remaining workers affected by the national minimum wage increase by 2009, a slight majority, 53%, work full time (more than 35 hours weekly), and another 31% work more than 20 hours but less than 34 hours each week (Table 3.39). While minorities are disproportionately represented among minimum wage workers, 61% are white. These workers also tend to be women (59% of the total). Table 3.39 also shows that minimum wage earners are concentrated in the retail and hospitality industries

FIGURE 3AB Minimum wage as a percent of average hourly earnings, 1964-2007

Source: Authors' analysis of Shapiro (1987) and CPS ORG data.

(46% of all minimum wage earners are employed there, compared to just 21% of all workers), but are underrepresented in other industries. The demographic breakdown of those affected by the spillover effects of the minimum wage increase—those indirectly affected—is more inclusive of full-time and adult workers but has a similar gender and racial/ethnic breakdown as the group directly affected by the minimum wage.

The level of the minimum wage strongly affects the wage gains of low-wage workers, particularly low-wage women whose wage is essentially set by the legislated minimum. Thus, the erosion of the minimum wage's value led to a precipitous drop in the wages of low-wage women in the 1980s and to a large increase in the 50/10 wage gap. The level of women's low wages (i.e., the 10th percentile) stabilized in the late 1980s after it had descended to its lowest possible level (i.e., near the minimum wage, where employers could still possibly hire) and as unemployment dropped. Thereafter, the 50/10 gap was flat or declined as unemployment fell to low levels in the late 1990s and as the federal government implemented two sets of increases in the minimum wage in the 1990s. Between 1999 and 2006, as the value of the minimum wage eroded and unemployment rose, the wages of low-wage women once again weakened and the 50/10 wage gap grew.

The technology story of wage inequality

Technological change can affect the wage structure by displacing some types of workers and by increasing demand for others. Many analysts have considered technological

TABLE 3.39 Characteristics of workers affected by minimum wage increase to $7.25 by 2009

	Directly affected*	Indirectly affected**	Total affected	Total workforce***
Number of workers (millions)	5.3	7.2	12.5	130.3
Percent of workforce	4.1%	5.5%	9.6%	100.0%
Gender				
Male	39%	42%	41%	52%
Female	61	58	59	48
Race / ethnicity				
White, non-Hispanic	61%	61%	61%	69%
Black, non-Hispanic	17	16	16	11
Hispanic, all races	18	18	18	14
Asian, non-Hispanic	2	2	2	4
Family status				
Parent	25%	28%	26%	36%
Married parent	15	18	17	29
Single parent	9	10	10	7
Age				
16-19	30%	15%	21%	5%
20 and older	71	85	79	95
Work hours				
1-19 hours	22%	13%	17%	5%
20-34 hours	36	27	31	13
Full time (35 + hours)	43	60	53	82
Industry				
Retail trade	24%	23%	23%	12%
Leisure and hospitality	29	18	23	9
Other	47	59	54	79
Occupation				
Sales	21%	18%	19%	11%
Service	41	33	37	17
Other	38	49	44	72

*   These are the workers earning between the state minimum wage and $7.25.
**   These are workers currently earning above $7.25, likely to be affected by "spillover effects."
***   Includes workers not covered by the minimum wage.

Source: EPI analysis of 2006 Current Population Survey data.

FIGURE 3AC Value of federal minimum wage compared to share of workforce covered by higher state minimums

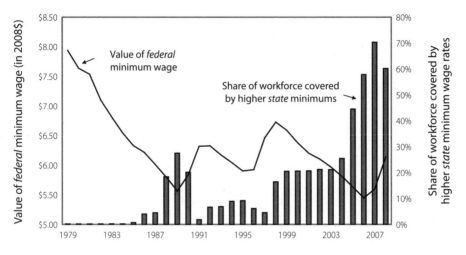

Source: Economic Policy Institute analysis of Current Population Survey data.

change a major factor in the recent increase in wage inequality. Unfortunately, because it is difficult to measure the extent of technological change and its overall character (whether it requires less skill from workers or more, and how much), it is difficult to identify the role of technological change on recent wage trends. More than a few analysts, in fact, have simply assumed that whatever portion of wage inequality is un-explained by measurable factors can be considered to be the consequence of techno-logical change. This type of analysis, however, only puts a name to our ignorance.

What is the technology story?

It is easy to understand why people might consider technology to be a major factor in explaining recent wage and employment trends. We are often told that the pace of change in the workplace is accelerating, and there is a widespread visibility of incredible new communications, entertainment, Internet, and other technologies. Given these ad-vances, it is not surprising that many non-economists readily accept that technology is transforming the wage structure. It needs to be noted, however, that technological advances in consumer products are not in and of themselves related to changes in labor market outcomes—it is the way goods and services are produced and consequent changes in the relative demand for different types of workers that affect wage trends. Since many high-tech products are made with low-tech methods, there is no close cor-respondence between advanced consumer products and an increased need for skilled workers. Similarly, ordering a book over the Internet rather than at a downtown book-store may change the type of jobs in an industry—we might have fewer retail workers in bookselling and more truckers and warehouse workers—but it does not necessarily change the skill mix.

The economic intuition for a large role for technology in the growth of wage inequality is that the growth of wage inequality and the employment shift to more-educated workers has occurred within industries and has not been caused primarily by shifts across industries (i.e., more service jobs, fewer manufacturing jobs). Research has also shown that technological change has traditionally been associated with an increased demand for more-educated or "skilled" workers. As we have noted, the wage premium for "more-educated" workers, exemplified by college graduates, has risen over the last two decades. This pattern of change suggests, to some analysts, an increase in what is called "skill-biased technological change" that is thought to be generating greater wage inequality.

Because wages have risen the most for groups whose supply expanded the fastest (e.g., college graduates), most economists have concluded that "demand factors" (i.e., shifts in demand and/or institutional factors, such as those discussed in earlier sections) are the driving force behind growing wage inequality. These economists reason that those groups with the relatively fastest growth in supply would be expected to see their wages depressed relative to other groups unless there were other factors working strongly in their favor, such as rapid expansion in demand. Rapid technological change favoring more-educated groups logically explains demand-side shifts leading to wider wage differences at the same time that supply is also increasing rapidly.

One complication in assessing any technology explanation is that technology's impact can vary in different periods, sometimes adversely affecting the least-educated and sometimes mid-level skilled workers the most. This means that almost any pattern or change in the pattern of wage inequality can be explained by technological change or some change in how technology affects different types of skills. The challenge is to empirically trace how technology affects the demand for different types of skills in different periods.

Reasons for skepticism about the technology story

There are many reasons to be skeptical of a technology-led increase in demand for "skill" as an explanation for growing wage inequality. Unfortunately, the "skills/technology" hypothesis frequently is presented as if evidence that technological change is associated with a greater need for skills or education is sufficient to show that technological change has led to the growth in wage inequality since 1979. This is not the case. Technological change certainly has generated the need for a more-educated workforce. However, the workforce has become far more educated: the share of the workforce without a high school degree has fallen sharply, and many more workers have college degrees (as Table 3.18 shows, 31.0% of workforce now has a four-year or advanced college degree, up from 14.6% in 1973). It is generally true that investment and technological change are associated with the need for more workforce skill and education— but this was true for the entire 20th century, and it therefore does not explain why wage inequality began to grow two decades ago. A convincing technology story must show that the impact of technology "accelerated" relative to earlier periods in order to explain why wage inequality started to grow in the 1980s, 1990s, and 2000s and did not grow in the prior decades.

Table 3.40 presents estimates of the changes in the relative wages, relative supply, and relative demand for college graduates (those with a four-year degree or more and some of those with an education beyond high school) for periods covering the last 90 years. These measures show whether college graduates are becoming better paid and more plentiful relative to those without a college degree. Using an assumed value for the elasticity of substitution (i.e., how easy it is to replace a college worker with one who does not have a college degree in the process of producing goods and services) one can calculate, as this table does, trends in relative demand for college graduates. In effect, the more the relative supply or the relative wage of college graduates increases, the more the relative demand for college graduates must have risen (or the increased relative supply would have led to lower relative wages).

What does the pattern in Table 3.40 tell us? First, the relative demand for college graduates grew over the entire period (except during the special circumstances of World War II, when wages grew faster for non-college workers) and a shift toward more college graduates occurred throughout this period. In this light we can safely say that skill-biased technical change has been ongoing for some time, leading to increasingly greater needs by employers for college graduates (or "skilled" workers).

The data in Table 3.40 are also informative about the last few decades that are the primary focus throughout this chapter. In the 1970s the wages of college graduates declined relative to other workers in response to a rapid growth in college graduates that overwhelmed the growing need for them. But their relative wages rapidly recovered and grew in the 1980s. It is this growth of the college wage at a time of rapid growth in overall wage inequality that has focused attention on education/wage gaps and turned to technological change as an explanation.

It is critical to note, however, that the trends since 1990 do not fit an explanation of a technologically driven demand for college-educated workers driving up their wages and therefore driving up wage inequality. Note that the relative demand for college graduates grew more slowly in the 1990s than in any period since World War II and that relative demand grew even more slowly in the 2000-05 period. This change in trend would suggest that the argument that we are in a time of historically rapid change in the need for education/skills in the workplace is not accurate, at least if one equates a college degree with skilled labor. In fact, during the entire period since 1980, the relative demand for college graduates grew no faster than during the prior 30 years **(Figure 3AD)**. So, given that wage inequality grew faster in recent decades but did not in earlier decades when technologically driven demands for college graduates were at least as rapid, it is difficult to say that a more rapid rise in technological change drove up wage inequality in recent years.

The fact that skill-biased technological change has not been more rapid in recent years, as evidenced by the measured growth in relative demand for college graduates, is even clearer when one digs a bit deeper into the measures used in Table 3.40. The measure

TABLE 3.40 Changes in the college wage premium and the supply and demand for college educated workers, 1915-2005

| | Annual change in college graduates, relative*: | | |
	Wage	Supply	Demand**
1915-40	-0.56	3.19	2.27
1940-50	-1.86	2.35	-0.69
1950-60	0.83	2.91	4.28
1960-70	0.69	2.55	3.69
1970-80	-0.74	4.99	3.77
1980-90	1.51	2.53	5.01
1990-2000	0.58	2.03	2.98
2000-05	0.34	0.89	1.42
1950-80	0.26	3.48	3.91
2000-05	0.97	2.18	3.76

* Comparisons of those with a college degree or more to those without a college degree.
** Calculated with elasticity of substitution set at 1.64.

Source: Authors' analysis of Goldin and Katz (2008).

of relative demand, as explained earlier, is deduced from changes in relative supply and the growth in relative wages. It is more accurate to say that this measure captures all non-supply factors that influence relative wages, including all institutional changes (minimum wage, unionization, norms, etc.) and all changes in relative demand (arising from technological change but also globalization, shifts in consumer demand toward services, and so on). In this light, technical change is just one component driving the measured relative demand for college graduates presented in Table 3.40. Given that other factors have been more important in the last few decades, including institutional ones, such as the lowering of the minimum wage and deunionization (which raise the relative wage of college graduates by lowering the wages on those without a college degree), and globalization, it seems certain that technical change was playing a *smaller* role in the last few decades than in the pre-1980 period.

Explaining education/wage gaps

The skills/technology story is frequently reduced to a tale about the growth of education/wage gaps, particularly the gap between college and high school wages. In this scenario, technology causes education/wage gaps to grow, and in turn wage inequality grows. It is easy to see that this particular tale is not valid. First, we have shown in earlier sections that changes in labor market institutions such as the minimum wage and unionization are responsible for some of the rise in education/wage differentials. Other

FIGURE 3AD Growth in relative demand for college graduates, 1950-2005

Source: Authors' analysis of Goldin and Katz (2008, Table 1).

factors, such as trade and consumer-driven industry shifts, also affect education and other skill differentials, and so there is not a complete correspondence of technology with skill differentials. The analysis above emphasized these points.

Second, the pattern of growth in the two key education differentials does not match the technology story. Since 2000 the wage gap between high- and middle-wage earners has continued to rise sharply (except during the first two years), as reflected in the 90/50 and 95/50 wage gaps presented in Figures 3K, 3L, and 3M and the data shown in Table 3.14. Yet the college/high school wage gap grew hardly at all in this period and was totally flat among women (see Table 3.14 and Figure 3N). What is true in recent years is also true in other periods: the growth of the wage gaps in the upper half of the wage scale rose continuously over the 1980s and 1990s even though the college wage premium shot up sharply in the 1980s but much less so in the 1990s.

The behavior of the education/wage gap between high school graduates and those without a high school degree is the one most in conflict with a technology story. This wage gap (Table 3.14) has been relatively stable over the entire 1973-2005 period. Thus, if those without a high school degree can be considered "unskilled," then the wage structure has not shifted much against these unskilled workers. This is probably because the lesser need for those without a high school degree was accompanied by a shrinkage in their share of the workforce, from 28.5% to 9.8% between 1973 and 2007 (Table 3.15). It is apparent, therefore, that shifts in education differentials have not driven the changes in wage inequality at the bottom, since the 50/10 wage gap (shown in Table 3.14 and Figures 3K and 3L) rose markedly in the 1980s and has fallen ever since, all while the education gap at the bottom was relatively stable.

Within-group wage inequality

As discussed above, there are two dimensions of wage inequality—between-group wage differentials, such as those relating to education and experience, and within-group wage inequality that occurs among workers of similar education and experience. We have already seen that the key education/wage differentials do not readily support a technology story. The same is true for the growth of within-group inequality, which accounts for roughly 60% of the growth of overall wage inequality since 1973 (see Table 3.21). The connection between growing wage gaps among workers with similar education and experience is not easily related to technological change unless interpreted as a reflection of growing economic returns to worker skills (motivation, aptitudes for math, etc.) that are not easily measured (that is, the regressions used to estimate education differentials cannot estimate these kinds of differentials). However, there are no signs that the growth of within-group wage inequality has been fastest in those industries where the use of technology grew the most. It is also unclear why the economic returns for measurable skills (e.g., education) and unmeasured skills (e.g., motivation) should not grow in tandem. In fact, between-group and within-group inequality have not moved together in the various sub-periods since 1973.

The timing of the growth of within-group wage inequality does not easily correspond to the technology story (see Table 3.21). For instance, consider what happened during the 1995-2000 period associated with a technology-led productivity boom: within-group wage inequality actually declined among women and was essentially flat among men. In the early 1990s, the so-called early stages of the "new economy," within-group wage inequality grew moderately, whereas it grew rapidly in the low-productivity 1980s. Within-group wage inequality did, however, start growing again as productivity accelerated further after 2000 but still lags far behind the 1980s pace. All in all, changes in within-group wage inequality do not seem to mirror the periods of rapid productivity growth or technological change.

Have the types of technologies deployed shifted?

The experience since the mid- to late 1980s does not accord with the conventional technology story, whose imagery is of computer-driven technology bidding up the wages of workers who have the most education and skills. In this picture the more-skilled do better than the middle-skilled and the middle-skilled do better than the least-skilled. It is certainly not the case that technology is leaving behind only a small group of unskilled workers with inadequate abilities—we have seen the continued wage gap between middle- and high-wage workers grow and have seen faltering wage growth in the middle of the wage scale except during the late 1990s. If technology were most adverse for unskilled or less-educated workers, then we would expect a continued expansion of the wage differential between middle-wage and low-wage workers (the 50/10 differential) and high-school-educated workers and "dropouts." Yet, the 50/10 differential was stable or declined among both men and women from 1986 or 1987 to 2005, and the high school/dropout wage differential was flat. Instead, we are seeing the top earners steadily pulling away from nearly all other earners—reflected in the 90/50 and 95/50 wage gaps.

Therefore, there seem to be factors driving a wedge between the top 10% and everyone else, rather than a skill-biased technological change aiding the vast majority but leaving a small group of unskilled workers behind. Further confirmation of the breadth of those left behind is that over the 1979-95 period wages were stable or in decline for the bottom 80% of men and the bottom 70% of women, and wages fell for the entire non-college-educated workforce (roughly 70-75% of workers).

These inconsistencies can be resolved if one believes that technology started having an adverse impact on middle-wage workers more than the least-skilled workers starting at the end of the 1980s or the early 1990s: the decline in the 50/10 wage ratio thereafter, in this view, is the result of technological displacement of middle-wage more harshly than low-wage jobs. At this point the research is not available to allow a determination of whether the "bias" of technology sharply shifted in the late 1980s. Our own analysis of year-to-year occupation shifts does not accord with this view; we do not find any sharp break in the impact of occupational shifts on the need for high-level workers, mid-level workers (high school or some college), or dropouts in the late 1980s or early 1990s that seems associated with the shift to a falling 50/10 wage gap.

Nevertheless, it is important to understand the implications of the hypothesized shift in "bias" such that middle-wage workers are most adversely affected by techno-logical change and that technology only favors those in the very top of the education and wage distribution (perhaps the upper 10% or the upper fifth of workers ranked by education levels). If so, then the policy response of making less-skilled workers into middle-skilled workers and middle-skilled workers into college graduates does not make sense, since this story suggests we have too many middle-skilled workers already. This bias shift story basically implies that the bottom 80-90% of the workforce is technologically disadvantaged and needs to become very highly educated. Perhaps if enough of the workforce makes that education transition, wage inequality will stop growing or even decline. However, given that the wages of entry-level college workers and those of all college graduates have declined or been flat over this business cycle (Tables 3.15-3.17 and 3.19), a strategy of vastly increasing the number of college graduates seems certain to drive down the wages of current and future college graduates. The possibility of increased offshoring of white-collar work may make such a strategy even more untenable in the future.

Executive pay

One distinct aspect of growing wage inequality is the gap between the very highest earners—those in the upper 1% or even upper 0.1%—and other high-wage earners at, say, the 90th percentile (who earn more than 90% of all workers). This was reviewed in an earlier section. This section now turns to the enormous pay increases received by chief executive officers (CEOs) of large firms and the spillover effects (the pay of other executives and managers rising in tandem with CEO pay) of these increases. These large pay raises go far beyond those received by other white-collar workers, though they are only one part of the growth in pay of very high earners.

The 1980s, 1990s, and 2000s have been prosperous times for top U.S. executives, especially relative to other wage earners. This can be seen by examining the increased divergence between CEO pay and a typical worker's pay over time (we use the average hourly compensation of production/nonsupervisory workers —who comprise about 80% of payroll employment—as our measure for a typical worker's pay; the trend since 1959 was illustrated in Figure 3B), as shown in **Figure 3AE**. In 1965, U.S. CEOs in major companies earned 24 times more than a typical worker; this ratio grew to 35 in 1978 and to 71 in 1989. The ratio surged in the 1990s and hit 299 at the end of the recovery in 2000. The fall in the stock market reduced CEO stock-related pay (e.g., options), causing CEO pay to tumble to 149 times that of the average worker in 2002. Since then, however, CEO pay has recovered and by 2007 was 275 times that of the typical worker. In other words, in 2007 a CEO earned more in one workday (there are 260 in a year) than the typical worker earned all year.

Figure 3AE also presents the ratio of *median* CEO compensation to that of the typical worker. This enables a comparison of a more typical (rather than average) CEO of a large firm to that of a typical worker. In 1995 the compensation of both the median and the average CEO were comparably larger, at 91 and 100 times that of a worker. Since then the pay of the average CEO grew more rapidly than that of the median CEO. Nevertheless, the gap between a median CEO and the typical worker more than doubled by 2007, reaching 194-to-1.

Table 3.41 presents more detail on the trends in CEO pay, both median and average, over the 1989-2007 period. CEO pay is based on a survey of 350 large publicly owned (i.e., they sell stock on the open market) industrial and service firms, and includes all of the components of direct compensation: salaries, bonuses, incentive awards, stock options exercised, stock granted, and so on. CEO compensation between 1989 and 2007 increased 167.3% for the average CEO and a still considerable 106.8% for the median CEO. This surge in pay occurred despite a drop of pay, especially for the average CEO, in the early 2000s due to the stock market decline. The compensation of a typical worker, in contrast, grew about 10% over the 1989 to 2007 period, almost of all that growth occurring in the late 1990s. During the recovery from 2002 to 2007, the pay for the average CEO surged 95.8% to reach $12.3 million annually, not as much as earned in 2000 at the end of the stock market bubble but a still hefty pay level. The median CEO saw a lesser growth in pay over the recovery, up 23.5%, though it was far larger than the pay increase of other workers in this time period (recall that the pay of both high school and college graduates was flat in the recovery).

Not only are U.S. executives paid far better than U.S. workers, they also earn substantially more than CEOs in other advanced countries. **Table 3.42** shows CEO pay in 13 other countries in 1988, 2003, and 2005 and an index (in the last two columns) that sets U.S. compensation equal to 100 (any index value less than 100 implies that that country's CEOs earn less than U.S. CEOs). The index shows that U.S. CEOs earn two and a quarter times the average of the 13 other advanced countries for which there are comparable data (note the non-U.S. average of 44%). In fact, in only one country, Switzerland, are CEOs paid even as much as 60% that of U.S. CEOs. This international pattern does not hold true for the pay of manufacturing workers; these jobs in other

FIGURE 3AE Ratio of average and median CEO total direct compensation to average worker pay, 1965-2007

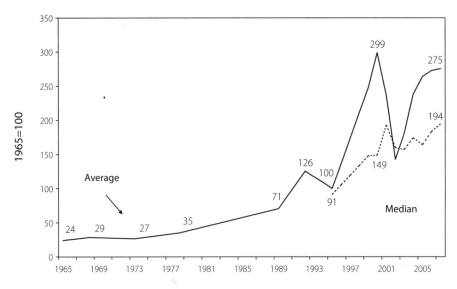

Source: Authors' analysis of *Wall Street Journal*/Mercer, Hay Group (2008).

advanced countries pay 85% of what U.S. workers earn. Not surprisingly, the ratio of CEO to worker pay was far larger in the United States in 2005 than in other countries, 39.0 versus 20.5. (Note that these cross-country comparisons employ different data and definitions than those used for historical U.S. trends in Table 3.41 and Figure 3AE and therefore yield a different CEO/worker pay ratio.) Lastly, Table 3.42 shows that

TABLE 3.41 Executive annual pay,* 1989-2007 (2007 dollars)

	1989	1995	2000	2002	2007	Percent change			
						1995-2000	2000-07	2002-07	1989-2007
			$(000)						
Median	$4,200	$4,963	$7,573	$7,034	$8,685	52.6%	14.7%	23.5%	106.8%
Average	4,606	5,444	15,196	6,285	12,309	179.2	-19.0	95.8	167.3

* Total direct compensation, including salary and bonuses, incentive awards, stock options exercised, and stock granted.

Source: Authors' analysis of *Wall Street Journal*/Mercer, Hay Group (2008).

TABLE 3.42 CEO pay in advanced countries, 1988-2005 ($2005)

Country	CEO compensation $ (000)			Percent change 1988-2005	Ratio of CEO to worker pay, 2005*	Foreign pay relative to U.S. pay, 2005 U.S. = 100	
	1988	2003	2005			CEO	Worker
Australia	$180,760	$737,162	$707,747	292%	15.6	33%	82%
Belgium	383,718	739,700	987,387	157	18.0	46	99
Canada	423,358	944,375	1,068,964	152	23.1	49	83
France	404,331	780,380	1,202,145	197	22.8	56	95
Germany	412,259	1,013,171	1,181,292	187	20.1	55	106
Italy	342,492	893,035	1,137,326	232	25.9	53	79
Japan	502,639	484,909	543,564	8	10.8	25	91
Netherlands	396,403	716,387	862,711	118	17.8	40	87
New Zealand	--	476,926	396,456	--	24.9	18	29
Spain	352,006	658,039	697,691	98	17.2	32	73
Sweden	234,670	743,160	948,990	304	19.2	44	89
Switzerland	510,567	1,263,450	1,390,899	172	19.3	64	130
United Kingdom	453,485	881,047	1,184,936	161	31.8	55	67
United States	805,490	2,386,762	2,164,952	169	39.0	100	100
Non-U.S. average	$383,057	$794,749	$946,931	173%	20.5%	44%	85%

* Ratio of CEO compensation to the compensation of manufacturing production workers.

Source: Authors' analysis of Towers Perrin (1988, 2003, and 2005).

CEO pay in other countries has tended to grow rapidly over the 1988-2005 period; in many countries CEO pay rose as fast as or faster than in the United States.

Jobs of the future

This section presents an analysis of the pay levels and education and skill requirements of the jobs that are projected by the Bureau of Labor Statistics to be created over the next 10 years. Some analysts examine which occupations are expected to grow at the fastest (and slowest) rates, while others examine which occupations will create the most (or least) absolute number of jobs. The purpose of this analysis is to assess whether the types of jobs that are expected to be created will significantly change the wages that workers earn or significantly raise the quality of work or the skill/education require- ments needed to fill tomorrow's jobs. This exercise requires an analysis of how the composition of jobs will change, that is, which occupations will expand or contract their *share* of overall employment.

Table 3.43 presents such an analysis for the 754 occupations for which the Bureau of Labor Statistics provides projections from 2006 to 2016. Through a shift-share analysis (weighting each occupation's characteristic, such as wage level, by its share of total employment) we can see what the characteristics of jobs are in 2006 and what they will be in 2016 if the projections are realized.

There are a few drawbacks to this analysis. First, it does not take into account how the jobs of a particular occupation (one of the 754 we analyze) will change over the next 10 years. (For example, will the education requirements of a loan officer or a parking lot attendant grow?) In other words, the changing "content" of particular jobs is a dimension of future skill requirements not captured by our analysis. Second, we have no point of historical comparison (due to lack of data availability owing to changing occupational definitions) for judging whether what is expected in the future is fast or slow relative to the past. However, there is still much to learn from how occupational composition shifts will affect the job and wage structure.

Table 3.43 shows that employment will shift to occupations with higher median annual wages, but the effect will be to raise annual wages by 1.1% over 10 years (or about 0.1% per year). This is not a large change compared to the real wage growth that occurs each year or to the composition effects evaluated in earlier years (using a dif- ferent occupation coding system). The analysis also shows that the jobs of the future will require greater education credentials but not to any great extent. In 2006, according to these data, the occupational composition of jobs requires that 27.7% of the workforce have a college degree or more. This share will rise by one percentage point to 28.7% by 2016 (**Figure 3AF**). The jobs will entail no need to expand the share of the workforce with only some college, a group roughly the same size as the required college-educated workforce. The demand for workers with a high school degree or less will fall slightly, from 43.6% to 42.6% over the 2006-16 period.

Table 3.43 also provides a detailed assessment of the education or training needed to be employed in an occupation. The results suggest a shift to the occupations that re- quire the most education or training (those requiring a bachelor's degree or more increase

TABLE 3.43 Effect of changing occupational composition on education and training requirements and earnings, 2006-16

Job characteristic	2006	2016	Change 2006-16
Annual earnings ($2004)	$38,087	$38,520	1.1%
Education level			
High school or less	43.5%	42.6%	-0.9%
Some college	28.7	28.7	0.0
College or more	27.7	28.7	1.0
Total	**100.0%**	**100.0%**	
Education/training			
Work experience in a related occupation	7.4%	7.1%	-0.2%
Short-term on-the-job training	35.3	34.8	-0.5
Moderate-term on-the-job training	20.0	19.6	-0.4
Long-term on-the-job training	7.7	7.4	-0.3
Postsecondary vocational award	5.4	5.6	0.2
Associate's degree	3.7	4.0	0.3
Bachelor's degree	12.1	12.8	0.7
Bachelor's or higher degree, plus work experience	4.2	4.2	-0.1
Master's degree	1.5	1.6	0.1
Doctoral degree	1.3	1.5	0.1
First professional degree	1.3	1.4	0.0
Total	**100.0%**	**100.0%**	

Source: Authors' analysis of BLS employment projections in Dohm and Shniper (2007).

their employment share by less than a percentage point) and, correspondingly, a shift from those occupations that require the least education and training (the bottom three categories lose a 1.1 percentage-point share of employment). Nevertheless, this method of gauging occupational skill requirements yields a lower estimate of the share of jobs requiring a college degree or more, just 21.4% in 2016; the other method, based on actual education in those occupations today, suggest a higher 28.7% of college graduates needed. So, using assessments of skill requirements in each occupation suggests a somewhat smaller growth in skill requirements and growth to a lesser level in 2016.

These projections show that occupational upgrading will continue in the future, as the jobs created will be in occupations with somewhat higher wages and educa-

FIGURE 3AF Education requirements of current and future jobs, 2006-16

Source: Authors' analysis of BLS employment projections in Dohm and Shniper (2007).

tional and training requirements. This trend has been evident over the last century (as explored earlier in the section on technological change), and the developments in the future do not appear to be extraordinary in any sense. Whether workers earn substantially more in the future than now will be determined primarily by how much earnings in particular occupations rise rather than by any expected change in the occupational composition of jobs.

Conclusion

The period since 2000 encompasses a few years in which the momentum from the late 1990s carried forward and brought real wage gains. However, real wages stopped growing when the recession took hold and unemployment and underemployment rose. Because of weak employment growth in the recovery, wage growth never picked up steam. Consequently, this period has seen the widest divergence between productivity and the wage or compensation of the typical worker of any recent recovery. The result was that the wages of a broad range of workers, including those with either a high school or college degree, failed to improve in the recovery from 2002 to 2007. Wage inequality has also continued to grow between those at the very top and other very high earners and between all the very high earners and other wage earners such as those earning high (90th percentile) wages or median wages.

Structural factors such as the shift to lower-paying industries, increased trade competition, and deunionization have generated wage inequities and eroding job quality. The eroded value of the minimum wage (relative to past levels), sluggish job creation, continued competitive pressures from low-wage countries, and immigration have also taken their toll on the pay of low- and middle-wage earners. Young workers' wages and benefits have faltered the most. Even young college graduates are facing disappointing prospects.

CHAPTER 4

Jobs
Diminished expectations

The job market is the primary mechanism through which the county's economic growth reaches working families. So following a recession, a robust job market—one with enough job creation to fully use the labor force's workers and their skills—is a critical component of a strong, lasting, and equitable recovery. By that measure, the recovery following the recession of 2001 fell short.

The recession of 2001 was followed by nearly two years of continued job loss, and it took an unprecedented *four years* to re-attain the number of jobs the economy supported prior to the recession. The first few years of the recovery of the 2000s have been aptly coined the "jobless" recovery—meaning that the recession of 2001 was officially over but the economy was still not generating job growth. Looking over the whole cycle, from 2000 to 2007, average annual job growth was 0.6%, well below the 1.8% annual job growth of the 1990s cycle and the 2.0% average of prior cycles. This historically weak job creation was costly for working families. The resulting lower rates of employment and consequent lack of upward pressure on wages translated into lost output and forgone increases in living standards. Poor job growth is one of the important factors underlying the ongoing divergence of overall economic growth and the wages and income of working families shown in earlier chapters.

In addition to weak job creation, the business cycle of the 2000s was lackluster by other relevant employment indicators. The unemployment rate increased by 0.7 percentage points from March 2001 (the peak of the last business cycle) to December 2007, despite the fact that the average age of workers increased and labor force participation rate shrank—both of which should have put downward pressure on the rate of unemployment. Furthermore, unemployment spells were much longer on average during the 2000s than they had been for previous cycles. Underemployment grew as well, with, for example, a significantly higher percentage of workers working "involuntarily" part-time in 2007 than in 2000.

The employment rate was also disappointing—it decreased by 1.5 percentage points over the 2000s cycle, in contrast to the 2.6 percentage-point average *increase* over prior cycles. The departure from previous cycles was especially dramatic for women, who saw their employment rates decrease by 1.8 percentage points after decades of dramatic increases.

Jobs

Figure 4A shows employment and labor force levels from 1979 to mid-2008. Over time, growth in the total number of jobs has more or less tracked growth in the size of the labor force, which is crucial; the economy must continually add jobs simply to keep up with population growth. Within the overall upward trend, however, there are clear fluctuations associated with business cycles. Historically, the number of jobs has peaked as the economy peaks, fallen during recessions, and begun to rise as the economy begins to expand. During the business cycle of the 2000s, however, the economy continued to shed jobs for almost two years into the official recovery, and there were over a million fewer jobs in August of 2003 than there had been at the end of the recession. It was not until February of 2005 that the economy re-attained the number of jobs it had had before the recession—but the labor force had grown by 4.4 million workers over that period.

FIGURE 4A Labor force and total nonfarm employment, 1979-August 2008

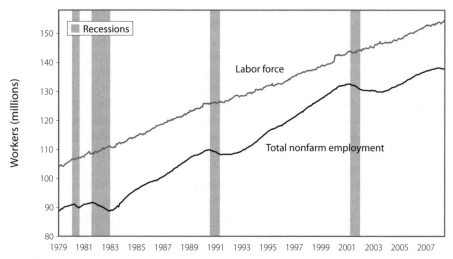

Source: Authors' analysis of BLS (2008b and 2008c) data.

FIGURE 4B Number of months to regain peak-level employment after a recession, current and prior business cycles

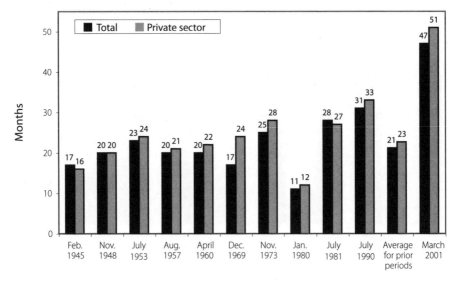

Source: Authors' analysis of BLS (2008b) data.

The next two figures directly compare job growth in the business cycle of the 2000s to that of previous cycles. **Figure 4B** shows that prior to the 2000s, it took an average of 21 months to regain peak-level employment after a recession, but that during the 2000s recovery, it took over twice that long—nearly four years. **Figure 4C** shows peak-to-peak annualized employment growth over all business cycles since 1960. Prior to the 2000s, employment grew 2.0% per year on average, just outpacing growth in the labor force, which grew 1.9% per year on average. In the 1990s, employment grew by 1.8% annually, strongly outpacing labor force growth, which grew at 1.3% annually over this period. In the 2000s, however, employment growth averaged only 0.6% a year, well below the growth needed to keep up with the ever-increasing labor force. If the economy had added as many jobs from March 2001 (the previous business cycle peak) to December 2007 (a period of 81 months) as it added in the first 81 months of the 1990s business cycle (July 1990 to April 1997), it would have added almost *7 million* more jobs than it did.

Gross job gains and losses
Interestingly, the weak job growth in the business cycle of the 2000s was driven not by high job loss, but instead by historically weak job creation. **Figure 4D** shows gross job gains (the number of jobs added in either opening or expanding establishments in the private sector) and gross job losses (the number of jobs lost in either closing or

FIGURE 4C Annualized peak-to-peak growth in employment, 1960-2007

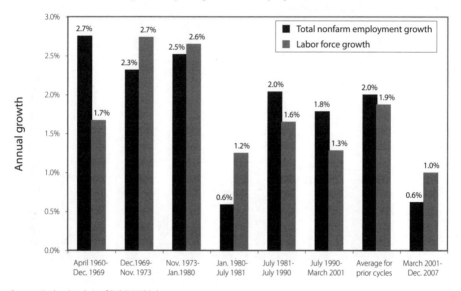

Source: Authors' analysis of BLS (2008b) data.

FIGURE 4D Gross job gains and losses, 1990q2 to 2007q4

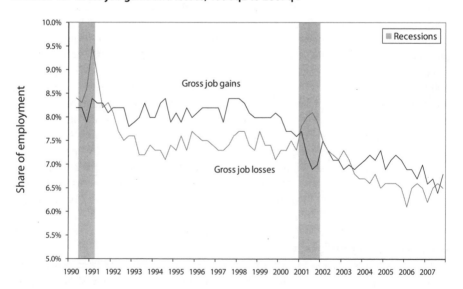

Source: Authors' analysis of Faberman (2004) and BLS (2008a) data.

contracting establishments in the private sector), each expressed as a percent of total private sector employment. As expected, during each recession job losses outweighed job gains, and a net loss of jobs resulted. In the 1990s, job gains outpaced losses again within a year of the end of the recession. In the 2000s, however, it took nearly two years for job gains to move back ahead of job losses. Interestingly, gross job gains never regained their pre-recession levels—but neither did losses. Throughout the 2000s recovery, both gains and losses were at lower levels than they were in the previous

FIGURE 4E Peak-to-peak annual growth rates by industry, 1979-2007

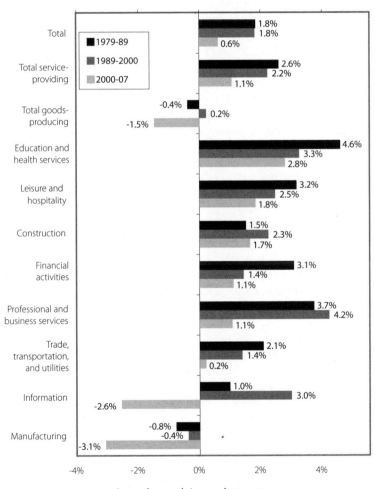

Annual growth in employment

Source: Authors' analysis of BLS (2008b) data.

business cycle. In other words, the 2000s were plagued not by high levels of job loss, but by a persistent failure to produce strong job gains.

Industry sectors

The industrial make-up of the U.S. economy has long been shifting away from producing goods to a more intensive service-producing economy. In 1969, one-third of jobs were in goods-producing industries; in 2007, it was only 16%. The ongoing shift can be seen in **Figure 4E**, which charts annualized employment growth by industry over the last three business cycles (grouping together the two business cycles of the early 1980s). The first set of bars again reflects the meager job growth of the current cycle compared to the earlier 1980s and 1990s cycles. The second and third sets of bars show the strong growth in the service-producing sector and contraction in the goods-producing sector. The remaining sets of bars show job growth among individual sectors.

The most recent cycle has had strong growth in the education and health services, leisure and hospitality, and construction. The sector that saw the largest decline was manufacturing (down 3.1% annually), with 61% of the decline occurring in the manufacturing of durable goods (especially in computer and electronic products, transportation equipment including motor vehicles and parts, and machinery) and the rest of the decline occurring in the manufacturing of nondurable goods (most noticeably in the apparel industry). Since manufacturing jobs traditionally have provided high wages and good benefits, the decline of manufacturing has meant a decline in a crucial source of good jobs. Chapter 3 further investigates the impact of industry shifts on wages and compensation.

Another sector that saw a large decline from 2000 to 2007 was information (down 2.6% annually after being *up* an average of 3.0% annually from 1989 to 2000). While information is a small sector (around 2% of employment), the dot-com bubble is evident. Employment in the information sector grew by 28% from 1995 to 2000—and then lost 56% of that increase by 2003. Employment in the sector has yet to recover; in 2007 information employment was still below the level it had achieved a decade earlier.

Job quality

Defining job quality is not straightforward. For example, a job would almost certainly be considered high quality if it paid well, offered good health and pension benefits, provided paid vacation, sick days, and family leave, and provided good working conditions, a good work schedule, and job security. A job with some but not all of those characteristics falls into a grayer area in terms of quality. John Schmitt (2007) of the Center for Economic and Policy Research has defined a "good" job modestly as a job that meets just three criteria—it must 1) pay at least $17 per hour (the median male earnings in 1979 adjusted to 2006 dollars), 2) offer health insurance, and 3) offer a retirement plan of some kind. He has tracked the prevalence of good jobs over time.

Figure 4F presents "good jobs" as a percent of total employment for recent business cycle peaks and for 2006. It also presents per capita GDP as a reference. The GDP values show that the country was getting richer over this period—per capita GDP

FIGURE 4F Good jobs* as percent of total employment, 1979-2006

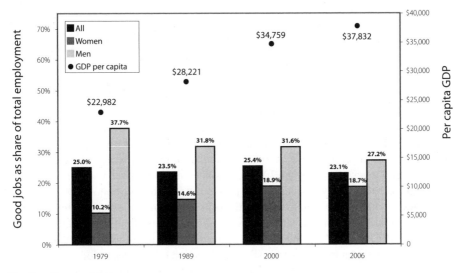

* See Figure Notes for definition.

Source: Schmitt (2007) and BEA (2008).

increased by 65% from 1979 to 2006. If those increased riches were being distributed broadly across the labor force, one would expect to see the share of good jobs increase accordingly. Instead, as the economy grew, the share of good jobs stagnated. From 2000 to 2006, the share of good jobs in the economy actually dropped 2.3 percentage points, such that in 2006 only 23.1% of jobs paid at least $17 per hour and offered both health and pension benefits.

It is important to keep in mind that the stagnation in good jobs occurred over a period when the workforce was becoming both older and more educated on average. All else equal, both of these factors would have *increased* the share of good jobs, as older and better educated workers tend to be better able to secure quality employment. The fact that the share of good jobs stagnated as the workforce aged and became better educated makes the lack of progress in good jobs even more troubling. Furthermore, the overall share of good jobs masks important differences by gender. From 1979 to 2000, women made enormous progress by the "good jobs" measure—the percent of working women who were in good jobs jumped from 10.2% to 18.9%. Over the 2000s, however, the share of women with good jobs was essentially flat (a 0.2 percentage point decline). For men, the situation was much grimmer. From 1979 to 2000, men experienced a 6.1 percentage point decline in the share with good jobs, and from 2000 to 2006 alone, that share dropped an additional 4.4 percentage points. The share of working men in good jobs has dropped substantially in the last three decades, despite the fact that the country experienced substantial economic growth over this period.

Unemployment

When workers are unemployed, they and their families lose wages. The economy as a whole also loses the goods or services they would have produced had they been working. In addition, the purchasing power of unemployed workers is cut, which can lead to a drop in consumer demand, and consequently unemployment for additional workers. **Figure 4G** shows the unemployment rate from January 1948 to August 2008 (the most recent data available as of this writing). Figure 4G reveals that unemployment is generally low at the beginning of a recession and spikes up sharply during a recession, peaking at or shortly after the end of a recession. Excluding the last two cycles, since 1948 it has taken an average of 2.8 months into an economic recovery for unemployment rates to peak. The last two cycles, however, have seen a different pattern emerge. Following the recession of the early 1990s, it took 15 months for unemployment to peak, and the lag was even longer following the 2001 recession, when it took the unemployment rate 19 months to peak. This was due in large part to the fact that for both of these business cycles, job creation was weak even after the official end of the recession (recall Figure 4B showed that following the early 1990s recession, it took about two and a half years to regain peak-level employment, and following the recession of the early 2000s, it took nearly four years). Another reason is simply a function of how recessions are officially dated; the business cycle dating committee puts much more weight on output measures than on labor market indicators when defining recessions. This means that when real

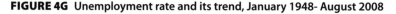

FIGURE 4G Unemployment rate and its trend, January 1948- August 2008

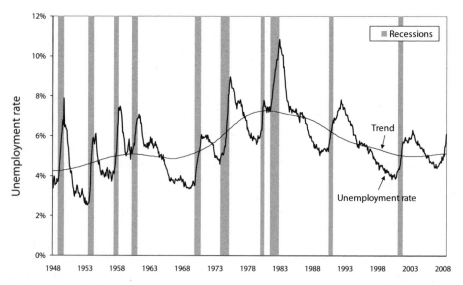

Source: Authors' analysis of BLS (2008c) data.

GDP begins rising after a downturn, the committee is likely to declare the end of a recession even if—as was the case after the downturns in the early 1990s and the early 2000s—the GDP growth results almost entirely from productivity growth, and is therefore accompanied by increasing unemployment.

During the recession of the early 2000s, the unemployment rate rose from 4.2% in the first quarter of 2001 (the peak of the previous business cycle) to 5.5% in the fourth quarter of 2001 (the official end of the recession). The unemployment rate continued on its upward climb for more than a year and a half after the end of the recession, topping out at 6.2% in the second quarter of 2003. It then began a decline as more people were able to find work during the economic expansion. The decline, however, lasted for only three-and-a-half years, with the unemployment rate reaching its lowest point in the fourth quarter of 2006, at 4.4%—still higher than at the end of the expansion of the 1990s. Starting in the first quarter of 2007, it again began a steady upward climb.

Figure 4G also charts a smoothed trend of the unemployment rate. The trend line shows that despite fluctuations, unemployment has been on an overall downward path since the recessions of the early 1980s, though it has flattened out since the mid-2000s. One of the driving factors of this decline has had nothing to do with improving labor market conditions, but simply with changes in the age composition of the labor force. The first panel of **Table 4.1** documents the aging of the labor force over this period by presenting the share of the labor force in different age categories over time. In the first quarter of 1980, slightly less than half (49.1%) of the labor force was age 35 or over, but by the fourth quarter of 2007, almost two-thirds (63.9%) of the labor force was age 35 or over, and 17.5% was 55 or over.

The second panel of Table 4.1 shows that, for any given year, unemployment rates drop dramatically with age. For example, since 1980, teenage workers have had unemployment rates that average about 13 percentage points higher than workers age 55 and over. Thus, the aging of the labor force would cause a decrease in overall unemployment rates *even if no individual age category experienced a decline in its unemployment rate*. From 1980q1 to 2007q4, the overall employment rate decreased by 1.5 points, but only one age category (20-24-year-olds) experienced a decline that big—all other categories experienced much smaller declines and the 55-and-over category actually experienced an increase.

Figure 4H shows the unemployment rate, along with what the unemployment rate would be if the age distribution of the labor force had not changed from the first quarter of 1980, (but where the unemployment rates *within* each age category changed as they actually did). In other words, the simulated unemployment rate demonstrates what the unemployment rate would be if the age distribution were held constant over time. The simulation shows that without the aging of the labor force over the last 28 years, the unemployment rate over the 2000s business cycle would average about 6% instead of about 5%. This is one example of how it is problematic to compare the unemployment rate of today to that of earlier periods. The below discussions of long-term unemployment and labor force participation offer further examples of how the unemployment rate of today is not entirely comparable with that of earlier periods.

TABLE 4.1 Labor force share and unemployment rate by age category, 1980q1-2007q4

	1980q1	1990q3	2001q1	2007q4	Percentage-point change 1980q1 to 2007q4
Share of labor force					
Age 16-19	8.9%	6.1%	5.7%	4.6%	-4.4
20-24	14.9	11.7	10.1	9.9	-5.0
25-34	27.1	28.5	22.6	21.6	-5.5
35-44	19.0	25.6	26.2	23.0	4.1
45-54	15.9	16.1	22.1	23.4	7.5
55 and over	14.2	11.9	13.3	17.5	3.4
All	100%	100%	100%	100%	--
Unemployment rate					
Age 16-19	16.5%	15.9%	13.8%	16.4%	-0.1
20-24	10.1	8.9	7.4	8.6	-1.5
25-34	5.9	5.7	4.0	4.8	-1.1
35-44	4.0	4.3	3.1	3.6	-0.4
45-54	3.5	3.4	2.8	3.4	-0.1
55 and over	3.0	3.2	2.7	3.1	0.1
All	6.3%	5.7%	4.2%	4.8%	-1.5

Source: Authors' analysis of BLS (2008c) data.

In addition to age, the overall unemployment rate masks enormous differences by other demographic characteristics, including race and ethnicity, gender, and educational attainment. **Table 4.2** looks at unemployment rates by gender and race/ethnicity. The overall unemployment rates show, unsurprisingly, low values for business cycle peaks and higher values for business cycle troughs. (Because unemployment increased for so long after the official troughs of the business cycles of the 1990s and 2000s, the quarter of maximum unemployment is also included for each of those cycles.)

Looking first at gender, the table shows that historically, the unemployment rate of women was higher than that of men—in 1969q4, for example, the unemployment rate for women was 1.8 points above that of men. During the recessions of the early 1980s, however, that trend reversed, and since that time women have generally had lower unemployment rates than men. This has been especially true during low points in the business cycle, as men's unemployment rates have tended to increase much more during economic downturns than women's. During the recession of the 2000s, women's

FIGURE 4H Actual and simulated unemployment rate, Jan 1980-August 2008

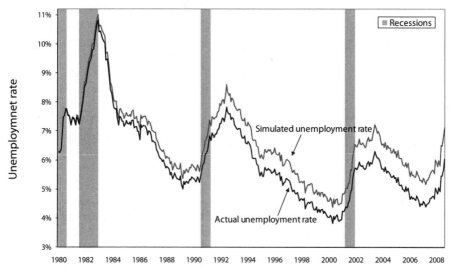

Source: Authors' analysis of BLS (2008c) data.

TABLE 4.2 Unemployment rates, 1969-2007

	Time period	Over-all	Male	Female	White	Black	His-panic	Female-male	Black-white	Hispanic-white
Peak	1969q4	3.6%	2.9%	4.7%	3.3%	n/a	n/a	1.8	n/a	n/a
Trough	1970q4	5.8	5.2	6.7	5.4	n/a	n/a	1.5	n/a	n/a
Peak	1973q4	4.8%	4.1%	5.9%	4.3%	9.0%	7.9%	1.8	4.7	3.6
Trough	1975q1	8.2	7.5	9.3	7.5	14.5	11.3	1.8	7.0	3.8
Peak	1980q1	6.3%	5.8%	6.9%	5.5%	13.0%	8.9%	1.1	7.5	3.4
Trough	1982q4	10.7	11.1	10.2	9.5	20.4	15.3	-0.9	10.9	5.8
Peak	1990q3	5.7%	5.7%	5.6%	4.9%	11.7%	8.2%	-0.1	6.8	3.3
Trough	1991q1	6.6	6.9	6.2	5.8	12.2	9.3	-0.7	6.4	3.5
Max. unemp.	1992q3	7.6	8.0	7.2	6.7	14.2	11.7	-0.8	7.5	5.0
Peak	2001q1	4.2%	4.3%	4.2%	3.7%	8.1%	6.0%	-0.1	4.4	2.3
Trough	2001q4	5.5	5.6	5.4	4.9	9.8	7.4	-0.2	4.9	2.5
Max. unemp.	2003q2	6.2	6.5	5.8	5.4	11.1	8.0	-0.7	5.7	2.6
Peak	2007q4	4.8%	4.9%	4.7%	4.3%	8.6%	5.9%	-0.2	4.3	1.6

Source: Authors' analysis of BLS (2008c) data.

unemployment rates increased by 1.6 percentage points, whereas men's increased by 2.2 points. Women have been more protected from business cycle fluctuations than men, in large part because they are overrepresented in many industries that do not tend to be highly cyclical, like education services and health services, and are underrepresented in many highly cyclical industries, like manufacturing and construction.

Considering race and ethnicity, the table shows that at any given time, black workers have been about twice as likely as white workers to be unemployed. During recessions, the black-white gap in unemployment rates has increased, as the unemployment rate of blacks increases more during economic downturns than that of whites. During the recession of the 2000s, the unemployment rates of whites increased by 1.7 percentage points, but that of blacks increased by 3.0 points. Hispanics also have higher unemployment rates than whites (though lower than blacks), and experience higher unemployment rates during recessions, though those differences have been gradually shrinking over time.

Table 4.3 shows more explicitly how the unemployment rates of various groups have fared over recent business cycles. Over the 1990s, unemployment rates of all groups fell substantially, with blacks in particular seeing enormous declines in unemployment. In the 2000s, however, that situation has reversed, with all groups except Hispanics at higher unemployment levels at the end of 2007 than at the previous business cycle peak in the first quarter of 2001.

Table 4.4 presents unemployment rates by educational attainment, with cross-tabulations by both gender and race/ethnicity, in four time periods—1992 (the year of maximum unemployment in the business cycle of the 1990s), 2000 (the peak of that

TABLE 4.3 Percentage-point change in unemployment rates between business cycle peaks

	1969q4-1973q4	1973q4-1980q1	1980q1-1990q3	1990q3-2001q1	2001q1-2007q4
Total	1.2	1.5	-0.6	-1.5	0.6
Male	1.2	1.7	-0.1	-1.4	0.6
Female	1.2	1.0	-1.3	-1.4	0.5
White	1.0	1.2	-0.6	-1.2	0.6
Male	1.0	1.4	-0.1	-1.2	0.6
Female	1.0	0.8	-1.3	-1.2	0.6
Black	n/a	4.0	-1.3	-3.6	0.5
Male	n/a	5.1	-0.5	-3.8	1.0
Female	n/a	2.5	-1.9	-3.5	0.2
Hispanic*	n/a	1.0	-0.7	-2.2	-0.1

* Seasonally adjusted data unavailable for Hispanics by gender.

Source: Authors' analysis of BLS (2008c) data.

TABLE 4.4 Unemployment rates by gender, race, and educational status (25 years or older), 1992-2007

	Educational status	1992	2000	2003	2007	Percentage-point change 1992-2000	2000-03	2003-07
Total	Less than high school	11.5%	6.3%	8.8%	7.1%	-5.1	2.5	-1.7
	High school	6.9	3.5	5.4	4.4	-3.4	2.0	-1.1
	Some college	6.0	2.8	5.2	3.9	-3.2	2.4	-1.3
	College graduates	3.2	1.7	3.1	2.0	-1.5	1.4	-1.1
Men	Less than high school	11.4%	5.4%	8.2%	6.6%	-6.0	2.7	-1.6
	High school	7.4	3.4	5.7	4.5	-4.0	2.3	-1.3
	Some college	6.1	2.7	5.4	3.7	-3.4	2.7	-1.8
	College graduates	3.3	1.5	3.3	2.0	-1.8	1.7	-1.3
Women	Less than high school	11.5%	7.8%	9.8%	8.2%	-3.7	2.0	-1.6
	High school	6.3	3.5	5.2	4.3	-2.8	1.8	-0.9
	Some college	5.9	3.0	5.0	4.1	-2.8	1.9	-0.9
	College graduates	3.0	1.8	2.9	2.1	-1.2	1.1	-0.8
White	Less than high school	10.7%	5.6%	7.8%	6.5%	-5.2	2.3	-1.3
	High school	6.0	2.9	4.8	3.9	-3.1	1.9	-0.9
	Some college	5.4	2.6	4.5	3.5	-2.8	1.9	-1.0
	College graduates	3.0	1.6	2.8	1.9	-1.4	1.2	-1.0
Black	Less than high school	15.3%	10.7%	13.9%	12.1%	-4.7	3.2	-1.8
	High school	12.4	6.4	9.3	7.3	-5.9	2.9	-2.1
	Some college	10.4	4.2	8.6	5.9	-6.2	4.4	-2.7
	College graduates	4.4	2.4	4.5	3.0	-2.0	2.1	-1.5
Hispanic	Less than high school	12.8%	6.3%	8.2%	6.0%	-6.5	1.9	-2.2
	High school	9.1	4.0	5.9	4.4	-5.1	1.9	-1.5
	Some college	8.4	3.3	5.8	4.4	-5.1	2.5	-1.5
	College graduates	5.0	2.2	4.1	2.3	-2.8	1.9	-1.8
Total		6.0%	2.9%	4.8%	3.6%	-3.1	1.8	-1.1

Source: Authors' analysis of BLS (2008c) data.

cycle), 2003 (the year of maximum unemployment in that business cycle), and 2007. The table shows that in any time period and for any gender, race, or ethnicity, there are large decreases in overall unemployment rates as educational attainment increases. The 2000-03 change shows that during economic downturns the least educated face higher increases in unemployment than those with higher levels of education—for example, between 2000 and 2003, workers without a high school diploma experienced unemployment increases of 2.5 percentage points overall, while workers with a college degree experienced unemployment increases of 1.4 percentage points. Conversely, during the expansion of the 1990s, while all workers saw sizeable drops in unemployment, the least educated workers made the biggest gains. During the expansion in the 2000s the gains were much smaller across the board, and, except for Hispanics without a high school education, the gains were smaller than the losses from 2000 to 2003, implying increases in unemployment rates from 2000 to 2007.

Over this time frame, there was somewhat more discrepancy in unemployment rates across educational categories for women than there was for men; in 2007, the difference in unemployment rates between women with college degrees and women without high school diplomas was 6.1 percentage points, while for men that number was 4.6 points. By race/ethnicity, the table shows that Hispanics experience the least discrepancy in unemployment rates across educational categories, while blacks experience the most. For whites, the difference in unemployment rates between workers with a college degree and workers without a high school diploma was 4.6 percentage

FIGURE 4I Unemployment rates of foreign-born and native-born workers, 1994-2007

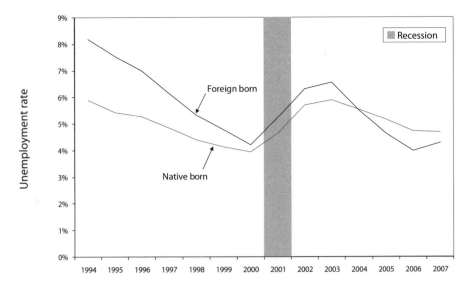

Source: Authors' analysis of CPS ORG data.

points. For Hispanics, this number was 3.7 percentage points, while for blacks it was two-and-a-half times that, at 9.1 percentage points. This big difference is largely driven by workers without a high school diploma—for blacks in this group, the unemployment rate is 12.1%, whereas for Hispanics it is 6.0%.

As the debate over immigration policy heats up, another interesting dissection of unemployment rates is by whether workers were born inside or outside the United States. **Figure 4I** gives this breakdown since 1994 (the earliest available year). What this figure shows is that the unemployment rate of immigrants over this period is more buffeted around by business cycles than those of native-born workers, that is, during expansions their unemployment rates drop more dramatically and during contractions they increase more dramatically. During the expansion of the 2000s, the immigrant unemployment rate fell below that of native-born workers for the first time, but appears poised to cross back above that of natives as the economy turns down again.

Long-term unemployment

A discussion earlier in this chapter showed how the aging of the workforce—which lowers the unemployment rate even if no individual age category experiences unemployment declines—points to problems with comparing the unemployment rate of today to that of earlier periods. Another issue is the fact that today's unemployed are spending much more time on average in unemployment than did unemployed workers in earlier periods. **Figure 4J** shows the unemployment rate over time, along with the share of the unemployed who have been unemployed for more than six months. The most striking aspect of this figure is the unprecedented gap between the unemployment rate and long-term unemployed share that emerged following the 2001 recession. In the first quarter of 2001—the peak of the previous business cycle—the share of the unemployed who were long-term unemployed was 11.4%. In the fourth quarter of 2007, the long-term share was 18.2%—an enormous increase in the share of the unemployed experiencing the hardship of being unemployed for more than six months.

Not only was the share of the unemployed who were long-term jobless alarmingly high in the 2000s, the average length of unemployment spells, unsurprisingly, was also much higher than the historical average. **Figure 4K** gives the average unemployment rate, the average share of the long-term unemployed, and the average length of unemployment spells for the 2000s recovery and for all prior periods combined. While the average unemployment rate of 5.3% for the 2000s recovery was slightly lower than the 5.6% historical average, the rest of the chart shows how the length of unemployment spells for those who did become unemployed had increased dramatically. Before the 2000s recovery, 12.1% of the unemployed were unemployed long-term (more than six months), on average. In the 2000s recovery, however, that share jumped to 19.4%. Similarly, before the 2000s recovery, the average length of an unemployment spell was 13 weeks, or three months. In the 2000s recovery, the average jobless spell was 17.9 weeks—over four months long. Figures 4J and 4K show that it was much harder for many workers to find work during the recovery of the 2000s than would be expected if one were to analyze the unemployment rate alone based on historical standards.

FIGURE 4J Long-term unemployment as a share of total unemployment, and the unemployment rate, 1979-2008q2

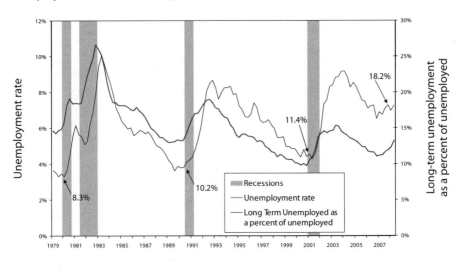

Source: Authors' analysis of BLS (2008c) data.

FIGURE 4K Unemployment and the 2000s recovery period

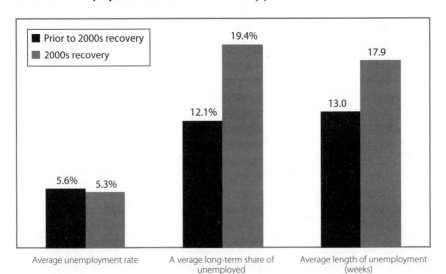

Source: Authors' analysis of BLS (2008c) data.

With so many more workers stuck in long-term unemployment, the question of who these workers are arises. **Table 4.5** gives shares of the total unemployed and the long-term unemployed by subgroup for 2000 and 2007. This table compares the shares of the unemployed to the shares of the long-term unemployed and reveals which subgroups of jobless workers are over- and under-represented among the long-term unemployed. For example, while 27.8% of the unemployed in 2007 were age 45 or older, 36.7% of the

TABLE 4.5 Shares of unemployment and long-term unemployment, 2000 and 2007

	2000			2007		
	Unem-ployment	Long-term	Percentage-point difference	Unem-ployment	Long-term	Percentage-point difference
All groups	100%	100%	0.0	100%	100%	0.0
Age						
16-24	36.9%	23.6%	-13.3	33.1%	22.5%	-10.6
25-44	41.1	43.1	2.0	39.1	40.8	1.7
45+	21.9	33.2	11.3	27.8	36.7	8.9
Education						
High school or less	65.8%	64.7%	-1.07	60.8%	59.5%	-1.3
Some college	22.1	21.1	-1.1	24.8	24.3	-0.5
College degree or more	12.1	14.2	2.2	14.4	16.2	1.8
Occupation						
White collar	43.4%	42.4%	-1	42.5%	44.0%	1.5
Blue collar	35.0	36.1	1.1	33.9	33.6	-0.3
Services	21.6	21.5	-0.1	23.7	22.4	-1.2
Gender						
Women	47.7%	44.3%	-3.4	45.2%	43.2%	-1.9
Men	52.3	55.7	3.4	54.8	56.8	1.9
Race/ethnicity*						
White	59.9%	51.0%	-8.9	60.7%	56.3%	-4.3
Black	22.4	29.9	7.5	21.0	28.6	7.6
Hispanic	17.7	19.1	1.4	18.3	15.1	-3.3

* See Table Notes.

Source: Authors' analysis of BLS (2008c) data.

long-term unemployed were 45 or older. In other words, these experienced workers were overrepresented among the long-term unemployed; if unemployed, workers age 45 and over were unusually likely to be unemployed long-term. On the other hand, while workers age 16-24 made up 33.1% of the unemployed, they made up only 22.5% of the long-term unemployed, meaning that young workers were underrepresented among the long-term unemployed. Education subgroups paint a similar picture; in 2007, while only 14.4% of unemployed workers had a bachelor's degree, 16.2% of the long-term unemployed had a bachelor's degree, meaning that the most educated workers were overrepresented among the long-term unemployed. The reverse was true for less-educated workers, who were underrepresented among the long-term unemployed.

When considering occupation, Table 4.5 shows that in 2007, white-collar workers were overrepresented among the long-term unemployed, and blue-collar workers were underrepresented—a reversal of the situation in 2000, when white-collar workers were underrepresented among the long-term unemployed and blue-collar workers were over-represented. These findings reveal that even the most educated and experienced workers were not sheltered from the run-up in long-term joblessness over the 2000s. Gender subgroups reveal that men are overrepresented among the long-term unemployed, while race and ethnicity subgroups show that whites are underrepresented among the long-term unemployed—though over the 2000s the white share of long-term unemployment increased by over 5 percentage points. African Americans are overrepresented among the long-term unemployed, and Hispanics are underrepresented.

Underemployment
Unemployment data include only workers who report that they are willing and able to work and have looked for work in the last four weeks; such data overlook workers who are not fully employed or who would like to be employed but are not actively seeking a job. **Table 4.6** presents data on underemployment, a broader measure than unemployment for gauging lack of success in the labor market. This alternative measure includes unemployed workers as well as: 1) those who are working part-time but who want and are available for full-time work ("involuntary" part-timers); 2) those who want and are available to work but are discouraged from looking for work because of weak job prospects ("discouraged" workers); and 3) others who are neither working nor currently looking for work but who want and are available for a job and have looked for work in the past year. (The second and third categories together are described as "marginally attached" workers.)

Generally, the underemployment rate—like its major component, the unemployment rate—is counter-cyclical, that is, as the economy expands or contracts, both the unemployment and underemployment rates decrease or increase, respectively. In 2003, the year of maximum underemployment in the business cycle of the 2000s, over one-tenth of the workforce was underemployed in some way, representing a large amount of lost output. As the economy expanded from 2003 to 2007, the underemployment rate declined, although, like the unemployment rate, it never entirely made up the ground it lost from 2000 to 2003, and in 2007 it was considerably higher (by 1.3 percentage points) than the 2000 rate, when truly tight labor markets prevailed. Later in the chapter,

TABLE 4.6 Underemployment, 2000-07 (in thousands)

	2000	2003	2007	2000-03	2003-07	2000-07
				Difference		
Underemployment						
Unemployed	5,692	8,774	7,078	3,082	-1,696	1,386
Involuntary part time*	3,227	4,701	4,401	1,474	-300	1,174
Marginally attached**	262	457	369	195	-88	107
Discouraged**	895	1,074	1,026	179	-48	131
Total underemployed	10,076	15,006	12,874	4,930	-2,132	2,798
Civilian labor force	142,583	146,510	153,124	3,927	6,614	10,541
Unemployment rate	4.0%	6.0%	4.6%	2.0	-1.4	0.6
Underemployment rate***	7.0%	10.1%	8.3%	3.1	-1.8	1.3

* Involuntary part-time workers are people employed part-time but who want and are available for full-time work.
** Marginally attached workers are people who currently are neither working nor looking for work but who want and are available for a job and have looked for work sometime in the recent past. Discouraged workers are a subset of the marginally attached who have indicated they are discouraged from looking for work because of weak job prospects.
*** Total underemployed workers as a percent of the civilian labor force plus all marginally attached workers.

Source: Authors' analysis of BLS (2008c) data.

Figure 4T shows that a significant portion of the increase in underemployment over the 2000s cycle can be explained by the increase in the share of people working part-time who would prefer to work full-time.

Labor force participation

The labor force participation rate is the percent of the population that is in the labor force, where a person is defined as being in the labor force if he or she is either employed (has a job) or unemployed (jobless but available for and looking for work). **Figure 4L** gives the labor force participation rate over time for people age 25-54 (prime working age). In the first quarter of 1980, the overall participation rate was 78.6%, which increased to 83.0% by the fourth quarter of 2007. The increase came entirely from women's increased participation, which jumped from 63.8% in the first quarter of 1980 to 75.4% in the fourth quarter of 2007. Men's participation actually decreased over this period, down from 94.4% to 90.8%.

Figure 4L shows that labor force participation does not tend to fluctuate with business cycles (which is unlike unemployment, shown earlier to be counter-cyclical, and also unlike employment, shown earlier to be pro-cyclical). Figure 4L also reveals that for the first time, there was an overall decrease in labor force participation during the business cycle of the 2000s. Both men's and women's labor force participation rate dropped from

FIGURE 4L Labor force participation rates, age 25-54, 1979-2008q1

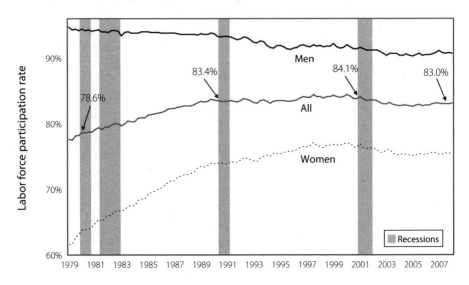

Source: BLS (2008c) data.

the first quarter of 2001 to the fourth quarter of 2007—men's by 0.8 percentage points and women's by 1.5 percentage points—for an overall drop of 1.1 percentage points.

When considering a labor force participation drop, the question that arises is whether the drop was cyclical (related to weak labor demand) or structural (people voluntarily leaving or not entering the workforce). One way to investigate this issue is to look at the labor force participation of young college graduates (25-34 years old). This subgroup of the population is expected to have very strong incentives and attachments to the labor market, so a drop in the labor force participation of this group is strong evidence of a lack of employment opportunity, not a voluntary exodus. **Figure 4M** gives the labor force participation rate over time for college graduates age 25 to 34. While the recent labor force participation of this group exhibits some business-cycle fluctuations, there was also a discernible shift down from the 1990s to the 2000s. Importantly, the shift was apparent among males as well as females, with males experiencing a decrease of 0.6 percentage points from 2000 to 2007, whereas their labor force participation rate had remained basically flat (increased 0.3 percentage points) over the business cycle of the 1990s.

The drop in labor force participation in the 2000s apparent in Figures 4L and 4M underscores another reason why it is problematic to compare the unemployment rate of today to that of earlier periods—to the extent that people dropped out of (or never entered) the labor force in the 2000s because they felt they would not be able to secure meaningful work, the unemployment rate understates the difficulty people experienced in finding work over this period. To quantify this effect, **Figure 4N** simulates what the

FIGURE 4M Annual labor force participation rate for college graduates (age 25-34), 1979-2007

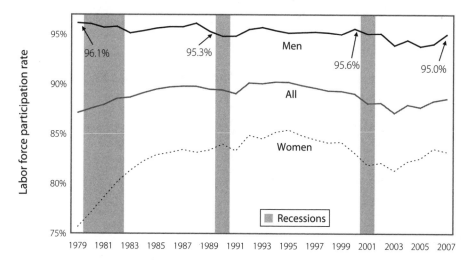

Source: Authors' analysis of BLS (2008c) data.

unemployment rate would have been over the cycle of the 2000s for 25-to-54-year-olds if the labor force participation rate had remained where it was in March of 2001, and if all the workers added to the labor force in that exercise are assumed to have been unemployed. The simulated unemployment rate in the fourth quarter of 2007 is 5.2%, which is 1.2 percentage points higher than the actual unemployment rate of 4.0%. In other words, if all workers making up the decline in the labor force participation rate from 2001 to 2007 had instead been in the labor force and without a job, the unemployment rate would have been 1.2 percentage points higher in 2007 than it actually was. Of course, it is not reasonable to assume that the entire decline in labor force participation from 2001 to 2007 was composed of would-be workers who chose not be a part of the labor force because they felt that if they did, they would face unemployment. However, the simulation provides an "upper bound" on the effect of decreasing labor force participation on unemployment and demonstrates that in periods of decreasing labor force participation—namely the cycle of the 2000s—it is likely that the unemployment rate understates labor market slack and it is therefore crucial to look at other measures in addition to the unemployment rate.

Employment

One important measure to consider is the employment rate, which is simply the percent of the population that is employed. The employment rate is conceptually different from

FIGURE 4N Actual and simulated* unemployment rates (25-54), 1979-2008q2

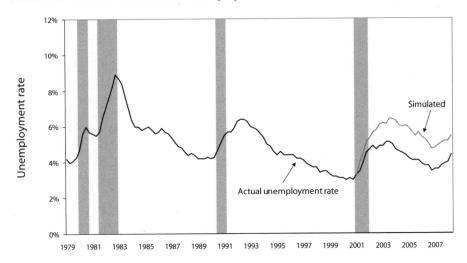

* What the unemployment would be if all workers making up the decline in the labor force participation rate from 2001 to 2007 had instead been in the labor force unemployed.

Source: Author's analysis of BLS (2008c) data.

FIGURE 4O Employment rates (25-54-year-olds), 1973-2008q2

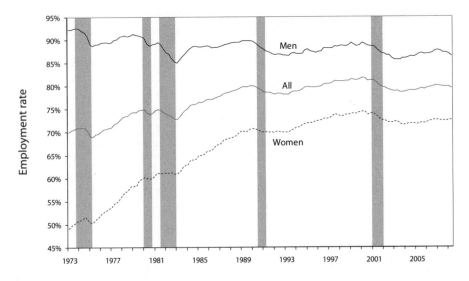

Source: BLS (2008c).

the unemployment rate, which is the percent of the labor force that is unemployed. By examining the employment rate, issues related to changes in the *labor force* are avoided. **Figure 4O** gives the employment rate over time for people age 25 to 54. Like the labor force participation rate, the employment rate has increased dramatically over time—from 70% in the first quarter of 1973 to 80% in the first quarter of 2008. Also like the labor force participation rate, all of the growth was due to women, whose employment rate increased enormously, from 49% in the first quarter of 1973 to 73% in the first quarter of 2008. Men's employment rate decreased over this same period from 92% to 87%.

Figure 4O shows that the employment rate is very sensitive to business cycles—with high levels at the beginning of a recession, sharp declines during a recession, and increases shortly after the end of a recession, generally attaining higher employment rates at the peak of a business cycle than existed at the previous peak. **Figure 4P** shows changes in the employment rate from one business cycle peak to the next. In the business cycle of the 1990s, women's employment increased 3.7 percentage points, and men's decreased by 0.1 percentage points, for an overall increase of 1.8 percentage points. The 2000s cycle saw a big reversal, however, with both men's and women's employment rates dropping—men's by 1.4 percentage points and women's by 1.8—for an overall drop of 1.5 percentage points.

Figure 4Q shows employment rates over time by gender and race/ethnicity. Among men, the group that saw the largest decline in employment from 1979 to 2007 was black men, with a decline of 4.8 percentage points. White men were not far behind, with a decline of 3.6 percentage points. Over the 1990s, the employment

FIGURE 4P Peak-to-peak change in employment rate (age 25-54)

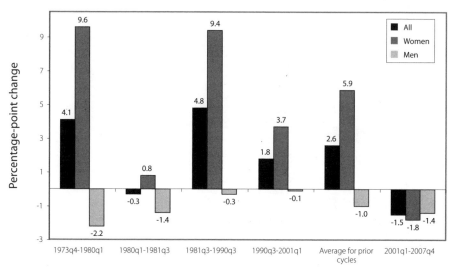

Source: BLS (2008c).

rate of black men decreased by only 0.5 percentage points, while that of white men decreased by 1.1 percentage points. In the 2000s, however, the employment rate of black men decreased by 1.7 percentage points, while that of white men decreased by 1.6 percentage points. Hispanic men were the only group of men to make gains—with employment rates 0.7 percentage points higher in 2007 than in 1979. All of their gains came over the 1990s. Their gains relative to other groups, however, continued in the 2000s, and by 2007 the employment rates of Hispanic and white men were virtually identical.

Among women, the employment gains between 1979 and 2000 were dramatic. For white women and Hispanic women, the steepest gains were in the 1980s (with

FIGURE 4Q Peak-to-peak change in employment rates by race and ethnicity, 1979-2007

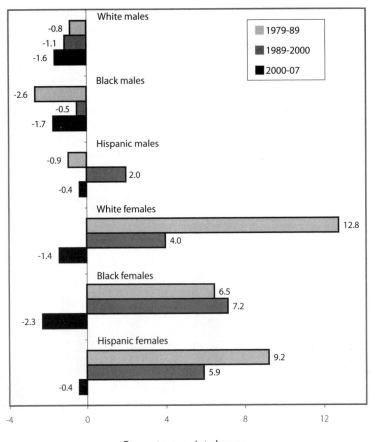

Percentage-point change

Source: BLS (2008c) data.

an increase of 12.8 percentage points for white women and 9.2 percentage points for Hispanic women from 1979 to 1989). For black women, the gains were steeper in the 1990s, with an increase of 7.2 percentage points from 1989 to 2000. All three groups of women experienced employment declines from 2000 to 2007, with the declines for black women, at 2.3 percentage points, the largest, and for Hispanic women, at 0.4 percentage points, the smallest. A final thing to note on Figure 4Q is that while for men, Hispanics have higher employment rates than blacks, for women the pattern is reversed and black women have higher employment rates than Hispanic women.

Importantly, the employment rates of those 55 years of age and older defied any cyclical response to the 2001 recession. The rates for men, long on the decline, reversed course in 1993 and have continued upward ever since. The rates for women, which were relatively flat after the mid-1970s, also increased significantly from 1993 onward. These changing trends are illustrated in **Figure 4R**. Two primary reasons why the employment rates of people age 55 and over have increased in the last 15 years are health insurance and pensions. First, most people get some portion of their health insurance coverage through their employer, and since health care costs have risen significantly, workers are working longer to cover them. Second, pensions are becoming less and less likely to provide adequate retirement income, while at the same time longevity is increasing. Thus, people are working longer to improve their economic security

FIGURE 4R Annual employment rates of workers 55 years and older, 1973-2007

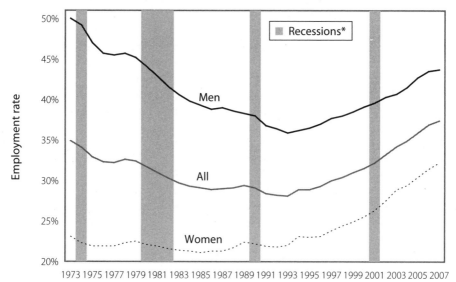

* Years are shaded only when the recession took place during at least two quarters of that year.

Source: BLS (2008c).

in retirement. Chapter 7 covers the issue of rising health costs in more depth, and Chapter 5 further covers the issue of falling retirement income adequacy.

Nonstandard work

Many workers, consistently or at some point in their working lives, are employed in a nonstandard work arrangement. Broadly defined, nonstandard work consists of employment arrangements that are not regular, full-time work; these include temporary, part-time, on-call, and self-employed workers. There are many reasons why a worker may be employed in a nonstandard job. On the supply side, many workers—students, older workers, workers with families—prefer jobs that offer more flexibility than the traditional 9-to-5 job. On the demand side, businesses hire nonstandard workers in a variety of capacities. Some put workers directly on their payrolls but assign them to an internal temporary worker pool. Others hire on-call workers and day-laborers. Some businesses hire independent contractors to perform work that would otherwise be done by direct-hire employees. Employers also use temporary help agencies and contracting firms to obtain workers on a temporary basis—sometimes, as discussed later in this section, for long periods. Hiring nonstandard workers is one way firms practice "just-in-time" employment strategies. Just-in-time employment allows firms to adjust labor the way they traditionally adjusted inventory levels—cyclically with demand fluctuations. Retaining workers through economic downturns and hiring full-time permanent workers while testing the strength and sustainability of the upturns is now a cost that many employers are not willing or able to incur.

Table 4.7 shows the distribution of employment by type of work arrangement. These data are from the 2005 Contingent Work Supplement (CWS), which is a household survey of workers. One caveat is that the CWS almost certainly undercounts nonstandard work, in part because it does not account for a worker's second or third job. Nevertheless, it is a rich source of data on nonstandard work. According to the 2005 CWS, 30.6% of workers were in nonstandard work arrangements, with by far the most prevalent form of nonstandard work being part-time work.

Broken down along gender lines, the table shows that women are much more likely to be in nonstandard work arrangements than men, with 35.2% of women and 26.5% of men working in nonstandard capacities. This is especially true with part-time work—19.0% of women and only 7.9% of men are employed in regular part-time work. In fact, a higher percentage of men than women work in nonstandard arrangements aside from regular part-time work. Men, for example, are much more likely to be self-employed independent contractors than are women.

Nonstandard workers, in general, tend not only to be paid less, but they are also less likely to receive benefits from their employers. Figures 7C and 7D in Chapter 7 show that nonstandard workers are much less likely to receive health insurance from their employer—only 20.8% of nonstandard workers receive health insurance from their job, as opposed to 71.8% of standard workers. **Figure 4S** paints a similar story with pensions. Over 70% of standard workers had access to a retirement plan at work

TABLE 4.7 Nonstandard workers in the U.S. workforce, 2005

	All	Women	Men
Nonstandard workers	30.6%	35.2%	26.5%
Regular part-time	13.2	19.0	7.9
Direct hire temporaries	2.1	2.3	2.0
Temp agency	0.9	1.0	0.8
Regular self-employed	4.4	5.1	3.8
Independent contractor (self-employed)	6.5	4.6	8.2
Independent contractor (wage & salary)	1.0	1.0	1.0
On-call / day laborers	2.0	2.0	2.0
Contract company employees	0.5	0.4	0.7
Standard workers	69.4%	64.8%	73.5%
All	100.0%	100.0%	100.0%

Source: Ditsler and Fisher (2006).

(and 65.7% participated). That stands in sharp contrast to nonstandard workers, where 27.0% had access to a retirement plan at work (and 22.8% participated).

Part-time work

As noted above, the most common form of nonstandard work is part-time work. Many workers prefer a part-time schedule because it allows time to pursue education, leisure, or family responsibilities. Nevertheless, part-timers generally have lower pay, less-skilled jobs, poor chances of promotion, less job security, inferior benefits (including vacation, health insurance, and pensions), and lower status overall within their places of employment. For these and other reasons, some part-timers would prefer to work full time. Those who work part-time schedules by choice would certainly prefer to receive the same compensation (i.e., the same hourly pay rate and prorated benefits) in exchange for performing the same work as their full-time coworkers.

According to the data in **Figure 4T**, 16.5% of workers worked part time in December 2007, meaning more than one out of six workers worked part time. (These numbers differ somewhat from those in Table 4.7 because here the definition of part time includes all part-time workers whereas Table 4.7 looked at "regular" part-time, which did not include part-time workers in other kinds of nonstandard employment.) Part-time workers are comprised of "voluntary" and "involuntary" part-timers. Voluntary part-timers are those who work part time for non-economic reasons, including medical reasons, personal obligations, and retirement or Social Security limits on

FIGURE 4S Access to job-based retirement plan by work arrangement, 2005

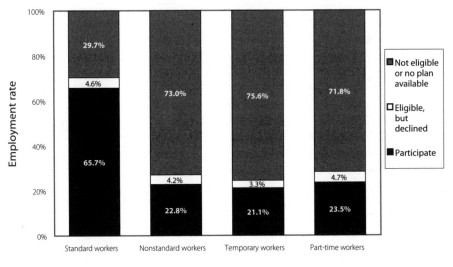

Source: Ditsler and Fisher (2006).

earnings, along with those who have an economic reason for working part time but who do not want to work full time and/or are unavailable to do so. Involuntary part-timers are those who want and are available for full-time work, but who work part time for economic reasons, including slack work or unfavorable business conditions, an inability to find full time work, and/or seasonal declines in demand. Note the break in the voluntary and involuntary series in 1994—in that year the survey implemented new methodology that was stricter in determining whether a worker was involuntarily part time, leading to a one-time drop in the percent of involuntary part-timers and an offsetting one-time increase in the percent of voluntary part-timers, making the data before and after 1994 not directly comparable.

The share of voluntary part-timers was remarkably stable both pre- and post-1994, coming in at 13.4% in December 2007. The share of involuntary part-timers was a very different story, exhibiting strong counter-cyclicality—tending to spike up during recessions and decline during recoveries. The 2000s recovery, however, largely bucked that trend, staying relatively flat such that in December 2007, the involuntary part-time rate was 3.2% of all employment, up from 2.4% at the peak of the previous business cycle (March 2001). As the economy has further slowed, the involuntary part-time rate has continued to climb and was at 3.9% as of this writing.

Temping

Figure 4U shows the percent of all workers who are in temporary help services. The series is pro-cyclical—decreasing during recessions as these are the first workers to be let

FIGURE 4T Part-time status, as a share of total employment, 1973-2008

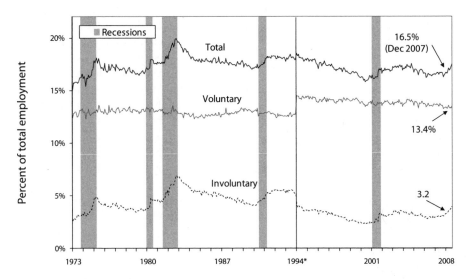

* 1994 CPS Survey change. See figure notes.

Source: Authors' analysis of BLS (2008c) data.

FIGURE 4U Employment in temporary help industry as share of non-farm employment, 1990-August2008

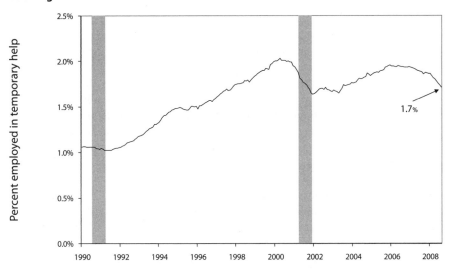

Source: Authors' analysis of 2008b data.

go, and increasing during expansions. The chart also shows a clear upward trend in temp work; this was especially true in the 1990s, when the percent of all workers who were temps increased from roughly 1% to roughly 2%. That percentage dropped to 1.6% over the recession of 2001, then increased back to 2% by the middle of 2006. As the economy has slowed since 2007, the temp share of employment is again declining.

Traditionally, the staffing of temporary workers was short-term as employers filled an employment need they knew to be temporary—to substitute for an employee on vacation or parental leave, or to do work that only existed for a certain season, for example. An important shift has been the dramatic increase in what is known as "permatemping." Permatemps are technically temporary but are often retained at one assignment full-time year after year, and often work side-by-side with regular employees who receive better pay and benefits. Hiring temporary employees has evolved from being not only a stopgap measure to fill short-term employment needs, but now also a strategy by employers to reduce costs and responsibility to employees. Ditsler and Fisher (2006) show that from 1995 to 2005 alone, the percent of temp agency workers who had been employed for one year or more in their current job assignment increased from 24.4% to 33.7%.

Job stability

Economic anxiety has often been linked to the feeling that job stability and long-term employment prospects declined considerably in recent decades. Job stability is a critical issue not only because it provides workers with a dependable paycheck, but also because longer job tenure is often associated with increased vacation time, vesting in retirement plans, and promotion and wage gains.

Job tenure

Table 4.8 provides the most basic information on job stability—the average number of years workers have been in their current job. This is presented for business cycle peaks since 1973 (tenure data are not available for the peak year 1989, so 1988 was used instead, and the latest data available as of this writing are from 2006). Since job tenure is sensitive to the age distribution in the population (younger workers' potential job tenure is necessarily shorter than that of older workers), data are presented by age category. From 1973 to 2006, average job tenure declined in all age categories—six months for workers age 25-34, 10 months for workers age 35-44, and one year for workers age 45-54.

In all age categories in all years, mean job tenure was higher for men, but over this period it decreased much more for men. In fact, for 35-44-year-olds, women's average tenure *increased* by seven months from 1973 to 2006 while men's decreased by a year and a half, and for 45-54-year-olds, women's tenure increased by 15 months while men's decreased by more than two years.

Across educational categories, the workers that saw the biggest declines in job tenure were those with the least education—for example, workers age 45 to 54 with a maximum education level of a high school diploma saw a decline in job tenure of

19 months from 1973 to 2006, whereas those with a college degree saw a decline of seven months. From 2000 to 2006, the overall patterns were roughly the same as over the entire period, though workers age 25 to 34 saw no additional erosion of job tenure during the 2000s. Workers age 35 to 44 saw a three-month decline in job tenure, and workers age 45 to 54 saw a five-month decline in job tenure. Over the 2000s, unlike the earlier period, both men and women in the two older age categories experienced declines in job tenure, though the decrease was more pronounced for men.

The mean job tenure data shed important light on job stability, but the share of jobs that are "long-term" may be more relevant to workers' perceptions of job security.

TABLE 4.8 Average years of job tenure by age, gender, and education, 1973-2006

	1973	1979	1988	2000	2006	Change (in months)	
						1973-2006	2000-06
Age 25-34							
All	4.0	3.8	4.0	3.5	3.5	-6	1
Male	4.3	4.2	4.2	3.6	3.7	-7	0
Female	3.5	3.4	3.9	3.3	3.4	-1	1
High school degree or less	4.3	4.0	4.3	3.7	3.6	-8	-1
Some college	3.7	3.9	4.0	3.6	3.6	-1	0
College degree or more	3.4	3.5	3.6	3.2	3.5	0	4
Age 35-44							
All	7.5	7.1	7.5	6.9	6.6	-10	-3
Male	8.5	8.5	8.5	7.5	7.0	-18	-6
Female	5.6	5.4	6.4	6.3	6.2	7	-1
High school degree or less	7.6	7.0	7.5	7.0	6.5	-12	-5
Some college	7.1	6.9	7.3	7.1	6.8	-4	-3
College degree or more	7.2	7.6	7.6	6.7	6.6	-8	-2
Age 45-54							
All	11.3	11.8	11.5	10.7	10.3	-12	-5
Male	13.1	13.9	13.5	11.7	11.0	-25	-8
Female	8.4	8.8	9.2	9.7	9.6	15	-1
High school degree or less	11.4	11.6	11.3	10.3	9.8	-19	-6
Some college	10.9	11.9	10.9	10.9	10.6	-4	-3
College degree or more	11.3	12.2	12.4	11.1	10.8	-7	-4

Source: Authors' analysis of Farber (2007).

Long-term jobs (ones that last, say, at least 10 years) typically are the kinds of employment situations that provide workers with the best potential for sustained wage growth, good fringe benefits, and a feeling of employment security. **Table 4.9** shows the share of workers in peak years that had been in their jobs for 10 or more and 20 or more years. From 1973 to 2006, the share of workers that had been in their job 10 years fell by over 5% for both workers age 35-44 and workers aged 45-54. Consistent with the mean job tenure data, men were much more likely to be in jobs long-term than women in every year and in every age category, but the percent in long-term jobs decreased for men and increased for women. In 2006, male workers age 45 to 54 were 10 percentage points less likely to have been in their job 10 years or longer than they were in 1973. Female workers age 45 to 54, on the other hand, were 5 percentage points more likely in 2006 than 1973 to have been in their jobs 10 years or longer. Also consistent with the mean job tenure data, Table 4.9 shows that the least educated workers saw the biggest declines in their likelihood of long-term employment over this period.

From 2000 to 2006, the overall patterns in long-term employment were roughly the same as over the entire period—workers aged 35-44 saw a 3.6 percentage point decline in the likelihood of being in their job for 10 years or more, and workers age 45 to 54 saw a 3.3 percentage point decline. Over the 2000s, unlike the earlier period, both men and women experienced declines—though the decrease was more pronounced for men.

Costs of displacement

When workers leave their jobs voluntarily but stay in the labor force, they generally move on to better circumstances in a new job with better pay or working conditions. When workers lose their jobs involuntarily, however, they typically pay a large economic price. One cost is difficulty in finding a new job. **Figure 4V** shows the labor force status post-displacement of workers who involuntarily lose their jobs "not for cause" (i.e., due to a plant closing, a layoff, or the abolition of a job). The likelihood of unemployment for these workers is, unsurprisingly, counter-cyclical—high during recessions and decreasing over expansions. However, during the 2000s business cycle, the percent of displaced workers that did not find re-employment showed little decline after the recession—over the 2003-05 period, one-third of workers who lost their jobs not for cause were either unemployed or had dropped out of the labor force altogether.

Among displaced workers who are able to find another job, wages at the new job tend to be lower than they had been in the lost job. **Figure 4W** shows the average weekly earning loss of displaced workers who move from full-time to full-time work. Again, this plot is counter-cyclical; during recessions, displaced full-time workers who find new full-time jobs face large wage losses, and those losses decrease over expansions. In the tight labor market of 1997-99, displaced workers faced almost no wage penalty in moving to a new job. In 2001-03, however, these workers faced a 13.6% drop in wages—the worst rate of the series. Farther into the 2000s expansion, displaced workers fared better; in 2003-05, the most recent data available, the decline in wages they faced was 6.7%.

Conclusion

Employment is the foundation of family income and economic well being. The great American jobs machine is arguably the most powerful mechanism in our economy for achieving broadly shared prosperity. But the faltering of that machine in the 2000s, as

TABLE 4.9 Share of employed workers in long-term jobs by age, gender, and education, 1973-2006

	1973	1979	1988	2000	2006	Percentage-point change 1973-2006	2000-06
With more than 10 years on current job							
Age 35-44							
All	29.9%	30.6%	32.6%	28.2%	24.6%	-5.3	-3.6
Male	36.9	39.9	38.7	31.9	26.9	-9.9	-5.0
Female	17.8	18.8	25.5	24.1	21.9	4.1	-2.2
High school degree or less	30.3	30.2	32.7	27.7	24.5	-5.9	-3.2
Some college	28.6	29.0	30.2	29.4	24.9	-3.8	-4.5
College degree or more	29.2	33.1	34.3	28.0	24.6	-4.6	-3.4
Age 45-54							
All	46.4%	48.7%	48.2%	44.6%	41.3%	-5.2	-3.3
Male	54.9	58.4	56.6	48.5	44.8	-10.1	-3.7
Female	32.2	35.4	38.4	40.6	37.5	5.3	-3.0
High school degree or less	46.4	47.2	47.1	41.7	37.6	-8.8	-4.1
Some college	45.0	47.9	43.8	44.8	42.2	-2.8	-2.6
College degree or more	47.9	55.1	54.1	47.7	44.7	-3.2	-3.0
With more than 20 years on current job							
Age 45-54							
All	21.9%	22.9%	22.5%	19.7%	17.4%	-4.4	-2.3
Male	29.2	31.8	30.7	23.7	20.3	-8.9	-3.4
Female	9.6	10.6	13.0	15.5	14.4	4.8	-1.1
High school degree or less	22.5	22.4	22.0	18.5	15.4	-7.1	-3.1
Some college	19.9	25.8	20.4	19.9	18.2	-1.7	-1.6
College degree or more	20.2	22.3	25.3	20.8	19.0	-1.1	-1.8

Source: Authors' analysis of Farber (2007).

FIGURE 4V Labor force status post-displacement, 1981-2005

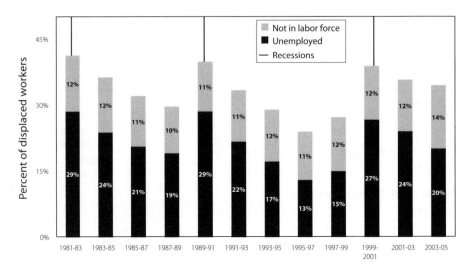

Source: Authors' analysis of Farber (2005).

FIGURE 4W Average decline in weekly earnings for displaced full-time workers who find new full-time work, 1981-2005

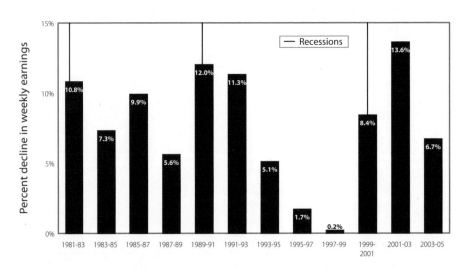

Source: Authors' analysis of Farber (2005).

it produced the weakest jobs recovery on record, has left lingering adversity for workers and their families. When jobs are plentiful, not only are workers more likely to find employment that matches their skills and experience, they are also in a better position to search for higher-paid employment and are in a better bargaining position with their employer to ask for higher levels of compensation. Job growth, however, was too tepid over the business cycle of the 2000s to boost living standards for most workers—even as the economy expanded and labor productivity posted impressive gains.

In other words, for most working families, the recovery of the 2000s felt like anything but a recovery. And by virtually all measures, the recovery has ended, and the economy is now heading into a potentially lengthy economic downturn. Without the cushion that a robust jobs expansion may have afforded them, many families are now facing a substantial threat to their living standards.

CHAPTER 5

Wealth
Unrelenting disparities

Much of the focus of the preceding chapters has been on the wages and incomes of American families. This chapter focuses on an analysis of wealth. Like wages and income, wealth has a crucial effect on a family's standard of living. Wealth—particularly liquid assets such as checking account balances, stocks, and bonds—can help families cope with financial emergencies related to unemployment or illness. Wealth also makes it easier for families to invest in education and training, start a small business, or fund retirement. More tangible forms of wealth, such as cars, computers, and homes, can directly affect a family's ability to participate fully in work, school, and community life. Chapter 2 on income mobility discussed the high degree of correlation in wealth across generations in the United States—that is, that children of poor parents are much more likely to be poor, and children of wealthy parents are much more likely to be wealthy—pointing to the existence of class barriers that violate a core American principal of equal opportunity for all.

This chapter further investigates wealth in America, uncovering some important features. First, the distribution of wealth is highly unequal—much more so than the distribution of wages and income that were the focus of earlier chapters. The wealthiest 1% of all households control a larger share of national wealth than the entire bottom 90%. The ownership of stocks is particularly unequal, with most Americans having no meaningful stake in the stock market. Housing equity also varies substantially by income levels and race.

Second, only households at the top of the income distribution are likely to be adequately prepared for retirement. For over a quarter of American households, income from Social Security, pensions, and personal savings are expected to replace less than half of their pre-retirement income.

Finally, for the typical household, debt has grown much faster than income in the last decade, fueled by increases in mortgages and home equity loans. In 2007, debt was

FIGURE 5A Growth of household net worth, 1965-2007

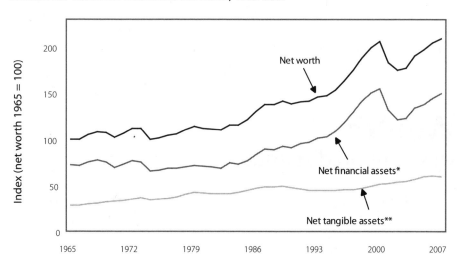

* Financial assets minus nonmortgage debt.
** Housing and consumer durables minus home mortgages.
Source: Authors' analysis of Federal Reserve Board (2008a) and Bureau of the Census data.

over 140% of disposable personal income. As housing prices collapse, the associated loss of home equity combined with large debt burdens are endangering the economic security of many Americans.

Net worth

The definition of wealth used in this chapter is net worth, that is, the sum of a family's assets—real estate, bank account balances, stock holdings, retirements funds (such as 401(k) plans and individual retirement accounts), and other assets—minus the sum of all of a family's liabilities—mortgages, credit-card debt, student loans, and other debts. Net worth excludes assets in defined-benefit pension plans because workers do not legally own the assets held in these plans and thus do not necessarily benefit or suffer from gains or losses in the value of assets used to pay the defined benefits. (Their companies are affected, however, because changes in asset values change the contributions companies have to pay to meet future defined benefits.) For similar reasons, this analysis also excludes Social Security and Medicare from net worth calculations (although the section projecting retirement income does include expected income from defined-benefit pension plans and from Social Security).

Figure 5A shows average net worth per household over time, along with net financial assets (financial assets minus nonmortgage debt) and net tangible assets (tangible assets—housing and consumer durables—minus home mortgages). One thing that is clear in the graph is the impact of the stock market bubble in the late 1990s and its crash in the early 2000s. From 1995 to 2000, average net worth increased 6.1% annually, but from 2000 to 2003, it decreased 5.0% annually. The surprisingly limited direct impact this stock market rollercoaster had on the large majority of households is discussed later in the chapter. Another thing to note in Figure 5A is the recent deceleration in the growth of net worth. From 2003—the end of the stock market crash—to 2006, the growth in average real net worth averaged 5.0% annually. From 2006 to 2007, however, it was 2.2%. This deceleration has been largely fueled by the bursting of the housing bubble starting in 2006, discussed later in the chapter.

The data used to make Figure 5A are from the Federal Reserve Board's Flow of Funds Accounts of the United States. These data are timely, but they do not allow an analysis of how wealth is distributed across the population. The Survey of Consumer Finances (SCF) is used to conduct a distributional analysis. This dataset, also collected by the Federal Reserve Board, is one of the country's primary sources of data on wealth. The major drawback of the SCF is that it is only conducted every three years; the latest data currently available are from 2004. It should be noted that the distributional effects of more recent economic events, like the bursting of the housing bubble, will not be reflected in much of the analysis that follows.

A key feature of the wealth distribution is that it is dramatically more unequal than either the distribution of wages or of incomes. **Table 5.1** shows income and wealth data from 2004, drawn from the SCF. The first column of Table 5.1 shows that in 2004, the 1% of households with the highest incomes received 16.9% of all income. By comparison, the wealthiest 1% of households owned 34.3% of all wealth. At the same time, the bottom 90% of households received only 57.5% of all income, but when considering the wealth distribution, that number is half as large, at 28.7%. The distribution is even more unequal when one examines wealth that provides direct financial returns ("financial assets"): the bottom 90% hold only 19.1% of all financial assets, less than half of the 42.2% owned by the wealthiest 1%.

Like income and wages, the distribution of wealth has become more unequal over time. **Figure 5B** illustrates the share of all wealth held by households in various

TABLE 5.1 Distribution of income and wealth, 2004

	Distribution of		
	Household income	Net worth	Net financial assets
All	100.0%	100.0%	100.0%
Top 1%	16.9	34.3	42.2
Next 9%	25.6	36.9	38.7
Bottom 90%	57.5	28.7	19.1

Source: Wolff (2006).

FIGURE 5B Distribution of wealth by wealth class, 1983-2004

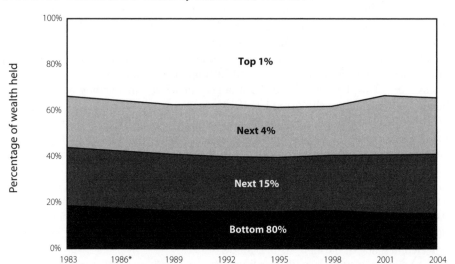

* See Figure Notes.

Source: Authors' analysis of Wolff (2006).

portions of the wealth distribution. Since 1983, the top 5% of wealth holders consistently held over 50% of all wealth, increasing from 56.1% in 1983 to 58.9% in 2004, while the bottom 80% of wealth holders consistently held less than 20%, decreasing from 18.7% in 1983 to 15.3% in 2004.

Table 5.2 provides a more detailed analysis of the distribution of wealth from 1962 to 2004. Table 5.2 shows that, in 2004, the top fifth of households held 84.7% of all wealth, while the middle fifth held only 3.8% (its lowest recorded share) and the bottom fifth actually had negative net worth—what they owed (net of what they owned) was equivalent to 0.5% of all net worth. From 1983 to 2004, the top fifth increased its wealth share by 3.4 percentage points, while the bottom four-fifths gave up the same percentage.

Table 5.3 puts dollar figures to the wealth shares in Table 5.2. In 2004, the average net worth of the top 1% of households was $14.8 million, an increase of $1.3 million from 2001—a 3.0% annual increase. Below these households on the wealth distribution, wealth holdings drop off sharply. The 4% of households just below the top 1%, for example, had an average net worth of $2.7 million in 2004, and households that were between the 80th and 90th percentiles on the wealth distribution had an average net worth of $576,300 in 2004. In 2004, the wealth of the median household was $77,900 (consisting primarily of home equity, as discussed later). This value was down $500, or -0.2% annually, from 2001. The wealth of the poorest households experienced an annual decline of 9.2% on average over the period from 2001 to 2004, such that these household had a net worth of $-11,400 in 2004. This was a devastating reversal for

TABLE 5.2 Changes in the distribution of wealth, 1962–2004

Wealth class*	1962	1983	1989	1998	2001	2004	Percentage-point change			
							1962-83	1983-89	1989-2001	2001-04
Top fifth	81.0%	81.3%	83.5%	83.4%	84.4%	84.7%	0.4	2.2	0.9	0.2
Top 1%	33.4	33.8	37.4	38.1	33.4	34.3	0.3	3.6	-4.0	1.0
Next 4%	21.2	22.3	21.6	21.3	25.8	24.6	1.2	-0.8	4.2	-1.2
Next 5%	12.4	12.1	11.6	11.5	12.3	12.3	-0.2	-0.5	0.7	0.0
Next 10%	14.0	13.1	13.0	12.5	12.9	13.4	-0.9	-0.1	-0.1	0.5
Bottom four-fifths	19.1%	18.7%	16.5%	16.6%	15.6%	15.3%	-0.4	-2.2	-0.9	-0.2
Fourth	13.4	12.6	12.3	11.9	11.3	11.3	-0.8	-0.3	-1.0	0.0
Middle	5.4	5.2	4.8	4.5	3.9	3.8	-0.2	-0.4	-0.9	-0.1
Second	1.0	1.2	0.8	0.8	0.7	0.7	0.2	-0.3	-0.1	0.0
Lowest	-0.7	-0.3	-1.5	-0.6	-0.4	-0.5	0.4	-1.2	1.1	-0.1
Total	100.0%	100.0%	100.0%	100.0%	100.0%	100.0%				

* Wealth defined as net worth (household assets minus debts).

Source: Wolff (2006).

TABLE 5.3 Changes in average wealth by wealth class, 1962-2004 (thousands of 2004 dollars)

Wealth class*	1962	1983	1989	1998	2001	2004	Annualized growth			
							1962-83	1983-89	1989-2001	2001-04
Top fifth	$680.8	$1,001.9	$1,178.7	$1,305.8	$1,711.6	$1,822.6	1.8%	2.7%	3.2%	2.1%
Top 1%	5,622.8	8,315.2	10,547.9	11,825.1	13,537.8	14,791.6	1.9	4.0	2.1	3.0
Next 4%	890.2	1,375.4	1,522.1	1,670.2	2,616.4	2,676.7	2.1	1.7	4.6	0.8
Next 5%	416.1	598.2	655.4	722.5	999.9	1,054.7	1.7	1.5	3.6	1.8
Next 10%	235.1	323.0	366.1	399.7	523.0	576.3	1.5	2.1	3.0	3.3
Bottom four-fifths	$40.1	$57.5	$58.1	$65.1	$78.9	$82.5	1.7%	0.2%	2.6%	1.5%
Fourth	112.7	154.8	173.9	186.9	229.6	243.6	1.5	1.9	2.3	2.0
Middle	45.7	64.3	68.2	70.7	80.0	81.9	1.6	1.0	1.3	0.8
Second	8.0	14.5	11.9	12.9	14.9	14.4	2.9	-3.3	1.9	-1.0
Lowest	-6.1	-3.7	-21.3	-10.3	-8.7	-11.4	2.4%	-33.9	7.2	-9.2
Median	$45.0	$63.3	$67.7	$70.3	$78.4	$77.9	1.6%	1.1%	1.2%	-0.2%
Average	168.2	246.4	282.3	313.2	405.5	430.5	1.8	2.3	3.1	2.0

* Wealth defined as net worth (household assets minus debts).

Source: Wolff (2006).

FIGURE 5C The ratio of the wealthiest 1% to median wealth in the United States

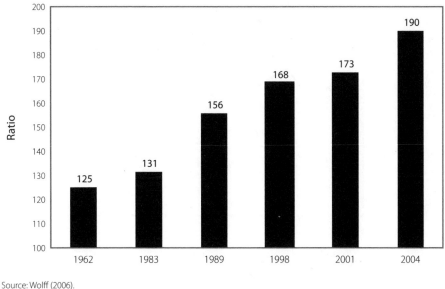

Source: Wolff (2006).

these households from the 1990s, with an annualized growth rate of 7.2% from 1989 to 2001.

Figure 5C shows the ratio of the average wealth of the top 1% to the wealth of the median household. In 1962, this number was remarkably high, at 125. In other words, in 1962, the wealthiest 1% of households averaged 125 times the wealth of the median household. That figure is, however, dwarfed by today's disparity—in 2004, the wealthiest 1% of households averaged 190 times the wealth of the median household, with particularly large increases in the 1980s and from 2001 to 2004.

Figure 5D shows the minimum, average, and maximum levels of wealth in 2007 dollars of the members of the "Forbes 400", an annual list of the 400 wealthiest people in the United States. The graph shows wealth holdings on a log scale, which compresses large differences to allow the three lines to fit on the same graph. Except for a temporary decline from 2000 to 2003 as the stock market plummeted, the average wealth of the "Forbes 400" grew steadily over virtually the entire period, increasing 681% between 1982 and 2007, from $493 million to $3.8 billion. In 2007, the price of admission to the Forbes 400 was $1.3 billion, up 716% from 1982, and the collective net worth of these 400 individuals was over $1.5 trillion (to put this in perspective, $1.5 trillion was 11% of GDP in 2007). Inequality also increased among the very wealthy between 1982 and 2007. The ratio of the maximum to the average wealth level of the Forbes 400 increased by 280% from 1982 to 1999, though much of that increase was erased as the ratio decreased from 1999 to 2007, due largely to the dramatic losses at the top in the stock

FIGURE 5D Annual net worth of "Forbes 400" wealthiest individuals

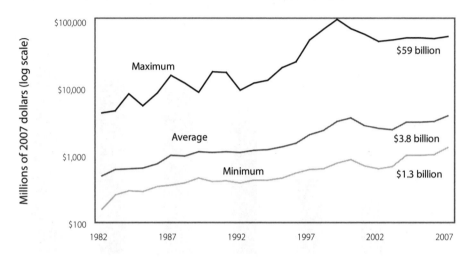

Source: Authors' analysis of Broom and Shay (2000) and Forbes (2008).

market crash of the early 2000s. Over the entire period from 1982 to 2007, the ratio of the maximum to the average wealth level increased by 77% among this group of super rich.

Another important feature of the wealth distribution is that a significant percentage of households have low net worth, and many have zero or negative net worth. **Table 5.4** reports the share of all households with zero or negative net worth (the first line) and net worth less than $12,000 (the second line). In 2004, 17.0% of all households had zero or negative net worth, while 29.6% had net worth less than $12,000. In other words,

TABLE 5.4 Households with low net worth, 1962-2004 (percent of all households)

Net worth	1962	1983	1989	1998	2001	2004	Percentage-point change			
							1962-83	1983-89	1989-2001	2001-04
Zero or negative	23.6%	15.5%	17.9%	18.0%	17.6%	17.0%	-5.6	2.4	-0.3	-0.6
Less than $12,000*	34.3	29.7	31.8	30.3	30.1	29.6	-4.6	2.1	-1.7	-0.5

* Constant 2005 dollars.

Source: Wolff (2006).

TABLE 5.5 Wealth by race, 1983-2004 (thousands of 2004 dollars)

Race	1983	1989	1992	1995	1998	2001	2004
Average wealth*							
Black	$54.20	$57.10	$61.30	$50.50	$67.50	$70.80	$101.40
White	287.90	340.60	329.60	300.40	371.90	496.80	534.00
Black-to-white ratio	0.19	0.17	0.19	0.17	0.18	0.14	0.19
Median wealth							
Black	$5.50	$2.50	$13.90	$9.10	$11.60	$11.40	$11.80
White	82.90	98.40	82.60	75.60	94.60	113.50	118.30
Black-to-white ratio	0.07	0.03	0.17	0.12	0.12	0.10	0.10
Households with zero or negative net wealth (%)							
Black	34.1%	40.7%	31.5%	31.3%	27.4%	30.9%	29.4%
White	11.3	12.1	13.8	15.0	14.8	13.1	13.0
Black-to-white ratio	3.0	3.4	2.3	2.1	1.9	2.4	2.3
Average financial wealth**							
Black	$27.30	$27.90	$34.90	$26.30	$43.60	$46.10	$61.50
White	212.10	257.50	253.80	233.60	295.30	394.30	402.50
Black-to-white ratio	0.13	0.11	0.14	0.11	0.15	0.12	0.15
Median financial wealth							
Black	$0.00	$0.00	$0.20	$0.20	$1.40	$1.20	$0.30
White	23.10	31.20	25.40	22.40	43.60	44.90	36.10
Black-to-white ratio	0.00	0.00	0.01	0.01	0.03	0.03	0.01

* Wealth defined as net worth (household assets minus debts).
** Financial wealth is liquid and semi-liquid assets including mutual funds, trusts, retirement, and pensions.
Source: Wolff (2006).

nearly a third of U.S. households have wealth holdings that are so low they are likely to be extremely vulnerable to financial distress and insecurity.

Racial divide

The data presented so far mask an important feature of the wealth distribution: wealth is very unequally distributed by race—far more so than either wages or income. The historical legacy of the black economic experience shows up in profound racial wealth disparities, presented in **Table 5.5**. The first section of Table 5.5 shows average wealth by race. In 2004, the average black household had a net worth that was 19% of the average white household, which, despite some fluctuations in the meantime, is the same as it was in 1983. The second section of Table 5.5 shows median wealth holdings by race. In 2004, the median black household had a net worth of $11,800, 10% of the net worth of the median white household, which was $118,000. The reason the black-to-white ratio for median wealth is lower than the black-to-white ratio for average wealth is that there is somewhat more inequality in wealth among blacks than among whites—that is, the ratio of median-to-average wealth is higher for blacks than for whites.

When considering low net worth, the experience of black households again differs significantly from that of white households. In 2004, at 29.4%, 2.3 times as many black households had zero or negative net worth than did white households, at 13.0%. This measure had improved dramatically in the 1990s—from black households being 3.4 times as likely as white households to have zero or negative net worth in 1989 to 1.9 times as likely in 1998. This was due largely to the fact that there was a 13.3 percentage point decline in black households with zero or negative net worth, from 40.7% in 1989 to 27.4% in 1998. However, after 1998, the percent of black households with zero or negative net worth increased to 29.4% by 2004.

The last two sections of Table 5.5 show that black households were especially unlikely to hold financial assets such as stocks and bonds. (Specific asset holdings are discussed in depth in the next section.) In 2004, the average financial wealth of black households was only 15% of the average financial wealth of white households. The median financial wealth for black households was just $300, less than 1% of the corresponding figure for whites. Again, the reason the black-to-white ratio for median financial wealth is lower than the black-to-white ratio for average financial wealth is that there is somewhat more inequality in financial wealth among blacks than among whites—that is, the ratio of median-to-average financial wealth is higher for blacks than for whites.

To summarize, the data on net worth reveal a highly unequal distribution of wealth. A large share of the population has little or no net worth, while the wealthiest 20% of the population has consistently held over 80% of all wealth and the top 1% has consistently held at least a third. Current economic trends offer no reason to believe that these wealth disparities will lessen any time soon.

Assets

The preceding section summarized the overall distribution of net worth. The focus of the remainder of the chapter shifts to the two components of net worth—assets and liabilities.

Households hold a variety of assets, from houses and boats to stocks and bonds. The distribution of assets among income and wealth classes varies significantly by the type of asset. Some assets, such as stocks and bonds, are highly concentrated among a relatively small number of households; other assets, such as houses, are more widely held.

TABLE 5.6 Distribution of asset ownership across households, 2004

| | Percentage of all holdings of each asset | | | | |
Wealth class	Common stock excluding pensions*	All common stock**	Non-equity financial assets***	Housing equity	Net worth
Top 0.5%	29.5%	27.6%	38.8%	8.1%	25.3%
Next 0.5%	9.7	9.3	10.3	4.4	9.1
Next 4%	28.6	28.4	23.1	19.9	24.6
Next 5%	13.3	13.5	9.3	13.5	12.3
Next 10%	11.0	11.9	9.3	19.5	13.4
Bottom 80%	7.9	9.4	9.1	34.6	15.3
Total	100.0%	100.0%	100.0%	100.0%	100.0%

* Includes direct ownership of stock shares and indirect ownership through mutual funds and trusts.
** Includes direct ownership of stock shares and indirect ownership through mutual funds, trusts, and IRAs, Keogh plans, 401(k) plans, and other retirement accounts.
*** Includes direct ownership of financial securities and indirect ownership through mutual funds, trusts, and retirement accounts, and net equity in unincorporated businesses.

Source: Wolff (2006).

The differences in these distributions are strongly related to overall wealth. Wealthy households, for example, tend to hold a much higher percentage of their wealth in stocks and bonds, whereas less-affluent households typically hold most of their wealth in housing equity.

Table 5.6 shows the distribution across wealth classes of several types of household assets in 2004. The wealthiest 5% of households (the sum of the first three data rows in the table) owned about two-thirds of assets of all types except housing equity. Housing equity, compared to other assets, is more equitably distributed across wealth classes, but is still very skewed. Instead of two-thirds, the top 5% held about one-third (32.4%) of housing equity. The entire bottom 80% also held about one-third (34.6%) of housing equity. The bottom 80% held just 7.9% of stock excluding pensions, and that share only increases to 9.4% when stocks in pension funds are considered.

Stocks

As **Figure 5E** illustrates, the stock market has been on quite a roller coaster over the last 15 years. The inflation-adjusted value of the Standard & Poor's 500 index of stocks increased 234% between 1990 and 2000, then dropped by over a third between 2000 and 2003, and then regained over 60% of those losses from 2004 to 2007. The stock market boom of the 1990s, along with the bust of the early 2000s and the rebound

FIGURE 5E Growth of U.S. stock market, 1955-2007

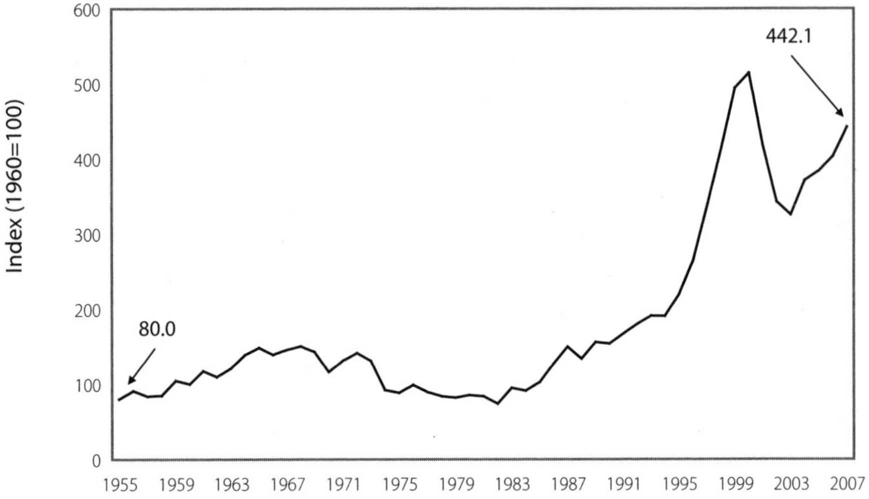

Source: Authors' analysis of the Economic Report of the President (2008) data.

that followed, have focused enormous media and public attention on the stock market. Data on stock ownership, however, show that the stock market, in practice, is of little or no direct financial importance to the large majority of U.S. households. Even in 1998, well into the stock market run-up, a majority of U.S. households had no stock holdings of any form, direct or indirect. (Households own stock directly when they buy shares in a particular company. Households own stock indirectly when they buy shares through a mutual fund that, in turn, holds a portfolio of stocks, or when household members make contributions to a 401(k)-style, defined-contribution pension plan that holds stocks for its beneficiaries.) In 2004, only 48.6% of households had stock holdings of any form, and only 34.9% of households had any stock holdings exceeding $6,000 (**Table 5.7**).

The top panel of **Table 5.8** provides a more detailed description of the distribution across wealth classes of stock ownership (both direct and indirect). Stock holdings for each wealth class increased on average between 1983 and 2001 and decreased on average between 2001 and 2004 (recall that the stock market collapsed between 2000 and 2003 and therefore the full impact was not yet evident in 2001). In 2004, the wealthiest 1% of households owned an average of $3.3 million in stocks (in 2004 dollars). The next 9% owned an average of $413,000. By comparison, the average stock holdings of the middle 20% of households was just $7,500, and the average for the bottom 40% was $1,400.

These data confirm that stock ownership is not very pervasive in the middle class. Of the $155,900 in average total assets held by the middle 20% of the wealth distribution, only $7,500—or 4.8%—was in stock. By comparison, the top 1% held an average of $15.3 million in assets, and 21.4% of that was in stock. **Figure 5F** shows the

TABLE 5.7 Share of households owning stock, 1989-2004

Stock holdings	1989	1992	1995	1998	2001	2004
Any stock holdings						
Direct holdings	13.1%	14.8%	15.2%	19.2%	21.3%	20.7%
Indirect holdings	24.7	28.4	30.2	43.4	47.7	44.0
Total	31.7	37.2	40.4	48.2	51.9	48.6
Stock holdings of $6,000 or more*						
Direct holdings	10.0%	11.4%	12.3%	13.6%	14.6%	13.5%
Indirect holdings	16.9	21.5	22.7	32.2	36.8	31.0
Total	22.6	27.3	28.8	36.3	40.1	34.9

* Constant 2003 dollars.

Source: Wolff (2006).

persistent and imbalanced distribution of stock market holdings by wealth class. Over the entire period from 1989 to 2004, the wealthiest 1% never held less than one third of total stock wealth, and the top 20% consistently held about 90% of all stock wealth.

Despite the collapse from 2000 to 2003, Figure 5E shows that the stock market still grew dramatically—by well over 100%—from 1989 to 2004. Unsurprisingly, given the unequal stock holdings at the beginning of the period, the growth was also distributed very unequally across wealth classes. **Figure 5G** shows the distribution of the growth of stock wealth from 1989 to 2004. There was almost no growth (0.5%) for the bottom 40%, and the middle 20% received only 1.2% of the rise in the overall value of stock holdings over the period. By comparison, 77.1% of the growth over the period went to the wealthiest 10% of households.

Stocks are also highly concentrated by household income. **Table 5.9** shows the share of all stock owned by households at different income levels in 2004. Predictably, higher income households were much more likely to own stocks. Households with incomes at or above $250,000 represented just 2.5% of all households, but 94.6% of these households owned some form of stock, and collectively they owned 44.0% of all stock. Comparatively, 28.3% of households made between $25,000 and $49,999, but only 41.8% of these households owned any form of stock and collectively they owned only 6.9% of all stock. Households with incomes above $100,000 held nearly three-quarters of all stock.

The concentration of stocks within upper income levels holds true even for stocks in retirement plans such as 401(k)s, where households with income above $100,000 hold 70% of the total. The main distributional difference between stock holdings in pension plans and other (direct) stock holdings is that pension assets are more evenly

TABLE 5.8 Average household assets and liabilities by wealth class, 1962-2004 (thousands of 2004 dollars)

Asset type	Top 1%	Next 9%	Next 10%	Next 20%	Middle 20%	Bottom 40%	Average
Stocks*							
1962	$2,791.8	$142.8	$15.9	$5.1	$1.3	$0.3	$44.4
1983	1,812.7	117.0	14.0	5.3	1.8	0.5	32.1
1989	1,368.3	150.3	29.5	10.3	4.3	0.7	33.8
1998	2,926.5	337.8	92.1	31.9	10.7	1.9	83.2
2001	3,806.1	546.4	140.6	44.0	12.8	2.0	113.4
2004	3,276.5	413.4	105.6	31.3	7.5	1.4	89.0
All other assets							
1962	$3,037.1	$524.4	$249.2	$138.5	$75.0	$17.8	$151.5
1983	6,976.6	905.5	366.1	188.3	92.7	19.5	251.5
1989	9,696.6	995.5	393.5	215.0	103.3	22.4	297.9
1998	9,226.1	957.5	384.0	209.9	113.1	27.6	285.1
2001	10,079.2	1,302.4	467.6	250.2	121.1	28.3	350.2
2004	12,060.6	1,524.7	573.7	305.8	148.4	35.2	420.5
Total debt							
1962	$206.2	$40.4	$29.9	$30.9	$30.6	$17.2	$27.6
1983	474.1	78.9	57.0	38.8	30.2	14.5	37.2
1989	517.0	105.3	56.9	51.4	39.4	27.8	49.4
1998	327.5	121.6	76.4	54.9	53.0	28.2	55.1
2001	347.5	130.5	85.3	64.6	53.9	27.2	58.1
2004	566.8	174.2	103.8	93.8	74.1	34.4	79.1
Net worth							
1962	$5,622.8	$626.8	$235.1	$112.7	$45.7	$0.9	$168.2
1983	8,315.2	943.6	323.0	154.8	64.3	5.4	246.4
1989	10,547.9	1,040.6	366.1	173.9	68.2	-4.7	282.3
1998	11,825.1	1,173.6	399.7	186.9	70.7	1.3	313.2
2001	13,537.8	1,718.4	523.0	229.6	80.0	3.1	405.5
2004	14,770.4	1,764.0	576.3	243.4	81.8	2.2	430.5

* All direct and indirect stock holdings.

Source: Wolff (2006).

FIGURE 5F Distribution of stock market wealth by wealth class, 1989-2004

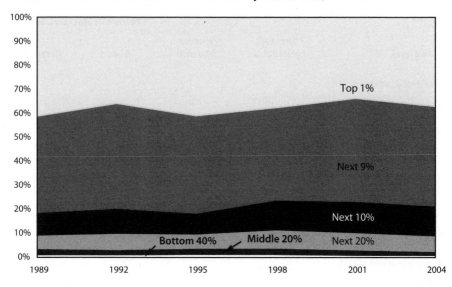

Source: Wolff (2006).

FIGURE 5G Distribution of growth in stock market holdings by wealth class, 1989-2004

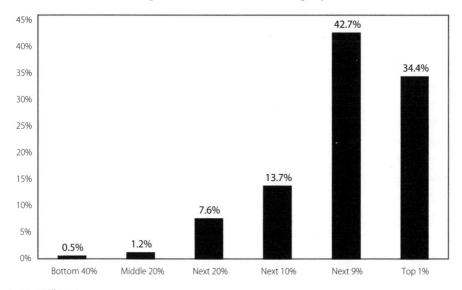

Source: Wolff (2006).

TABLE 5.9 Concentration of stock ownership by income level, 2004

Income level	Share of households	Percent who own	Percent of stocks owned	
			Shares	Cumulative
Publicly traded stock				
$250,000 or above	2.5%	67.7%	56.4%	56.4%
$100,000-249,999	13.6	44.9	22.9	79.4
$75,000-99,999	9.4	32.4	5.6	84.9
$50,000-74,999	17.4	25.1	8.3	93.3
$25,000-49,999	28.3	12.8	4.7	98.0
$15,000-24,999	13.7	8.3	0.9	98.9
Under $15,000	15.2	4.6	1.1	100.0
All	100.0	20.7	100.0	
Stocks in pension plans*				
$250,000 or above	2.5%	79.4%	25.5%	25.5%
$100,000-249,999	13.6	75.1	44.0	69.6
$75,000-99,999	9.4	62.5	10.5	80.0
$50,000-74,999	17.4	49.4	10.8	90.8
$25,000-49,999	28.3	31.0	7.3	98.1
$15,000-24,999	13.7	12.1	1.3	99.4
Under $15,000	15.2	5.8	0.6	100.0
All	100.0	38.0	100.0	
All stocks**				
$250,000 or above	2.5%	94.6%	44.0%	44.0%
$100,000-249,999	13.6	86.6	29.2	73.2
$75,000-99,999	9.4	77.5	7.8	81.0
$50,000-74,999	17.4	62.5	9.9	90.9
$25,000-49,999	28.3	41.8	6.9	97.8
$15,000-24,999	13.7	19.6	1.2	98.9
Under $15,000	15.2	11.8	1.1	100.0
All	100.0	48.6	100.0	

* All defined-contribution stock plans including 401(k) plans.
** All stock directly or indirectly held in mutual funds, IRAs, Keogh plans, and defined-contribution pension plans.

Source: Wolff (2006).

distributed *among high-income households*. The highest income group—households with an annual income above $250,000—controlled 56.4% of all publicly traded stock, while the second highest income group—households with an annual income from $100,000 to $249,999—controlled 22.9%. By comparison, the highest income group controlled 25.5% of stock holdings in pension plans, while the second highest income group controlled 44%. At the same time, the bottom three-fourths of households—those with annual incomes of $74,999 or less—held only 20% of all stock in pension plans (and only 15% of publicly traded stock).

This section has exposed the fallacy that all or even most American households are greatly invested in the stock market—either directly or indirectly through pension plans. Less than half of households have any stock holdings, and only about a third have stock holdings—either direct or indirect—that are worth more than $6,000. What the data show is that to a large extent, low- and moderate-income households depend on labor income alone to meet their financial obligations.

Home ownership

While much attention is paid to the ups and downs of the stock market, the fact is that housing equity is actually a far more important form of wealth for most households. The second section of Table 5.8, which shows the distribution of all non-stock assets by household wealth, makes this point indirectly. In 2004, the middle 20% of households

FIGURE 5H Home ownership rates, 1965-2007

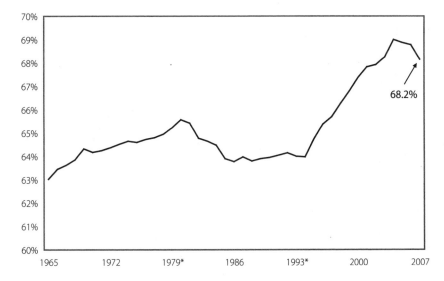

* Data for 1979, 1993, and 2002 have been adjusted to account for annual revisions.

Source: Authors' analysis of U.S. Census Bureau (2008b) data.

TABLE 5.10 Home ownership rates by race and income

Income/race	Home ownership rates						Percentage-point change			
	1979	1989	1999	2001	2005	2007	1979-89	1989-99	1999-2005	2005-07
By income*										
Top 25%	87.0%	84.5%	87.4%	88.0%	89.4%	–	-2.5	2.9	2.0	–
Next 25%	72.3	68.6	73.1	73.4	78.5	–	-3.6	4.5	5.4	–
Next 25%	56.2	56.3	57.8	59.7	63.3	–	0.0	1.5	5.5	–
Bottom 25%	46.2	46.4	49.4	50.9	51.0	–	0.2	2.9	1.6	–
All races	65.0%	64.0%	66.8%	67.8%	68.9%	68.1%	-1.0	2.8	2.1%	-0.8%
White	68.9%	69.3%	73.2%	74.3%	75.8%	75.2%	0.4	3.9	2.6%	-0.6%
Black	44.7	42.1	46.3	47.7	48.2	47.2	-2.6	4.2	1.9	-1.0
Hispanic	42.6	41.6	45.5	47.3	49.5	49.7	-1.0	3.9	4.0	0.2
Asian	–	–	53.1	53.9	60.1	60.0	–	–	7.0	-0.1

* Data only available through 2005.

Source: Authors' analysis of U.S. Bureau of the Census (2005, 2008a) data and the CPS March Supplement.

held $148,400 in non-stock assets, and only $7,500 in stocks. In other words, non-stocks assets—which are overwhelmingly housing equity—made up over 95% of their total wealth.

Census data graphed in **Figure 5H** show home ownership rates over time. The graph shows a dramatic decade-long run-up in home ownership from 64% in 1994 to 69% in 2004, and then the loss of about a fifth of that increase from 2004 to 2007—a decline that shows no signs of flattening out. The last time the trend fell that steeply was in the deep recession of the early 1980s. (The current housing crisis is discussed below.)

As with other measures of wealth, home ownership rates vary dramatically by demographic group. **Table 5.10** presents data collected through the biennial American Housing Survey on home ownership by income and race. Table 5.10 and **Figure 5I** show that in 2005 (the most recent data available by income), 89.4% of households in the top 25% of the income distribution were homeowners, compared to just 51.0% in the bottom 25%. Table 5.10 and **Figure 5J** also show that white households are much more likely than other households to own a home—in 2007, 75.2% of white households owned a home, whereas 47.2% of black households, 49.7% of Hispanic households, and 60.0% of Asian households owned a home. While all race/ethnicity groups made gains from the mid-1990s to 2005 and then experienced a decline or flattening from 2005 to 2007, black households experienced the largest recent drop—1 percentage point—from 2005 and 2007.

FIGURE 5I Home ownership rates by income, 2005

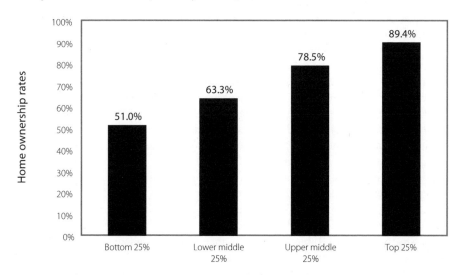

Source: Authors' analysis of U.S. Census Bureau (2005) data.

FIGURE 5J Home ownership rates by race, 1975-2007

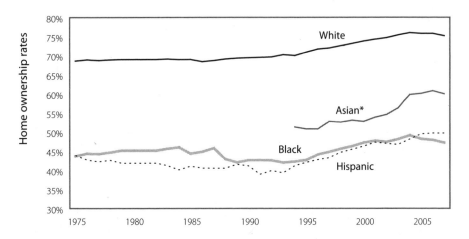

* Asian includes Native Hawaiian/Pacific Islander. Data are unavailable prior to 1994 for this population.

Note: Where data are unavailable from 1979 to 1982, they are substituted by the 1978/1983 average..

Source: U.S. Bureau of the Census (2008a) and the CPS March Supplement.

Retirement income adequacy

The concept of retirement adequacy is an important component of wealth. Expected retirement income is a key determinant of when (or even if) a worker will retire. A common test of retirement income adequacy is the ability in retirement to replace at least half of current income, based on expected pension, Social Security benefits, and returns on personal savings. **Table 5.11** shows the proportion of households that did not meet this test. In 2004, 27.2% of households headed by someone age 47 to 64 expected their retirement income to be inadequate by this measure.

Like other aspects of wealth, expected retirement adequacy was not uniformly distributed. African American or Hispanic households were more likely to expect to have low incomes in retirement—39% of these households expected to be unable to replace half of current income. By comparison, 24.1% of white non-Hispanic households expected to have inadequate means in retirement. Education also had a big impact on retirement security—almost half (47%) of the households where the household head had less than a high school degree expected to have inadequate retirement income, whereas only 21% of college grads faced that level of retirement insecurity. The second-to-last panel of Table 5.11 shows that retirement adequacy varied little by family status in 2004, but that over time households headed by single females have become more likely to expect retirement adequacy. The last panel of Table 5.11 shows that there were large differences by homeowner status, as homeowners were much less likely to expect inadequate retirement income.

TABLE 5.11 Retirement income inadequacy, 1989-2004

	Percent of households aged 47-64 with expected retirement income less than one-half of current income				
				Percentage-point change	
Group	1989	2001	2004	1989-2001	2001-04
All	30.5%	28.1%	27.2%	-2.3	-0.9
*By race/ethnicity**					
Non-Hispanic white	27.3%	25.4%	24.1%	-2.0	-1.3
African American or Hispanic	42.1	40.0	39.0	-2.1	-1.0
*By education***					
Less than high school	39.2%	29.2%	46.6%	-10.0	17.4
High school degree	24.7	29.0	28.8	4.3	-0.2
Some college	18.8	30.1	34.7	11.3	4.6
College degree or more	20.8	25.4	21.2	4.6	-4.2
By family status					
Married couple	26.5%	24.1%	26.6%	-2.4	2.5
Single male	22.6	26.5	29.0	3.9	2.5
Single female	43.8	39.0	27.7	-4.8	-11.3
By homeowner status					
Owns a home	24.9%	25.1%	22.5%	0.2	-2.6
Renter	49.8	40.1	44.4	-9.7	4.3

* Asian and other races are excluded from the table because of small sample sizes.
** Households are classified by the schooling level of the head of household.

Note: A 7% real return on assets is assumed for financial wealth and net worth. Households are classified by the age of the head of household. Retirement income is based on marketable wealth holdings and all expected pension and Social Security benefits.

Source: Wolff (2006).

Whether looking at stocks, homes, or retirement wealth, the distribution of assets is highly unequal. The wealthy own an extremely disproportionate share of all assets, especially financial assets such as stocks. Housing equity is, by far, the most important form of wealth held by typical American households. (The potential impact of the current crisis in the housing markets on the net worth of typical homeowners is addressed below.)

TABLE 5.12 Household debt by type, 1949-2007

		As a share of disposable income		
	All debt as a share of all assets	All debt*	Home mortgage**	Home equity loans***	Consumer credit
1949	6.2%	33.1%	19.7%	--	10.2%
1959	10.3	58.8	37.1	--	16.3
1973	12.6	66.3	39.1	--	19.7
1979	13.8	73.5	46.1	--	19.8
1989	14.8	85.8	56.6	5.01%	20.1
2000	15.1	102.8	67.0	5.67	24.2
2007	19.9	141.3	103.3	11.00	25.1
Average annual percentage-point change					
1949-59	0.4	2.6	1.7	--	0.6
1959-73	0.2	0.5	0.1	--	0.2
1973-79	0.2	1.2	1.2	--	0.0
1979-89	0.1	1.2	1.1	--	0.0
1989-2000	0.0	1.5	0.9	0.1	0.4
2000-07	0.7	5.5	5.2	0.8	0.1

* Includes subcategories not listed here, including security credit and commercial mortgages.
** Includes loans made under home equity lines of credit and home equity loans secured by junior liens.
*** Data for 1989 refer to 1990.

Source: Federal Reserve Board (2008a).

Liabilities

Assets are one side of the balance sheet that tallies net worth; the other side is liabilities, or debts. It is important to note that debt is not *necessarily* a problem for households. In fact, access to credit generally represents a tremendous economic opportunity for households, since they can use it to buy houses, cars, invest in education, and other big-ticket consumer goods and necessities that provide services over many years. Debt can also be used to cope with short-term economic setbacks such as unemployment or illness. Debt becomes a burden only when required debt payments begin to crowd out other economic obligations or opportunities.

As **Table 5.12** indicates, in 2007 the total value of all forms of household debt was at its highest on record—nearly 20% of all assets. All debt, as a share of annual disposable personal income, was also at its highest at 141.3%. Mortgage debt has greatly

FIGURE 5K Debt as a percentage of disposable income, 1947-2007

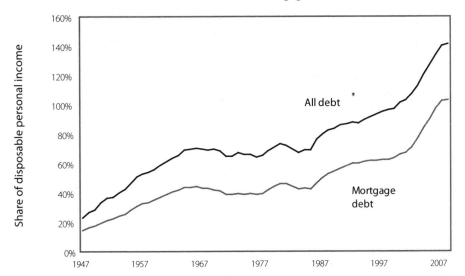

All debt and mortgage debt

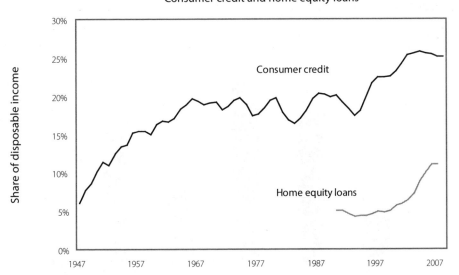

Consumer credit and home equity loans

* Data for home equity loans are unavailable prior to 1990.

Source: Authors' analysis of Federal Reserve Board (2008a) data.

increased over time and was at 103.3% of annual disposable personal income in 2007, while consumer credit debt (mostly credit card debt and auto loans) was one-quarter of disposable income. The historical trajectory of debt levels and the notable highs reached in 2007 are depicted in **Figure 5K**. The top graph shows that all debt rose from about 25% of disposable income at the end of World War II to over 60% by the early 1960s. Overall debt levels then remained roughly constant through the mid-1980s, when they began to increase rapidly again. By 2007, overall debt was at 141% of disposable income. In 1947 mortgage debt was about 14% of disposable income, but by 2007 that share had increased to 106%. Furthermore, as home ownership rates and home values increased, so did home equity loans, as shown in the bottom half of Figure 5K. The steep growth rate in home equity loans indicates that households were increasingly spending their accumulated equity rather than saving it.

Table 5.12 and Figure 5K show that debt is a more important feature of the household economy than at any time in modern history. Over the last decade especially, many American households have become dangerously overleveraged. As earlier chapters have shown, wages and income have largely stagnated, and without being able to count on these means for maintaining living standards, many families have taken advantage of often extremely low interest rates to finance consumption through debt. More families than ever before now live with the insecurity of knowing that a financial emergency such as a serious illness, loss of employment, or even an increase in interest rates could mean being unable to maintain debt repayments. For many families,

FIGURE 5L Distribution of growth in debt, 1989-2004

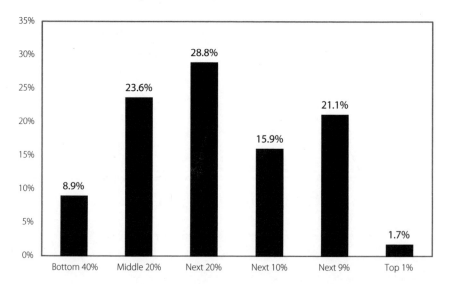

Source: Wolff (2006).

the bursting of the housing bubble—and the associated decline in the value of their homes—has been just that financial emergency. The housing meltdown is further discussed below.

Table 5.12 and Figure 5K show data at the aggregate level. The aggregate data, however, mask the distribution of debt, presented in the third section of Table 5.8. The debt distribution has several striking features. First, debt is more equally distributed than assets or net worth. In 2004, for example, the average household in the top 1% had a net worth over 180 times greater than that of the average household in the middle 20%. In the same year, however, the average debt held by the top 1% was about seven-and-a-half times greater than the average for the middle 20%. Second, for typical households, debt levels were high compared to the value of assets. In 2004, the average outstanding debt of households in the middle 20% was $74,100. This debt level was about 10 times greater than the corresponding $7,500 average for stock holdings and about 50% of the total value of all other assets, including the family home.

Figure 5L shows how the total increase in debt between 1989 and 2004 was distributed across wealth classes. The middle 20% of households on the wealth distribution acquired 23.6% of all debt growth from 1989 to 2004, while the next 20%—those between the 60th and 80th percentile on the wealth distribution—acquired 28.8% of total growth in debt over this period. The wealthiest 1% of households, on the other hand, acquired only 1.7% of all debt between 1989 and 2004.

TABLE 5.13 Financial obligations ratio, 1980-2007 (as a percent of disposable personal income)

	Renters	Homeowners		
	Total	*Total*	*Mortgage*	*Consumer*
1980	24.2%	13.7%	8.3%	5.4%
1989	25.0	15.3	9.9	5.4
1995	26.2	15.0	9.6	5.4
2000	29.8	15.5	9.2	6.3
2007	25.9	18.0	11.7	6.4
Percentage-point change				
1980-89	0.8	1.6	1.6	0.1
1989-2000	4.8	0.2	-0.7	0.9
2000-07	-3.8	2.5	2.5	0.0

Source: Federal Reserve Board (2008a).

Debt service

As stated above, debt is not necessarily a problem—on the contrary, access to credit can represent great economic opportunities. Problems arise, however, when debt payments begin to crowd out other economic obligations. A useful measure for assessing debt burden is the financial obligations ratio—the ratio of debt payment (including minimum required payments on mortgages, consumer debt, automobile leases, and rent) to disposable personal income. **Table 5.13** gives the average household financial obligations ratio separately for renters and homeowners. In 2007, renters spent an average of 25.9% of their disposable on minimum debt payments, whereas homeowners spent an average of 18.0% (11.7% on mortgages and 6.4% on consumer debt). Over the full period from 1980 to 2007, the financial obligations ratio for renters changed little—increasing 1.8 percentage points, or 7.4%, over this period. For homeowners, the ratio increased from 13.7% in 1980 to 18.0% in 2007—an increase of 4.3 percentage points, or 31.7%. This increase was mostly driven by mortgages. Since 2000 alone, mortgage payments as a share of disposable income increased on average from 9.2% to 11.7%—an increase of 2.5 percentage points, or 27.1%.

It is important to note that the financial obligation ratio does not capture many additional costs incurred by low-income families who find themselves needing to turn to nontraditional lending services (such as pawn shops) and rapid-cash providers (such as non-bank check-cashing services). These entities often charge extraordinary fees compared to traditional lending institutions and constitute significant sources of debt service expenses for many low-income families.

TABLE 5.14 Household debt service as a share of household income, by income percentile, 1989-2004

Household income	1989	1998	2001	2004	Percentage-point change	
					1989-2004	2001-04
Top fifth						
Top 10%	8.7%	10.3%	8.1%	9.3%	0.6	1.2
Next 10%	15.7	16.8	17.0	17.3	1.6	0.3
Bottom four-fifths						
Fourth	16.9%	19.1%	16.8%	18.5%	1.6	1.7
Middle	16.3	18.6	17.1	19.4	3.1	2.3
Second	13.0	16.5	15.8	16.7	3.7	0.9
Lowest	14.1	18.7	16.1	18.2	4.1	2.1
Average	12.9%	14.9%	12.9%	14.4%	1.5	1.5

Source: Bucks, Kennickell, and Moore (2006).

Another measure of household debt service—the debt service ratio—is reported by income percentile in **Table 5.14**. Like the financial obligations ratio, the debt service ratio is a ratio of minimum debt payment to disposable personal income. The difference between these two measures is that the debt service ratio is narrower—it does not include, for example, rental payments, but instead only includes payments on mortgage and consumer debt. Table 5.14 shows that in 2004, households in the top 10% of household income spent 9.3% of their income meeting the minimum required debt payments, compared to 19.4% of income for middle-income households. Those at the top had the lowest debt service and the smallest increase over the 1989-2004 period. The bottom three-fifths of households saw the largest increase over the 1989-2004 period.

Hardship

Debt service payments equal to more than 40% of household income constitute a level of debt generally considered to represent economic hardship. **Table 5.15** looks at such hardship by income percentiles. In all years, high debt burden was negatively associated with income. In 2004, just 1.8% of households in the top 10% had high debt burdens, whereas that number was 13.7% for households in the middle 20% and 27.0% for households in the bottom 20%. Note that data in this table include renters but not rental payments as debt, which suppresses these numbers, particularly at the lower end of the income scale.

TABLE 5.15 Share of households with high debt burdens,* by income percentile, 1989-2004

Percentile of household income	1989	1998	2001	2004	Percentage-point change 1989-2004	Percentage-point change 2001-04
Top fifth						
Top 10%	1.9%	2.8%	2.0%	1.8%	-0.1	-0.2
Next 10%	3.4	3.5	3.5	2.4	-1.0	-1.1
Bottom four-fifths						
Fourth	5.8%	9.8%	6.5%	7.1%	1.3	0.6
Middle	11.0	15.8	12.3	13.7	2.7	1.4
Second	14.5	18.3	16.6	18.6	4.1	2.0
Lowest	24.6	29.9	29.3	27.0	2.4	-2.3
Average	10.0%	13.6%	11.8%	12.2%	2.2	-1.4

* A high debt burden is a ratio of debt to income greater than 40%.

Source: Bucks, Kennickell, and Moore (2006).

TABLE 5.16 Share of households late paying bills, by income percentile, 1989-2004

Percentile of household income	1989	1998	2001	2004	Percentage-point change 1989-2004	2001-04
Top fifth						
Top 10%	2.4%	1.6%	1.3%	0.3%	-2.1	-1.0
Next 10%	1.1	3.9	2.6	2.3	1.2	-0.3
Bottom four-fifths						
Fourth	5.9%	5.9%	4.0%	7.1%	1.2	3.1
Middle	5.0	10.0	7.9	10.4	5.4	2.5
Second	12.2	12.3	11.7	13.8	1.6	2.1
Lowest	18.2	12.9	13.4	15.9	-2.3	2.5
Average	7.3%	8.1%	7.0%	8.9%	1.6	1.9

Source: Bucks, Kennickell, and Moore (2006).

FIGURE 5M Consumer bankruptcies per 1,000 adults

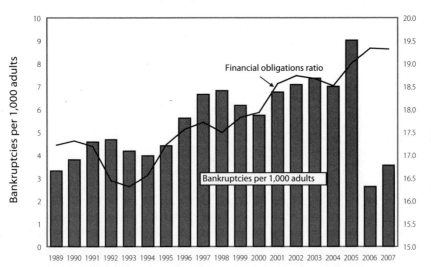

Source: Authors' analysis of American Bankruptcy Institute (2008) data, Federal Reserve Board (2008b) data, and the Economic Report of the President (2008).

Table 5.16 shows another measure of the impact of debt on economic hardship: the share of households, by income level, that were late paying bills. In 2004, about 9% of all households were 60 days or more late in paying at least one bill. Not surprisingly, the share of households behind on their bills was strongly related to income. Very few (0.3%) of the highest income group were late in paying bills, while 15.9% in the lowest income range were behind on at least one bill. Table 5.16 also illustrates a rise in the percentage of late-paying households between 2001 and 2004 for the lowest four-fifths of the income groups.

The ultimate indicator of debt-related difficulties is personal bankruptcy. **Figure 5M** graphs the rate of personal bankruptcies from 1989 through 2007, along with the average financial obligations ratio (including both renters and homeowners). Up to 2005, the rate of bankruptcies steadily increased as the debt burden grew. In 2005, nine out of every 1,000 adults declared personal bankruptcy. In October 2005, however, new bankruptcy laws went into effect that made filing for bankruptcy more complicated and dramatically more expensive. As a result, the number of bankruptcy filings plummeted 70% from 2005 to 2006—from 2 million filers to 600,000 filers. Part of this difference can undoubtedly be attributed to a run-up in filings just prior to the date the new regulations were implemented, but looking between 2004 and 2007—i.e., leaving out the years around the time of the legislation—the number of filings still dropped by about half. The financial obligations ratio, however, *increased* by 4.3% over this same period, implying that the drop in bankruptcy filings was indeed due to the new bankruptcy legislation and not to any structural declines in the debt burden. Research has shown

FIGURE 5N Home prices and home ownership rates, 1989-2008q2

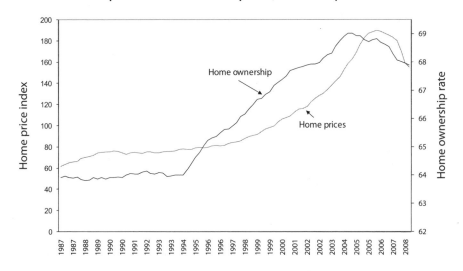

Source: Authors' analysis of S&P/Case-Shiller (2008) and U.S. Census Bureau (2008b) data.

that, even before the new bankruptcy laws, severe misfortune preceded the vast majority of personal bankruptcies, with more than half of bankruptcies resulting from medical emergencies and a large share of the rest resulting from either job loss or divorce. Figure 5M shows that the new bankruptcy laws have made it much more difficult for families in a financial crisis to get out from under their debts and make a fresh start.

The housing meltdown

So far, this section covering liabilities has investigated debt levels, debt service (i.e., debt payments), and debt-related hardship, examining these measures both on average and as they are distributed across wealth classes. Housing-related issues have arisen many times in this discussion; Table 5.12 and Figure 5K show that mortgage debt and home equity loans as a percentage of disposable income have dramatically increased, especially since the late 1990s, and Table 5.13 shows that the sharp increase in the financial obligations ratio (the ratio of debt payment to disposable income) for homeowners between 2000 and 2007 was driven almost entirely by mortgages. This section focuses directly on housing issues.

Figure 5N shows the increase in home prices from 1987 to 2007 as measured by the Standard & Poor's/Case-Shiller U.S. National Home Price Index. The dramatic run-up in home prices from the mid-1990s to 2005 is clear, with double-digit or near-double-digit annual increases from mid-2002 to 2005. The growth in home prices reached its peak in the first quarter of 2005, at an annual increase of 15.7%. After that, however, the rate of increase plummeted, and in the first quarter of 2007, the country logged its first annual decrease in home prices since 1991. Home prices experienced

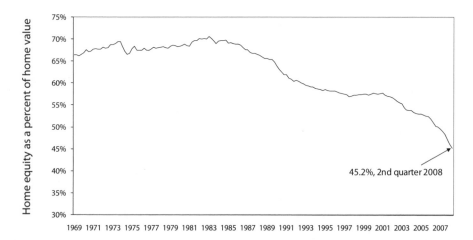

FIGURE 50   Homeowners' equity as a percent of home value, 1969-2008q2

Source: Authors' analysis of Federal Reserve Board (2008a) data.

a 18.2% decrease from their peak level (in the second quarter of 2006) to the second quarter of 2008, and the decline shows no signs of easing. The bursting of the housing bubble has enormous implications for the home equity wealth of homeowners.

The value of a home is defined as the current market value—i.e., its price, or how much the home would sell for if it were put on the market. Home equity is the value of a home minus the outstanding balances of mortgages (including home equity loans). **Figure 5O** shows the ratio of homeowners' equity to the value of their homes—i.e., the percent of home value that homeowners own outright. After hovering between 67% and 70% until the late 1980s, this ratio began a descent that was particularly steep starting in the first quarter of 2001. This means that as home prices were logging double-digit annual increases in the early-to-mid 2000s, the percent of home value that homeowners owned outright was actually *decreasing*. This was driven largely by an increase in home equity loans (as shown in Figure 5K). Believing home prices would continue to rise, homeowners used their accumulated equity to finance spending. Unsurprisingly, as housing prices began to fall in the second half of 2006, home equity as a percent of home value fell sharply, dropping 5.8 percentage points from the second quarter of 2006 to the second quarter of 2008. For the first time on record, the percent of home value that homeowners own outright has dropped below 50%—meaning that banks now own more of the nation's housing stock than people do. As discussed earlier in this chapter, home equity is the primary source of wealth for a large majority of households, and therefore declines in home equity have devastating effects on the economic security of many, if not most, homeowners.

Another reason home equity was dropping as a share of home value even as home prices were skyrocketing was that to get into the housing market, an unprecedented number of buyers were making home purchases with small (or zero) down payments. Figure 5N plots home ownership rates along with home prices. The increase in home ownership is strongly correlated with housing prices, as families scrambled to get into the housing market during the run-up in home prices due to a widespread belief that home prices would continue their steep ascent and thus buying a home would be a smart investment, and that waiting to buy a home would mean soon being priced out of the market. Many of these families had various credit risk factors, such as low income, a small down payment, or a troubled or nonexistent credit history, and therefore they assumed mortgages at higher than market interest rates (subprime mortgages) and/or at adjustable rates that would reset much higher, believing they would later be able to refinance at more favorable terms. However, once housing prices began to drop, refinancing became more difficult, homeowners began to see their home equity fall, and mortgage delinquencies began to climb.

Figure 5P shows the volume of prime and subprime mortgage originations from 2001 to 2006. The percent of new mortgages that were subprime went from 10% in 2001 to 29% just five years later. A large chunk of this increase was due to an increase in predatory lending practices that was left largely unchecked by federal and state regulatory authorities during the booming housing market. **Figure 5Q** shows the percent of subprime mortgages by race and ethnicity in 2006; blacks were twice as likely as whites to assume subprime mortgages, and Hispanics were 1.8 times as likely. Since

FIGURE 5P Volume of prime and subprime mortgage originations, 2001-06

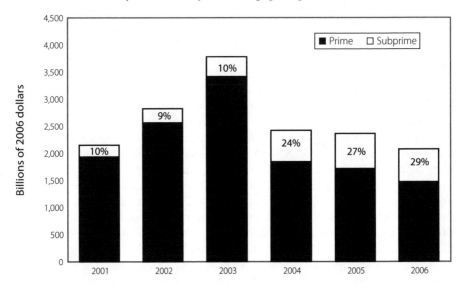

Source: Leigh and Huff (2007).

FIGURE 5Q Subprime share of loans for home purchase by race, 2006

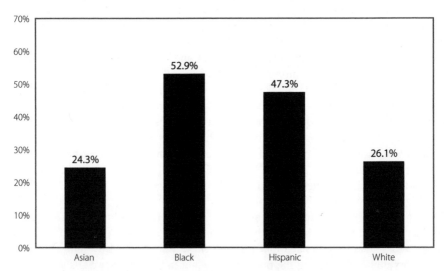

Source: Leigh and Huff (2007).

FIGURE 5R Foreclosures per 1,000 owner-occupied households, 2005-August 2008

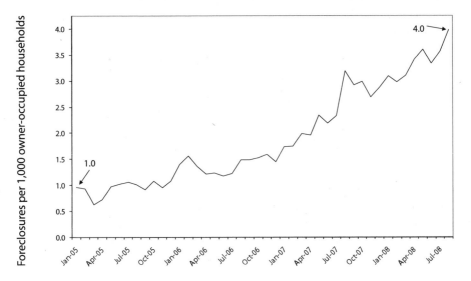

Source: Authors' analysis of RealtyTrac (2008) and Bureau of the Census (2008b) data.

homeowners with subprime mortgages are much more likely than other homeowners to face foreclosure, this figure implies that a much higher proportion of black and Hispanic homeowners are likely to lose their homes—and any equity they had there—during the current housing crisis.

Figure 5R shows the number of foreclosure filings per 1,000 owner-occupied households from January 2005, near the peak of the boom, to August 2008. In January 2005, one out of every 1,000 owner-occupied households faced a foreclosure filing. By August 2008, however, that number had quadrupled, such that four out of every 1,000 owner-occupied households faced a foreclosure filing—one in every 250 owner-occupied households. This was equivalent to over 300,000 households, which translates into 3.6 million households annually. Without government measures to guarantee some security to vulnerable homeowners, millions more may be faced with the loss of their homes.

The housing bubble—ignored by central bankers who did nothing to moderate its expansion—has burst, causing millions of people to lose their homes, tens of millions to see most of their savings disappear as falling house prices eliminate the equity in their homes, and a profound economic slowdown. This is the second recession in this decade to be caused by the bursting of an obvious speculative asset bubble (the first was the recession of 2001, which was caused by the collapse of the dot-com bubble). The question of what the Federal Reserve Board should do in the future to acknowledge and deal with bubbles before they cause an economic crisis should now be of the utmost importance.

Conclusion

The data presented here establish that the distribution of wealth is highly unequal—much more so than the distribution of wages and income that were the focus of earlier chapters. Stocks and other financial assets are particularly concentrated among the very wealthy, but housing equity also varies substantially by income and race. There is also enormous variation in households' adequacy of retirement savings.

The biggest story in the wealth picture since 2001, however, is the huge run-up in debt as a percentage of disposable income, fueled by increases in mortgages and home equity loans. Mounting debt squeezed the net worth of the typical household and put economic strains on a large percentage of low- and middle-income families. As housing prices collapse, the loss of home equity on top of large debt burdens will be an enormous issue for many homeowners. As this chapter has shown, for the vast majority of homeowners, home equity is the main source of wealth. For many homeowners approaching retirement, a decline in home equity means the loss of retirement security. There has also been a sharp increase in the number of homeowners of all ages who are drawing down or even liquidating 401(k) accounts to prevent foreclosure. The extent of the effects of the housing bubble on wealth levels of the typical homeowner remains to be seen, but high average debt levels along with plunging home prices suggest that the damage may be severe and long-lasting.

CHAPTER 6

Poverty
Growth failed to reach low-income families

Other chapters discussed income, wealth, and mobility trends affecting families of all income classes. This chapter focuses exclusively on families with low incomes.

The first challenge in this analysis is definitional. Dividing lines between income groups are, of course, somewhat arbitrary, and there are many ways to define "low income." The most common definition in American income analysis uses the official poverty lines of the U.S. government. While there is some value to this measure—it is consistent over time, and many useful time series employ the official measure—it is widely considered to be an inadequate measure of the concept of poverty.

The concept of poverty, or inadequate income to meet the basic needs given societal norms, involves two basic measurement challenges: defining income and defining the threshold below which families are judged to be poor. This chapter will present measures using various alternative definitions of both income and poverty thresholds. For example, some of the evidence this chapter tracks uses twice the official poverty line as a threshold. While this measure will lead to higher shares of low-income persons compared to the official measure, evidence on basic-needs family budgets presented below suggests it is a much more realistic measure of material well-being.

This chapter also presents measures that adjust income in common sense ways. For example, the official measure ignores the value of food stamps, a near-cash benefit received by some low-income families. Some of the analysis in this chapter corrects that, adding the cash value of this benefit back into income. Better measures also subtract taxes paid and add tax credits, since poverty is best understood as a post-tax measure (because families provide for themselves with post-tax income).

Analyzing both the official series—enhanced by a broad set of better, alternative measures—establishes a number of revealing facts about poverty in America:

- Under the official poverty measure, 12.5% of the population, over 37 million people (including 13.3 million children), were poor in 2007. But under an updated, comprehensive measure that corrects the shortcomings of the official measure, many millions more people would be classified as poor. In 2006, the poverty rate was 17.7%, compared to 12.3% under the official measure. That is an extra 16 million poor persons, compared to the official undercount.

- Under either an official or more accurate alternative measure, a larger share of the population was poor or low-income in 2006 than in 2000, despite the economic recovery that occurred over those years. While the 2000s business cycle was not the first in which poverty increased (poverty rose over the 1980s cycle, too), the increase is especially problematic because it occurred despite significantly faster productivity growth than in earlier periods.

- An analysis of the factors responsible for the increase in poverty in the 2000s suggests that greater inequality of income explains almost all of the full percentage-point increase.

- The backsliding against poverty in the 2000s is most notable among the least advantaged, who happened to be the same groups that made the most progress in the 1990s. One particularly disheartening example is young (less than six years old) African American children. Almost half were officially poor in 1995, going down to one-third in 2000. That share has since climbed back up to 39.5%.

- Similarly, the poverty of mother-only families increased significantly over the 2000s. Evidence regarding their incomes and work in the paid labor market suggests that the anti-poverty safety net in the United States has been less counter-cyclical, that is, less effective in reducing economic hardship when the economy and job market are underperforming.

- As low-income policy has come to depend more on paid work as the main pathway out of poverty, the quality of jobs in the low-wage labor market, along with work-supports (public benefits tied to work), have become more important determinants of poverty outcomes. (The fact that one-fourth of the labor force earns low wages by one widely used measure thus poses a binding constraint on progress against low incomes.)

The official poverty measure

The official poverty rate in 2007 (the latest data) was 12.5%, meaning that 37.3 million persons lived in families with incomes below the poverty threshold for their family size.

Most poverty analysts strongly believe that the official poverty statistics are inadequate to the task of determining who is poor in America. The thresholds used to determine poverty status were developed almost half a century ago, and have been updated only for inflation. Thus, they fail to reflect how changes in living standards over half a century are reflected in family expenditures. As the median income has risen over time, for example, the poverty thresholds have lagged behind, meaning that, by definition, the poor are falling ever further below the middle class. In 1960, the poverty line for a family of four was about half of median family income; now it is less than a third (about 30%).

Spending patterns have changed over time, too. For example, thanks to both policy changes and evolving norms, more family members work in the paid labor market now than in the past, and so families are incurring greater work-related expenditures. Many analysts believe that such costs, most notably child care, should be subtracted from the income of working families when determining poverty.

The poverty measure also fails to account for important changes in tax and transfer policy. Because official poverty status is determined using pretax income, the measure fails to capture the poverty-reducing impact of expansions in the earned income tax credit (EITC), a more than $40 billion wage subsidy program targeted at the working poor. Other objections include the failure to account for regional differences in the cost of living and the failure to count out-of-pocket expenditures on health care.

In short, the official measure is widely criticized for inadequately representing *both* needs and income. (This chapter offers a comprehensive new measure that finds a much higher poverty rate when using the most up-to-date methods.)

This is not surprising, considering the current official thresholds. In 2007, for example, a single parent with two children was poor if the family income (before taxes but counting cash transfers like welfare benefits) was below $16,705; for two parents with two children, the income threshold was $21,027. But detailed studies of family budgets, which take into account all expenses that families must incur to live safely while meeting their basic needs, show income needs of about *twice* that amount. For example, the Economic Policy Institute calculates basic, "no-frills" budgets for low-income, working families in various cities. The median budget for a family of four with two children was $44,600 in 2008; for a single parent with two children, the budget was $38,500.

Yet despite all these criticisms, the official measure has some utility in studying poverty. First, it has a long history, and many informative time series use that metric. Second, while the official statistics omit many families whose incomes are insufficient to meet their basic needs, the statistics still provide information about the most economically disadvantaged families. Third, presenting poverty analysis alongside twice-poverty analysis (the share and number of persons with family incomes below twice the poverty threshold for their family types; e.g., for a family of four with two children, this threshold is about $42,000 in 2007), provides a more complete picture of the share of Americans facing income constraints.

Figure 6A and **Table 6.1** show the long-term trends in both poverty and twice poverty. The two trends are similar, although twice poverty tends to be slightly more responsive to the business cycle; this is probably the case because, as they move higher up the income scale, families tend to be more attached to the workforce and thus have incomes that are more responsive to the economic cycle. The large decline in poverty rates over the 1960s was due both to economic factors discussed below and the

FIGURE 6A Poverty and twice-poverty rate, 1959-2006

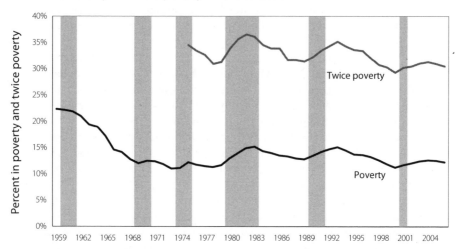

Note: Periods of recession are shaded.

Source: U.S. Census Bureau. For detailed information on figure sources, see Figure Notes.

significant expansion of Social Security benefits, which helped reduce poverty among the elderly by 20 percentage points between 1959 and 1979.

Once this long slide ended in the early 1970s, poverty rates became more insensitive to economic expansions. For example, Table 6.1 shows that poverty rates rose slightly, by about 1 point, between 1979 and 1989, while twice poverty was essentially unchanged. The latter 1990s, however, serve as an instructive exception and are investigated throughout the chapter. Poverty fell by 2.5 percentage points between 1995 and 2000, and twice poverty fell by 4.3 points. Almost 7 million persons were lifted above the twice-poverty threshold in these years.

Poverty trends in the 2000s, however, tell a much different and much less sanguine story. Despite the relatively mild recession of 2001 (at least in terms of duration and GDP decline), poverty rose consistently from 2001 to 2004, was little changed in 2005, and fell 0.3 percentage points in 2006, only to rise again slightly, to 12.5% in 2007. Assuming that 2007 was the peak year of the 2000s business cycle, that leaves the poverty rate higher at the end of the cycle than at the beginning. Given the rise of joblessness in 2008, it is very likely poverty could rise as high as 13% in 2008 and higher in 2009, as unemployment is likely to continue to rise that year as well.

Thus, much as in the 1980s cycle, economic growth failed to reach the bottom of the income scale, or as is commonly noted in such cases: "the rising tide lifted the yachts, not the rowboats." There is, however, an important and notable difference between the economies of 1980s and that of the 2000s, as shown in **Figure 6B**. Between 1979 and 1989, when poverty actually rose by 1.1 points, productivity growth was rela-

TABLE 6.1 Percent and number of persons in poverty and twice poverty, 1959-2007

Year	Poverty rate	Number in poverty (000)	Twice poverty rate	Number in twice poverty (000)
1959	22.4%	39,490	n/a	n/a
1967	14.2	27,769	n/a	n/a
1973	11.1	22,973	n/a	n/a
1979	11.7	26,072	31.3%	69,769
1989	12.8	31,528	31.4	77,241
1995	13.8	36,425	33.6	88,614
2000	11.3	31,581	29.3	81,731
2007	12.5	37,276	30.5	91,103
Percentage-point changes				
1959-79	-10.7	-13,418	n/a	n/a
1979-89	1.1	5,456	0.1	7,473
1989-2000	-1.5	53	-2.1	4,489
1995-2000	-2.5	-4,844	-4.3	-6,884
2000-07	1.2	5,695	1.2	9,373

Source: U.S. Census Bureau.

tively slow, increasing by 1.4% per year. But in the 2000s, productivity grew at a much faster annual rate of 2.5%. This extra percent per year means there was much more income created per hour worked; had more of that extra income flowed to the lower end of the income scale, poverty would surely have fallen in the 2000s. In this regard, the 2000s result can be viewed as a worse outcome because the potential for poverty reduction was greater than in the 1980s.

Racial and ethnic differences in poverty rates

Table 6.2 and **Figure 6C** show persistent differences in poverty rates by race and ethnicity. Given their lower income (see Chapter 1), poverty rates for minorities are consistently higher than those of whites. The rate for African Americans, for example, was at least three times that of whites through 1989. However, poverty among blacks and Hispanics was much more responsive than that of whites to the faster and more broadly distributed income growth during the 1990s—and particularly during the latter 1990s full-employment period—and by 2000 the poverty rate for blacks was their lowest on record. The importance of this period of tight labor markets, and their poverty-reducing impact, is a theme returned to throughout the chapter.

FIGURE 6B Change in poverty and productivity, 1979-89 and 2000-07

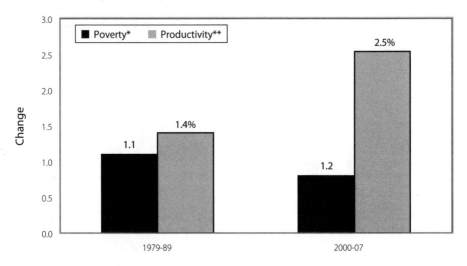

* Percentage-point change.
** Annualized percent change.

Source: Authors' analysis of U.S. Census Bureau and Bureau of Labor Statistics data.

FIGURE 6C Poverty rates by race/ethnicity, 1973-2006

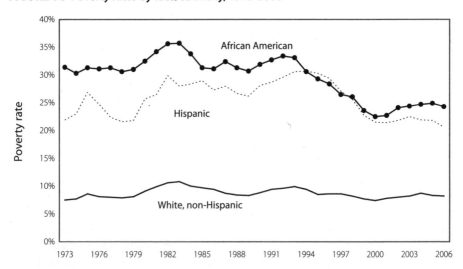

Source: U.S. Census Bureau.

TABLE 6.2 Persons in poverty, by race/ethnicity, 1959-2007

Year	Total	White	Black	Hispanic
1959	22.4%	18.1%	n/a	n/a
1967	14.2	11.0	39.3%	n/a
1973	11.1	8.4	31.4	21.9%
1979	11.7	9.0	31.0	21.8
1989	12.8	10.0	30.7	26.2
1995	13.8	11.2	29.3	30.3
2000	11.3	9.5	22.5	21.5
2007	12.5	10.5	24.5	21.5
Percentage-point changes				
1959-79	-10.7	-9.1	n/a	n/a
1979-89	1.1	1.0	-0.3	4.4
1989-2000	-1.5	-0.5	-8.2	-4.7
1989-95	1.0	1.2	-1.4	4.1
1995-2000	-2.5	-1.7	-6.8	-8.8
2000-07	1.2	1.0	2.0	0.0

Source: U.S. Census Bureau.

Once again, the 2000s reflect very different poverty dynamics than the 1990s. Whereas African American poverty fell faster than white poverty in the 1990s, it rose more quickly in the 2000s (2 points for blacks compared to 1 for whites). Interestingly, poverty for Hispanic workers was flat in the 2000s, the only racial/ethnic group to not lose ground by this measure. One probable cause of this difference relates to the housing boom in the 2000s, as Hispanics were disproportionately employed in that sector. Related trends in poverty by immigration status are examined below (immigrants are disproportionately represented among Hispanics).

Child and family poverty

Consistent research has revealed the life-altering disadvantages of an economically deprived childhood. Children that grow up poor are more likely to develop significant and lasting cognitive and physical deficits compared to non-poor children. In 2007, 18% or about 13 million of the nation's children (persons less than age 18) were officially poor (**Table 6.3**); as described below, an improved, updated poverty measure finds higher children poverty rates (21.4% in 2006). Again, rates are much higher among minorities, with about a third of African American children and 29% of Hispanic children living in poverty.

Among children under six, for whom the damage inflicted by poverty is particularly severe, the rates are consistently higher than the overall child rates. In 2007, about 20% of young children were poor, though the rate was almost double for black children, and almost 10 points higher—29%—for Hispanics.

TABLE 6.3 Percent of children in poverty, by race, 1979-2007

Year	Total	White	Black	Hispanic
Children under 18				
1979	16.4%	11.8%	41.2%	28.0%
1989	19.6	14.8	43.7	36.2
1995	20.8	16.2	41.9	40.0
2000	16.2	13.1	31.2	28.4
2007	18.0	14.9	34.5	28.6
Percentage-point changes				
1979-89	3.2	3.0	2.5	8.2
1989-2000	-3.4	-1.7	-12.5	-7.8
1989-95	1.2	1.4	-1.8	3.8
1995-2000	-4.6	-3.1	-10.7	-11.6
2000-07	1.8	1.8	3.3	0.2
Children under 6				
1979	18.1%	13.3%	43.6%	29.2%
1989	22.5	16.9	49.8	38.8
1995	24.1	18.6	49.2	42.8
2000	17.2	14.1	32.9	28.9
2007	20.6	17.3	39.5	31.1
Percentage-point changes				
1979-89	4.4	3.6	6.2	9.6
1989-2000	-5.3	-2.8	-16.9	-9.9
1989-95	1.6	1.7	-0.6	4.0
1995-2000	-6.9	-4.5	-16.3	-13.9
2000-07	3.4	3.2	6.7	2.2

Source: U.S. Census Bureau.

In the 2000s, child poverty rose 1.8 percentage points overall, though like the overall trends shown in the last table, poverty rose more quickly for black children and fell for Hispanic kids. The increases in the 2000s were even larger for young children, suggesting that young families did more poorly than older ones. The increase for young African American children—up 6.7 points—is really quite disheartening, as it significantly reverses much of the progress made in the 1990s against this particularly damaging social indicator. Back in 1995, before the sharp slide in poverty among young black children, almost half were poor, a truly alarming level of economic hardship for young children. But thanks to the dramatic progress in the latter 1990s, that share fell to one-third in 2000. By 2007, it was back up to 39.5%.

Child poverty rates are fully a function of a family's income. **Table 6.4** shifts the unit of observation from persons to families, which in Census terminology refers to two or more persons related through blood, marriage, or adoption (i.e., one-person households are excluded). In general, family poverty rates are lower than poverty rates for persons, reflecting both the relatively high number of poor children and the inclusion of unrelated individuals in the person counts but not in the family counts.

The patterns over time are similar to those shown in the previous tables, with consistently increasing rates of family poverty at business cycle peaks from 1973 to 1989. The poverty rates for African American families were essentially unchanged over these years, at about 28%. Over the 1990s, however, they fell by 8.5 percentage points; the 2000 rate of 19.3% is the lowest on record and marks the first time poverty for black families fell below 20%. Poverty among Hispanic families grew sharply, by 3.6 points, through 1995, but thereafter reversed course and fell even more quickly than it did for blacks; by 2000, Hispanics, too, posted the lowest rate on record.

The last two columns of Table 6.4 show the poverty rates of two family types with children: single mothers and married couples. Poverty rates for the latter are much lower, in part because such families can tap two earners when both spouses work in the paid labor market. Turning to trends, however, the poverty rates of mother-only families fell significantly through the 1970s, stagnated in the 1980s, and fell sharply in the 1900s. As shown below, this recent decline relates to a sharp upturn in the labor market participation of these single parents.

Family poverty reversed course in the 2000s, with the largest increases accruing to lower-income groups, including families headed by an African American and a single mother. This latter point regarding the 2000s increase among single mothers has important policy implications for welfare reform, a set of policy changes targeted at the demographic group. Based on the poverty trends for mother-only families in the 1990s and 2000s, the policy changes appear to be "pro-cyclical" in that they help reduce poverty in a strong economy/job market but fail to do so in a weaker one. This hypothesis is explored more thoroughly below.

The depth of poverty
This section examines two measures of the depth of poverty: the poverty gap and the share of the poor with incomes less than half the poverty threshold (i.e., the deeply impoverished).

TABLE 6.4 Family poverty, by race/ethnicity of family head and for different family types, 1959-2007

	Race/ethnicity of family head				Families with children	
	All	**White**	**Black**	**Hispanic**	**Married couples**	**Female head**
1959	18.5%	15.2%	n.a.	n.a.	n.a.	59.9%
1967	11.4	9.1	33.9%	n.a.	n.a.	44.5
1973	8.8	6.6	28.1	19.8%	n.a.	43.2
1979	9.2	6.9	27.8	20.3	6.1%	39.6
1989	10.3	7.8	27.8	23.4	7.3	42.8
1995	10.8	8.5	26.4	27.0	7.5	41.5
2000	8.7	7.1	19.3	19.2	6.0	33.0
2007	9.8	7.9	22.1	19.7	6.7	37.0
Percentage-point changes						
1959-73	-9.7	-8.6	n.a.	n.a.	n.a.	-16.7
1973-79	0.4	0.3	-0.3	0.5	n.a.	-3.6
1979-89	1.1	0.9	0.0	3.1	1.2	3.2
1989-2000	-1.6	-0.7	-8.5	-4.2	-1.3	-9.8
1989-95	0.5	0.7	-1.4	3.6	0.2	-1.3
1995-2000	-2.1	-1.4	-7.1	-7.8	-1.5	-8.5
2000-07	1.1	0.8	2.8	-0.5	0.7	4.0

Source: U.S. Census Bureau.

Since a poverty threshold is a fixed-income level, families are considered poor whether they are $1 or $1,000 below the poverty line. Thus, another useful way to gauge the depth of poverty is the "poverty gap": the average income deficit (the dollar gap between a poor family's income and its poverty threshold) experienced by poor families or individuals. For example, **Table 6.5** shows that, in 2007, the average poverty gap was about $8,500. This figure is the highest in the table, meaning that poor families are, on average, poorer now than in earlier periods.

Figure 6D plots both family poverty rates and the average family poverty gap. Over the 1960s through the mid-1970s, both the poverty rate and the poverty gap declined, meaning that fewer families were poor and, of those who were, they were on average less poor over time. The strong labor market, along with the expansion of cash transfers over this period, including both Social Security (which significantly reduced

TABLE 6.5 Average poverty gap, 1967-2007 (2007 dollars)

Years	Families
1959	$7,633
1973	6,826
1979	7,316
1989	7,900
1995	8,157
2000	8,213
2007	8,523
Annual growth rates	
1959-73	-0.8%
1973-79	1.2
1979-89	0.8
1989-2000	0.4
1989-95	0.5
1995-2000	0.1
2000-07	0.5

Source: U.S. Census Bureau.

the poverty of the elderly) and welfare benefits, contributed to these trends. As shown in Table 6.5, the average family poverty gap fell 0.8% annually over this period.

Both family poverty and the poverty gap rose steeply over the recessionary period in the early 1980s, and, as shown in the figure, the two series diverged in the mid-1980s. In fact, the growth rates in the bottom section of the table reveal that the poverty gap has risen consistently over business cycle peaks. Thus, while the 1973 and 2000 poverty rates were about the same (8.8% in 1973 and 8.7% in 2000), the average poor family was over $1,400 (2007 dollars) worse off in the latter year.

The poverty gap series shows an interesting divergence from much of the data series observed thus far in that it shows no improvement over the latter 1990s. In fact, the average poor family was slightly worse off in 2000 than in 1995. This suggests that those families that exited poverty over this period were those whose incomes placed them closer to the poverty threshold, leaving behind the least well-off among the poor and raising the average poverty gap. **Figure 6E**, the share of the poor below half the poverty line, corroborates this interpretation. For a family of four with two children, this threshold amounted to about $10,500 in 2007. After increasing from around 30% to around 40% through the 1980s, the share of the deeply poor has changed little,

FIGURE 6D Family poverty gap and family poverty rates, 1959-2006

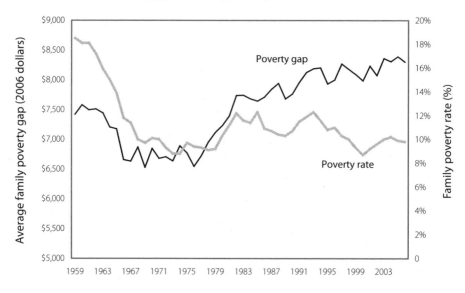

Source: U.S. Census Bureau.

FIGURE 6E Percent of the poor below half the poverty line, 1975-2006

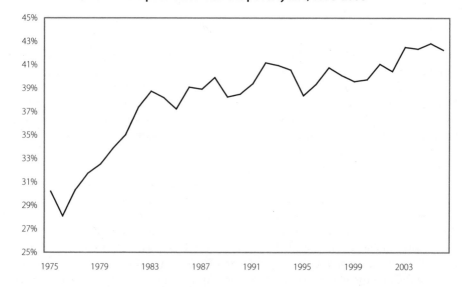

Source: U.S. Census Bureau.

reinforcing the notion that the poor of today have lower average income levels than the poor in earlier periods.

To some extent, the trend toward more deeply poor families within the poverty population is not surprising, given the strong shift of public policy toward work over cash assistance. The families most able to take advantage of both the strong labor market of the latter 1990s and the income supports tied to work, like the EITC, were likely to both climb out of poverty and do so from relatively close to the income threshold. Those left behind are probably the least likely to be able to take advantage of either a strong market economy or work-based supports.

That said, it is unsettling to recognize that, since 2000, the poverty rate, the average poverty gap, and the share below half poverty have been on the rise. In other words, since this last economic peak, more families are poor and average incomes are lower. Clearly, the anti-poverty momentum of the latter 1990s has disappeared.

Immigration and poverty

Immigration to America has led to a highly charged debate in recent years. One prevailing view of poverty suggests that immigrants are a main cause of the problem, but the data belie that claim. While it is true that some immigrants (though, as shown below, not naturalized citizens) have higher poverty rates than native-born persons, the trends are similar and, in fact, immigrant poverty rates fell significantly faster over the 1990s than did rates for the native-born (see **Table 6.6** and **Figure 6F**). So, while more immigrants have joined the U.S. population, at least over this period (the only period for which the Census Bureau publishes such annual data) their likelihood of being poor has fallen.

However, it could still be the case that simply adding more immigrants, even with their diminished propensity toward poverty, boosts the overall poverty rate. A simple experiment shows this did not occur over this period. The share of the immigration population increased from 9% to 13% between 1993 and 2006. Had the share remained constant at 9%, the overall poverty rate would have been 12.3% in 2007, just 0.2 points lower than the actual rate that year. In other words, the decline in immigrant poverty largely offset the higher poverty effect of the growth of the immigrant population.

The table reveals another point that is particularly germane to the immigration debate. Part of the debate has revolved around whether immigration policy should smooth the path to citizenship for noncitizens, including undocumented immigrants. The data in the table reveal that the poverty rate among noncitizens is consistently more than twice that for naturalized immigrants. Some of this big difference is likely attributable to different characteristics (e.g., immigrants from wealthier countries are more likely to be naturalized), relative skill levels between the two groups, and date of arrival. But even when we control for such factors, the significant differences in poverty rates remain, suggesting that naturalized citizens face certain economic advantages, such as in the job market, that give them a leg-up on noncitizens. The implication is that a smoother path to citizenship would help noncitizens become more integrated into the economy.

Alternative poverty measures

In the mid-1990s, a government-appointed panel convened by the National Academy of Sciences (NAS) was asked to update the way in which poverty is measured in America. The NAS measure has many advantages over the official approach, and the Census Bureau has implemented a variety of versions of NAS recommendations. The key differences between the official measure and the Census publications of the NAS measures include the following:

• The NAS thresholds are based on actual expenditures on food, clothing, and shelter, and thus reflect increases in living standards.

• The NAS income measure is after-tax, and thus reflects the poverty reduction effects of tax credits.

• NAS includes non-cash benefits in income (though it does not include the value of publicly provided health care).

• NAS deducts some work expenses, like child care expenditures for working families, from income.

• NAS subtracts out-of-pocket medical expenses, including premium payments.

• NAS factors in regional differences in the cost of living.

Using variants of these measures, the Census Bureau has generated a consistent time series back to 1999 of 12 different NAS-based approaches. For example, some measures account for geographical differences and out-of-pocket medical spending, while others do not.

TABLE 6.6 Poverty rates by nativity, 1993-2007

| | | | Foreign born | | |
	All	*Native*	*Total*	*Naturalized*	*Non-citizen*
1993	15.1%	14.4%	23.0%	10.1%	28.7%
2000	11.3	10.8	15.4	9.0	19.2
2007	12.5	11.9	16.5	9.5	20.3
1993-2000	-3.8%	-3.6%	-7.6%	-1.1%	-9.5%
2000-07	1.2	1.1	1.1	0.5	2.1

Source: U.S. Census Bureau.

FIGURE 6F Poverty, native and foreign born, 1993-2006

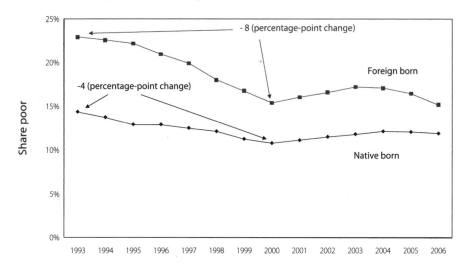

Source: U.S. Census Bureau.

FIGURE 6G Poverty rates, official compared to NAS alternatives, 1999 to 2006

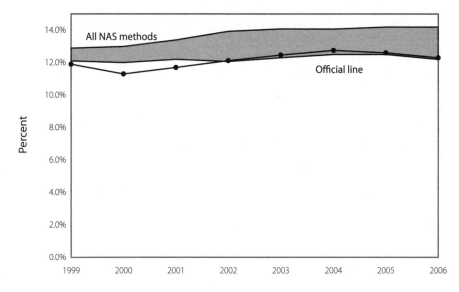

Source: National Academy of Sciences and U.S. Census Bureau.

A fundamental question is do these improved measures generate lower or higher poverty rates relative to the official measure? By plotting the full range of the Census Bureau's different measures, **Figure 6G** illustrates the answer: the NAS measures (12 are included here) are uniformly higher than the official measure. On average over the period covered by the graph, the NAS rates are about 1 percentage point above the official rate, which would mean around 3 million more persons living in poverty.

However, not all of the Census alternatives hew closely to the best practices identified by NAS. For example, some of the Census measures adjust the poverty thresholds using the consumer price index (CPI) instead of changes in expenditures on basic necessities. The latter is an important advance recommended by NAS. Fortunately, two poverty measurement experts (Thesia Garner of the BLS and Kathleen Short of the Census Bureau, 2008) have recently derived both thresholds and income definitions that go the farthest yet in establishing a poverty measure that uses the NAS concepts.

The official and their alternative poverty thresholds for a family of two parents and two children are shown in **Table 6.7**. Note that the alternative thresholds are higher both in level and trend, with the alternative threshold growing about 14 percentage points faster than the official (43% versus 29%). The reasons for this difference stem from the fact that, based on the expenditures of low-income families, the alternative measure weighs certain items, such as housing and medical expenditures, more heavily than the CPI. Since the prices of these components grew significantly faster than average prices over this period, the alternative thresholds grew more quickly as well.

This does not, however, necessarily imply that the alternative measure will show higher poverty rates, because the two measures differ significantly on the income, or resource, side of the equation. As noted, the alternative income definition is far more inclusive than the official measure. For example, while the alternative thresholds are higher, if more low-income workers receive the earned income tax credit (a wage subsidy for low-wage workers), or if policy changes expand such benefits, incomes as measured under a NAS standard will increase. The pretax official measure, on the other hand, will not record these changes.

TABLE 6.7 Official and alternative poverty thresholds, 1996-2006: Family of four (two parents, two children)

	Official	Alternative	Official/alternative
1996	$15,911	$18,096	88%
2006	20,444	25,834	79%
Change	28.5%	42.8%	-8.8%

Source: Garner and Short (2008).

As shown in **Figure 6H** and in the first column of **Table 6.8**, the alternative measure is both higher and rises more quickly than the official measure. In 1996, the official rate stood at 13.7%, while the alternative rate was 17.1%. By 2005, the official rate, at 12.3%, was lower than its 1996 rate; the alternative rate—17.7%—was slightly higher. As shown in Figure 6H, the gap between the two rates rose from 3.4 points in 1996 to 5.4 points in 2006. In terms of counting the poor, the alternative measure implies that compared to the official measure, there were 16 million more poor persons in 2006.

The fact that millions more people face serious income constraints in meeting their basic needs compared to the official measure is an extremely important finding in this area of research. It obviously implies that we are failing to accurately measure material deprivation, but that much was known. Perhaps, more importantly, because access to many public benefits is tied to the official poverty measure, this finding suggests that these programs reach too few persons.

It is also noteworthy that the difference between the two measures grows wider over time. As noted, this has much to do with the different expenditure weights in the thresholds, particularly the fact that housing expenditures, such as mortgage payments, play a larger role in the alternative measure compared to the official. Also, childcare costs and other work expenses grew more quickly in the 2000s than in the latter 1990s, and these costs are subtracted from income in the alternative measure. In other words, over the 2000s, the alternative thresholds grew more quickly than the CPI (and thus, more quickly than the official thresholds), and the alternative income measure grew more slowly than income as officially measured due to increased expenses.

FIGURE 6H Official versus alternative poverty rates, 1996-2006

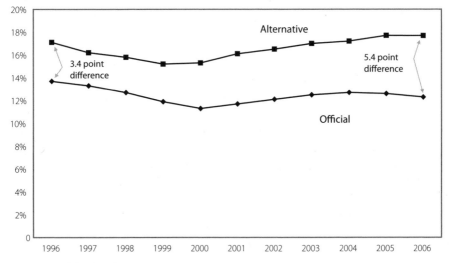

Source: Garner and Short (2008).

TABLE 6.8 Official and alternative poverty rates, 1996-2005, by demographics

Official	All	Children	Non-elderly adults	Elderly	White	African American
1996	13.7%	20.5%	11.4%	10.8%	11.2%	28.4%
2000	11.3	16.1	9.4	10.2	9.4	22.0
2005	12.3	17.4	10.8	9.4	10.3	24.3
Percentage-point change						
1996-2005	-1.4	-3.1	-0.6	-1.4	-0.9	-4.2
2000-05	1.0	1.3	1.4	-0.8	0.9	2.3
Alternative						
1996	17.1%	22.8%	14.4%	18.0%	14.3%	32.8%
2000	ᵛ15.3	19.6	12.8	18.5	13.2	26.8
2005	17.7	21.4	15.5	21.8	15.2	31.7
Percentage-point change						
1996-2005	0.6	-1.4	1.1	3.8	1.1	-1.1
2000-05	2.4	1.8	2.7	3.3	2.2	4.9

Source: Garner and Short (2008).

Table 6.8 compares alternative and official rates for various subgroups of the population. Poverty rates grow more quickly, or fall less quickly, for each group over the full period. For example, the official measure for African Americans falls 3.5 percentage points over these years, while the alternative measure falls only 0.9 points. In the 2000s, black alternative poverty grows almost 3 percentage points faster than did the official rate. While more research is needed to explain this finding, one possibility is that the safety net was less effective in the 2000s than in earlier years, a possibility explored later in the chapter. This shows up as higher poverty under the alternative measure, since it means fewer additions to income compared to the official income measure.

Elderly poverty rates are much higher and grow considerably faster under the alternative measure, largely stemming from the inclusion of out-of-pocket medical costs, which are subtracted from income. Trends and levels for children, on the other hand, are closer under the two different approaches.

Relative poverty

Another way to measure poverty—one with great intuitive appeal—tracks the poor while accounting for changes in prevailing income levels among the non-poor. Such measures are called "relative" in that they usually set the poverty threshold as a percent of the median income, which moves each year and typically rises in nominal terms. The utility of this measure (the norm in international comparisons) is that it tells how the poor are faring relative to middle-income families. In fact, since the poverty line is adjusted only for inflation, anytime the median income grows in real terms, that is, faster than inflation, the poor lose relative ground. Note, for example, that the poverty threshold for a four-person family used to be about 50% of the median income for such families back in 1959, compared to about 30% in 2006. This decline occurred because median income grew faster than prices, implying that the officially poor fell further behind the middle class.

Figure 6I plots official poverty and relative poverty—the share of person in families with one-half of median income—from 1979 to 2006 (the income concept used in the relative calculation is similar to the NAS measure). The official rate is considerably more cyclical, falling over the expansion of the 1980s and, significantly more so, in the 1990s. For example, after peaking at 15.1% in 1993, the official rate fell to 11.3% in 2000. But relative poverty fell less than a percentage point, from 18.5% to 17.7%.

The reason for these different trends is that real median income rose in the 1990s (see Chapter 1), so the relative threshold of half the median was rising as well in real terms. Figure 6I shows that in absolute terms the poor gained a great deal of ground. But in relative terms their incomes grew at about the same rate as middle incomes, so the poor remained about the same distance from the middle class as before.

FIGURE 6I Official and relative poverty, 1979-2006

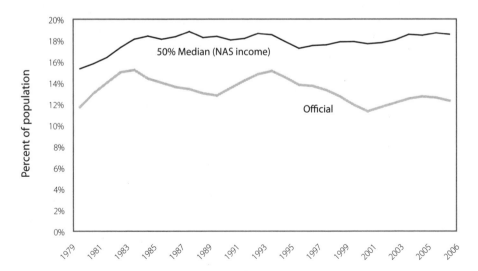

Source: Authors' analysis of CPS March Supplement data.

Because the relative measure tracks the social/economic distance between the poor and the middle class (in a way that absolute measures do not), it reveals the impact of changes in inequality on poverty. The share of the population that is poor in relative terms has hovered around 18% since the mid-1980s, showing that many more persons are poor in relative terms—their income is less than half the median—than in absolute terms. The fact that such a significant share of the population remains relatively distant from the mainstream is an important dimension of the poverty problem.

The determinants of low incomes

Addressing the problem of poverty in America, however it is defined, requires an accurate diagnosis of its causes. As with any complex social phenomenon, many factors play a role, and this section highlights those that researchers have identified as the most salient, including growth, inequality, family structure, education, and race (the role of immigration was discussed earlier).

Full employment

Much discourse regarding poverty reduction covers a range of ideas from strengthening anti-poverty programs, to creating greater incentives to work, to addressing perceived cultural shortcomings. While redistributive transfer programs are important poverty determinants, history also shows that one of the most effective anti-poverty programs is an economy that generates good jobs in a very tight labor market.

The U.S. economy has few institutions to strengthen the bargaining clout of the least advantaged. In the absence of greater union power or higher minimum wages, for example, it is particularly challenging for less-advantaged workers, including those with lower levels of education, to improve their living standards. The erosion of these clout-enhancing institutions is one factor driving inequality higher, which, as stressed below, leads to higher poverty rates than would otherwise prevail.

On the other hand, a tight labor market, such as the one that existed in the latter 1990s, is one of the best tools for lifting the wages and incomes of the least well off simply because there are more and better jobs available for the working poor in such periods. Moreover, this relationship has become even more important in the 1990s, as poverty policy has become ever more focused on work in the paid labor market as the primary pathway out of poverty. Unfortunately, periods of full employment have been more the exception than the rule in recent decades.

The importance of full employment is at least threefold. First, tight labor markets force employers to bid up wages to get and keep the workers they need. Second, full employment helps to generate a more equitable distribution of growth, and thus helps to remove the wedge that inequality creates between overall growth and poverty reduction. Third, the demand for labor in a full employment economy draws persons into the job market (and extends the work hours of those already in the job market) who, under slack conditions, would be without work.

TABLE 6.9 Changes in poverty rates and various correlates, 1959-2006

	Poverty rates	Productivity*	Unemploy- ment	Inequality**	Low-wage growth***	Per-capita GDP
1959-73	-11.3	2.8%	-0.6	-0.8%	na	2.9%
1973-89	1.8	1.3	0.4	10.4	-0.3%	2.0
1989-2000	-1.5	2.0	-1.3	4.3	1.0	1.9
1995-2000	-2.5	2.5	-1.6	1.7	2.3	2.9
2000-06	1.0	3.0	0.6	2.3	0.0	1.4

Note: Poverty rates and unemployment are percentage-point changes; productivity and low-wage growth are annualized changes; inequality is percent change in Gini coefficient.

* Nonfarm business sector
** Gini coefficient
*** 20th percentile real wage

Source: U.S. Census Bureau, Bureau of Labor Statistics, Bureau of Economic Analysis, and authors' analysis of CPS-ORG data.

Table 6.9 relates some of the relevant indicators of strong (or weak) employment demand to poverty rates. The table presents growth rates of poverty along with a set of economic variables, including a measure of inequality, discussed in greater detail in the next section. Broadly speaking, in periods of fast productivity growth and tight job markets, like the 1960s and the latter 1990s, poverty is diminished. Of course, much more was going in both these periods, as is always the case. In the 1960s, another cause for poverty's large drop was an increase in Social Security benefits that led to a decline in poverty rates among elderly persons. The latter 1990s featured an expansion of work supports, as discussed in Table 6.11 below.

The mid-1970s through the 1980s were years of relatively low productivity growth, rising and generally high unemployment rates, and increasing inequality. This is a potent recipe for higher poverty rates, and poverty rose 1.8 points over those years.

The 1990s started much the same way, but the latter 1990s were a different story. Productivity growth was strong, accelerating more than 1% over the 1973-89 rate, meaning that the workforce was generating that much more output per hour each year. While it is a consistent belief among economists that higher productivity growth creates a path to higher living standards, in an era of greater inequality this relationship is strained. For that potential to be realized, other forces need to be in place to ensure an equitable distribution of income growth. In the latter 1990s, full employment played that role. The unemployment rate fell 1.6 points between 1995 and 2000, hitting 4.0% in 2000. The growth of inequality was diminished, as measured by the Gini coefficient, which grew 1.7% between 1995 and 2000, compared to 2.5% from 1989 to 1995. And, most critically, low wages (the real wage at the 20th percentile) grew at an annual rate of 2.3%, almost the same as productivity.

Here lies a critical chain of economic events, in terms of poverty reduction. Faster productivity growth, by creating more income per hour worked, provides the potential for significant poverty reduction, but only if that income reaches the lower end of the income scale. For that to occur, full employment conditions need to prevail in the job market. This combination—faster productivity growth occurring in the context of very tight job markets—will lead to faster growth in low-wages, and this in turn will help drive poverty rates lower. These dynamics are especially salient in the context of today's poverty policy, where work in the paid labor market is promoted as a primary path out of poverty.

Figure 6J compares these linkages in two comparable time periods of the business cycle: the last five years of both the 1980s and 1990s cycle. Unemployment in this Figure is given as the rate in the cycle's final year, typically the low point for jobless-ness before it begins to rise in the downturn. In the 1980s, productivity was relatively slow and unemployment never fell below 5% (the average for the cycle, 1979-89, was 7.1%). In the absence of either productivity rising at least 2% and unemployment close to 4%, inflation-adjusted low wages went nowhere, even in the five best years of that cycle, rising only 0.1% per year.

In the latter 1990s, these positive productivity and unemployment conditions were present, and low wages grew at a real annual rate close to that of productivity. Most notably, as has been stressed throughout, poverty fell sharply, especially for minorities, in these years.

FIGURE 6J   Real low-wage growth, productivity, and unemployment: Three five-year periods

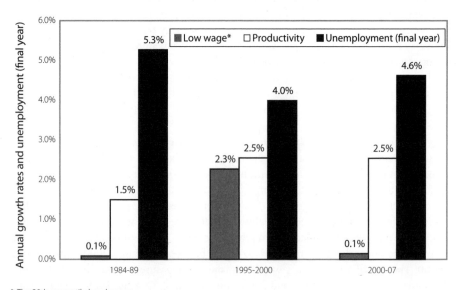

* The 20th percentile hourly wage.

Source: U.S. Bureau of Labor Statistics and authors' analysis of CPS-ORG data.

For completeness, Figure 6J includes the path of these three indicators in the 2000s (note that these are not comparable cyclical years, but the full cycle, assuming that cycle ended in 2007). These data provide something of a natural experimental test of the theories discussed above, because the 2000s saw productivity grow at the same pace as the latter 1990s, but with weaker job markets (see Chapter 4). In this regard, we can ask whether the poverty reducing chain—fast productivity and full employment leading to faster low-wage growth and poverty reduction—works if one of the chain's links is missing, in this case, full employment. The answer appears to be no. Without low unemployment to boost the bargaining power of low-wage workers, the faster growth eluded them, as reflected in a low-wage growth rate analogous to that of the 1980s. The result was, of course, higher poverty at the end of the 2000s cycle, despite truly impressive productivity growth.

Income inequality

Chapters 1 and 2 included fairly detailed discussions of the role of inequality as a factor explaining stagnant income growth. Here too, in a discussion of low-income families, the role of inequality is critical. As income inequality grows, poverty rates become less responsive to overall growth, because too little of that growth reaches the lower end of the income scale. In fact, as Table 6.10 will reveal, in the 2000s, the growth in inequality explains almost the full percentage point increase in poverty in that period.

Poverty analyst Sheldon Danziger offers one simple way to demonstrate the important change in the relationship between macroeconomic growth and poverty reduction. He constructs a simple statistical model between poverty and GDP growth through the early 1970s, and based on this historical relationship, predicts the path of poverty based on growth alone.

The result is shown in **Figure 6K**. The model forecasts poverty quite accurately through the mid-1970s, when economic growth was broadly shared (see Chapter 1, Figure 1H, top panel). But since then, poverty has cyclically fluctuated within a fairly narrow range, with the level in 2006—12.3%—identical to that of 1975. Again, it should be stressed that while current poverty measures are inadequate, better measures would very likely show a similar trend (and, as shown above, the most accurate alternative measure suggests the official poverty trend is biased downward).

If, however, poverty continued to be driven by per capita GDP growth, it would have hit zero by 1985. That is, had factors such as inequality not begun to play such an important role as a poverty determinant, poverty reduction would have likely continued apace since the mid-1970s. Note that we are not claiming that a zero poverty rate would have really occurred, or even that this is a realistic goal, absent very substantial interventions in market outcomes. But clearly, growth and poverty reduction became unlinked in the mid-1970s, just as inequality was taking off.

Some poverty analysts argue that a more important factor than either growth or inequality is family structure. As shown in earlier tables, single-parent families have a significantly higher propensity to be poor, in large part because they have one adult earner, putting an obvious constraint on their families' earnings capacity. The

FIGURE 6K Poverty rate, actual and simulated, 1959-2006

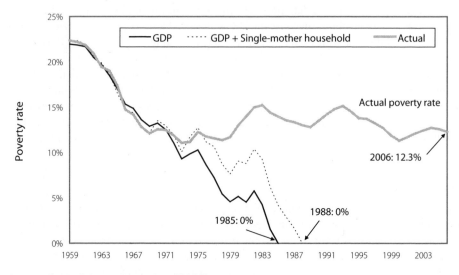

Source: Authors' analysis using Danziger (unpublished).

increase in the share of these families over time is thus often highlighted as an important determinant.

While this effect has been poverty-inducing, its impact has fallen sharply over the years and has played a very small role in poverty outcomes in more recent years, as shown below. This theory is also tested in the context of Figure 6K, asking how the "bottom line" would have changed if we control for the rising share of mother-only families. If this factor was as important as its advocates claim, adding it to the model should help close the large gap between predicted and actual poverty rates.

Instead, controlling for the increase in the share of single-mother families has very little impact on the predictions of this simple model. Instead of going to zero in 1985, the predicted measure hits zero three years later, in 1988. Thus, at least by this simple modeling approach, family structure explains little of the sharply diminished response of poverty to overall growth.

Putting it all together: Growth, inequality, family structure, education, and race

Table 6.10 decomposes the role played by each of a set of factors commonly associated with changes in poverty over the past 37 years (see Appendix B for an explanation of the methodology). The "actual change" line shows how much poverty rates changed over the years in question, which is almost not at all over the full period (0.1 percentage points). But all the internal factors in the Table have pushed and pulled in different directions over the years with varying degrees of impact.

Starting with the most recent period, 2000-06, increasing inequality has been the most important factor, explaining almost the full percentage -point increase of poverty over these years. Other factors had little impact and generally cancelled each other out. In other words, controlling for race, education, and family structure, had income growth been more broadly shared over this period, poverty would not have deepened from its 2000 trough.

The historical findings in the table show education and overall economic growth to be the two biggest poverty-reducing factors, while family structure and inequality push the other way. The racial composition of the population—the growth of minority populations with higher likelihoods of poverty—has contributed relatively little over time, and only 0.1 percentage points in the 2000s. Except in the 2000s, when average income growth was weak, the expanding economy reduced poverty by about 2 percentage points in each cycle. This finding harks back to Figure 6K above, which established that, simply based on the real growth of GDP per person, poverty would have ended in the early 1980s.

The family structure component deserves closer attention, and **Figure 6L** plots its impact. Many critics of economic explanations for poverty's lack of responsiveness to growth—factors such as inequality or the absence of full employment—cite family structure as the most important factor. They often argue that too many people make misguided choices regarding family formation, as seen by the increase in mother-only families over time, and these choices lead to higher poverty rates. In this line of thinking, more jobs, stronger growth, and less inequality are secondary policy solutions to marriage.

There is, of course, a rationale for these arguments. Mother-only families have much higher poverty rates, and as the last column in Table 6.10 shows, their formation

TABLE 6.10 The impact of economic, demographic, and education changes on poverty rates

	1969-79	1979-89	1989-2000	2000-06	1969-2006
Actual change	-0.5	1.2	-1.5	1.0	0.1
Total demographic effect	0.5	-0.2	-0.6	0.0	-0.3
Race	0.3	0.4	0.4	0.1	1.1
Education	-1.5	-1.2	-1.1	-0.3	-4.1
Family structure	2.0	0.7	0.4	0.2	3.3
Interaction	-0.2	-0.1	-0.2	-0.1	-0.6
Economic change	-1.1	1.4	-0.9	1.0	0.4
Growth	-1.7	-1.8	-2.1	0.1	-5.6
Inequality	0.7	3.2	1.2	0.9	6.0

Source: Authors' analysis based on Danziger and Gottschalk (1996).

has led to an increase in poverty of 3.3 percentage points over time. However, notice the sharp fall in the impact of this factor, as shown in Figure 6L. In each succeeding cycle, family-structure changes explain less of the increase in poverty rates, with the effect largely fading out by the 2000s, when the shift to more economically vulnerable families contributed on 0.2 points to the growth in poverty rates. This progress has to do both with the slower growth rate of this family type over time, as well as their faster income growth, most recently in the 1990s, as discussed below.

Figure 6M plots that last column of the previous table, showing the impact of the various factors over the full analysis period. Inequality and growth were largely off-setting, but their impacts are quantitatively large. Had growth been equally distributed, which, in this analysis means that all families' incomes would have grown at the average real growth rate, poverty would be 6 points lower, essentially half of what it is today.

Educational upgrading is often a forgotten factor in this analysis. The low-income population has become considerably more highly educated over time, even with the influx of less-educated immigrants. Since more highly educated families have higher incomes, the third bar in the figure reveals that this has been a potent force in lowering poverty rates.

In sum, our diagnosis of poverty's determinants reveals that the unequal distribution of income has been a major factor in keeping poverty rates from falling in periods of strong economic growth. In the 2000s in particular, the workforce has been highly pro-ductive, yet poverty has risen. This rise has little to do with family formation choices. In

FIGURE 6L The impact of family structure changes on poverty rates, 1969-2006

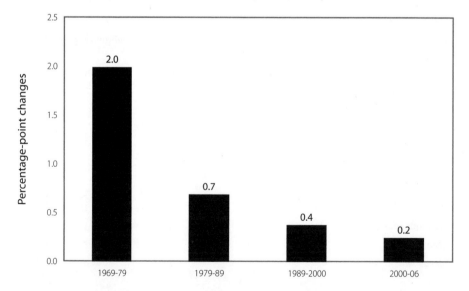

Source: Authors' analysis based on Danziger and Gottschalk (1996).

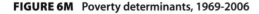

FIGURE 6M Poverty determinants, 1969-2006

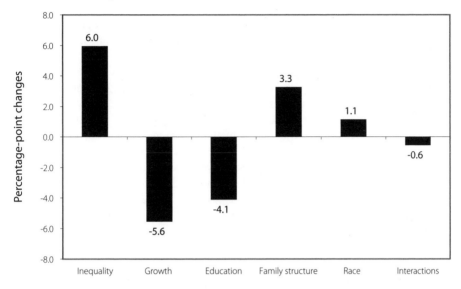

Source: Authors' analysis based on Danziger and Gottschalk (1996).

a policy climate where poverty reduction is closely tied to work in the paid labor market, job and earnings opportunities for low-wage workers must become a focal point for anti-poverty policy. The next section turns to the analysis of these labor market issues.

Tight job markets and work supports: A potent combination

Under the rubric of welfare reform, a number of policy changes occurred in the 1990s that had considerable impact on low-income families, particularly those headed by single parents, the vast majority of which are headed by women. Those low-income, mother-only families who interacted with the welfare system faced a set of changes in rules and practices with far-reaching consequences. Many more of these women went to work in the paid job market, and they significantly increased their hours worked and earnings. Nevertheless, their average wages remained low, typically well below $10 per hour.

Given these low wages, the loss of welfare benefits, and the requirement to spend more time working outside the home, many of these women were faced with a real challenge closing the gap between what they earned and what their family budgets required for them to make ends meet. Two policy changes over this period helped: the higher minimum wage enacted in 1996, and the expansion of the system of work supports. The latter policy set is explored in some detail below.

First, however, note the dramatic expansion in annual hours worked by low-income women with children (those with family incomes below twice poverty). **Figure 6N** compares their increase in work hours with that of low-income married women with children. Clearly, the push of changes associated with welfare reform played a role, as women affected by the policy changes ratcheted up their work hours much more than women with similar incomes but who were unaffected by the new policies. Single mothers' hours rose from 840 in 1993 to about 1,170 in 2000, the equivalent of adding more than two months of full-time work.

Those added hours led to higher incomes, but given both low hourly wages and costs associated with paid work, such as child care, low-income single-mother families still faced great difficulty meeting their families' material needs. Work supports are public benefits tied to work, designed to help close the gap between what these families can earn in the job market and what they actually need to make ends meet. This system was expanded over the 1990s (as shown in Table 6.11).

One of the most important work supports is the earned income tax credit, a wage subsidy for workers in low-income families. Since its inception in the mid-1970s, the amount of the credit has increased, and as shown in **Table 6.11**, a parent with two children now can receive over $4,000 from the EITC. But while this was one of the largest expansions in work supports, Table 6.11 shows that many others were, and remain, important to closing the income/needs gap.

The table simulates the effect of work supports on the income of a single-parent family with two children in Chicago, where the parent works full-time for $8 per hour. That is, these are the available set of work supports to this type of a low-income, working family in Chicago, but, as discussed below, very few families receive this much assistance. The top panel shows income and the bottom panel lists expenses,

FIGURE 6N Annual hours worked, low-income women with children, 1979-2006

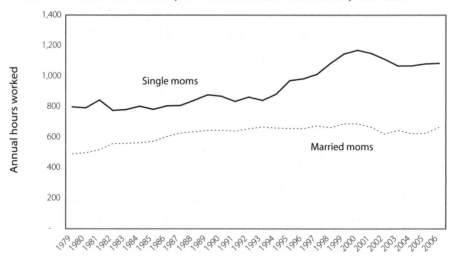

Source: Authors' analysis of CPS March Supplement data.

including tax liabilities (tax credits, like the EITC, are in the top panel). Moving across the table, more work supports are added to the family's income, and the table's bottom line shows the result of expenses minus these changing income values (note that the bottom line begins as a negative, as expenses surpass income). For example, column two adds both the federal and state EITC (some states offer a small add-on to the federal program). Together, these work supports add about $4,350 to the family's income, lowering the net negative on the bottom line.

The rest of the table adds food stamps, publicly provided health insurance, child care, and housing assistance (the latter three are factored into the table by reducing expenses, not raising income), and together, they turn the bottom line from net negative to net positive. To do so, however, invokes some significant additions to income, and some particularly large reductions to expenses. Expenses are reduced by over $17,000 in this simulation.

How realistic is this scenario? These work supports all exist, of course, but their receipt is far from universal. Many families fail to access work supports for which they are eligible. The EITC has very high take-up rates, but the child care subsidy only reaches about 15% of eligible families. Research on work-support receipt finds that far less than 10% of working families with incomes below the poverty line receive the set of available supports shown above. A detailed discussion of the reasons for this lack of take-up go beyond the scope here. In some cases, complex program design and lack of outreach are the culprits. In other cases, such as housing vouchers and some health insurance subsidies (like the State Children's Health Insurance Program, or SCHIP), budget constraints—the fact that the programs are under-funded—prevent full take up. Whatever the causes, given the importance of these supports to family income, this is clearly an area where low-income policy could be greatly improved.

Fading safety net?

Among the themes stressed in this chapter are the importance of both full employment and work supports, especially in the 1990s, as well as the failure of poverty to decline in the 2000s, despite fast productivity growth. These themes are usefully explored in a recent study by the Congressional Budget Office (CBO), which looks at the income trends of low-income families with children (in this case, "low-income" refers to families in the bottom fifth of the income scale). The study covers the early 1990s through the mid-2000s, focusing on both overall income growth as well as that of in-come components, such as earnings and work supports, including tax credits and other government benefits.

A particularly notable finding in this work, one which is the focus of this section, is the failure of the safety net to work in the necessary counter-cyclical fashion in the 2000s. That is, anti-poverty programs that are supposed to boost incomes of low-in-come families when work is less available, appear to be functioning less effectively.

Figure 60 focuses on single mothers (average 2005 income: $13,700), though the trend is similar for all low-income families with children. Each bar represents the annual growth rate of income or an income component, shown separately for the 1990s

TABLE 6.11 The effects of work supports on family resources and expenses, assuming full receipt: Single mother of two with full-time employment at $8 an hour, Chicago

	Employment alone (no work support)	Employment plus: EITCs	Employment plus: EITCs food stamps public health insurance	Employment plus: EITCs food stamps public health insurance child care subsidy	Employment plus: EITCs food stamps public health insurance child care subsidy housing voucher
Annual resources					
Earnings	$16,640	$16,640	$16,640	$16,640	$16,640
Federal EITC	0	4,158	4,158	4,158	4,158
State EITC	0	208	208	208	208
Food stamps	0	0	3,977	3,005	2,355
Total resources	$16,640	$21,006	$24,983	$24,011	$23,361
Annual expenses					
Rent and utilities*	$10,812	$10,812	$10,812	$10,812	$4,415
Food	5,302	5,302	5,302	5,302	5,302
Child care*	9,924	9,924	9,924	962	962
Health insurance*	2,212	2,212	0	0	0
Transportation	900	900	900	900	900
Other necessities	4,351	4,351	4,351	4,351	4,351
Payroll and income taxes	791	791	791	791	791
Total expenses	$34,292	$34,292	$32,080	$23,118	$16,721
Net resources					
(Resources minus expenses)	$-17,652	$-13,286	$-7,097	$893	$6,640

* This chart shows income and expenses from the perspective of the family. Because health insurance, child care, and housing benefits are paid directly to the provider, families experience them as reduced expenses rather than increased income.

Source: Cauthen (2007).

FIGURE 6O Low-income growth, single-mother families with children, 1991-2005

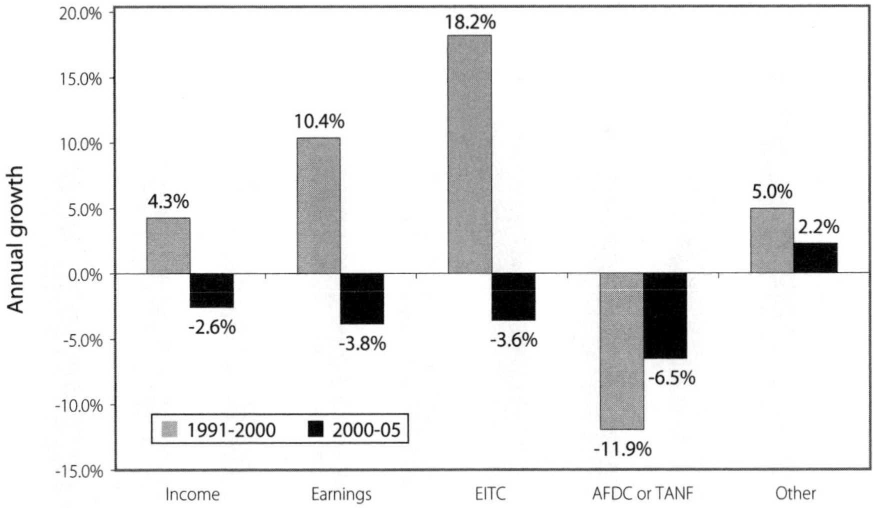

Source: Authors' analysis of CBO data.

and the 2000s. Over the course of the 1990s, the new welfare reform rules interacted with tight labor markets and a significant expansion of the EITC to generate histori-cally large income gains and significant poverty reduction for these families. As shown in the fourth set of bars, welfare benefits fell sharply, but, at least while the job market boomed, this decline was more than offset by earnings and the EITC.

But when the job market faltered in the 2000s, not only did earnings fall, but the safety net failed to catch these vulnerable families as their employment opportunities took a recessionary hit. The result was a real income decline of 2.6% per year, amounting to a $1,900 dollar loss in the 2000-05 period.

The growth of EITC benefits reversed sharply, from 18.2% per year in the 1990s, to -3.6% in the 2000s. Perhaps of greatest concern, welfare benefits (TANF—Tempo-rary Assistance for Needy Families) failed to pick up the slack. True, they fell more slowly in the 2000s than in the 1990s (-6.5% compared to -11.9% per year), but they failed to play their intended counter-cyclical role.

This last point is critical. While the welfare-to-work aspects of welfare reform have often been viewed as a policy success, the results since 2000 should give pause to policy makers. The combination of a booming labor market and generous subsidies did, in fact, prove to be a powerful anti-poverty combination in the 1990s. But without the former ingredient, that is, in the absence of robust job creation and plentiful employment oppor-tunities, the real incomes of low-income families with children have steadily eroded.

Another example of the diminished effect of the safety net is shown in **Figure 6P**, which plots the share of children lifted from deep poverty by the safety net, that is, by

FIGURE 6P Diminished effect of safety net: Share of children lifted above deep poverty

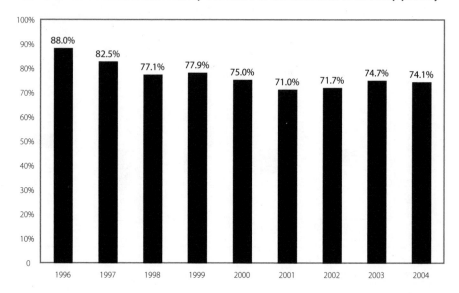

Source: Center for Budget and Policy Priorities.

the cash and non-cash benefits that are designed to reach the deeply poor. In 1996, 88% of children in families with income below half the poverty line were lifted above that threshold thanks to cash benefits from welfare, the EITC, the cash value of food stamps, and so on.

Eight years later, in 2004, that share had fallen to 74.1%, a 14 percentage-point drop in the share of children lifted from deep poverty. In terms of numbers of kids, that drop meant that over 900,000 more children languished in deep poverty than would have been the case if the safety net had been as effective in 2004 as in 1996. As it was, 1.7 million children remained below 50% of poverty after means-tested benefits, suggesting that the diminished effectiveness of the safety net led to a doubling of the number of kids remaining below 50% of poverty.

Certainly, fewer welfare benefits were reaching poor families, but that trend is a well-known outcome of welfare reform. Much less well known is the drop in EITC benefits shown in the previous figure. As Figure 6N reveals, low-income, mother-only families experienced a significant decline in their hours worked in the 2000s, as did many other families, including those with middle incomes (see Table 1.1). These facts—loss of welfare benefits, diminished work hours, and the declining EITC—suggest that the safety net has become too pro-cyclical: as shown in Figure 6O, it gives families a solid boost in strong economies, but fails to protect them from weak ones.

This loss of counter-cyclicality is particularly critical as the economy enters another downturn. If we fail to correct this apparent shortcoming, the most economically vulnerable families are at greater risk now than in prior recessions. Also, by putting more money in the hands of families that will surely spend it, these counter-cyclical policies play a useful role in stimulating the macroeconomy. Such spending is clearly associated with "multiplier effects," generating economic activity that would otherwise not occur, and helping to offset the economic slowdown.

The role of the low-wage job market

Given the elevated role of work in the lives of poor and near-poor families, conditions in low-wage labor markets play an increasingly important role in evaluating progress against poverty. This section examines the characteristics of low-wage workers and their historical wage trends.

Table 6.12 looks at the characteristics of low-wage workers, defined the same way as in Table 3.7 (as the hourly wage that would lift a family of four above the poverty threshold, $10.20 an hour in 2007, given full-time, full-year work). Just over one-quarter of the workforce earned this wage level in 2007, and their average hourly wage was about $8, about two-fifths of the average wage.

Comparing the percentages in the two columns reveals categories in which low-wage workers are overrepresented. Such workers are disproportionately female, minority, non-college-educated, and young. They also are more likely to work in low-wage industries such as retail trade and service industries, and less likely to work in durable manufacturing (non-durable manufacturing—the manufacture of things like food and apparel—pays much less than durable), transportation, finance and information services, and government. By occupation, low-wage workers are overrepresented in sales (e.g., cashiers) and services, where they staff the low-paying jobs such as security guards, food preparation, or home health aides in health services. They are least likely to be managers and professionals and significantly less likely to be covered by union contracts.

Immigrant workers are over-represented in low-wage jobs, as they are 16% of the workforce but 22% of low-wage earners. Of that 22%, about 5% are recent immigrant arrivals, in the United States less than five years. They too are over-represented in the low-wage workforce.

Some commentators have argued that many low-wage workers live in higher-income families. However, the final panel of Table 6.12 shows that while some low-wage workers—about 30%—live in families with income greater than $50,000, most reside in low- and low-middle-income families. About 44% of low-wage workers live in the lowest-income families, those with less than $25,000, compared to 28% in the total workforce.

The critical role of full employment is particularly germane in the low-wage labor market. Figure 6Q makes this point by showing the impact on real wage growth of a 1 percentage-point decline in the unemployment rate. Note the steep downward staircase, particularly for men, revealing that those at the lower end get the biggest wage boost from tighter job markets. According to these results, based on data from 1973 to 2006, a year with lower unemployment leads to a 2% real wage boost for low-wage men and a 1.5% boost for women. Compare this with the smaller gain to high-wage workers of well below 1%.

Figure 6R shows these dynamics in action, by tracking the pay of low-wage workers over time. Many of the wage-depressing factors discussed in Chapter 3 were in play throughout the 1980s, as wages fell for low-wage men and were relatively stagnant for women. The latter 1990s, however, a time when unemployment fell quickly to

TABLE 6.12 Characteristics of low-wage workers, 2007 (Part 1 of 2)

	Low-wage	Total workforce
Share of workforce	26.5%	100.0%
Number	32,486,770	122,815,179
Average wage	$8.04	$19.50
Gender		
Female	57.0%	47.9%
Male	43.0	52.1
Race/ethnicity		
White	56.0%	67.4%
African American	14.7	11.4
Hispanic	23.4	14.8
Asian	3.8	4.6
Other	2.2	1.8
Education		
Less than high school	21.5%	9.8%
High school	37.5	29.6
Associates	7.2	9.8
Some college	24.4	19.8
College or more	9.5	31.0
Age		
18-25	35.8%	16.5%
26-35	22.4	23.6
35+	41.7	59.9

Table continues

TABLE 6.12 Characteristics of low-wage workers, 2007 (Part 2 of 2)

	Low-wage	Total workforce
Industry		
Financial and information services	4.2%	7.1%
Manufacturing	8.8	12.2
Durable	4.9	7.8
Non-durable	3.9	4.4
Construction	5.4	7.1
Transportation and utilities	3.7	5.5
Services	50.9	44.5
Trade	21.1	14.3
Wholesale	2.3	3.1
Retail	18.9	11.2
Information	1.5	2.6
Government	2.3	5.3
Other industries	2.0	1.4
Occupations		
Managers/professionals	11.4%	35.0%
Admin/office support	14.7	14.5
Operations/transportation	22.8	23.2
Services	33.8	16.2
Sales	15.6	10.5
Other occupations	1.7	0.6
Union status		
Non-union	94.1%	86.4%
Union	5.9	13.6
Family income		
Less than $25K	44.3%	28.3%
$25K-$50K	25.9	21.8
More than $50K	29.8	49.9

Source: Authors' analysis of CPS-ORG data.

FIGURE 6Q Percent change in wage given 1 point decline in unemployment

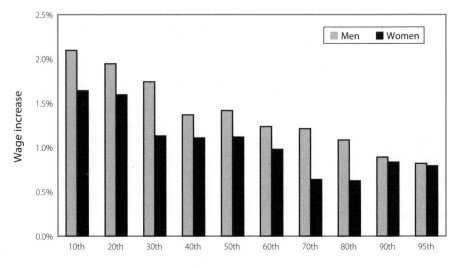

Source: Authors' analysis of CPS-ORG data.

FIGURE 6R Real hourly wages of low-wage workers, 1973-2007

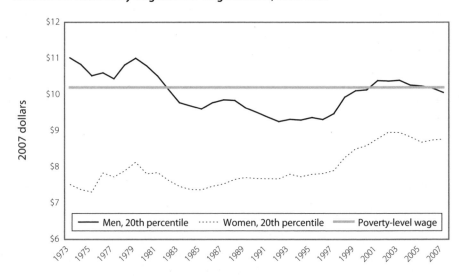

Source: Authors' analysis of CPS-ORG data.

historically low levels, stand out as a period of real wage growth for low-wage workers and of significant progress against poverty.

The tail end of these series, when real low wages began to falter, is also instructive regarding the poverty-inducing effect of higher unemployment. The recession of 2001 was relatively mild in terms of gross domestic product, but the loss of full employment took a clear toll on low-wage growth (and also on poverty, up 1 point between 2000 and 2006, as shown in Table 6.1).

The final point in Figure 6R addresses real wage levels. The straight line in the figure—the wage needed to raise a family of four above poverty—serves as a benchmark against which to judge the adequacy of low-wage levels relative to what families need to make ends meet. With the earnings boost in the latter 1990s, low-wage males reached this benchmark, though women remained below it. But for most of the period, 20th percentile wages have lagged this benchmark, meaning that the universe of low-wage workers (i.e., including those earning below the 20th percentile) earned below the poverty-level wage. From a policy perspective, this gap underscores the need for wage subsidies and work supports that will help close the distance between what these workers earn and what they need.

Conclusion

The last few decades have been extremely instructive regarding poor and low-income families in the American economy. Measurement advances have vastly improved on our ability to accurately assess the extent of material deprivation in our society, given both the costs of basic needs and societal norms. Applying those advances finds that poverty is actually much higher in the United States than under the official measure. In 2006, the official rate was 12.3%, compared to 17.7% under the alternative, implying that under the more accurate measure, 16 million more people are poor.

Comparing the 1990s and the 2000s is equally instructive. In the 1990s, the combination of full-employment job markets and expanded work supports were complementary to policies that emphasized work in the paid labor market as the primary pathway out of poverty. The low-income population decreased in those years, and the declines in poverty and twice poverty were largest for minority and mother-only families, two groups particularly vulnerable to poverty.

In the 2000s, these trends reversed. The economy expanded, and productivity growth was on a par with the latter 1990s, yet poverty was higher at the end of the 2000s business cycle than at the beginning. The culprit was increased income inequality: the growth that occurred failed to reach low-income families, and poverty rates rose most quickly among the least advantaged. At the same time, policy changes have rendered the U.S. safety net less counter-cyclical, that is, less effective at preventing income losses among low-income families in periods of economic weakness. At this point, the damaging impact of high and growing inequality and the ineffectiveness of policies intended to protect families from market failures are exposing America's most economically vulnerable families to undo hardship and lasting disadvantages.

CHAPTER 7

Health

Life expectancy gap grows as coverage declines

by Elise Gould

Much of this book has focused on wages, income, and wealth across the population. This chapter turns to an examination of another important measure of workers' living standards—health care, particularly employer-provided health insurance, life expectancy, and health care costs.

Vast improvements have been made in health insurance coverage and health status over the last half century. Living standards are better in general, and Americans have the advantage of a more-extensive and far-reaching health care system than ever before. These improvements, though true on average, do not reflect the inequality in the U.S. health care system. While Americans, on average, are healthier and living longer, many are left without adequate insurance coverage or access to the great advances of our health care system. Nowhere are these disparities clearer than in life expectancies, where the gap between the socioeconomically best- and worst-off grew from 2.8 years in 1980 to 4.5 years in 2000.

This chapter begins with recent trends in employer-provided health insurance for the non-elderly population—by various individual and family characteristics. Since the previous business-cycle peak in 2000, fewer people receive this valuable benefit (down 5.4 percentage points), particularly among the less educated and lower income. Children experienced the greatest declines in employer-provided coverage (down 6.2 percentage points), although they have the greatest access to the public health insurance safety net that has kept many of them from becoming uninsured.

The data in this chapter suggest growing disparities in access to insurance, health security, and health outcomes by income, race, and education. Previous chapters have demonstrated the great divide between those at the top of the income distribution and those in the middle and the bottom. Here we reveal how those inequalities play out in the health care landscape. While average life span in the United States has grown, much of the increase is due to large gains at the top; gains at the bottom have been minimal. Disparities also remain by race: the infant mortality rate of blacks is 2.3 times higher than whites.

One area that affects everyone in the United States is rising health costs. The costs to employers and workers of purchasing coverage and the costs of purchasing health care services are growing much faster than overall inflation and wages. Premiums increased 115% from 1999 to 2007, as compared to increases of 29% and 24% in workers' earnings and wages, respectively. Rising expenses incur an increasing burden on working families, even for those lucky enough to have insurance through an employer.

This chapter concludes with a comparison of the United States with several Organization for Economic Cooperation and Development (OECD) countries in health spending, infant mortality, and life expectancy. While spending on health care in the United States exceeds that of other advanced economies, there is little benefit to show for these higher expenditures in terms of better health outcomes.

Employer-provided health insurance among non-elderly Americans

Chapter 3 (on wages) discussed the rate of employer-provided health insurance for strongly attached workers who get insurance from their own job. This chapter broadens the discussion of employment-based insurance to encompass all types of workers and their dependents. Employment-based coverage remains the predominant form of insurance for Americans under 65, particularly those with ties to the formal labor market. Because the vast majority of those 65 and older have access to Medicare, this chapter focuses on the non-elderly. Not surprisingly, the results here mirror those found earlier in the book.

About 2.7 million fewer people under the age of 65—including workers, their spouses, and their children—had health insurance provided by an employer in 2007 than in 2000. The percent of the non-elderly population with employer-provided health insurance fell from 68.3% in 2000 to 62.9% in 2007, a decline of 5.4 percentage points, despite a productivity-rich and highly profitable recovery (**Table 7.1**).

Although these declines in coverage occurred for all groups regardless of age, sex, race, nativity, education, or household income level, some experienced bigger declines than others. Those with only a high school education and those in the second-to-lowest household income quintile continue to be the hardest hit since 2000. High school graduates were not only less likely than college graduates to have employer-provided insurance (56.4% vs. 80.0%), but they experienced declines in coverage twice as large (9.2 vs. 3.6 percentage-point drops).

Health insurance coverage rates are also dramatically different by age, race, and ethnicity. Since 2000, children under 18 (-6.5 percentage points), adults 18-24 years old (-5.1), and adults 25-54 years old (-6.1) experienced significant declines in em-ployer-provided health coverage. The smaller losses in employer-provided coverage for older Americans may be attributed to the rising employment among this group since 2000.

TABLE 7.1 Employer-provided health insurance, population under 65 years old, 2000-07

	Health insurance coverage (%)		Percentage-point change
	2000	*2007*	*2000-07*
Under 65 population	68.3%	62.9%	-5.4
Age			
0-17 years	65.9%	59.5%	-6.5
18-24 years	53.5	48.4	-5.1
25-54 years	72.9	66.8	-6.1
55-64 years	68.1	67.8	-0.3
Gender			
Male	68.2%	62.5%	-5.7
Female	68.3	63.2	-5.1
Race			
White, non-Hisp.	75.6%	70.8%	-4.6
Black	56.1	51.6	-4.5
Hispanic	45.8	41.4	-4.4
Other	64.3	61.7	-2.6
Nativity			
Native	70.4%	65.1%	-5.3
Foreign born	52.2	47.4	-4.8
Education*			
Less than H.S.	39.0%	30.1%	-8.9
High school	65.6	56.4	-9.2
Some college	73.3	67.0	-6.3
College	83.5	80.0	-3.6
Post-college	87.6	85.8	-1.9
Household income fifth			
Lowest	28.7%	21.9%	-6.8
Second	61.7	53.6	-8.1
Middle	77.4	71.6	-5.7
Fourth	85.6	81.9	-3.7
Highest	88.4	86.4	-1.9

* Education reflects own education for individuals 18 and over and reflects family head's education for children under 18.

Source: Authors' analysis of BLS (2008c) data.

In 2007, 70.8% of whites had employer-provided coverage as compared to 51.6% of blacks and 41.4% of Hispanics. However, each of these groups experienced declines in coverage in excess of 4 percentage points. Being born outside the United States also has a significant impact on the likelihood of having employer-provided health insurance: 65.1% of native-born residents had coverage in 2007 as compared to 47.4% of those foreign born. However, the decline in coverage was pervasive across both groups. A growing immigrant population has not been a major driving force in the fall in overall coverage, particularly since there was a *larger* fall in employer-provided coverage among the native born (5.3 vs. 4.8 percentage-point drop).

Employer-provided coverage fell for all groups across the income scale, and households with the lowest incomes had the lowest coverage rates. Only about one in five individuals in the bottom fifth of the household income scale had employer-provided health insurance, whereas more than four in five individuals in the highest income fifth had coverage. Individuals in households in the second fifth saw the largest declines in coverage, falling 8.1 percentage points, from 61.7% in 2000 to 53.6% in 2007, or nearly 3.9 million fewer Americans with employer-provided coverage in that income group alone.

Children experience lower access to private health coverage
Insurance plays an invaluable role in providing children access to health care. When children lack coverage they experience the burden of health services delayed, including

FIGURE 7A Employment-based health insurance and Medicaid/SCHIP for children under 18 in the United States, 2000-07

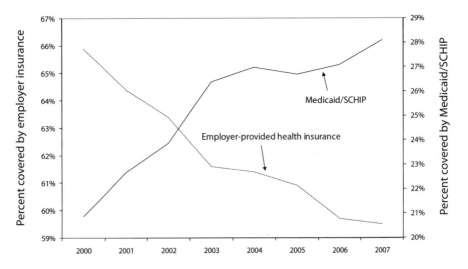

untreated illnesses, higher incidence of health problems, higher avoidable hospitalizations, and future financial risks placed on the family. In the short run, poor health undermines a child's achievement in school (e.g., untreated vision, hearing, and oral health problems can all cause distractions from learning). In the long run, better health improves future prospects and increases earnings, which benefits both the future adults and their communities in the form of a better economy and higher government revenues.

Traditionally, workers and their families rely on employer-provided health insurance. By 2007, only 59.5% of children under 18 had such coverage, down 6.5 percentage points from 65.9% in 2000 (see Table 7.1).

As children lost employment-based coverage in the 2000s, they experienced overall gains in public coverage, a trend seen throughout the country. **Figure 7A** demonstrates that, over the last six years, the percent of children covered by the employment-based system has declined, and the percent of children covered by the public system has increased, which presumably has helped to keep more children from becoming uninsured. The share of children receiving Medicaid/State Children's Health Insurance Program (SCHIP) has leveled off since 2004, contributing to a rise in the number of uninsured children for two years in a row.

These results do not identify whether individual children switched from private to public coverage. In fact, some children may lose employer-provided coverage and simply become uninsured, while others move from being uninsured to gaining public coverage. Recent increases in public coverage (excepting the slight decline in 2005) have been the only factor mitigating the continued decline in the percent of uninsured children over the past few years (when employment-based coverage has been leaving more kids uncovered).

Critics of public health insurance argue that some people will simply drop their private insurance and opt for public coverage. These results, however, *do not* indicate that public coverage is causing employment-based insurance to decline. In fact, both trends are signs of the 2000s slack labor market. In the recent economy, fewer employers offer affordable coverage and more kids fall into the eligible range for public insurance. **Figure 7B** provides direct evidence that public insurance is not simply replacing private coverage. Most SCHIP enrollees (72.2%) were not covered by private coverage six months before enrollment in the public program. Another 13.6% lost coverage within a six-month period prior to SCHIP enrollment due to a lost job, an employer dropping coverage, or a change in family structure (as in divorce, separation, or death of a covered spouse).

This leaves only 14.2% of SCHIP cases that went directly from private to public coverage. More than half of these cases (7.7%) cited an inability to afford private coverage as the reason for shifting over to SCHIP; the cost of the family premium through their job was prohibitively high.

Churning in and out of insurance coverage
Uninsured Americans do not form a static group from one year to the next or even one month to the next. There is a group that is consistently uninsured through time, but many more Americans go in and out of various states of coverage.

FIGURE 7B Status of enrollees of the State Children's Health Insurance Program (SCHIP), 2002

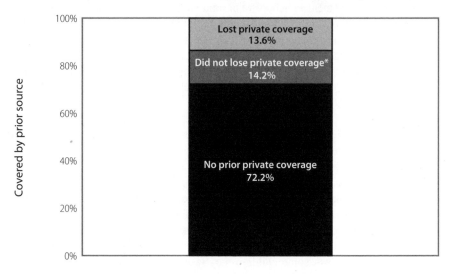

* Includes enrollees that found SCHIP coverage more affordable (7.7%), those with a general preference for SCHIP (1.8%), and reason unknown (4.7%).

Source: Sommers et al. (2007).

Tracking people over time, **Figure 7C** demonstrates the extent of shifting in and out of various states of coverage among Americans under 65 from 2001 to 2003. Over a third of the non-elderly are uninsured for at least one month over this three-year period, and a full quarter are uninsured for more than four months. While examining the uninsured at a point in time is useful, it understates the extent to which a larger share of Americans have spells without coverage and it misses the scope of the long-term coverage problem.

Disparities in health insurance and life expectancy

As shown in Table 7.1, access to employment-based coverage varies by race, nativity, education, and family income. Disparities also exist in access to insurance by type of job, wherein those with nonstandard jobs (part time or part year) have little to no employment-based coverage. This section examines more closely some of these disparities and long-term differences in health outcomes.

Substandard access for nonstandard workers

Nonstandard workers, in general, are not only often paid less (see the analysis of part-time workers in Chapter 4), but they also are less likely to receive benefits from their employers and more likely to be uninsured. Nonstandard work includes part-time jobs,

FIGURE 7C Duration without coverage, between 2001-03

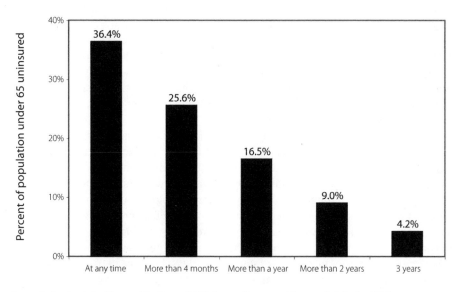

Source: Authors' analysis of Bureau of the Census (2001), Survey of Income and Program Participation (SIPP).

FIGURE 7D Source of health insurance, 2005

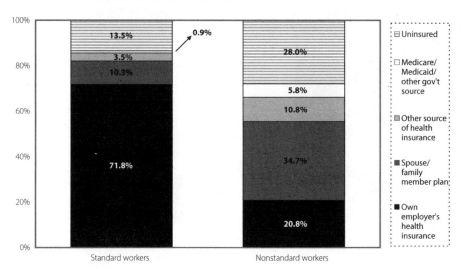

Source: Ditsler and Fisher (2006).

the self employed, independent contractors, and temporary jobs, among others. Over 30% of workers in the United States are nonstandard. **Figure 7D** gives the source of health insurance for both standard and nonstandard workers. Standard workers are much more likely to be insured and to be insured through employer-provided health insurance. In 2005, 86.5% of standard workers were insured, compared to 72.1% of nonstandard workers. Of those percentages, 71.8% of standard workers were insured through their own employer, while just 20.8% of nonstandard workers were. Although nonstandard workers were more likely to receive health insurance from a spouse or other family member's plan, overall nonstandard workers were more than twice as likely as standard workers to be uninsured.

The problem of access to employer-provided health insurance for the nonstandard workforce is clear in **Figure 7E**. In 2005, the majority (61.1%) of nonstandard workers was not eligible for employer-provided insurance, and just about one in five were insured by their employer's plan. In contrast, 14.9% of standard workers were not eligible, and 71.8% were insured through their employer. Many employers fail to provide benefits based on a particular work arrangement, such as denying benefits to part-time workers. This is exacerbated by the fact that many workers are working part time when they would prefer full-time work with benefits (see Chapter 4 for more on this).

Figure 7E indicates that 85.2% of standard workers, but only 39.0% of nonstandard workers, were eligible for employer-provided health insurance from their own employer.

FIGURE 7E Access to health insurance via own employer, 2005

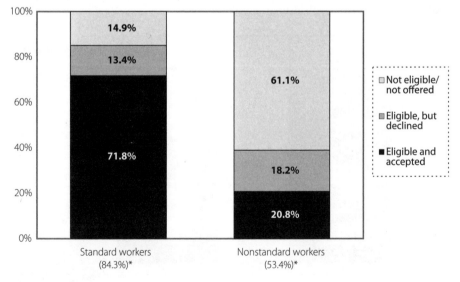

* Health insurance take-up rates in parentheses.

Source: Ditsler and Fisher (2006).

TABLE 7.2 Life expectancy (in years) by socioeconomic deprivation groups*, 1980-2000

	Life expectancy			Absolute difference with 10th decile		
	1980-82	*1989-91*	*1998-2000*	*1980-82*	*1989-91*	*1998-2000*
Both sexes						
Decile 1	73.0	73.9	74.7	2.8	3.5	4.5
Decile 2	73.8	74.8	75.8	2.0	2.6	3.4
Decile 3	73.8	74.8	76.1	2.0	2.6	3.1
Decile 4	74.0	75.1	76.4	1.8	2.3	2.8
Decile 5	74.1	75.4	76.7	1.7	2.0	2.5
Decile 6	73.9	75.2	76.7	1.9	2.2	2.5
Decile 7	74.5	75.9	77.4	1.3	1.5	1.8
Decile 8	74.9	76.3	78.3	0.9	1.1	0.9
Decile 9	75.1	76.4	78.3	0.7	1.0	0.9
Decile 10	75.8	77.4	79.2	0.0	0.0	0.0
Males						
Decile 1	68.7	69.8	71.5	3.8	4.7	5.4
Decile 2	69.8	71.0	72.8	2.7	3.5	4.1
Decile 3	69.8	71.1	73.1	2.7	3.4	3.8
Decile 4	70.1	71.5	73.5	2.4	3.0	3.4
Decile 5	70.3	71.9	73.9	2.2	2.6	3.0
Decile 6	70.1	71.6	73.8	2.4	2.9	3.1
Decile 7	70.8	72.4	74.7	1.7	2.1	2.2
Decile 8	71.3	72.8	75.7	1.2	1.7	1.2
Decile 9	71.5	73.0	75.8	1.0	1.5	1.1
Decile 10	72.5	74.5	76.9	0.0	0.0	0.0
Females						
Decile 1	77.5	78.0	78.0	1.3	2.1	3.3
Decile 2	77.9	78.6	78.7	0.9	1.5	2.6
Decile 3	77.7	78.5	78.9	1.1	1.6	2.4
Decile 4	77.8	78.6	79.1	1.0	1.5	2.2
Decile 5	77.9	78.8	79.4	0.9	1.3	1.9
Decile 6	77.7	78.7	79.4	1.1	1.4	1.9
Decile 7	78.2	79.2	80.0	0.6	0.9	1.3
Decile 8	78.4	79.6	80.8	0.4	0.5	0.5
Decile 9	78.5	79.7	80.7	0.3	0.4	0.6
Decile 10	78.8	80.1	81.3	0.0	0.0	0.0

* Socioeconomic deprivation group refers to a deprivation index based on 11 census-based, county-level social indicators including education, occupation, wealth, income distribution, unemployment rate, poverty rate, and housing quality; 1 being least well-off and 10 being most well-off.

Source: Authors' analysis of Singhl and Siahpush (2006).

Furthermore, nonstandard workers, even when eligible, were less likely to "take-up" their employer's insurance coverage: the take-up rates for eligible standard and eligible nonstandard workers were 84.3% and 53.4%, respectively (located in parentheses in Figure 7E). The two most common reasons cited for not enrolling in an employer's plan were that workers had coverage from another (probably cheaper or better quality) source, or that the plan being offered was too expensive. (Refer to Chapter 3 for more details on workers health coverage through the job.)

Growing inequality in life expectancy

Having examined the disparities in insurance coverage by socioeconomic status (i.e., family income and education), we now turn to issues of life expectancy. While life expectancy has grown on average across the United States, some segments of the population have experienced more improvement than others. **Table 7.2** compares life expectancy by socioeconomic class, ranked by decile from 1 (worst-off) to 10 (best-off). The data suggest that there are growing disparities in life expectancy by socioeconomic status.

In 1980, the worst-off group had a life expectancy 2.8 years lower than the best-off group (73.0 and 75.8 years, respectively). Twenty years later in 2000, this disparity had grown to a 4.5 year differential. The worst-off socioeconomic group had a life expectancy of 74.7 years as compared to 79.2 for the best-off. This increased disparity, however, was not only found between the extremes of the socioeconomic scale—the

FIGURE 7F Absolute difference in life expectancy between top and bottom decile socioeconomic deprivation groups,* 1980-2000

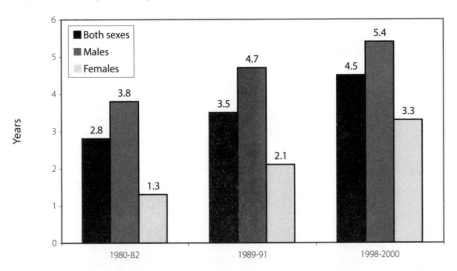

* See note to Table 7.2.

Source: Authors' analysis of Singhl and Siahpush (2006).

gap between the life expectancy of the middle group (the 5th decile) and the best-off (10th decile) climbed from 1.7 in 1980 to 2.5 by 2000.

When comparing these trends by gender, the evidence suggests that the disparities are higher for males (**Figure 7F**). Since 1980 females consistently had a higher life expectancy than males across the socioeconomic spectrum, although this gender gap had narrowed somewhat by 2000.

Furthermore, research on working men finds that increases in longevity are not balanced across the income ladder. According to a new Social Security Administration working paper (Waldron 2007), a male in the top half of the earnings distribution who turned 60 in 1972 could expect to live 1.2 years longer than one in the bottom half. By 2001, that gap had grown to 5.8 years. **Figure 7G** shows how the growth in life expectancy over the 29-year period was primarily due to longevity advances among the top half of the earnings distribution. These data show that life expectancy for men increased on average by 4.2 years, and that the 6.5 year gain in life expectancy by the best-paid half reaped 77% of the total gains in life expectancy. (It is also interesting to note that Meara, Richards, and Cutler [2008] find growing disparities in life expectancy by education level.)

Similar to improvement in overall life expectancy, the United States has experienced significant reductions in infant mortality. As **Figure 7H** shows, although both blacks and whites have seen marked improvements in infant mortality, a large disparity remains. The infant mortality rate among blacks was still 2.3 times that of whites in 2004.

FIGURE 7G Life expectancy for male Social Security-covered workers (age 60) by earnings group, 1972 and 2001

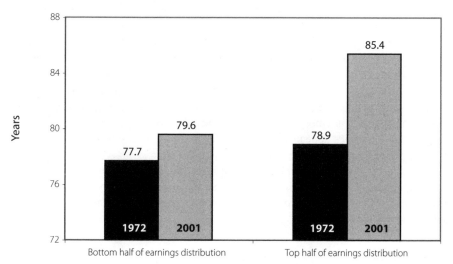

Source: Authors' analysis of Waldron (2007).

FIGURE 7H Racial disparities in infant mortality rates, 1980-2004

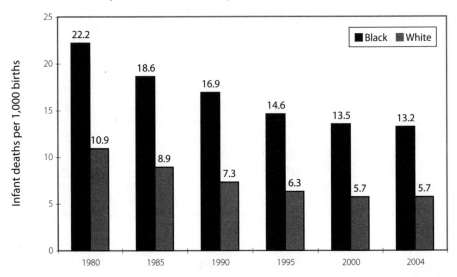

Source: U.S. Department of Health and Human Services (2005, 2007).

Health insecurity unequal by race and ethnicity

Employer-based health insurance is eroding for all Americans, but among the major racial and ethnic groups, Hispanic workers are the most likely to work for small firms and in industry sectors that do not offer employment-based insurance, according to a recent study by the National Council of La Raza (2008). (Chapter 3 documents their lower coverage on the job.) **Figures 7I** shows that among whites, African Americans, and Hispanics, the latter experience the most health care insecurity. As compared to 17% of whites and 20% of African Americans, 26% of Hispanics do not visit the doctor out of a concern over costs. Hispanics are most likely to take money out of personal or retirement savings to pay for health-related expenses, and among those with health insurance, Hispanics are most worried about losing their coverage. All of these indicators suggest that Hispanics appear to experience the most insecurity when it comes to employer-provided health care coverage.

Thus far we have documented growing insecurity and disparities in coverage. So what explains this increase in the uninsured and the losses in employer-provided coverage? One answer is the rapid growth in insurance and health care costs. The next section details these trends.

Rising costs

The cost of purchasing employment-based health insurance has grown dramatically in the last several years. As shown in **Figure 7J**, premiums grew 115.3% between

FIGURE 7I Racial differences in health care insecurity, 2007

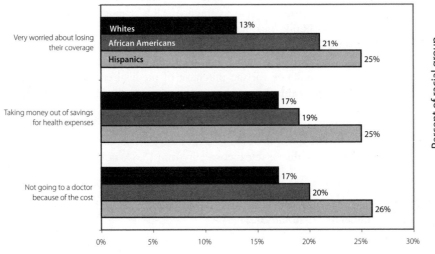

Source: The Rockefeller Foundation (2007).

FIGURE 7J Growth rate index of health premiums, workers' earnings and overall inflation, 1999-2007

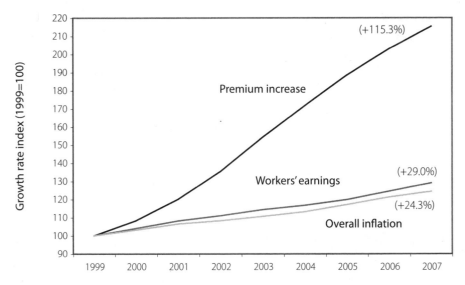

Source: Authors' analysis of Kaiser Family Foundation (2007).

1999 and 2007, a time when workers' earnings only grew 29.0% and overall inflation grew 24.3%.

In 2007, the total cost of the average employer-provided health insurance premium for family plans was $12,106, with an average of $8,824 paid for directly by the working family. Median family income in the United States was just under $60,000 in 2007 (see Chapter 1). While the cost of the premium alone looms large in families' budgets, the premium is only one way that families share in the costs of securing health care. Out-of-pocket expenditures for the purchase of medical care and services, for instance, have also grown. **Table 7.3** combines these costs to illustrate the total family out-of-pocket burden.

The total out-of-pocket burden for a family is measured in comparison to after-tax family income in 1996 and 2003. In 2003, 19.2% of the U.S. population had health care burdens in excess of 10% of disposable income, up from 15.8% in 1996. In other words,

TABLE 7.3 Percent of persons with total family out-of-pocket burdens by insurance and poverty status (under 65), 1996 and 2003

	1996		2003	
	Burden >10% of disposable income	Burden >20% of disposable income	Burden >10% of disposable income	Burden >20% of disposable income
Total U.S. population	15.8%	5.5%	19.2%	7.3%
Insurance status				
Private employment-related insurance	14.2%	3.8%	18.2%	5.5%
Private nongroup insurance	50.0	19.8	53.4	21.1
Public insurance	15.1	8.3	19.4	10.7
No coverage	12.7	6.7	14.5	8.8
Poverty status (% of federal poverty line)				
Poor (<100%)	25.9%	17.7%	33.3%	24.0%
Near poor/low income (100 to <200%)	24.1	6.7	23.7	9.9
Middle income (200% to <400%)	15.6	3.7	22.7	6.2
High income (≥400%)	7.1	1.5	9.7	1.6
Health status				
Perceived health to be fair or poor	--	--	32.3%	15.7%
Limitations in activities of daily living*	--	--	31.4	15.1

* Pertaining to both physical and sensory activity (i.e., visual and hearing impairments).

Source: Banthin and Bernard (2006).

nearly 20% of the U.S. population spent more than 10% of their after-tax income on health care premiums and purchases of health goods and services in 2003. Burdens in excess of 20% of disposable income were found in 7.3% of the U.S. population in 2003, up from 5.5% in 1996.

Medical cost burdens vary by insurance type and poverty status. The highest burdens are found in families with private, non-group insurance, that is, insurance purchased on the individual market. This is due to the fact that premiums are often higher and coverage is often less comprehensive in the non-group market. In addition, higher cost burdens are associated with fair or poor health; 32.3% of those in fair or poor health spent more than 10% of their disposable income on medical expenses in 2003, and 15.7% spent more than 20%. Those who are both in poor health and have to buy health coverage in the non-group market are doubly burdened.

Table 7.3 also demonstrates that family burdens decline as income rises. One-third of the poor spend more than 10% of their income on health care, and nearly one-quarter spend over 20%. Those with higher incomes spend a much lower percent of their family income on health care; less than 10% spend more than 10% of their disposable income on health coverage, and only 1.6% spend more than 20%. But the poor and high income alike saw increases from 1996 to 2003 in the share of those with serious burdens from health care costs.

Even for those who are fortunate to have health insurance coverage through their job, the share of premiums paid for by their employer may be crowding out wage gains. From 1980 to 2006, health insurance is shown to eat up a larger part of compensation, as wages and salaries take up less (**Figure 7K**). At the start of the last peak (2000), 5.7% of total compensation was spent on health insurance premiums. By 2006, health insurance spending made up 7.2% of total compensation. This increase occurred as wages and salaries fell 2.5 percentage points as a share of total compensation.

While a one-for-one trade-off would not be expected, higher health costs must be paid for somehow, either by cutting back on other forms of worker compensation and/or reducing firms' profits. That said, higher health insurance costs are not the primary driver for overall wage trends, and they cannot explain the key trends identified in earlier chapters of this book. Certainly health care costs cannot explain any part of the wage stagnation experienced by the 45% of workers who do not even receive insurance through their job (see Chapter 3 on wages). Furthermore, the slowdown in wage growth in this recovery cannot be attributed to health costs, which slowed even more than wage growth (see Figure 7K).

International comparisons

This chapter has demonstrated that one of the most pressing issues in the United States is health insurance and access to health care. But how does the United States compare to other countries in terms of health spending and outcomes? Although the United States spends more on health care than other countries with similar per capita income and populations, it has worse health outcomes, on average. As compared to these comparable Organization for Economic Cooperation and Development (OECD) countries, the United States is the only one without universal coverage.

FIGURE 7K Employer contributions to health insurance and wages as a share of total compensation,* 1979-2006

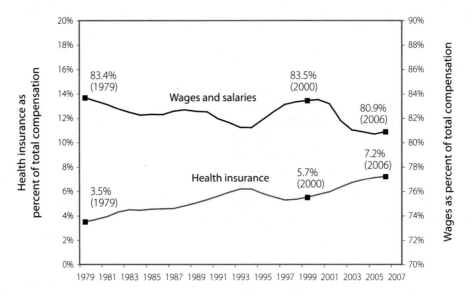

* Total compensation, other insurance, and pension funds.

Source: Authors' analysis of Bureau of Economic Analysis (2008) data.

Americans who have adequate health insurance are provided good health care, but, in the United States, many people have no health insurance whatsoever. In 2006, about 47 million Americans did not have any form of health insurance coverage. As shown earlier in this chapter, the incidence of employer-provided health coverage has been decreasing. At the same time, costs of obtaining coverage and purchasing private health care is increasingly difficult for most low- to middle-income workers, let alone those who are among the unemployed or otherwise disenfranchised. Those with pre-existing conditions or family members with chronic illnesses find it near impossible to purchase adequate insurance on their own.

Figure 7L illustrates the amount of public and private expenditures on health care as a percentage of GDP in 2005. The United States spent more on health care per capita than any of the other countries. In total, the United States spent 15.3% of its GDP on health care—Switzerland (11.6%) and France (11.1%) were a distant second and third. The countries that spent the least were Finland (7.5%), Ireland (7.5%), and Japan (8.0%). Strikingly, it was only in the United States that private expenditures were greater than public expenditures on health care. Overwhelmingly, for the other OECD countries, public expenditures on health care accounted for the majority of overall spending on health.

FIGURE 7L Public and private expenditures on health care spending (as percent of GDP), 2005

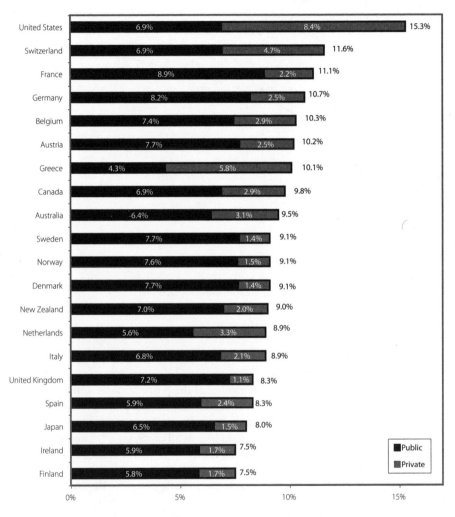

Percent of gross domestic product

* Any discrepancies in total expenditure are due to rounding.

Source: OECD (2007g).

Of course, health spending is not the whole of health care; it is essential to know the relationship between health care spending and outcomes. Based on OECD data, **Figure 7M** illustrates the simple relationship between life expectancy at birth and per capita health care spending. Higher per capita health spending is generally associated

FIGURE 7M Life expectancy at birth and health spending per capita, 2005

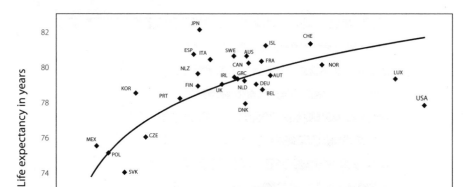

Health spending per capita, U.S. dollars

* See the Figure Notes for a guide to the country abbreviations.

Source: Authors' analysis of OECD (2007g) data.

with a higher life expectancy (as is indicative of the positive slope of the line). However, this relationship tends to be less pronounced with higher per capita spending. The United States was a clear outlier. It had the highest per capita health care spending, but its life expectancy was ranked in the bottom half of all of the OECD countries (not just those of similar size and GDP). The United States spent over twice as much as Japan, but Americans' life expectancy is lower by over four years.

Another important health outcome is infant mortality rate. As **Figure 7N** indicates, in 1979 infant mortality rates (per 1,000 live births) were very high for many OECD countries. The highest rates were in Greece (18.7), Italy (15.4), and Austria (14.7). Moreover, the lowest rates at that time were Sweden (7.5), Finland (7.6), and Japan (7.9)—all of which were higher than the highest rates in 2005. All peer countries made significant progress in reducing infant mortality between 1979 and 2005 (an average decline of 63%). As with life expectancy, the U.S. infant mortality rate—while it decreased by nearly 50% from 1979 to 2005—was the highest amongst these OECD countries in 2005. In 2005, Sweden (2.4) had the lowest infant mortality rate, while Greece, Germany, Spain, and Austria decreased their rates by more than 70% during this period.

Although there are many factors that influence health outcomes, it is clear that the contribution of health care goes a long way in explaining the differences in the health

FIGURE 7N Infant mortality, per 1,000 live births

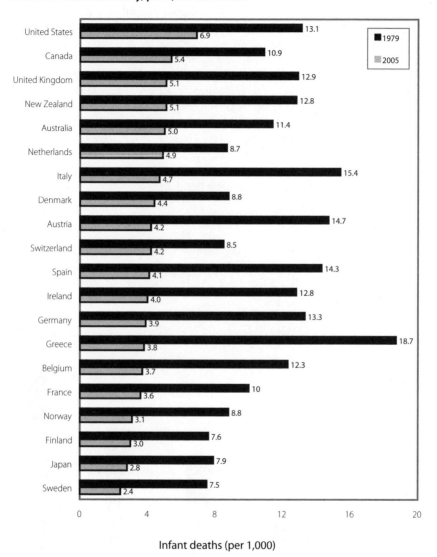

Infant deaths (per 1,000)

Source: OECD (2007g).

outcomes described here. Many in the United States enjoy premier health care, while others have none. Compared to the Untied States, other countries are more committed to the health and well-being of their citizens through more-universal coverage and more-comprehensive health care systems.

The Commonwealth Fund International Health Policy Survey offers some insight into health care costs and health care received. **Figure 70** charts responses to a survey question that asked adults whether they went without needed care due to costs. The lighter bars in the figure include responses from all surveyed adults, and the darker bars represent the responses from adults with below-average incomes. Forty percent of adults surveyed in the United States reported they went without needed care due to costs. This percentage increased to 57% for respondents with below-average incomes. For all adults and those with below-average income, survey respondents in the United Kingdom reported the lowest incidence of forgoing needed health care due to costs. This is true despite the fact that the United Kingdom spends a relatively low 7.2% of its GDP on public health expenditures and covers 100% of its citizens. Compared to the United States, all of the other countries surveyed had smaller shares of their population that went without health care because of costs, even though the United States spends a larger share of its national income on health care.

Conclusion

Economic well-being is measured along many dimensions. This chapter detailed troubling trends in health insurance that have only worsened during the most recent recovery. These findings indicate that fewer Americans have access to employment-

FIGURE 70 Percent of adults going without needed health care due to costs, 2004

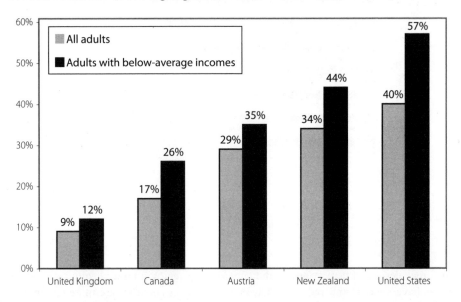

Source: Schoen and Osborn (2004).

based coverage, that rising costs are eroding family incomes, and that widening disparities exist in insurance coverage and health outcomes by race, income, and education. Costs are rising for both working families and firms, and it is not clear what the United States gains by the money it spends, as compared to other developed countries.

CHAPTER 8

International comparisons
How does the United States stack up against its global peers?

The preceding chapters have examined the current U.S. economy using historical outcomes as a benchmark. This chapter compares the economic performance of the United States to 19 other industrialized countries belonging to the Paris-based Organization for Economic Cooperation and Development (OECD), one of the world's most reliable sources of comparable statistics. The 19 countries used for comparison were selected because, aside from the United States, they are the 19 richest OECD countries (as measured by income per capita in 2007) who also have a population of at least a few million people. These countries are the global peers of the United States—economies facing the same global conditions with respect to trade, investment, technology, the environment, and other factors that shape economic opportunities. The comparison thus provides an independent yardstick for gauging the strengths and weaknesses of the U.S. economy. It also sheds light on the advisability of other countries adopting the "United States model"—specifically, features of the U.S. economy such as weaker unions, lower minimum wages, less-generous social benefits, and lower taxes—as a strategy for addressing their economic problems, real or perceived.

Two dominant themes emerge from this chapter. First, while the United States is a very rich country—currently second only to Norway in per capita income—it also has both the highest level of inequality and the highest level of poverty (including child poverty) of its peers. In other words, much less of the vast income of the United States is reaching the lower end of the income distribution. While it is true that many families in the United States are well-off, a great many are not, especially when compared to low- and moderate-income families in other advanced countries.

Second, it is far from a foregone conclusion that economies that have strong welfare states and labor protections are also necessarily less productive, less employment-generating, and less "flexible" than the U.S. economy. Many peer countries with strong unions, high minimum wages, generous social benefits, and high taxes have caught up with, and in many cases surpassed, U.S. productivity while achieving low unemployment levels. Both Norway and the Netherlands, for example, have higher productivity than the United States and lower unemployment rates. It is an important point that so many peer countries have been successful and productive within very different economic models.

For ease of comparison, in each table that follows, the seven largest economies are first listed in order of size (these countries form the group of the seven major industrialized nations, or G-7: United States, Japan, Germany, United Kingdom, France, Italy, and Canada), followed by the remaining 13 countries in alphabetical order.

Per capita income and productivity

A country's standard of living refers to both the value of goods and services available to its citizens and to the way those goods and services are distributed across the population. This section tackles the former by looking at per capita income (the total value of goods and services produced in the domestic economy per member of the population) and productivity (the total value of goods and services produced in the domestic economy per hour worked). Later in the chapter, the focus turns to income distribution measures.

Because countries have different currencies, it is important to be clear about what exchange rates are used to make income measures internationally comparable. This section uses purchasing-power parity (PPP) exchange rates. PPPs are not based on international currency market exchange rates but rather on the price of buying a given "basket" of goods and services—i.e., PPPs equalize the purchasing power of currencies in their home countries. While the calculation of PPPs presents many practical and conceptual problems, the use of PPPs provides by far the best measure of relative living standards for two reasons. First, PPPs are much less volatile than market exchange rates, and second, PPPs reflect long-term differences in costs of living across countries. It is important to note, however, that the pattern of growth in per capita income is similar regardless of whether PPPs or market exchange rates are used.

Per capita income in the United States has been among the highest in the world for the entire post–World War II period. **Table 8.1** shows per capita income levels and growth rates for the United States and its peers from 1950 to 2007. In 1950, with many peer countries still rebuilding after World War II, U.S. per capita income was well ahead of all the peer economies except Switzerland. The United States remained second only to Switzerland up to the early 1980s, when it was also surpassed by Norway. Since the early 1990s, the United States has been second only to Norway.

What these rankings disguise are the large relative gains made by almost all the other countries on the list. Of the 19 countries for which data are available since 1950, the United States is ranked *17th* in terms of per capita income growth from 1950-2007.

TABLE 8.1 Per capita income using purchasing-power parity, 1950-2007 (2007 dollars)

Country	Per capita income					Annual growth rates				
	1950	1979	1989	2000	2007	1950-79	1979-89	1989-2000	2000-07	1950-2007
United States	$13,881	$27,278	$33,477	$41,236	$45,604	2.4%	2.1%	1.9%	1.4%	2.1%
Japan	2,793	19,142	26,093	30,158	33,303	6.9	3.1	1.3	1.4	4.4
Germany	–	–	26,365	31,159	33,880	–	–	1.5	1.2	–
United Kingdom	10,236	19,422	24,211	29,737	34,827	2.2	2.2	1.9	2.3	2.2
France	7,661	21,757	25,768	30,430	32,906	3.7	1.7	1.5	1.1	2.6
Italy	5,367	19,494	24,474	28,772	30,649	4.5	2.3	1.5	0.9	3.1
Canada	11,009	24,415	28,851	33,759	37,812	2.8	1.7	1.4	1.6	2.2
Australia	$11,194	$21,628	$25,816	$32,637	$38,451	2.3%	1.8%	2.2%	2.4%	2.2%
Austria	6,092	22,105	26,892	34,008	38,596	4.5	2.0	2.2	1.8	3.3
Belgium	8,409	21,339	25,778	31,804	35,751	3.3	1.9	1.9	1.7	2.6
Denmark	10,201	22,499	26,830	33,742	37,185	2.8	1.8	2.1	1.4	2.3
Finland	6,205	17,989	24,720	28,844	35,304	3.7	3.2	1.4	2.9	3.1
Greece	3,623	16,845	19,130	22,913	30,369	5.4	1.3	1.7	4.1	3.8
Ireland	5,417	13,125	17,068	34,184	45,204	3.1	2.7	6.5	4.1	3.8
Netherlands	9,491	23,282	26,519	35,221	38,118	3.1	1.3	2.6	1.1	2.5
New Zealand	12,352	17,945	20,481	23,637	27,382	1.3	1.3	1.3	2.1	1.4
Norway	10,034	26,632	33,554	46,362	53,011	3.4	2.3	3.0	1.9	3.0
Spain	3,721	15,416	19,689	26,143	29,774	5.0	2.5	2.6	1.9	3.7
Sweden	9,980	21,799	25,950	30,475	36,425	2.7	1.8	1.5	2.6	2.3
Switzerland	14,583	29,042	33,684	36,097	38,842	2.4	1.5	0.6	1.1	1.7
Average excluding U.S.	$8,243	$20,771	$25,362	$31,583	$36,199	3.5%	2.0%	2.0%	2.0%	2.8%
Ratio of U.S. to non-U.S. average	1.68	1.31	1.32	1.31	1.26	0.67	1.02	0.94	0.73	0.76

Source: Authors' analysis of The Conference Board and Groningen Growth and Development Centre (2008).

Only Switzerland and New Zealand have lower rates of per capita income growth over the last six decades. While in 1950 the per capita income of the United States was 68% higher than the average of its peers, in 2007 the per capita income of the United State was 26% higher than its peer average. It should be noted that the slower growth in the United States is not just a function of the enormous growth in Europe following World War II. In recent years, the U.S. growth rate, at 1.4% annually from 2000 to 2007, is ranked 13th out of the 20 countries. **Figure 8A** illustrates the growth rates over time of the United States compared to the other comparison countries collectively. The upshot of Table 8.1 and Figure 8A is that while the U.S. standard of living as measured by per capita income has historically been significantly higher than most of its peers, those peers have been quickly closing the gap.

Table 8.2 shows levels and growth rates over time of productivity—the value of goods and services an economy can produce, on average, in an hour of work. Other nations' productivity levels are presented as a percentage of the U.S. level. Productivity growth provides the basis for increasing living standards and is therefore a key element in any examination of differences across countries. An important trend to note when examining productivity growth in the peer economies is that, as with per capita income, there was a dramatic slowdown after the mid-1970s in every case. Growth across the board was much faster in the 1950s and 1960s than it was in the 1980s, 1990s, and first half of the 2000s. Within that overall trend, the U.S. economy has historically been far more productive than its peers. For example, in 1950, the United States was over five

FIGURE 8A Annual growth rates of per capita income using PPPs, 1950-2007 (2007 dollars)

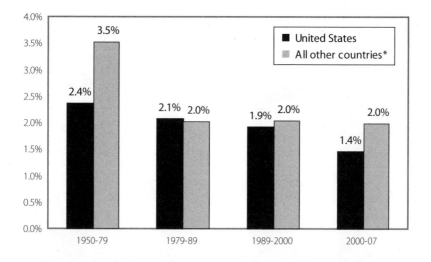

*Average of all countries listed in Table 8.1, not including the United States.

Source: Authors' analysis of The Conference Board and Groningen Growth and Development Centre (2008).

TABLE 8.2 Productivity levels and growth, 1950-2007 (2007 dollars)

Country	GDP per hour worked (U.S.=100)					Annual growth rates			
	1950	1979	1989	2000	2007	1950-79	1979-89	1989-2000	2000-07
United States	100	100	100	100	100	2.3%	1.3%	1.6%	2.0%
Japan	18	57	67	72	71	6.4	2.9	2.3	1.9
Germany	–	–	94	98	95	–	–	2.1	1.4
United Kingdom	63	73	80	87	89	2.8	2.3	2.4	2.3
France	42	85	99	103	99	4.8	2.8	2.1	1.3
Italy	40	90	98	99	87	5.2	2.2	1.6	0.3
Canada	84	89	86	86	81	2.5	0.9	1.7	1.1
Australia	76	84	81	85	82	2.6%	1.0%	2.0%	1.6%
Austria	34	83	92	108	103	5.5	2.3	3.1	1.4
Belgium	52	95	105	110	102	4.4	2.4	2.1	0.9
Denmark	57	83	89	93	85	3.6	2.0	2.0	0.8
Finland	34	60	72	82	83	4.3	3.1	2.8	2.3
Greece	27	73	72	66	71	5.9	1.2	0.8	3.1
Ireland	31	58	74	89	92	4.4	3.9	3.3	2.5
Netherlands	61	101	106	106	100	4.1	1.8	1.7	1.2
New Zealand	–	60	66	62	58	–	2.2	1.0	1.1
Norway	62	108	119	136	135	4.3	2.3	2.9	1.8
Spain	25	68	87	82	71	5.9	3.8	1.1	0.0
Sweden	58	85	82	84	87	3.6	1.1	1.8	2.6
Switzerland	81	99	96	88	83	3.0	0.9	0.9	1.1
Average excluding U.S.	50	81	88	91	88	4.3%	2.2%	2.0%	1.5%
Ratio of U.S. to non-U.S. average	2.01	1.24	1.14	1.10	1.13	0.53	0.60	0.83	1.33

Source: Authors' analysis of The Conference Board and Groningen Growth and Development Centre (2008).

times as productive as Japan and over twice as productive as France and Italy. However, the productivity growth of many peer countries has been so dramatic over the last six decades that in 2007, four peer economies—Norway, Austria, Belgium, and the Netherlands—matched or exceeded U.S. productivity. Furthermore, while in 1950 the U.S. productivity level was more than twice as high as the average of its peers, in 2007 it was only 13% higher.

U.S. productivity growth has, however, experienced a recent surge. **Figure 8B** illustrates data from Table 8.2 for two time periods, 1989-2000 and 2000-07, for the G-7. From 1989-2000, the United States ranked last among G-7 countries (and 16th overall) in productivity growth, but from 2000 to 2007 the United States experienced strong growth on average and is trailing only the United Kingdom (while ranking sixth overall). Though not captured in this chart, it is worth noting that the U.S. productivity surge actually took place between 1996 and 2004, while growth since that time has slowed dramatically.

Some economists have accounted for the relatively low U.S. productivity growth up to the 1990s by arguing that it is much harder to lead than to follow, to innovate than to imitate. In this view, productivity growth would be faster outside the United States because other economies have the advantage of being able to rapidly assimilate technological improvements pioneered in the United States. While this view may have made sense as late as the 1960s or 1970s, the data show that by the 1990s, several peer countries had productivity levels that matched or exceeded that of the United States, and many others had narrowed the gap considerably. This suggests that there may be features intrinsic to peer economies that provide them with an important edge over the United States when it comes to productivity growth. In particular, the ability of France,

FIGURE 8B Productivity growth rates in G-7 countries

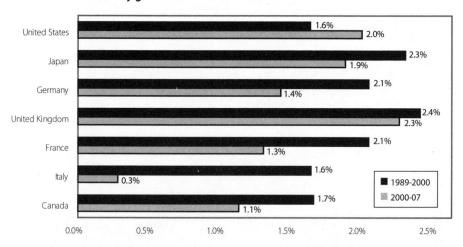

Source: Authors' analysis of The Conference Board and Groningen Growth and Development Centre (2008).

Belgium, the Netherlands, and Norway to reach U.S. productivity levels in the 1990s suggests these countries' comprehensive welfare and collective-bargaining systems have not stymied income growth or improvements in economic efficiency relative to the more free-market–oriented United States. (Figure 8C, discussed in the next section, further supports this view.)

Employment and hours worked

The per capita income figures in Table 8.1 may appear, at face value, to be at odds with the productivity figures in Table 8.2. Per capita income (i.e., GDP per capita) in the United States is generally much higher relative to peer countries than is U.S. productivity (i.e., GDP per hour worked). For example, in 2007, the U.S. per capita income trailed only Norway and was 26% higher than the average of its peer countries, whereas the U.S. productivity level trailed Norway, Austria, Belgium, and the Netherlands and was only 13% higher than the average of its peer countries. What accounts for U.S. per capita income being so much more impressive than U.S. productivity? The discrepancy stems from two important differences across countries: the share of the total population employed and the average number of hours worked each year by those with jobs. This section compares employment, unemployment, and hours worked across countries.

Employment rates vary across countries because of differences in not just job prospects, but also school enrollment rates for adults, early retirement rates, women's non-market responsibilities (especially child care), and other cultural norms. **Table 8.3** gives the percentage employed among people aged 15-64 for the peer economies. It shows that while historically the United States tended to employ more of its working-age population than the majority of its peers, the gap has closed substantially, especially from 2000 to 2006. Currently, the U.S. employment-to-population ratio is in the middle of the peer-country pack.

Table 8.4 shows the average annual hours worked of employed people from 1979 to 2006. Historically, the United States was in the middle of the pack for average working hours. Over the last three decades, however, workers in other countries have reduced their hours dramatically (by an average of over 10%) in comparison to the United States (which saw working hours reduced by less than 2%). Workers from the historic leader in annual hours—Japan—experienced a reduction in average hours of 16.1% from 1979 to 2006. Currently, U.S. workers work more hours on average than any of the comparison countries, with workers from the Netherlands, Norway, and Germany working the fewest hours on average.

The data on employment rates and average hours worked suggest a simple exercise to assess how much of the U.S. advantage in GDP per capita is due to productivity, how much is due to success in providing jobs to potential workers, and how much is due to differences in average hours worked. **Table 8.5** uses the fact that per capita income is equal to the product of productivity, average hours worked per worker, and the employment-to-population ratio. The first column of the table gives the percent difference in per capita income between each country and the average of all the countries in the table. For example, the per capita income in 2006 in the United States was 25% higher than the

TABLE 8.3 Employment rates (ages 15-64), 1979-2006

Country	1979	1989	2000	2006	Percentage-point change		
					1979-89	1989-2000	2000-06
United States	67.9%	72.5%	74.1%	72.0%	4.6	1.6	-2.1
Japan	66.8	67.7	68.9	70.0	0.9	1.2	1.1
Germany	65.0	63.5	65.6	67.2	-1.5	2.1	1.6
United Kingdom	--	72.0	72.2	72.5	--	0.2	0.3
France	64.3	59.7	61.1	62.3	-4.6	1.4	1.2
Italy	53.4	52.0	53.9	58.4	-1.4	1.9	4.5
Canada	65.4	70.8	70.9	72.9	5.4	0.1	2.0
Australia	64.4%	68.2%	69.3%	72.2%	3.8	1.1	2.9
Austria	--	--	68.2	70.2	--	--	2.0
Belgium	--	53.8	60.9	60.4	--	7.1	-0.5
Denmark	--	75.3	76.4	76.9	--	1.1	0.5
Finland	68.9	74.2	67.0	68.9	5.3	-7.2	1.9
Greece	--	55.2	55.9	61.0	--	0.7	5.1
Ireland	55.7	50.0	64.5	68.1	-5.7	14.5	3.6
Netherlands	54.0	60.2	72.3	72.4	6.2	12.1	0.1
New Zealand	--	67.5	70.7	75.2	--	3.2	4.5
Norway	69.6	73.9	77.9	75.5	4.3	4.0	-2.4
Spain	54.7	50.8	57.4	65.7	-3.9	6.6	8.3
Sweden	79.2	82.9	74.2	74.5	3.7	-8.7	0.3
Switzerland	--	--	78.4	77.9	--	--	-0.5
Average excluding U.S.	63.5%	64.6%	67.7%	69.6%	1.0	2.4	1.9

Source: Authors' analysis of OECD (2007d, 2007c) data.

peer average, while per capita income in France was 10% lower than the average. The next three columns break down the first column (difference in per capita income) into the three constituent parts described above. It is important to note that while theoretically the last three columns should sum to the first, that is not always the case because some measurement error is virtually inevitable in this kind of decomposition (the data in each of the columns come from different sources within countries).

Table 8.5 shows that while per capita income in the United States was 25% higher than the peer average, only 12 of those percentage points can be attributed to higher

TABLE 8.4 Average annual hours worked, 1979-2006

Country	1979	1989	2000	2006	Change in hours (Number of hours) 1979-89	1989-2000	2000-06	(Percent) 1979-2006
United States	1,834	1,855	1,841	1,804	21	-14	-37	-1.6%
Japan	2,126	2,070	1,821	1,784	-56	-249	-37	-16.1
Germany	–	–	1,473	1,436	–	–	-37	–
United Kingdom	1,818	1,786	1,711	1,669	-32	-74	-43	-8.2
France	1,856	1,699	1,591	1,564	-157	-108	-27	-15.7
Italy	1,949	1,899	1,861	1,800	-50	-38	-61	-7.6
Canada	1,832	1,801	1,768	1,738	-31	-34	-30	-5.1
Australia	1,823	1,785	1,777	1,714	-38	-8	-64	-6.0%
Austria	–	–	1,632	1,655	–	–	23	–
Belgium	–	1,741	1,554	1,571	–	-187	17	–
Denmark	1,624	1,532	1,554	1,577	-92	22	24	-2.9
Finland	1,869	1,802	1,750	1,721	-67	-53	-29	-8.0
Greece	–	2,075	2,080	–	–	5	–	–
Ireland	–	1,999	1,719	1,640	–	-280	-79	–
Netherlands	–	1,497	1,372	1,391	–	-125	19	–
New Zealand	–	1,821	1,830	1,787	–	9	-44	–
Norway	1,580	1,511	1,455	1,407	-70	-55	-48	-10.9
Spain	2,022	1,822	1,815	1,764	-199	-7	-51	-12.8
Sweden	1,530	1,565	1,625	1,583	34	60	-42	3.4
Switzerland	1,819	1,709	1,685	–	-110	-25	–	–
Average excluding U.S.	1,821	1,771	1,688	1,635	-72	-67	-30	-10.2%

Source: Authors' analysis of OECD (2007c) data.

TABLE 8.5 Decomposition of per capita income, 2006

Country	Per capita income	Productivity	Average hours worked per worker	Employment-to-population ratio
United States	25%	12	10	3
Japan	-9	-22	8	6
United Kingdom	-6	-3	1	-1
France	-10	9	-5	-13
Canada	3	-9	6	0
Australia	3%	-9	4	0
Belgium	-3	12	-5	-15
Denmark	2	-4	-4	8
Finland	-6	-9	4	-3
Netherlands	3	12	-17	7
New Zealand	-26	-38	7	6
Norway	43	49	-19	10
Spain	-19	-21	6	-5
Sweden	-2	-3	-4	2

Source: Authors' analysis of OECD and The Conference Board and Groningen Growth and Development Centre (2008) data. See also Tables 8.1, 8.2, and 8.4.

productivity, whereas 10 percentage points are due to the fact that U.S. workers work more annual hours on average, and 3 percentage points are due to the fact that the United States employs a larger portion of its population. French productivity rates are 9% higher than the average, but a smaller-than-average share of the French population works, which reduces relative per capita income there by 13 percentage points, and those in France who do work tend to work fewer hours than the peer average, which further reduces relative per capita income in France by five percentage points. As a result, even though French workers are 9% more productive than the peer average, France has a per capita income that is 10% lower than the peer average. Norwegian productivity rates are 49% higher than the average, and a larger-than-average share of the Norwegian population works, which increases relative per capita income there by 10 percentage points. Workers in Norway, however, tend to work fewer hours than the peer average, which reduces relative per capita income by 19 percentage points, and as a result, the Norwegian per capita income is 43% above the peer average. The basic lesson of this table is that an important portion of the higher per capita income in the United States comes not from working more efficiently than its peer countries, nor from being more successful in providing jobs to potential workers, but rather from each worker simply working longer hours on average. Many peer nations, on the other hand, have taken a sizeable chunk of their productivity gains in the last several decades in the form of reduced hours. This is frequently an explicit policy choice—France, for example, adopted a 35-hour work week in January 2000, reduced from 39 hours.

An important complement to work is leisure. **Table 8.6** reveals one important reason for the differences in annual hours worked between the United States and its peer countries—differences in annual leave policies. The average statutory minimum paid vacation for the peer countries of the United States is 4.1 weeks. The United States

TABLE 8.6 Work and leave policies

Country	Full-time employees			
	Statutory paid minimum vacation (weeks)	Statutory paid public holidays (days)	Total (weeks)	Average annual weeks worked, 2005*
United States	0.0	0.0	0.0	46.7
Japan	2.0	0.0	2.0	--
Germany	4.0	10.0	6.0	41.7
United Kingdom	4.0	0.0	4.0	43.3
France	6.0	1.0	6.2	41.4
Italy	4.0	13.0	6.6	42.5
Canada	2.0	8.0	3.6	44.8
Australia	4.0	7.0	5.4	--
Austria	4.4	13.0	7.0	42.2
Belgium	4.0	10.0	6.0	44.0
Denmark	4.0	9.0	5.8	41.6
Finland	5.0	9.0	6.8	41.7
Greece	4.0	6.0	5.2	45.0
Ireland	4.0	9.0	5.8	44.6
Netherlands	4.0	0.0	4.0	43.1
New Zealand	4.0	7.0	5.4	--
Norway	5.0	2.0	5.4	41.0
Spain	4.4	12.0	6.8	43.3
Sweden	5.0	0.0	5.0	38.8
Switzerland	4.0	0.0	4.0	--
Average excluding U.S.	4.1	6.1	5.3	42.6

* Considers 52 weeks per year minus statutory public holidays, minimum paid leave, maternity/parental leave, sickness and disability leave, and leave for other reasons.

Source: Ray and Schmitt (2007) and OECD (2007e).

TABLE 8.7 Work and family policies

| Country | Maternity leave entitlements (in weeks), 2005 | | Public expenditure on child care support per child in U.S. dollars (using PPPs), 2003 |
	Total entitlement	Share of entitlement paid (FTE)*	
United States	12	0.0	$1,803
Japan	12	8.4	1,252
Germany	14	14.0	3,084
United Kingdom	52	15.3**	1,850
France	16	16.0	4,009
Italy	21	16.8	--
Canada	15	9.4	--
Australia	52	--	$ 874
Austria	16	16.0	3,251
Belgium	15	11.53***	1,900
Denmark	18	18.0	8,009
Finland	18	11.7	4,186
Greece	17	17.0	--
Ireland	26	14.4****	1,430
Netherlands	16	16.0	2,025
New Zealand	12	6.0	672
Norway	26	20.8	6,085
Spain	16	16.0	1,234
Sweden	15	12.0	5,530
Switzerland	16	16.0	919
Average excluding U.S.	21	14.0	$2,894

*   Full-time equivalent of leave in weeks, as if the claimant were to receive 100% of average earnings. Paid leave as listed here is the federal minimum standard and does not include parental or family leave benefits, or disability insurance for which a mother may qualify in a particular country.

**   Calculated at 90% for initial 6 weeks, followed by either: a flat rate (approximately 30% of average wage) for remaining 33 weeks (as calculated here) or 90% of average weekly earnings, whichever is lower (effective April 2007).

***   Paid at 82% for first four weeks and 75% for the remaining 11.

****   Paid at 80% for first 18 weeks plus eight weeks unpaid.

Source: OECD Family Database, OECD Social Expenditure Database, International Social Security Association (2006), and the United Nations (2005a and 2005b).

is the only country among its peers with no statutory vacation time. Furthermore, most of the peer countries also mandate a number of paid holidays, so that on average, the peer countries mandate 5.3 weeks of paid vacation and holiday leave, whereas the United States mandates neither.

In all countries, because some employers offer paid vacations above the statutory minimum and because some workers take unpaid vacations, the actual holidays and vacations taken by workers exceed the statutory minimum on average. The last column of Table 8.6 gives the average annual weeks worked by full-time workers. The differences between weeks worked and 52 weeks (i.e., working full year) include not just holidays and vacations, but also sick leave, disability leave, maternity leave, and leave for other reasons. Nonetheless, this column offers a revealing indicator of how much time off full-time workers in the United States have compared to full-time workers in peer countries. The average full-time U.S. worker, at 46.7 weeks per year, works more than the average worker in any peer countries, and about one month more than the overall average, which is 42.6 weeks. These figures present good evidence that the labor/leisure decision is structurally different in the United States compared to its global peers.

Table 8.7 shows another facet of the labor market that, because of women's historically greater responsibility for family and child care, is closely related to the labor force participation of women—maternity leave and child care benefits. In the United States, the Family Medical Leave Act of 1993 guarantees 12 weeks of unpaid maternity leave. That ranks the United States last among its peer countries in generosity of mandated maternity leave benefits. The most generous countries in terms of length of total leave (i.e., paid leave plus unpaid leave) are Australia and the United Kingdom, at one year of guaranteed leave each. The most generous countries in terms of paid leave are Norway (which offers 26 weeks at an 80% reimbursement rate, which is equivalent to 100% reimbursement for 20.8 weeks) and Denmark (which offers full reimbursement for 18 weeks). Data on public expenditures per child on child care support paint a similar story—the United States spent $1,803 per child, which was less than a fourth of what was spent in Denmark, less than a third of what was spent in Norway and Sweden, less than half of what was spent in Finland and France, and well below spending in Austria, Germany, the Netherlands, Belgium, and the United Kingdom.

Table 8.8 shows employment rates over time by gender. In 2006, the U.S. employed 66.1% of its female working-age population—ninth among the group of 20 peer countries. The patterns over time in the gender employment gap (the male employment rate minus the female employment rate) display interesting trends. In the United States and in its peer countries, women made dramatic employment gains in the 1980s relative to men, closing the employment gap by 9.2 percentage points in the United States and 9.6 percentage points on average elsewhere. In the 1990s, women continued to make relative employment gains, though at a slower rate—with gains of 4.5 percentage points in the United States and 6.2 on average elsewhere. From 2000 to 2006, the gains continued in the peer countries, with a decrease in the employment gap of 3.0 percentage points on average, but slowed dramatically in the United States, with a decrease of 0.8 points. In 2006, the United States had a gender employment

TABLE 8.8 Employment rates by gender, 1979-2006

Country	Women				Men				Gender employment gap				Percentage-point change in gender employment gap		
	1979	1989	2000	2006	1979	1989	2000	2006	1979	1989	2000	2006	1979-89	1989-2000	2000-06
United States	55.1%	64.1%	67.8%	66.1%	81.6%	81.4%	80.6%	78.1%	26.5%	17.3%	12.8%	12.0%	-9.2	-4.5	-0.8
Japan	51.3	54.8	56.7	58.8	82.8	80.6	80.9	81.0	31.5	25.8	24.2	22.2	-5.7	-1.6	-2.0
Germany	49.0	50.8	58.1	61.5	81.5	75.9	72.9	72.9	32.5	25.1	14.8	11.4	-7.4	-10.3	-3.4
United Kingdom	–	62.2	65.6	66.8	–	81.8	78.9	78.4	–	19.6	13.3	11.5	–	-6.3	-1.8
France	50.4	49.7	54.3	57.1	78.3	70.0	68.1	67.5	27.9	20.3	13.8	10.4	-7.6	-6.5	-3.4
Italy	32.5	35.2	39.6	46.3	75.1	69.2	68.2	70.5	42.6	34.0	28.6	24.2	-8.6	-5.4	-4.4
Canada	51.0	62.4	65.6	69.0	79.8	79.1	76.2	76.8	28.8	16.7	10.6	7.8	-12.1	-6.1	-2.8
Australia	46.4%	56.4%	61.4%	65.5%	82.1%	79.8%	77.1%	78.8%	35.7%	23.4%	15.7%	13.3%	-12.3	-7.7	-2.4
Austria	–	–	59.4	63.5	–	–	76.8	76.9	–	–	17.4	13.5	–	–	-3.9
Belgium	–	39.7	51.9	53.6	–	67.9	69.8	67.0	–	28.2	17.9	13.4	–	-10.3	-4.5
Denmark	–	69.5	72.1	73.2	–	80.9	80.7	80.6	–	11.4	8.6	7.4	–	-2.8	-1.2
Finland	64.3	71.4	64.5	67.3	73.5	77.0	69.4	70.5	9.2	5.6	4.9	3.2	-3.6	-0.7	-1.7
Greece	–	37.6	41.3	47.5	–	74.1	71.3	74.6	–	36.5	30.0	27.1	–	-6.5	-2.9
Ireland	32.2	34.5	53.3	58.8	78.5	65.6	75.6	77.3	46.3	31.1	22.3	18.5	-15.2	-8.8	-3.8
Netherlands	32.5	45.2	63.0	66.0	74.9	74.7	81.3	78.7	42.4	29.5	18.3	12.7	-12.9	-11.2	-5.6
New Zealand	–	57.6	63.5	68.4	–	77.7	78.2	82.1	–	20.1	14.7	13.7	–	-5.4	-1.0
Norway	58.1	67.5	74.0	72.3	80.7	80.1	81.7	78.6	22.6	12.6	7.7	6.3	-10.0	4.9	-1.4
Spain	29.6	30.6	42.0	54.0	80.2	71.1	72.7	77.3	50.6	40.5	30.7	23.3	-10.1	-9.8	-7.4
Sweden	72.0	80.7	72.2	72.1	86.2	85.1	76.2	76.8	14.2	4.4	4.0	4.7	-9.8	-0.4	0.7
Switzerland	–	–	69.4	71.1	–	–	87.3	84.7	–	–	17.9	13.6	–	–	-4.3
Average excluding U.S.	47.4%	53.3%	59.4%	62.8%	79.5%	75.9%	76.0%	76.4%	32.0%	22.6%	16.6%	13.6%	9.6	6.2	3.0

Source: Authors' analysis of OECD (2007c and 2007d).

TABLE 8.9 Employment growth, 1979-2006

Country	Annual growth rate (%)		
	1979-89	*1989-2000*	*2000-06*
United States	1.7%	1.4%	0.9%
Japan	1.1	0.5	-0.2
Germany	0.5	2.6	0.3
United Kingdom	0.6	0.2	0.7
France	0.2	0.8	0.7
Italy	0.4	0.0	1.4
Canada	2.0	1.2	1.9
Australia	2.4%	1.4%	2.1%
Austria	0.9	1.0	0.8
Belgium	0.0	1.1	0.6
Denmark	0.7	0.3	0.4
Finland	1.1	-0.6	0.8
Greece	1.0	1.0	1.4
Ireland	-0.5	3.8	3.2
Netherlands	2.3	2.4	0.7
New Zealand	2.0	1.5	2.7
Norway	0.8	1.0	0.7
Spain	0.4	1.9	4.1
Sweden	0.6	-0.6	0.7
Switzerland	1.8	0.9	0.8
Average excluding U.S.	1.0%	1.1%	1.3%

Source: Authors' analysis of OECD Annual Labor Force Statistics.

gap of 12 percentage points, lagging behind eight of its peers—Finland (3.2), Sweden (4.7), Norway (6.3), Denmark (7.4), Canada (7.8), France (10.4), Germany (11.4), and the United Kingdom (11.5).

An important thing to note in Table 8.8 is that women's relative employment gains over this period have come both from generally increasing women's employment and generally decreasing men's employment. For U.S. women, there was a dramatic increase in employment in the 1980s, which continued but at a slower rate in the 1990s and then actually reversed from 2000 to 2006. In the peer countries, the increase in employment rates among women has been relatively continuous over the entire period from 1979 to 2006. In the United States, men's employment rates were roughly flat over the 1980s, declined slightly in the 1990s, and declined a significant amount—2.5 percentage points—from 2000 to 2006. Men in the peer countries generally experienced a much steeper decline during the 1980s, a similar slight decline during the 1990s, and a slight increase in employment from 2000 to 2006.

The capacity of the U.S. economy to sustain high employment rates for men and women is an important economic accomplishment. **Table 8.9** puts U.S. job creation into historical and international context by presenting annual employment growth rates in the 20 peer countries over time. In the 1980s, Australia had the highest annual growth rate, at 2.4%, followed by the Netherlands, Canada, New Zealand, and then the United

TABLE 8.10 Standardized unemployment rates, 1979-2006

Country	1979	1989	2000	2006
United States	5.8%	5.3%	4.0%	4.6%
Japan	2.1	2.3	4.7	4.1
Germany	2.7	5.6	7.2	8.4
United Kingdom	4.7	7.1	5.4	5.3
France	5.6	8.8	9.1	9.4
Italy	5.8	9.7	10.1	6.8
Canada	7.5	7.5	6.8	6.3
Australia	6.3%	6.0%	6.3%	4.9%
Austria	--	--	3.7	4.8
Belgium	9.1	7.4	6.9	8.2
Denmark	--	6.8	4.3	3.9
Finland	6.5	3.1	9.8	7.8
Greece	--	6.7	11.2	8.9
Ireland	--	14.7	4.3	4.4
Netherlands	5.8	6.6	2.9	3.9
New Zealand	1.7	7.1	6.0	3.8
Norway	2.0	5.4	3.4	3.5
Spain	7.7	13.9	11.1	8.6
Sweden	2.1	1.5	5.6	7.0
Switzerland	--	--	2.7	--
Average excluding U.S.	5.0%	7.1%	6.6%	6.1%

Source: OECD.stat and OECD (2007c).

TABLE 8.11 Unemployment rates by education level (persons aged 25-64), 2005

Country	Unemployment rate			Ratio of:	
	Less than high school	High school	College	Less than high school to college	High school to college
United States	9.0%	5.1%	2.6%	3.5	2.0
Japan	--	4.9	3.1	--	1.6
Germany	20.2	11.0	5.5	3.7	2.0
United Kingdom	6.6	3.2	2.0	3.3	1.6
France	12.4	7.3	6.0	2.1	1.2
Italy	7.7	5.3	5.7	1.4	0.9
Canada	9.8	5.9	4.6	2.1	1.3
Australia	6.3%	3.5%	2.5%	2.5	1.4
Austria	8.6	3.9	2.6	3.3	1.5
Belgium	12.4	6.9	3.7	3.4	1.9
Denmark	6.8	4.0	3.7	1.8	1.1
Finland	10.7	7.4	4.4	2.4	1.7
Greece	8.2	9.2	7.0	1.2	1.3
Ireland	6.0	3.1	2.0	3.0	1.6
Netherlands	5.8	4.1	2.8	2.1	1.5
New Zealand	3.8	2.4	1.9	2.0	1.3
Norway	7.3	2.6	2.1	3.5	1.2
Spain	9.3	7.3	6.2	1.5	1.2
Sweden	8.5	6.0	4.5	1.9	1.3
Switzerland	7.7	3.7	2.7	2.9	1.4
Average excluding U.S.	8.8%	5.3%	3.8%	2.4	1.4

Source: Authors' analysis of OECD (2007b).

States, at 1.7% annually. In the 1990s, Ireland had the highest annual growth rate, at 3.8%, followed by Germany, the Netherlands, Spain, New Zealand, and then Australia and the United States at 1.4%. From 2000 to 2006, the United States—which was in a recession during the early part of this period—had lower than average growth rates in employment compared to its peers. Over this period, Spain had the highest growth rate at 4.1%, and the United States was ranked eighth among its peers, at 0.9%.

Table 8.10 reports the unemployment rate in the 20 peer countries. The rates reported in this table are calculated using a standardized definition of unemployment from the OECD so as to be internationally comparable. Over the late 1990s, the United States and many of its peers experienced falling unemployment rates. The jobless rate remained low in the United States in 2000 at 4.0%, and only four countries had rates below 4.0%—Switzerland (2.7%), the Netherlands (2.9%), Norway (3.4%), and Austria (3.7%). Between 2000 and 2006, while its peer countries experienced a decrease in unemployment of 0.3% on average, the United States saw an increase from 4.0% to 4.6%, so that by 2006 the United States was ranked seventh in unemployment among its global peers, behind Norway (3.5%), New Zealand (3.8%), Denmark (3.9%), the Netherlands (3.9%), Japan (4.1%), and Ireland (4.4%).

Some economists have argued that Europe's labor market institutions—institutions like strong unions, high minimum wages, and generous social benefits—have priced low-wage workers out of jobs. **Table 8.11** assesses this claim by looking across countries at ratios of unemployment rates by education level. In general, unemployment rates are higher for workers with lower levels of education, so that the ratio of the unemployment rate of, say, workers without a high school diploma to that of workers with a college degree will be significantly larger. If strong labor market institutions in Europe have indeed hurt job creation for less-educated workers, then the ratio of the unemployment rate of lower-educated workers to that of higher-educated workers should be *larger* in Europe than in the United States, which has much weaker labor market institutions. The data, however, run completely counter to this supposition. In 2005, the latest year for which international unemployment data by education level are available, the unemployment rate for workers with less than a high school education in the United States was 3.5 times as high as the rate for college-educated workers. The peer average was much lower at 2.4, and only two countries had the same or higher ratio—Germany (3.7) and Norway (3.5). The unemployment rate for workers with at most a high school diploma in the United States was twice as high as the rate for college educated workers, whereas the non-U.S. average ratio was 1.4, with only one other country, Germany, tying the U.S. level. Thus, Europe's strong labor market institutions do not appear to have priced workers with a high school degree or less out of the market—if anything, the European institutions are associated with substantially *lower* relative unemployment rates for less-educated workers.

It is important to note that these institutions are also associated with other positive economic outcomes. For example, the top of **Figure 8C** shows union coverage (the percent of workers covered by union contracts) for 2000 plotted against an inequality measure. The measure of inequality used in this plot is the "90-10" ratio, which measures how many times more income a household in the 90th income percentile has compared to a household in the 10th income percentile (this and other inequality measures are discussed in depth below). The United States stands out as the country with the highest level of inequality and, at 14%, the lowest level of union coverage. Apparent in this figure is the strong correlation between union coverage and low levels of inequality. The bottom half of Figure 8C goes on to plot union coverage against productivity, demonstrating that countries with higher levels of unionization also tend to have higher levels of productivity. The correlation here is not as strong, but it clearly shows that productivity is not at all suffering in

FIGURE 8C Collective bargaining coverage in relation to inequality and productivity, 2000

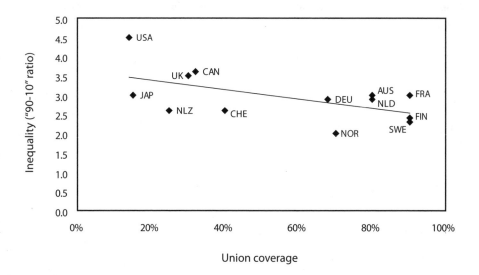

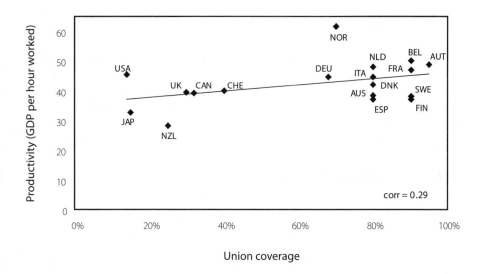

Note: See figure note to Figure 7M for a guide to the country abbreviations.

Source: Authors' analysis of OECD (2004, 2005) data and The Conference Board and Groningen Growth and Development Centre (2008) data.

TABLE 8.12 Annual growth in real hourly compensation, 1979-2006

Country	1979-89	1989-2000	2000-06
United States	0.5%	1.1%	1.0%
Germany	--	--	-0.1
France	--	--	--
Italy	--	0.2	0.7
Canada	0.2	0.9	1.0
Australia	--	--	1.2%
Austria	--	1.5%	0.0
Denmark	1.2%	1.2	1.8
Finland	3.1	1.6	2.1
Greece	--	--	2.6
Netherlands	--	--	1.4
Norway	0.7	2.1	3.1
Spain	--	--	0.1
Sweden	--	--	2.3

Source: Authors' analysis of OECD (2007h) data.

countries where a high percentage of the workforce is covered by union contracts. While there is much discussion in policy making circles about the potential costs of protective labor market institutions, Figure 8C should remind readers that these institutions also carry potential benefits, both to individual workers and to the wider economy, and that these benefits should be as prominent in discussions about them as any potential costs.

Wages and compensation

Obviously, the vast majority of workers in the United States and its peer countries rely heavily on their wages and other work-related benefits for their economic security and well-being. The level, growth, and distribution of wages and benefits are therefore important economic indicators. **Table 8.12** shows the inflation-adjusted annual growth rates of average hourly worker compensation (wages plus fringe benefits) in the private sector for countries where these data are available. The table shows that U.S. compensation growth has been weak compared to most of its peers. From 2000 to 2006, the period for which the most data are available, U.S. average hourly worker compensation grew at 1.0% annually, ranked eighth of the 13 available countries and behind the peer average of 1.3% annual growth.

TABLE 8.13 Relative hourly compensation of manufacturing production workers, 1979-2006 (U.S.=100)

Country	Percent of civilian labor force in manufacturing	Relative hourly compensation of manufacturing production workers, 1979-2006 (U.S.=100)							
		Using market exchange rates				Using purchasing power parities			
	2006	1979	1989	2000	2006	1979	1989	2000	2006
United States	11.3%	100	100	100	100	100	100	100	100
Japan	18.3	61	88	112	85	56	64	78	79
Germany	22.0	--	--	115	144	--	--	129	130
United Kingdom	13.0	64	74	86	114	68	77	89	95
France	15.5*	87	89	79	105	68	84	91	91
Italy	21.2	80	102	74	105	97	108	98	97
Canada	12.8	91	107	84	108	94	101	101	102
Australia	10.4%	84	89	73	110	77	82	96	103
Austria	--	90	101	97	128	88	106	117	117
Belgium	--	120	102	102	134	93	110	125	119
Denmark	--	120	103	109	149	82	85	105	103
Finland	--	89	120	91	126	77	87	99	103
Greece	--	38	39	39	68	53	64	62	76
Ireland	--	61	71	68	109	64	76	76	86
Netherlands	13.9*	129	106	98	136	99	109	120	121
New Zealand	--	55	56	43	61	65	62	65	62
Norway	--	119	132	115	172	78	94	111	124
Spain	--	60	63	54	79	66	76	80	83
Sweden	15.0	127	124	105	133	88	95	105	108
Switzerland	--	118	118	107	129	87	97	97	95
Average excluding U.S.	16.1%	89	94	87	116	78	87	97	100

* Refers to 2005 data.

Source: Authors' analysis of BLS (2008) and OECD (2008) data.

The most extensive international data on compensation covers a narrower group of workers—production workers in manufacturing, which generally comprise around 70% of manufacturing workers. One benefit of focusing on these workers is that it allows the examination of compensation growth excluding very high earners, who overwhelmingly tend to be managers and supervisors, not production workers. The first column in **Table 8.13** shows the relative size of the manufacturing sector recently by presenting the percent of the civilian labor force in manufacturing in 2006. The U.S. manufacturing sector was 11.3% of its labor force in 2006—the lowest in the G-7 and 4.8 percentage points below the average of its peers for which data are available.

The rest of Table 8.13 compares average hourly compensation of manufacturing production workers in peer countries to the corresponding levels in the United States. Here, national compensation rates were converted into U.S. dollars using both market exchange rates and purchasing-power parity exchange rates. Market exchange rates reflect the relative value of American goods, services (including labor), and assets in international markets, and therefore the compensation figures calculated using these rates capture the relative costs to an employer of hiring U.S. labor, reflecting aspects of international competitiveness. Purchasing-power parity exchange rates, on the other hand, better reflect the ability of the compensation levels in each country to guarantee a specific standard of living. What this implies is that market exchange rates should be used for international comparisons of competitiveness, while purchasing-power parity exchange rates should be used for international comparisons of living standards.

Using market exchange rates, the United States was ranked seventh out of its peers in terms of compensation of production workers in 1979; peer countries averaged 89% of U.S. compensation. By 2006, however, the United States was ranked 16th. Furthermore, those countries offering compensation above the United States generally paid *well* above the United States; the average of peer countries was 16% above the U.S. level and up to 72% above the U.S. level in Norway. Over the last three decades, U.S. manufacturing has become a low-wage sector among its peers. In fact, in only four countries—New Zealand, Greece, Spain, and Japan—did manufacturing workers earn less than in the United States.

Using PPP exchange rates, which are used to compare living standards between production workers in the United States and in peer countries, the trends are essentially the same though U.S. workers have fared marginally better—reflecting the fact that consumption goods (housing, food, transportation, clothing, etc.) tend to be cheaper in the United States. In 1979, the United States was ranked first out of its peers in terms of compensation of production workers, and peer countries averaged 78% of U.S. compensation. By 2006, however, 10 of its peers had overtaken the United States, and the level of U.S. compensation matched the average of its peers. **Table 8.14** looks more carefully at the growth of real hourly compensation in manufacturing on a PPP basis. Among U.S. production workers in the 1980s, real hourly compensation actually fell 0.3% per year, compared to an average growth rate in peer countries of 0.8% per year. In the 1990s, U.S. growth, at 0.4% annually, was again among the slowest—significantly lower than the peer country average of 1.2%, which included strong annual gains in Japan (2.2%), Denmark (2.4%), and Norway (1.9%). From 2000 to 2006, U.S. compensation growth, at 0.6%, was again near the bottom of the pack, but the growth in peer countries had slowed somewhat to an average of 1.1%.

TABLE 8.14 Annual growth in real hourly compensation (using PPP exchange rates) of manufacturing production workers, 1979-2006

Country	1979-89	1989-2000	2000-06
United States	-0.3%	0.4%	0.6%
Japan	0.9	2.2	0.9
Germany	--	--	0.6
United Kingdom	1.0	1.7	1.7
France	1.8	1.1	0.7
Italy	0.7	-0.5	0.4
Canada	0.4	0.4	0.7
Australia	0.4%	1.8%	1.7%
Austria	1.5	1.3	0.5
Belgium	1.4	1.5	-0.2
Denmark	0.0	2.4	0.3
Finland	0.8	1.6	1.3
Greece	1.4	0.1	4.2
Ireland	1.4	0.4	2.7
Netherlands	0.6	1.3	0.8
New Zealand	-0.9	0.9	-0.3
Norway	1.5	1.9	2.6
Spain	1.0	0.9	1.2
Sweden	0.4	1.3	0.9
Switzerland	0.7	0.4	0.2
Average excluding U.S.	0.8%	1.2%	1.1%

Source: Authors' analysis of BLS (2008) data.

Household income inequality

To this point, the data presented have largely consisted of economy-wide, annual averages. A country's standard of living, however, refers not just to the value of goods and services available to its population as a whole (as presented in the per capita income figures in Table 8.1), but also to the way those goods and services are distributed *across* the population. Earlier sections tackled the former; this section tackles the latter by looking at a number of measures of income inequality. These measures take into account the fact that economic outcomes can strongly diverge for different populations

TABLE 8.15 Household income inequality, 2005

Country	Gini coefficient 2005	Ratio of 90th-to-10th percentile, 2005
United States*	0.37	4.86
Japan	--	3.12
Germany	0.28	3.13
United Kingdom	0.34	3.51
France	0.28	3.10
Italy	0.33	--
Canada	0.32	3.74
Australia*	0.31	3.12
Austria	0.26	--
Belgium	0.28	--
Denmark	0.24	2.64
Finland	0.26	2.42
Greece	0.33	--
Ireland	0.32	3.57
Netherlands	0.31	2.91
New Zealand	--	3.50
Norway	0.28	2.21
Spain	0.32	3.53
Sweden	0.23	2.33
Switzerland	--	2.61
Average excluding U.S.	0.29	3.03

* See Table Notes.

Source: OECD (2005), CIA (2008), and Luxembourg Income Study (2007).

within a nation. Because individuals make important decisions about employment and consumption as part of a family or broader household, much of the analysis in this section will examine household data.

Table 8.15 presents two basic measures of household income inequality. The first is the Gini coefficient, a standard measure of inequality that ranges from zero (perfect equality of income across household) to one (all income concentrated at the very top of the income distribution). In 2005, the United States had the highest Gini coefficient, at 0.37, and was well above the peer country average. Sweden and Denmark have the least inequality by this measure, with Gini coefficients of 0.23 and 0.24, respectively.

The second measure in Table 8.15 is the "90-10" ratio, which measures how many times more income a household in the 90th income percentile has compared to a household in the 10th income percentile. The higher the ratio, the more inequality exists. Again, the U.S. ratio—which shows that a 90th percentile household has an income almost five times as high as a 10th percentile household—was the highest and much higher than the average of the peer countries. The countries with the lowest inequality by this measure were Norway, at a ratio of 2.21, and Sweden, at 2.33.

Figure 8D presents yet another set of inequality measures for 2005. One is the ratio of the 10th percentile household to the median household, which is a measure of how poor the poorest 10th of the population is in relation to the typical household; a lower number implies more inequality. The U.S. value of 48% means that the 10th percentile household has an income that is less than half of the typical household's income. This is the lowest value in Figure 8D and is far below the peer average of 62%. The other measure given in the chart is the ratio of the 90th percentile household to the median household, which is a measure of how rich the richest 10th of the population is in relation to the typical household; a higher number implies more inequality. The U.S. value

FIGURE 8D Relative household income dispersion, 2005

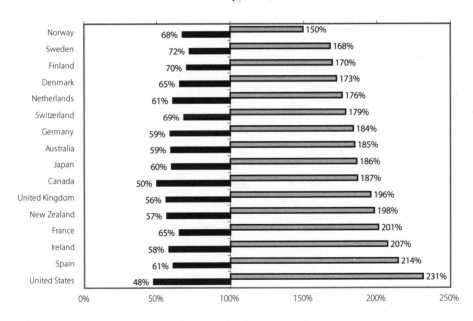

Percent of U.S. median income received by:

Low-income (10th percentile) households   High income (90th percentile) households

FIGURE 8E Household income dispersion relative to the U.S. median, 2005

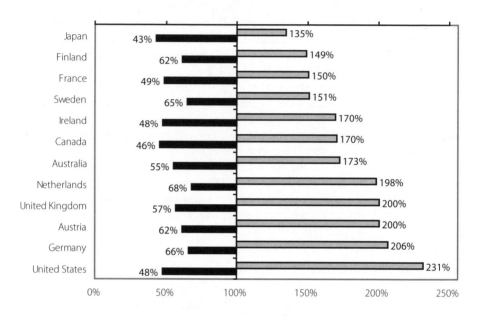

Percent of U.S. median income received by:

Low-income (10th percentile) households   High income (90th percentile) households

Source: Authors' analysis of OECD Database on Earnings Distribution and OECD (2007c) data.

of 231% means that the 90th percentile household has an income that is 2.3 times that of the typical household's income. This is the highest value of the chart and is far above the peer average of 185%. Once again, inequality in the United States dominates that of its peers.

Figure 8D showed that 10th percentile earners in the United States are worse off relative to the U.S. median than are 10th percentile earners in any peer country, relative to their own countries' medians. Median earnings, however, vary across countries. Thus, comparing 10th percentile earners in peer countries to the U.S. median is also useful, allowing the comparison of the absolute living standards of low-income households in the United States to the low-income households in peer countries. These results, along with results for high-income households, are presented in **Figure 8E**. The figure shows that despite the relatively high median income in the United States, inequality in the United States is so severe that low-income households in the United States are actually worse off than low-income households in all but four peer countries. While 10th percentile earners in the United States make 48% of the U.S. median, 10th percentile

FIGURE 8F Top 0.1% income share in selected countries

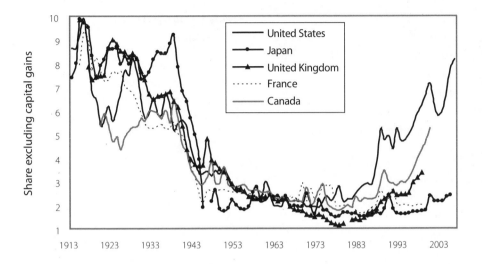

Source: Smeeding and Piketty (2003, 2006), Smeeding and Moriguchi (2007), and Smeeding and Alvaredo (2007).

earners in peer countries average 56% of the U.S. median. Not surprisingly, high-income households are much better off in the United States.

Figure 8F shows historical distributions of the top 0.1% income shares—i.e., the percent of a country's income earned by the highest one-tenth of 1% of earners. Because of limitations associated with collecting top incomes in household survey data, the best data for the very high end of the income distribution come from income tax returns and are not available for all peer countries. Figure 8F presents data for the G-7 countries except Germany and Italy. The figure shows that there was a steady decline in the top 0.1% share from the early 1900s—when the top 0.1% income share averaged about 9% for the charted countries—until the mid-1970s—when the top 0.1% income share averaged about 2%. Over this period, the top 0.1% share in the United States was generally in the middle of the peer country pack. In 1973, however, the U.S. level began a steady upward climb that dramatically outpaced its peers. By 1998, the last year data are available for all the charted countries, the top 0.1% income share in the United States was 3.2 times what it had been in 1973, while the peer average in 1998 was only 1.7 times what it had been in 1973. Despite a temporary downturn during the recession of the early 2000s, the U.S. top 0.1% income share has continued to rise and in 2006 was at 8.1—meaning that the top 0.1% of the population collected 8.1% of the nation's income. The figure shows that the last time the United States experienced that level of income share going to the very top of the income distribution was in the robber baron days of the early 1900s.

TABLE 8.16 Poverty rates, 2000

Country	Poverty line (50% of median)		
	Total poverty	Children	Elderly
United States	17.0%	21.9%	24.7%
Germany	8.3	9.0	10.1
France	8.0	7.9	9.8
Italy	12.7	16.6	13.7
United Kingdom	12.4	15.3	20.5
Canada	11.4	14.9	5.9
Australia	14.3%	15.8%	29.4%
Austria	7.7	7.8	13.7
Belgium	8.0	6.7	16.4
Denmark	9.2	8.7	6.6
Finland	5.4	2.8	8.5
Ireland	16.5	17.2	35.8
Netherlands	7.3	9.8	2.4
Norway	6.4	3.4	11.9
Spain	14.3	16.1	23.4
Sweden	6.5	4.2	7.7
Switzerland	7.6	6.7	18.4
Average excluding U.S.	9.8%	10.2%	14.6%

Source: Luxembourg Income Study.

Poverty

So far this chapter has shown that the United States has a very high per capita income, but also pronounced inequality, especially when compared with its peer countries. In addition to the measures of inequality discussed in the last section, another key measure of the distribution of a country's income across its population—and therefore a key measure of living standards—is how well its most vulnerable citizens fare. This section finds that the United States—with the second-highest per capita income of its peers— also has the highest level of poverty. In other words, the income of the United States is not reaching the bottom end of the income distribution. **Table 8.16** summarizes international data on poverty rates in 2000, the latest data available. Following the standard methodology for international comparisons of poverty, the table defines the poverty rate

FIGURE 8G Child poverty rates before and after taxes and transfers, 2000

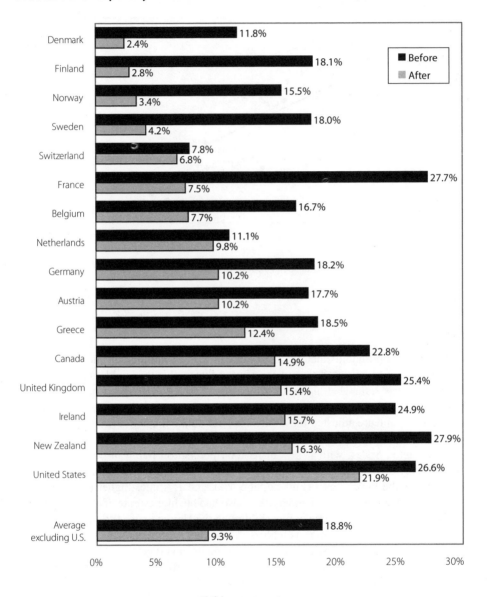

Child poverty rate

Source: Corak (2005).

FIGURE 8H Social expenditure versus child poverty, 2001

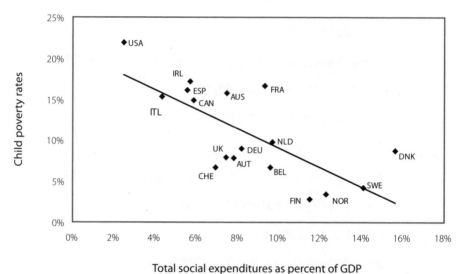

Total social expenditures as percent of GDP

Note: See figure note to Figure 7M for a guide to the country abbreviations.

Source: Authors' analysis of OECD Social Expenditure Database and the Luxembourg Income Study.

as the share of households that received 50% or less of the median income in each country. It should be noted that in the United States, this threshold amounted to an income that was somewhat higher than the official poverty rate (see Chapter 6). Like the official U.S. definition of poverty, the poverty rates in Table 8.16 take into account cash transfers and are adjusted for family size, but unlike the U.S. definition, they also account for taxes and tax credits.

The United States, with 17.0% of its total population living in poverty, had the highest level of overall poverty among its peers—over three times as high as the country with the lowest level (Finland, at 5.4%), and 1.7 times higher than the peer-country average of 9.8%. The United States also had the highest rate of child poverty at 21.9%, meaning more than one in five children in the United States is living in poverty. This level is almost eight times as high as the country with the lowest level (Finland, at 2.8%), and over twice as high as the peer-country average of 10.2%. Finally, the United States had the third-highest rate of elderly poverty (24.7%)—over 10 times as high as the country with the lowest level (the Netherlands, at 2.4%), and 1.7 times higher than the peer-country average of 14.6%.

International differences in labor market institutions such as minimum wages and unionization explain a large part of the differences in international poverty rates, but **Figure 8G** shows that variations across countries in tax and transfer programs for low-income households are also extremely important. While Table 8.16 shows poverty rates after taxes and transfers, Figure 8G shows child poverty rates both before and after taxes and transfers (some of the rates in Table 8.16 do not exactly match those in Figure 8G because of varying reference years; see Table and Figure Notes). The child poverty rate before taxes and transfers in the United States was 26.6%, which was only about 1.4 times the average of peer countries of 18.8%. In other words, "market" child poverty rates in the United States are not far off from those in peer countries. Once taxes and transfers were accounted for, however, the child poverty rate in the United States was 21.9%, about 2.4 times the non-U.S. average of 9.3%. In other words, taxes and transfers reduced child poverty in peer countries by 50% on average, but in the United States they reduced child poverty by only 18%.

Figure 8G showed the effect taxes and transfers can have on child poverty, but it does not give information about spending levels. **Figure 8H** shows total social expenditures as a percent of GDP by country (total social expenditures do not include pension or health benefits, but include all other income supports and social services). The figure plots these social expenditures against child poverty levels, providing a clear picture of the relationship between social spending and poverty. The United States stands out as the country with the lowest expenditures and the highest child poverty rate. The United States devotes 2.5% of its GDP to social expenditures, well below all peer countries, who average 8.3%. Figures 8G and 8H dramatically show that other peer countries are much more likely than the United States to step in where markets have failed to lift their most disadvantaged citizens out of poverty. This suggests that the relatively low expenditures on social welfare are at least partially implicated in the high poverty rates in the United States.

Conclusion

This chapter has compared the performance of the U.S. economy with that of its global peers. It shows that the United States is among the richest, most productive economies in the world, though its strength relative to its global peers in this regard is often overstated. Additionally, compared to its peers, the U.S. economy yields highly varied results regarding the living standards of its citizens. The United States has more inequality, higher poverty rates (including child poverty), and workers who work longer and have far fewer days off than any of its peers.

Supporters of the U.S. economic model generally acknowledge the high inequality in the United States but argue that the U.S. model provides greater mobility, greater employment opportunities, and greater dynamism than do economies with greater employment protections and higher levels of social spending. The evidence, however, provides little support for this view. As the data in this chapter reveal, many peer economies with more public spending and employment protections do as well or better than the United States on key macroeconomic measures, from productivity to job growth to unemployment. Furthermore, as discussed in Chapter 2, the United States has less economic mobility than several of its peer countries.

The best interpretation of the available evidence is that since World War II, the United States and many of its peers have experienced stunning rates of economic growth and a great potential for growth in their citizens' living standards. That said, outcomes have not been entirely rosy. No peer country has seen a return to the productivity growth of the 1950s and 1960s, inequality has increased in all but a few countries, and several peer countries have seen joblessness remain at high levels. The evidence in this chapter, which underscores the diversity of experiences among peer countries in providing income and employment security, suggests that those who look exclusively to the United States for economic solutions, instead of its global peers, will miss a great deal.

Appendix A

This appendix explains the various adjustments made to the U.S. Census Bureau's March Current Population Survey (CPS) data and the methodology used to prepare the data in the tables discussed on the following pages.

The data source used for our analyses of family incomes and poverty is the March CPS microdata set. Each March, approximately 60,000 households are asked questions about their incomes from a wide variety of sources in the prior year (for example, the income data in the 2007 March CPS refer to 2006). For the national analysis in Chapter 1, we use the data relevant to the year in question.

In order to preserve the confidentiality of respondents, the income variables on the public-use files of the CPS are top-coded, that is, values above a certain level are suppressed. Since income inequality measures are sensitive to changes in the upper reaches of the income scale, this suppression poses a challenge to analysts interested in both the extent of inequality in a given time period and the change in inequality over time. We use an imputation technique, described below, that is commonly used in such cases to estimate the value of top-coded data. Over the course of the 1990s, Census top-coding procedures underwent significant changes, which also must be dealt with to preserve consistency. These methods are discussed below.

For most of the years of data in our study, a relatively small share of the distribution of any one variable is top-coded. For example, in 1989, 0.67% (i.e., two-thirds of the top 1%) of weighted cases are top-coded on the variable "earnings from longest job," meaning actual reported values are given for over 99% of those with positive earnings. Nevertheless, the disproportionate influence of the small group of top-coded cases means their earnings levels cannot be ignored.

Our approach has been to impute the average value above the top-code for the key components of income using the assumption that the tails of these distributions follow a Pareto distribution. (The Pareto distribution is defined as $c/(x^{(a+1)})$, where c and a are positive constants that we estimate using the top 20% of the empirical distribution (more precisely, c is a scale parameter assumed known; a is the key parameter for estimation). We apply this technique to three key variables: income from wage and salary (1968-87), earnings from longest job (1988-2000), and income from interest (1968-92). Since the upper tail of empirical income distributions closely follows the general shape of the Pareto, this imputation method is commonly used for dealing with top-coded data (West, undated). The estimate uses the shape of the upper part of the distribution (in our case, the top 20%) to extrapolate to the part that is unobservable due to the top-codes. Intuitively, if the shape of the observable part of the distribution suggests that the tail above the top-code is particularly long, implying a few cases with very high income values, the imputation will return a high mean relative to the case where it appears that the tail above the top-code is rather short.

Polivka (1998), using an uncensored dataset (i.e., without top-codes), shows that the Pareto procedure effectively replicates the mean above the top-code. For example, her analysis of the use of the technique to estimate usual weekly earnings from the earnings files of the CPS yields estimates that are generally within less than 1% of the true mean.

As noted, the Census Bureau has lifted the top-codes over time in order to accommodate the fact that nominal and real wage growth eventually renders the old top-codes too low. For example, the top-coded value for "earnings from longest job" was increased from $50,000 in 1979 to $99,999 in 1989. Given the growth of earnings over this period, we did not judge this change (or any others in the income-component variables) to create inconsistencies in the trend comparisons between these two time periods.

However, changes made in the mid- and latter 1990s data did require consistency adjustments. For these years, the Census Bureau both adjusted the top-codes (some were raised, some were lowered; the new top-codes were determined by using whichever value was higher: the top 3% of all reported amounts for the variable, or the top 0.5% of all persons), and used "plug-in" averages above the top-codes for certain variables. "Plug-ins" are group-specific average values taken above the top-code, with the groups defined on the basis of gender, race, and worker status. We found that the Pareto procedure was not feasible with unearned income, given the empirical distributions of these variables, so for March data (survey year) 1996 forward we use the plug-in values. Our tabulations show that, in tandem with the procedure described next regarding earnings, this approach avoids trend inconsistencies.

The most important variable that we adjust (i.e., the adjustment with the largest impact on family income) is "earnings from longest job." The top-code on this variable was raised sharply in survey year 1994, and this change leads to an upward bias in comparing estimates at or around that year to earlier years. (Note that this bias is attenuated over time as nominal income growth "catches up" to the new top-code, and relatively smaller shares of respondents again fall into that category.) Our procedure for dealing with this was to impose a lower top-code on the earnings data that we grew over time by the rate of inflation, and to calculate Pareto estimates based on these artificial top-codes. We found that this procedure led to a relatively smooth series across the changes in Census Bureau methodology. For example, we find that, while our imputed series generates lower incomes among, say, the top 5% of families (because we are imposing a lower top-code) in the mid-1990s, by the end of the 1990s our estimates were only slightly lower than those from the un-adjusted Census data. For 2001 forward we do not have any top-code adjustments.

Table 1.2: We decompose the growth of average family income in the following manner (all monetary values are in real terms). We begin with log changes in family income over the relevant time periods—this is the value to be decomposed between annual hours, hourly wages, and other (non-labor) income. For example, in Table 1.2, this equals 14.2% for the lowest fifth over the 1989-2000 period. Family earnings grew 28.3% over this period, and we multiply this value by earnings/income averaged over the two years. For this period, that ratio is 0.505. This result represents the earnings contribution (14.3%) that appears in the table. In order to decompose this value further into the wage and hours shares, we use weights derived from their growth over the period as shown in the table. The hours share, 1989-2000, is thus computed as (14.4%/ (14.4%+13.9%))*14.3%, or 7.3%, where 14.4% and 13.9% are the log growth rates of annual hours and annual earnings. The share of income growth attributed to the change in "other" is derived by multiplying its growth over the period by the ratio of other/ income, again averaged over the two years (note that for the lowest fifth, this is simply one minus the 0.505 value noted above). It is the nature of this type of log decomposi-tion that if the "other" category is a relatively large share of the total, the decomposition will not perfectly sum to the total, but this is not the case here.

Tables 1.21–1.22: The source for these tables is the March CPS datasets described above. The analysis focuses on married-couple families with children, spouse present, where both spouses were between 25 and 54 years of age. The distributional analysis places 20% of families, not persons, in each fifth.

The annual hours variable in the March data is the product of two variables: weeks worked per year, and usual hours per week. Since allowable values on the latter variable go up to 99, this product can be over 5,000. Such values are clearly outliers, and we decided to exclude cases with annual hours greater than 3,500, which led to the exclu-sion of between 2% and 5% of cases over the years of our analysis.

For the analysis of income with and without wives earnings in Table 1.22, we create separate quintile cutoffs for the distributions with and without wives' earnings.

Table 6.10: The methodology for this decomposition is taken from Danziger and Gottschalk (1995, Chapter 5). The change to be explained is the difference in poverty rates between t0 and t1. We first isolate the effect of average income growth by assigning the average growth between the two time periods to all families in t0 and recalculate the poverty rate (we adjust each family's poverty line for the increase in the CPI over this period). This procedure holds the demographic composition and the shape of the income distribution constant in t0 while allowing incomes to grow equally for all families. Thus, the difference between this simulated poverty rate and the actual t0 poverty rate is attributable to the growth in average income.

We repeat this exercise for each demographic group in t0 (we use three family types: married couples, female headed families, and persons living alone (a small residual group of male-headed families is included with married couples, since it was too small to separate out), two races—white and non-white—and three education categories of the family head—less than high school, high school and some college, and college or more). By weighting each of these simulated t0 rates by their t1 population shares, we can simulate a t0 poverty rate that reflects the average income growth and demographic composition of t1. The difference between this simulated rate and the one discussed in the above paragraph gives the contribution of demographic change over the time period. Finally, since this second simulated rate incorporates the mean growth and demographic change between the two periods, but not the change in the shape of the distribution, the difference between this second simulated rate and the actual rate for t1 equals the change in poverty rates attributable to changes in inequality over the two periods.

Appendix B

This appendix provides background information on the analysis of wage data from the Current Population Survey (CPS), which is prepared by the U.S. Census Bureau for the Bureau of Labor Statistics (BLS). Specifically, for 1979 and beyond, we analyze microdata files provided by the BLS that contain a full year's data on the outgoing rotation groups (ORG) in the CPS. (For years prior to 1979, we use the CPS May files; our use of these files is discussed below.) We believe that the CPS ORG files allow for a timely, up-to-date, and accurate analysis of wage trends keeping within the familiar labor force definitions and concepts employed by BLS.

The sampling framework of the monthly CPS is a "rolling panel," in which households are in the survey for four consecutive months, out for eight, and then back in for four months. The ORG files provide data on those CPS respondents in either the fourth or eighth month of the CPS (i.e., in groups four or eight, out of a total of eight groups). Therefore, in any given month the ORG file represents a quarter of the CPS sample. For a given year, the ORG file is equivalent to three months of CPSs (one-fourth of 12). For our analysis, we use a sample drawn from the full-year ORG sample, the size of which ranges from 160,000 to 180,000 observations during the 1979 to 1995 period. Due to a decrease in the overall sample size of the CPS, the ORG was shrunk to 145,000 cases from 1996 to 1998, and our current sample comes in at about 170,000 cases.

Changes in annual or weekly earnings can result from changes in hourly earnings or from more working time (either more hours per week or weeks per year). Our analysis is centered around the hourly wage, which represents the pure price of labor (exclusive of benefits), because we are interested in changing pay levels for the workforce and its sub-groups. We do this to be able to clearly distinguish changes in earnings resulting from more (or less) work rather than more (or less) pay. Most of our wage analysis, therefore, does not take into account that weekly or annual earnings may have changed because of longer or shorter working hours or lesser or greater opportunities for employment. An exception to this is Table 2.1, where we present annual hours, earnings, and hourly weighted wages from the March CPS.

In our view, the ORG files provide a better source of data for wage analysis than the traditionally used March CPS files. In order to calculate hourly wages from the March CPS, analysts must make calculations using three retrospective variables: the annual earnings, weeks worked, and usual weekly hours worked in the year prior to the survey. In contrast, respondents in the ORG are asked a set of questions about hours worked, weekly wages, and (for workers paid by the hour) hourly wages in the week prior to the survey. In this regard, the data from the ORG are likely to be more reliable than data from the March CPS. See Bernstein and Mishel (1997) for a detailed discussion of these differences.

Our sub-sample includes all wage-and-salary workers with valid wage and hour data, whether paid weekly or by the hour. Specifically, in order to be included in our sub-sample, respondents had to meet the following criteria:

* age 18-64;

* employed in the public or private sector (unincorporated self-employed were excluded);

* hours worked within the valid range in the survey (1-99 per week, or hours vary— see discussion below); and,

* either hourly or weekly wages within the valid survey range (top-coding discussed below).

For those who met these criteria, an hourly wage was calculated in the following manner. If a valid hourly wage was reported, that wage was used throughout our analysis. For salaried workers (those who report only a weekly wage), the hourly wage was their weekly wage divided by their hours worked. Outliers, that is, persons with hourly wages below 50 cents or above $100 in 1989 CPI-U-X1-adjusted dollars, were removed from the analysis. Starting from year 2002, we use CPI-RS-adjusted dollars instead. These yearly upper and lower bounds are presented in **Table B-1**. CPS demographic weights were applied to make the sample nationally representative.

The hourly wage reported by hourly workers in the CPS is net of any overtime, tips, or commissions (OTTC), thus introducing a potential undercount in the hourly wage for workers who regularly receive tips or premium pay. OTTC is included in the usual weekly earnings of hourly workers, which raises the possibility of assigning an imputed hourly wage to hourly workers based on the reported weekly wage and hours worked per week. Conceptually, using this imputed wage is preferable to using the reported hourly wage because it is more inclusive. We have chosen, however, not to use this broader wage measure, because the extra information on OTTC seems unreliable. We compared the imputed hourly wage (reported weekly earnings divided by weekly hours) to the reported hourly wage; the difference presumably reflects OTTC.

TABLE B.1 Wage earner sample, hourly wage upper and lower limits, 1973-2007

Year	Lower	Upper	Year	Lower	Upper
1973	0.19	38.06	1991	0.55	109.84
1974	0.21	41.85	1992	0.57	113.15
1975	0.23	45.32	1993	0.58	116.53
1976	0.24	47.90	1994	0.60	119.52
1977	0.25	50.97	1995	0.61	122.90
1978	0.27	54.44	1996	0.63	126.53
1979	0.30	59.68	1997	0.65	129.54
1980	0.33	66.37	1998	0.66	131.45
1981	0.36	72.66	1999	0.67	134.35
1982	0.39	77.10	2000	0.69	138.87
1983	0.40	80.32	2001	0.71	142.82
1984	0.42	83.79	2002*	0.70	140.05
1985	0.43	86.77	2003*	0.72	143.26
1986	0.44	88.39	2004*	0.74	147.06
1987	0.46	91.61	2005*	0.76	152.10
1988	0.48	95.40	2006*	0.78	156.90
1989	0.50	100.00	2007*	0.81	161.45
1990	0.53	105.40			

* Upper limit adjusted by CPI-RS.

Source: Authors' analysis.

This comparison showed that significant percentages of the hourly workforce appeared to receive negative OTTC. These error rates range from a low of 0% of the hourly workforce in the period 1989-93 to a high of 16-17% in 1973-88, and persist across the survey change from 1993 to 1994. Since negative OTTC is clearly implausible, we rejected this imputed hourly wage series and rely strictly on the hourly rate of pay as reported directly by hourly workers, subject to the sample criteria discussed above.

For tables that show wage percentiles, we "smooth" hourly wages to compensate for "wage clumps" in the wage distributions. This is a standard technique that corrects for the widespread phenomenon of workers reporting their wages as being the closest "round" wage—for example, people making hourly wages of $6.98 or $7.03 all reporting wages of $7.00. The technique involves breaking the hourly wage distribution into 50-cent intervals, starting at 25 cents. To find the smoothed wage associated with a given percentile, we first identify the 50-cent interval within which the percentile falls. We then find (1) what percent of workers make wages within or

TABLE B.2 Pareto-imputed mean values for top-coded weekly earnings, and share top coded, 1973-2007

| | Share | | | Value | |
| | *Percent hours* | | | | |
Year	All	Men	Women	Men	Women
1973	0.11%	0.17%	0.02%	$1,365	$1,340
1974	0.16	0.26	0.01	1,385	1,297
1975	0.21	0.35	0.02	1,410	1,323
1976	0.30	0.51	0.01	1,392	1,314
1977	0.36	0.59	0.04	1,384	1,309
1978	0.38	0.65	0.02	1,377	1,297
1979	0.57	0.98	0.05	1,388	1,301
1980	0.72	1.23	0.07	1,380	1,287
1981	1.05	1.82	0.10	1,408	1,281
1982	1.45	2.50	0.18	1,430	1,306
1983	1.89	3.27	0.25	1,458	1,307
1984	2.32	3.92	0.42	1,471	1,336
1985	2.78	4.63	0.60	1,490	1,343
1986	0.80	1.37	0.15	2,435	2,466
1987	1.06	1.80	0.20	2,413	2,472
1988	1.30	2.19	0.29	2,410	2,461
1989	0.48	0.84	0.08	2,710	2,506
1990	0.60	1.04	0.11	2,724	2,522
1991	0.71	1.21	0.17	2,744	2,553
1992	0.77	1.28	0.22	2,727	2,581
1993	0.86	1.43	0.24	2,754	2,580
1994	1.25	1.98	0.43	2,882	2,689
1995	1.34	2.16	0.43	2,851	2,660
1996	1.41	2.27	0.46	2,863	2,678
1997	1.71	2.67	0.65	2,908	2,751
1998	0.63	0.98	0.25	4,437	4,155
1999	0.71	1.12	0.21	4,464	4,099
2000	0.83	1.38	0.24	4,502	4,179
2001	0.92	1.46	0.34	4,477	4,227
2002	0.91	1.44	0.33	4,555	4,252
2003	1.07	1.69	0.40	4,546	4,219
2004	1.19	1.90	0.42	4,611	4,195
2005	1.30	2.02	0.51	4,623	4,264
2006	1.49	2.26	0.65	4,636	4,328
2007	1.69	2.55	0.76	4,658	4,325

Source: Authors' analysis.

below that interval, and (2) what percent of workers make wages below that interval. Finally, based on these cumulative percentages, we linearly interpolate the wage value associated with the percentile. For example, suppose that the median (50th percentile) worker reports a wage that falls within the $9.76-$10.25 interval. Further suppose that 51% of all workers make wages within that interval or below, and 48% of workers make wages below that interval. To find the hourly wage of the 50th percentile worker, we simply interpolate between $9.76 and $10.25, assuming that the 50th percentile worker will fall two-thirds of the way from $9.76 to $10.25, (since 50% falls two-thirds of the way from 48% to 51%). In other words, the "smoothed" wage of the median worker is $9.76 + ($10.25-9.76)*(50-48)/(51-48) = $10.09.

For the survey years 1973-88, the weekly wage is top-coded at $999.00; an extended top-code value of $1,923 is available in 1986-97; the top-code value changes to $2,884.61 in 1998-2005. Particularly for the later years, this truncation of the wage distribution creates a downward bias in the mean wage. We dealt with the top-coding issue by imputing a new weekly wage for top-coded individuals. The imputed value is the Pareto-imputed mean for the upper tail of the weekly earnings distribution, based on the distribution of weekly earnings up to the 80th percentile. This procedure was done for men and women separately. The imputed values for men and women appear in **Table B-2**. A new hourly wage, equal to the new estimated value for weekly earnings, divided by that person's usual hours per week, was calculated.

In January 1994, a new survey instrument was introduced into the CPS; many labor force items were added and improved. This presents a significant challenge to the researcher who wishes to make comparisons over time. The most careful research on the impact of the survey change has been conducted by BLS researcher Anne Polivka (1996, 1997). Interestingly, Polivka does not find that the survey changes had a major impact on broad measures of unemployment or wage levels, though significant differences did surface for some sub-groups (e.g., weekly earnings for those with less than a high school diploma and those with advanced degrees, the unemployment rate of older workers). However, a change in the reporting of weekly hours did call for the alteration of our methodology. In 1994 the CPS began allowing people to report that their usual hours worked per week vary. In order to include non-hourly workers who report varying hours in our wage analysis, we estimated their usual hours using a regression-based imputation procedure, where we predicted the usual hours of work for "hours vary" cases based on the usual hours worked of persons with similar characteristics. An hourly wage was calculated by dividing weekly earnings by the estimate of hours for these workers. The share of our sample that received such a wage in the 1994-2005 period is presented in **Table B-3**. The reported hourly wage of hourly workers was preserved.

BLS analysts Ilg and Hauzen (2000), following Polivka (1999), do adjust the 10th percentile wage because "changes to the survey in 1994 led to lower reported earnings for relatively low-paid workers, compared with pre-1994 estimates." We make no such adjustments for both practical and empirical reasons. Practically, the BLS has provided no adjustment factors for hourly wage trends that we can use—Polivka's work is for weekly wages. More importantly, the trends in 10th percentile hourly

TABLE B.3 Share of wage earners assigned an hourly wage from imputed weekly hours, 1994-2007

Year	Percent hours vary
1994	2.0%
1995	2.1
1996	2.4
1997	2.4
1998	2.5
1999	2.4
2000	2.4
2001	2.5
2002	2.5
2003	2.5
2004	2.7
2005	2.7
2006	2.5
2007	2.4

Source: Authors' analysis.

wages differ from those reported by Ilg and Hauzen for 10th percentile weekly earnings. This is perhaps not surprising, since the composition of earners at the "bottom" will differ when measured by weekly rather than hourly wages, with low-weekly earners being almost exclusively part-timers. Empirically, Ilg and Hauzen show the unadjusted 50/10 wage gap jumping up between 1993 and 1994, when the new survey begins. In contrast, our 50/10 wage gap for hourly wages falls between 1993 and 1994. Thus, the pattern of wage change in their data differs greatly from that in our data. In fact, our review of the 1993-94 trends across all of the deciles shows no discontinuities whatsoever. Consequently, we make no adjustments to account for any effect of the 1994 survey change. Had we made the sort of adjustments suggested by Polivka, our measured fall in the 50/10 wage gap in the 1900s would be even larger and the overall pattern—falling 50/10, rising 90/50, and especially the 95/50 wage gaps—would remain the same.

When a response is not obtained for weekly earnings, or an inconsistency is detected, an "imputed" response is performed by CPS using a "hot deck" method, whereby a response from another sample person with similar demographic and economic characteristics is used for the nonresponse. This procedure for imputing missing wage data appears to introduce artificial differences between union and nonunion members. We restrict our sample to the observations with non-imputed wages only for union wage premium analysis (Table 3.32).

Demographic variables are also used in the analysis. Starting in January 2003, individuals are asked directly if they are Spanish, Hispanic, or Latino. Persons who report they are Hispanic also may select more than one race. For consistency purposes, our race variable comprises four mutually exclusive categories across years:

- white, non-Hispanic;

- black, non-Hispanic;

- Hispanic, any race;

- all others.

In January 2003, the CPS used the 2002 Census Bureau occupational and industry classification systems, which are derived from the 2000 Standard Occupational Classification (SOC) system and the 2002 North American Industry Classification System (NAICS). The new classification system creates breaks in existing data series at all levels of aggregation. Since we have built in "old" and "new" industry and occupation systems in our underline 2000-02 data, we use year 2000 as a break point to create consistent analysis with the "old" code for pre-2000 analysis and the "new" code for post-2000 analysis.

Beginning in 1992, the CPS employed a new coding scheme for education, providing data on the respondent's highest degree attained. The CPS in earlier years provided data on years of schooling completed. The challenge to make a consistent wage series by education level is to either make the new data consistent with the past or to make the old "years of schooling" data consistent with the new educational-attainment measures. In prior versions of *The State of Working America*, we achieved a consistent series by imputing years of schooling for 1992 and later years, that is, making the "new" consistent with the "old." In this version, however, we have converted the "old" data to the new coding following Jaeger (1997). However, Jaeger does not separately identify four-year college and "more than college" categories. Since the wages of these sub-groups of the "college or more" group have divergent trends, we construct pre-1992 wages and employment separately for "four-year college" and "advanced." To do so, we compute wages, wage premiums, and employment separately for those with 16, 17, and 18-plus years of schooling completed. The challenge is to distribute the "17s" to the 16 years (presumably a four-year degree) and 18-plus years (presumably advanced) groups. We do this by using the share of the "17s" that have a terminal four-year college degree, as computed in the February 1990 CPS supplement that provides both education codings: 61.4%. We then assume that 61.4% of all of the "17s" are "college-only" and compute a weighted average of the "16s" and 61.4% of the "17s" to construct "college-only" wages and wage premiums. Correspondingly, we compute a weighted average of 38.6% (or 1 less 61.4%) of the "17s" and the "18s" to construct advanced "wages and wage premiums." Distributing the "17s" affects each year differently depending on the actual change in the wages and premiums for "17s" and the changing relative size of the "17s" (which varies only slightly from 2.5% of men and women from 1979 to 1991).

We employ these education categories in various tables in Chapter 3, where we present wage trends by education over time. For the data for 1992 and later, we compute the "some college" trends by aggregating those "with some college but no degree beyond high school" and those with an associate or other degree that is not a four-year college degree.

Table Notes

Introduction

1   *The major indicators of the 2000s economy from the perspective of working families.* GDP is from U.S. Department of Commerce, BEA (2008). Productivity is from BLS, for nonfarm business. Jobs data are from U.S. Department of Labor, BLS (2008b) data; while unemployment, under-employment, labor force participation and median weekly earnings are from U.S. Department of Labor BLS (2008c) data. Annual hours is an EPI calculation based on CPS March Supplement data (see Appendix A). Median income and poverty is based on the 2008 annual release of U.S. Bureau of the Census income and poverty data.

2   *Middle-income growth in the 1990s and 2000s: Earnings and hours.* Authors' analysis of the CPS March Supplement data (see Appendix A). See also Table 1.2, middle fifth.

3   *Income growth and income shares of the top 10% of earners.* Analysis of Piketty and Saez (2008) updated from Piketty and Saez (2003) data.

4   *Share of income growth by income group.* Based on an analysis of Pikkety and Saez (2008) updated from Piketty and Saez (2003) data recomputed using the CPI-U-RS inflation measure for deflating real incomes This analysis identifies the shares of the per houshelod income growth that accrued to each income segment.

5   *Economic indicators for African Americans, Hispanics, and all workers.* 1990s represents 1989 to 2000; 2000s is 2000 to 2007.

Chapter 1

1.1   *Median family income.* U.S. Census Bureau, Historical Income Tables, Families, Table F-5.

1.2   Income growth in the 1990s and 2000s and the roles of earnings, hours, and hourly wages. Authors' analysis of March CPS data; see Appendix A for explanation.

1.3   *Median family income by race/ethnic group.* U.S. Census Bureau, Historical Income Tables, Families, Table F-5.

1.4   *Full employment, African American family income, unemployment, and inflation.* CBO NAIRU estimates: http://www.cbo.gov/doc.cfm?index=9706 (see "Key Assumptions in CBO's projections of Potential Output"); Family income, see source re Table 1.3, unemployment and inflation, BLS.

1.5   *Median family income by age of householder.* Census homepage, Historical Income Tables, Families, Table F-11.

1.6   *Median family income by family type.* Census homepage, Historical Income Tables, Families, Table F-7.

1.7   *Shares of family income going to income fifths and to the top 5%.* Census homepage, Historical Income Tables, Families, Table F-2.

1.8   *Real family income by income group, 1947-2006, upper limit of each group.* Census homepage, Historical Income Tables, Families, Table F-1.

1.9   *Household income shares.* CBO Household Income series: http://www.cbo.gov/doc.cfm?index=8885. Data are for all households.

1.10   *Effective federal tax rates for all households, by comprehensive household income quintile.* See Table 1.9.

1.11   *Effective tax rates for selected federal taxes.* See Table 1.9.

1.12   *Federal and state/local revenue as a share of GDP.* See U.S. Department of Commerce, BEA (2008), Tables 3.2 and 3.3.

1.13   *Composition of federal and state/local tax revenue, by progressive and regressive components.* See Table 1.12.

1.14   *Impact of 2001-06 tax cuts on 2008 income.* Tax Policy Center,T06-0281 (http://www.taxpolicycenter.org/numbers/displayatabcfm?Docid=1363&Doc TypeD=2).

1.15   *Family income by income categories.* Data provided by U.S. Bureau of the Census.

1.16   *The impact in inequality on income shares.* Authors' analysis of ASEC data. See Appendix A.

1.17   *Sources of income by income group and distribution of income types.* Based on tabulations from the Urban-Brookings Tax Policy Center Microsimulation Model (version 0305-3A) and provided by Peter Orzag.

1.18   *Shares of market-based personal income by income type.* From U.S. Department of Commerce, BEA (2008), Table 2.1. Capital gains data are from the Internal Revenue Service Statistics on Income series and include gains as well as losses (see http://www.irs.gov/taxstats/article/0,,id=175788,00. html). The capital gains data for 2007 are an estimate based on the growth in CBO forecasts for capital gains from 2006 to 2007 (see http://www.cbo.gov/ ftpdocs/89xx/doc8917/Chapter4.8.1.shtml, #1069855, Table 4-3).

1.19   *Shares of income by type and sector.* Based on U.S. Department of Commerce, BEA (2008), Table 1.13 (available in June 2008). The "corporate and business" sector includes "corporate" and "rest of world." Capital income consists of profits, and net interest. The "government/nonprofit" sector includes the household, non-profits, government enterprise, and general government sectors. The capital income in this sector is the interest and rent earned plus the surplus of government enterprises. The capital and labor income in the corporate sector are not adjusted for the increased presence of 'spread income' or 'realized option income' that is counted as wages but more appropriately should be considered capital income. The data in Table 1.20 do make an adjustment.

1.20   *Corporate sector profit rates and shares.* These estimates start with the corporate income from U.S. Department of Commerce, BEA (see note to Table 1.13). Corporate income is corporate profits (with IVA and CCAdj) plus net interest. Compensation is line 10. "After-tax profit rates" account for a tax rate based on the quotient of taxes on corporate income and applied to capital income, as previously defined. Corporate capital data are from the BEA series, the Current-Cost Net Stock of Private Nonresidential Fixed Assets. This is updated to 2007 based on growth in Flow of Funds data on tangible assets. The "capital-output ratio" is corporate capital divided by capital income.

An important adjustment is made to account for the increased presence of 'spread income' or 'realized option income' that is counted as wages but more appropriately should be considered capital income. An estimate of realized option income is subtracted from wages in the corporate sector and added to the capital income in the sector. This income rose to be as high as 2.6% of all wages in 2000 from 0.0% in 1994. These options, when counted as capital income, raised the estimate of capital income by roughly 15% in 2000 but by only about 6% in 2004. This adjustment relies on estimates of realized option income presented in CBO (2008) and Jaquette et al. (2003). Jaquette (2003) provides estimates of the absolute amount and the wage share for the 1997-2001 period in Tables 1 and 2. CBO (2008) provides estimates of realized option income as a share of wages from 1994 to 2004 in Figure 7. For 1994 the share is zero and our estimates for 1995 and 1996 are based on a straight-line extrapolation from the 1994 and 1997 shares. The 2002 and 2003 shares were provided by Scott Jaquette of CBO. The share for 2004 was set to that of 1997 based on the CBO figure, and it was assumed that this wage share prevailed over the 2005-07 period as well. Based on the estimates of the realized options share of wages in this period, estimates of the absolute amount of realized options (the share times the total NIPA wage bill) were made and used to adjust corporate wage and capital income.

1.21   *Annual hours of work, married men and women, 25-54, with children, by income fifth.* Authors' analysis of ASEC data. See Appendix A.

1.22   *Real income growth of prime-age, married-couple families with children, and married women's contribution.* Authors' analysis of CPS ASEC data. See Appendix A.

Chapter 2

2.1   *Income mobility between quintiles.* Data provided by Greg Acs, from Acs and Zimmerman (2008).

2.2   *Intergenerational wealth, parents to children.* See Charles and Hurst (2003).

Chapter 3

3.1   *Median wage, compensation growth, and productivity growth in recoveries.* Productivity data are from the BLS and measure output per hour in the non-farm business sector. The wage data are the median hourly wage from Table 3.5 (the sample definition and details of computations of the CPS-ORG wage data are in Appendix B). The wage data are converted to "compensation" using the compensation to wage ratios presented in Table 3.3 and used in Figure 3B.

3.2   *Trends in average wages and average hours.* Productivity data are from the BLS and measure output per hour in the non-farm business sector. The wage-level data are based on the authors' tabulations of March CPS files using a series on annual, weekly, and hourly wages for wage and salary workers (the sample definition in the CPS-ORG wage analysis is used; see Appendix B). The weekly and hourly wage data are "hour weighted," obtained by dividing annual wages by weeks worked and annual hours worked. The 1967 and 1973 values are derived from unpublished tabulations provided by Kevin Murphy from an update of Murphy and Welch (1989). Their values include self-employment as well as wage and salary workers. The values displayed in this table were bridged from CPS 1979 values using the growth rates in the Murphy and Welch series. Hours of work were derived from differences between annual, weekly, and hourly wage trends.

3.3   *Growth of average hourly wages, benefits, and compensation.* The data in the top panel are computed from the U.S. Department of Commerce, Bureau of Economic Analysis (2008) NIPA tables. "Wages and salaries" are calculated by dividing wage and salary accruals (Table 6.3) by hours worked by full-time and part-time employees (Table 6.9). "Total compensation" is the sum of wages and salaries and social insurance. Social insurance is total compensation (Table 6.2) minus the sum of volunteer benefits (sum of health and non-health benefits; see (Table 6.11) and wages and salaries. "Benefits" is the difference between total compensation and wages and salaries. These data were deflated using the NIPA personal consumption expenditure (PCE, chain-weighted) index, with health insurance adjusted by the PCE medical care (chained) index. These data include both public- and private-sector workers.

Employer Costs for Employee Compensation (ECEC) comes from the U.S. Department of Labor, BLS (2008d) data, and provide cost levels for March for private-industry workers, available starting in 1987. We categorize wages and salaries differently than BLS, putting all wage-related items (including paid leave and supplemental pay) into the hourly wage (so that 'wages' is comparable to workers' W-2 earnings). Benefits, in our definition, include only payroll taxes, pensions, insurance, and "other" benefits. The sum of wages and salaries and benefits makes up total compensation. It is important to use the current-weighted series rather than the fixed-weighted series because composition shifts (in the distribution of employment across occupations and industries) have a large effect. Employer costs for insurance are deflated by the medical care component of the CPI-U-RS. All other pay is deflated by the CPI-U-RS for "all items." Inflation is measured for the first quarter of each year.

3.4   *Hourly and weekly earnings of private production and nonsupervisory workers.* From the U.S. Department of Labor, BLS (2008b) Current Establishment Survey data, deflated using CPI-U-RS.

3.5   *Wages for all workers by wage percentile.* Based on analysis of CPS wage data described in Appendix B.

3.6   *Wages for male workers by wage percentile.* Based on analysis of CPS wage data described in Appendix B.

3.7   *Wages for female workers by wage percentile.* Based on analysis of CPS wage data described in Appendix B.

3.8   *Distribution of employment by wage level and race category, All and White.* Based on analysis of CPS wage data described in Appendix B. The poverty-level wage is calculated using the preliminary estimate of the four-person weighted average poverty threshold in 2007 divided by 2,080 hours which is 10.20. This figure is deflated by CPI-U-RS to obtain the poverty-level wage levels for other years. The threshold is available at the Census Web site. We calculated more intervals than we show but aggregated for simplicity of presentation (no trends were lost). The data are for non-Hispanic whites.

3.9   *Distribution of employment by wage level and race category, black and Hispanic.* See note to Table 3.8.

3.10   *Changes in the distribution and level of wage and salaries.* Data taken from Kopczuk, Saez, and Song (2007), Table A-3. Data for 2006 extrapolated from 2004 data using growth rates from Social Security Administration (SSA) wage statistics (http://www.ssa.gov/OACT/COLA/awidevelop.html). SSA provides data on share of total wages and employment in annual wage brackets such as for those earning between $95,000.00 and $99,999.99. We employ the midpoint of the bracket to compute total wage income in each bracket and sum all brackets. Our estimate of total wage income was 99.1% of the actual. We used interpolation to derive cutoffs building from the bottom up to obtain the 0-90% bracket and then estimating the remaining categories. This allowed us to estimate the wage shares for upper wage groups. To obtain absolute wage trends we used the SSA data on the total wage pool and employment and computed the real wage per worker (based on their share of wages and employment) in the different groups in $2007.

3.11   *Growth of specific fringe benefits.* Based on ECEC data described in note to Table 3.3.

3.12   *Change in private-sector employer-provided health insurance coverage.* Based on tabulations of March CPS data samples of private wage-and-salary earners ages 18-64 who worked at least 20 hours per week and 26 weeks per year. Coverage is defined as being included in an employer-provided plan where the employer paid for at least some of the coverage.

3.13   *Change in private-sector employer-provided pension coverage.* These data are from the March CPS on pension coverage using the sample described in the note to Table 3.12.

3.14   *Dimensions of wage inequality.* All of the data are based on analyses of the CPS ORG data described in Appendix B. The measures of "total wage inequality" are natural logs of wage ratios (multiplied by 100) computed from Tables 3.6 and 3.7. The exception is that the 1979 data for women are 1978-80 averages. This was done to smooth the volatility of the series, especially at the 10th percentile. The "between group inequalities" are computed from regressions of the log of hourly wages on education categorical variables (high school omitted), experience as a quartic, marital status, race, and region (4). The college/high school and high school/less-than-high-school premiums are simply the coefficient on "college" and "less than high school" (expressed as the advantage of "high school" over "less than high school" wages). The experience differentials are the differences in the value of age (calculated from the coefficients of the quartic specification) evaluated at 25, 35, and 50 years. "Within-group wage inequality" is measured as the root mean square error from the same log wage regressions used to compute age and education differentials.

3.15   *Real hourly wage for all by education.* Based on tabulations of CPS wage data described in Appendix B. See Appendix B for details on how a consistent measure of education was developed to bridge the change in coding in 1992.

3.16   *Real hourly wage for men by education.* See note to Table 3.15.

3.17   *Real hourly wage for women by education.* See note to Table 3.15.

3.18   *Educational attainment of workforce employment.* Based on analysis of CPS wage earners. The data are described in Appendix B. The categories are as follows: "less than high school" is grade 1-12 or no diploma; "high school/ GED" is high school graduate diploma or equivalent; "some college" is some college but no degree; "associate college" is occupational or academic associate's degree; "college B.A." is a bachelor's degree; and "advanced degree" is a master's, professional, or doctorate degree.

3.19   *Hourly wages of entry-level and experienced workers by education.* Based on analysis of CPS wage data described in Appendix B.

3.20   *Hourly wages by decile within education groups.* Based on analysis of CPS wage data described in Appendix B.

3.21   *Decomposition of total and within-group wage inequality.* Data are from the CPS ORG sample described in Appendix B. "Overall wage inequality" is measured as the standard deviation of log wages. "Within-group wage inequality" is the mean square error from log wage regressions (the same ones used for Table 3.14). "Between-group wage inequality" is the difference between the overall and within-group wage inequalities and reflects changes in all of the included variables: education, age, marital status, race, ethnicity, and region.

3.22   *Hourly wage growth by gender, race/ethnicity.* Based on analysis of CPS wage data described in Appendix B.

3.23   *The gender wage ratio.* Wages and ratio are based on 50th percentile from Tables 3.6 and 3.7, CPS ORG data.

3.24   *Impact of rising and falling unemployment on wage levels and wage ratios.* The unemployment rate is from BLS (2008c). Wage data are based on analysis of quarterly CPS wage data (see Appendix B). The "simulated effect of change on unemployment" was calculated by regressing the log of nominal wages on lagged wages, unemployment, productivity growth, and seasonal dummies for each included percentile, by gender. Using these models, wages were predicted given a simulated unemployment rate series where in one case the unemployment rate maintained its 1979 level through the third quarter of 1987 (preventing its actual increase), and in the other case maintained its 1995 level through the fourth quarter of 2000 (preventing its actual decrease). "Unemployment contribution to change" shows the wage simulated by the model in the final quarter of the simulation period compared to the actual wage.

3.25   *Employment growth by sector.* Employment levels by industry are from the U.S. Department of Labor, BLS (2008b) Current Employment Statistics. Compensation by industry is from the U.S. Department of Labor, BLS (2008d) Employer Costs for Employee Compensation (ECEC) series for March 2005, Table 10 for private-sector workers. Compensation for certain industries is based on U.S. Department of Commerce, BEA (2008) NIPA data for compensation per full-time equivalent worker. College intensity by industry is computed form the CPS ORG data described in Appendix B.

3.26   *Annual pay of expanding and contracting industries.* These data reflect the average (annual) wages, benefits, and compensation of the net new employment in each period based on changes in industry composition. The employment data are payroll counts from the U.S. Department of Labor, BLS (2008b) establishment survey and the pay data are from U.S. Department of Commerce, BEA (2008) NIPA data (calculated per payroll employee). The pay of the net new employment is a weighted average of the pay by industry where the weights are the changes in each industry's employment share over the time period.

3.27   *Effect of trade on composition of employment by education level.* Bivens (2008).

3.28   *Estimated relative wage impact of trade based on Krugman CGE Model.* Based on Bivens' (2008) re-analysis of Krugman (1995).

3.29   *Characteristics of offshorable jobs.* Authors' analysis of data of Blinder (2007), matching Blinder's occupational codes to the BLS, Occupational Employment Statistics (OES) survey <http://www.bls.gov/oes/>. See Bernstein, Lin, and Mishel (2007) for details.

3.30   *Share of Mexican and other immigrants in workforce.* Data from Figure 1 in Borjas and Katz (2005) and authors' computations of the Current Population Survey for 2000 and 2007.

3.31   *Percent distribution of educational attainment of immigrants.* From Table 2 in Borjas and Katz (2005) and authors' computations of the Current Population Survey for 2000 and 2007.

3.32   *Union wage premium by demographic group.* "Percent union" is tabulated from CPS ORG data (see Appendix B) and includes all those covered by unions. "Union premium" values are the coefficients on union in a model of log hourly wages with controls for education, experience as a quartic, marital status, region, industry (12) and occupation (9), and race/ethnicity, and gender where appropriate. For this analysis we only use observations that do not have imputed wages. This is because the imputation process does not take union status into account and therefore biases the union premium toward zero. See Mishel and Walters (2003).

3.33   *Union premiums for health, retirement, and paid leave.* Based on Table 4 in Mishel and Walters (2003), which draws on Buchmueller, DiNardo, and Valletta (2001).

3.34   *Union impact on paid leave, pension, and health benefits.* Based on Table 3 in Mishel and Walters (2003), which draws on Pierce (1999), Tables 4, 5, and 6.

3.35   *Effect of declining union power on male wage differentials.* This analysis replicates, updates, and expands on Freeman (1991), Table 2. The analysis uses the CPS ORG sample used in other analyses (see Appendix B). The year 1978, rather than 1979, is the earliest year analyzed because we have no union membership data in our 1979 sample. The "union wage premium" for a group is based on the coefficient on collective bargaining coverage in a regression of hourly wages on a simple human capital model (the same one used for estimating education differentials, as described in note to Table 3.14), with major industry (12) and occupation (9) controls in a sample for that group. The change in union premium across years, therefore, holds industry and occupation composition constant. "Percent union" is the share covered by collective bargaining. Freeman's analysis assumed the union premium was unchanged over time. We allow the union premium to differ across years so changes in the union effect are driven by changes in the unionization rate and the union wage premium. The analysis compares the change in the union effect on relative wages to the actual change in relative wages (regression-adjusted with simple human capital controls plus controls for other education or occupation groups).

3.36   *Union wage premium for subgroups.* Builds on Mishel and Walters (2003), Table 2.3A and Gundersen (2003), Table 5.1 and Appendix C. Premium estimates by fifth are from: Schmitt (2008); Card, Lemieux, and Riddle (2002); and Gittleman and Pierce (2007). Union coverage by fifth is from Schmitt (2008).

3.37   *Impact of unions on average wages of high school graduates.* Based on Table 5 in Mishel and Walters (2003).

3.38   *Value of the minimum wage.* Historical values of minimum wage from Shapiro (1987) and authors' updates. Deflated using CPI-U-RS.

3.39   *Characteristics of workers affected by potential federal minimum wage increase to $7.25 by 2009.* See Table 1 in Minimum Wage Issue Guide at < http://www.epi.org/content.cfm/issueguides_minwage >.

3.40   *Changes in the college wage premium and the supply and demand for college educated workers.* See Goldin and Katz (2008), Table 1. The authors used the original data to break out the most recent period, 2000-05.

3.41   *Executive annual pay.* The 1992-2005 data are from a *Wall Street Journal/ William M. Mercer* survey (of 350 large industrial and service companies) of CEO compensation. "Realized direct compensation" includes salary, bonus, gains from options exercised, value of restricted stock at grant, and other long-term incentive award payments. These data were made available by the Mercer Company and the data from 1994 onwards are in a report for the Business Roundtable by Cook (2006). The average compensation for 1989 is backed out of the 1995 data by extrapolating the 1989-95 trend in the Pearl Meyer/*Wall Street Journal* data for that period.
    The bigger challenge is how to update the series between 2005 and 2007 because of two shifts. One is that the definitions of executive pay provided in proxy statements changed in 2006 making comparability to 2005 problematic. The biggest change in 2006 is that CEO pay, total direct compensation (TDC), included the value of all long-term incentives granted during 2006; the prior proxy definition of CEO pay by contrast included all unvested stock and option awards, including long-term incentives granted in previous years, not just in 2006. The second shift is that the Wall Street Journal used a new firm, the Hay Group, to produce its 2007 executive pay data and the survey sample shifted: Mercer used the first *350* companies with annual revenues in excess of *$1 billion*

that reported proxy statements for the last fiscal year while the Hay Group selects only the first 200 companies with annual revenues in excess of $5 billion. To carry forward the 2005 data to 2006 we relied on the Mercer calculations of the growth of CEO pay in their survey of 2006 compensation (which extrapolates forward the pay levels of those in the Mercer sample of 350 large firms). We went to the published data for all 350 companies <http://online.wsj.com/public/resources/documents/Execpay_ceocomp07. pdf>. There, each CEO's TDC was reported, as well as his or her percent change from the comparable 2005 TDC. This percent change reflects the growth rate of each executive's TDC from the previous year *under the 2006 definition of TDC*, and is therefore an "apples-to-apples" growth rate. The cost of obtaining a consistent definition is that the sample is not all CEOs but those who continued employment from 2005 into 2006.

To link 2006 levels to 2007 levels we used the changes in compensation in the Hay Group survey. In order to get trend data for the Hay study, we asked Steven Sabow, previously of Mercer, to do a data run for us. Though Hay Group only had data for realized TDC in 2007, it had expected TDC in both 2006 and in 2007. He was able to run this data on expected TDC for us in those two years, and so we now have data on the growth of expected TDC from 2006-07. (Expected TDC is the sum of salary + bonus + expected long-term incentive payments, e.g., value of payments at date of grant. Realized TDC is the sum of salary + bonus + realized long-term incentive payments, e.g., vested value of payments.)

3.42   *CEO pay in advanced countries.* Total CEO compensation in dollars and the ratio of CEO to production-worker pay are from Towers Perrin (1988, 2003, and 2005). The table uses unweighted average for non-U.S. countries. These data are from a different sample (smaller firms) as the data in Table 3.41 and therefore the U.S. data differ.

3.43   *Effect of changing occupational composition on wages and education.* This is a shift-share analysis based on the changes in the employment shares of 754 occupations, and their skill and education levels, according to the most recent BLS projections, in Dohm and Shniper (2007). The education intensities, training requirements, and median annual wage for each occupation are available at <ftp://ftp.bls.gov/pub/special.requests/ep/OPTDData/ >.

Chapter 4

4.1   *Labor force share and unemployment rate by age category.* Authors' analysis of U.S. Department of Labor, BLS (2008c) data at official business cycle peaks and the fourth quarter of 2007.

4.2   *Unemployment rates.* Data are from U.S. Department of Labor, BLS (2008c), Table A-1.

4.3   *Percentage-point change in unemployment rates between business cycle peaks.* Monthly unemployment data are from BLS (2008c).

4.4   *Unemployment rates by gender, race, and educational status.* Data are taken from BLS (2008c), for persons 25 years and older.

4.5   *Shares of unemployment and long-term unemployment.* Occupational categories represent only those who reported a civilian occupation. Race/ethnicity shares are calculated using white, black, and Hispanic workers only.

4.6   *Underemployment.* Data is taken from BLS (2008c), Table A-12. Regarding involuntary part-time, see also note to Figure 4T.

4.7   *Nonstandard workers in the U.S. workforce.* Nonstandard work refers to any work arrangement other than employment in a full-time, full-year wage and salary job. From Ditsler and Fisher (2006), based on analysis of the 2005 Contingent Work Supplement from the February CPS.

4.8   *Average years of job tenure by age, gender, and education.* Analysis of Farber (2007), based on data provided to EPI by the author.

4.9   *Share of employed workers in long-term jobs by age, gender, and education.* See note to Table 4.8.

Chapter 5

5.1   *Distribution of income and wealth.* Unpublished analysis of Survey of Consumer Finances (SCF) data prepared in April 2006 by Edward Wolff for the Economic Policy Institute. Data from the 2007 SCF were not available at the time of this writing.

5.2   *Changes in the distribution of wealth.* See note to Table 5.1.

5.3   *Changes in average wealth by wealth class.* See note to Table 5.1.

5.4   *Households with low net worth.* See note to Table 5.1.

5.5   *Wealth by race.* See note to Table 5.1.

5.6   *Distribution of asset ownership across households.* Assets considered here are liquid and semi-liquid assets including mutual funds, trusts, retirement, and pensions. It does not include assets such as vehicles, primary residence, or other real estate investments. Also see note to Table 5.1.

5.7   *Share of households owning stock.* See note to Table 5.1.

5.8   *Average household assets and liabilities by wealth class.* See note to Table 5.1.

5.9   *Concentration of stock ownership by income level.* See note to Table 5.1.

5.10   *Home ownership rates by race and income. Home ownership by race* is the authors' analysis of U.S. Department of Commerce, Bureau of the Census (2008a), Table 20, Homeownership Rates by Race and Ethnicity of Householder from 1994 on. Data prior to 1994 are taken from CPS March Supplement, provided by the Bureau of the Census upon request. "Black" refers to non-Hispanic blacks, "White" refers to non-Hispanic whites, and "Hispanic" refers to Hispanics of any race. *Homeownership by income* is the authors' analysis of the U.S. Department of Commerce, Bureau of the Census (2005), published every two years.

5.11   *Retirement income inadequacy.* See note to Table 5.1.

5.12   *Household debt by type.* Disposable personal income is personal income less tax and like tax payments. Personal taxes include income, estate and gift, and personal property taxes and motor vehicle licenses. Like-tax payments include passport fees, fines and forfeitures, and donations. Data are taken from Federal Reserve Board (2008a), B.100 Balance Sheet of Households and Nonprofit Organizations via Data Download, Z.1 Statistical Release for March 6, 2008. Data for home equity loans are taken from Table L.218 and is unavailable prior to 1990.

5.13   *Financial obligations ratio.* Data refer to annual averages from the Federal Reserve Board (2008b), Household Debt Service and Financial Obligations Ratios. Per the FRB: the *financial obligations ratio (FOR)* adds automobile lease payments, rental payments on tenant-occupied property, homeowners' insurance, and property tax payments to the debt service ratio (an estimate of the ratio of debt payments on outstanding mortgage and consumer debt, to disposable personal income. See note to Table 5.12 for disposable personal income definition). The *homeowner mortgage FOR* includes payments on mortgage debt, homeowners' insurance, and property taxes, while the *homeowner consumer FOR* includes payments on consumer debt and automobile leases.

5.14   *Household debt service as a share of household income, by income percentile.* Data are taken from Bucks, Kennickell, Moore (2006), Table 14, p.34.

5.15   *Share of households with high debt burdens, by income percentile.* Data are taken from Bucks, Kennickell, Moore (2006), Table 14, p.35.

5.16   *Share of households late paying bills, by income percentile.* See note to Table
        5.14.

Chapter 6

6.1   *Percent and number of persons in poverty and twice poverty.* See U.S. Census
        Bureau, Historical Poverty Income Tables, Persons, Table 2.

6.2   *Persons in poverty, by race/ethnicity.* See U.S. Census Bureau, Historical
        Poverty Income Tables, Persons, Table 3.

6.3   *Percent of children in poverty, by race.* See U.S. Census Bureau, Historical
        Poverty Income Tables, Persons, Table 3.

6.4   *Family poverty, by race/ethnicity of family head and for different family
        types.* See U.S. Census Bureau, Historical Poverty Income Tables, Families,
        Table 4.

6.5   *Average poverty gap.* Unpublished time series provided by the U.S. Census
        Bureau. Annual updates are available online (http://pubdb3.census.gov/
        macro/032007/pov/new28_001_01.htm).

6.6   *Poverty by nativity.* See U.S. Census Bureau, Historical Poverty Income
        Tables, Persons, Table 23.

6.7   *Official and alternative poverty thresholds for a family of four.* Official
        thresholds can be found online (http://www.census.gov/hhes/www/poverty/
        threshld.html). For alternative thresholds, see Garner and Short (2008).

6.8   *Official and alternative poverty rates, by demographics.* For official poverty
        rates see note to Table 6.1. For alternative poverty rates, see Garner and Short
        (2008).

6.9   *Changes in poverty rates and various correlates.* For "poverty rates" see
        note to Table 6.1; for "productivity" see BLS, measures of output per hour in
        the non-farm business sector; for "per capita income" see U.S. Department
        of Commerce, BEA (2008), NIPA Table 2.1; for "unemployment" see BLS;
        for "Inequality" see U.S. Bureau of the Census, Historical Income Tables,
        Families, Table F-4, and note to Figure 1I; and for "low-wage growth" see
        authors' analysis of CPS ORG hourly wages as described in Appendix B.

6.10   *The impact of economic, demographic, and education changes on poverty
        rates.* See Appendix A. Method based on Danziger and Gottschalk (1996).

6.11   *The effects of work supports on family resources and expenses, assuming full receipt.* See Cauthen (2007), Table 2.

6.12   *Characteristics of low-wage workers.* Authors' analysis of CPS ORG data; see Appendix B.

Chapter 7

7.1   *Employer-provided health insurance, population under 65 years old.* Authors' analysis of the March Current Population Survey, 2001-07. Taken from Gould (2007a), Table 3, "Employer-provided health insurance, population under 65 years old, 2000-06" and updated to 2007.

7.2   *Life expectancy (in years) by socioeconomic deprivation groups.* Authors' analysis of Singhl and Siahpush (2006), "Table 3, Number of deaths and life expectancy at birth (in years) by sex and socioeconomic deprivation groups, U.S., 1980–2000," based on data from the U.S. National Vital Statistics System, 1980–2000.

7.3   *Percent of persons with total family out-of-pocket burdens by insurance and poverty status.* Total burden includes out-of-pocket premiums for private expenditures on health care services, for persons under age 65. Data were calculated using Medical Expenditure Panel Surveys (MEPS) data.

Chapter 8

8.1   *Per capita income using PPPs.* GDP is converted to 2007 dollars and based on PPP exchange rates of 2005, per the Conference Board and Groningen Growth and Development Centre (2008).

8.2   *Productivity levels and growth.* Productivity refers to GDP per hour worked. See notes to Table 8.1.

8.3   *Employment rates.* Data for 1979-2000 are taken from the OECD (2007d) <http://dx.doi.org/10.1787/172580205657>. Data for 2006 are taken from OECD (2007c) <http://dx.doi.org/10.1787/024835322607>, in which data for Germany and France are estimated by applying changes between 2005 and 2006 from the European Labor Force Survey, to national estimates for 2005. Employment rates refer to persons aged 15 to 64 (16 to 64 in Norway, Sweden, Spain, and the UK) who are in employment, divided by the working-age population.

8.4   *Average annual hours worked.* See OECD.stat (Labor-Labor Force Statistics) and OECD (2007c) <http://dx.doi.org/10.1787/025031458255>, Table F, page 263 for 1979 and 2006, "Average annual hours actually worked per person in employment." This accounts for hours worked over the year divided by the average number of people in part-time and full-time employment. Hours worked data in Greece and Switzerland were unavailable for 2006 at the time of publication.

8.5   *Decomposition of per capita income.* For sources, refer to Table 8.1 for per capita income, Table 8.2 for productivity, and Table 8.4 for hours worked. Employment-to-population ratio is calculated from OECD (2008), where latest available data are substituted for the following countries: Australia (2003), Japan (2005), and Canada (2005). See also OECD.stat (Annual National Accounts-Main Aggregates).

8.6   *Work and leave policies.* Average Annual Weeks Worked is taken from the OECD (2007e) calculations of individual countries' surveys including European Union Labor Force Survey (EULFS), Statistics Canada Labor Force Survey, the Australia Labor Force Survey, and the Current Population Survey (CPS) for the United States. Data for statutory minimum vacation days and public holidays assume a five-day workweek. Note that the European Union's Working Time Directive (1993, 93/104/EC) requires a paid leave floor of four weeks, or 20 days per year, for all EU member countries.

8.7   *Work and family policies.* Maternity data for all countries except Australia and the UK are taken from OECD (2007f). Data for Australia were taken from the UN Statistics Division, Statistics and Indicators on Women and Men (2005b) and United Nations (2005a). Data for the UK were updated to 2005 legislation that went into effect April of 2007; see UK's Department for Work and Pensions <http://www.dwp.gov.uk/lifeevent/benefits/statutory_maternity_pay.asp#what> and the International Social Security Association (2006). Child care data are extracted from the OECD Family Database (variable PF10.2) and attributed to: OECD Social Expenditure Database 1980-2003. Note: The International Labor Organization Maternity Protection Convention (2000) stipulates the period of leave to be at least 14 weeks.

8.8   *Employment rates by gender.* Data for 1979-2000 is taken from OECD (2007d). Data for 2006 is taken from OECD (2007c). See note to Table 8.3 for country notes.

8.9   *Employment growth.* Employment refers to civilian employment based on Annual Labor Force Statistics (ALFS), accessible through OECD.stat. Note: U.S. employment data of the ALFS is based averages of the Current Population Survey, released monthly.

8.10   *Standardized unemployment rates.* Standardized unemployment rates refer to
        the percentage of unemployed persons as a percent of the civilian labor force.
        Data for 1979 and 1989 are based on OECD.stat (Main Economic Indicators,
        Comparative Subject Tables Release 12). Data for 2000 and 2006 are taken
        from the OECD (2007c). < http://dx.doi.org/10.1787/024830722817 >

8.11   *Unemployment rates by education level.* See OECD (2007b): Unemployment
        rates and educational attainment by gender in 2005. This was published in
        November of 2007 as a revision of OECD (2007c).

8.12   *Real compensation growth per year.* "Labor compensation per hour" in national
        currency for the total economy taken from OECD (2007h) in OECD.stat (Unit
        Labor Costs-Annual Indicators) and converted to real currency using the Price
        Index provided for each country, prior to calculating growth rates. Countries
        are limited due to available data.

8.13   *Relative hourly compensation of manufacturing production workers.* Percent
        of Civilian Labor Force in Manufacturing is taken from the U.S. Department
        of Labor, BLS (2008), Comparative Civilian Labor Force Statistics, Ten
        Countries,1960-2006, Table 7: Percent Distribution of Civilian Employment
        Approximating U.S. Concepts by Economic Sector. According to BLS
        approximations, production workers make up about 60% to 80% of the total
        manufacturing workforce in the United States. Index of compensation using
        market exchange rates is taken directly from U.S. Department of Labor,
        BLS (2008), International Comparisons of Hourly Compensation Costs for
        Production Workers in Manufacturing, Supplementary Tables, Table 1, "Indexes
        of hourly compensation costs in U.S. dollars." Index of hourly compensation
        in U.S. dollars using PPPs is based on Table 2, "Hourly compensation costs in
        U.S. dollars," converted using purchasing-power parities for GDP taken from
        OECD (2008), extracted from OECD.stat (Annual National Accounts-Main
        Aggregates-PPPs & Exchange Rates).

8.14   *Annual growth in real hourly compensation of manufacturing production
        workers.* All data are from the BLS (2008), adjusted to real 2006 dollars. See
        International Comparisons of Hourly Compensation Costs for Production
        Workers, Supplementary Tables, 1975-2006, Table 2, "Production Workers:
        Hourly compensation costs in U.S. dollars in manufacturing, 34 countries or
        areas and selected economic groups 1975-2006."

8.15   *Household income inequality.* Gini coefficients are taken from the CIA
        Factbook (see Table 8.16b: where Australia is 2006), with the exception
        of the United States, which was only available for the year 2007. Thus, for
        comparative purposes, the Gini Coefficient for the United States is taken from
        the Luxembourg Income Study for the year 2004. 90-10 ratios are based on
        OECD (2005). Also see notes to Figure 8C.

8.16   *Poverty rates.* From LIS (retrieved 2006), "Relative Poverty Rates for the Total Population, Children and the Elderly." Data are unavailable for Japan, Greece, and New Zealand. All data are for 2000 except for Switzerland (2002), Netherlands, Poland, and the UK (1999), Denmark (1997), and Australia and France (1994).

Figure Notes

Introduction

A   *Job growth: 2000s cycle versus average of past cycles.* Based on BLS (2008b) data according to NBER business cycle peaks. See also Figure 4B (months to gain peak level employment) and Figure 4C (employment growth).

B   *Jobs and joblessness.* Taken from U.S. Department of Labor, BLS (2008b) for jobs data, and BLS (2008c) for unemployment and underemployment data.

C   *Real paychecks falling in the downturn.* Hourly and weekly earnings are from BLS (2008b) for non-supervisory production workers. Wages and benefits are taken from BLS (2008d), Employer Costs for Employer Compensation (ECEC) data.

D   *Change in average real family income following peak years, by selected income fifths.* Authors' analysis of U.S. Census Bureau, Historical Income Tables, Families, Table F-3.

E   Forecasted real family income losses given rising unemployment. Based on Goldman Sachs projected unemployment of 2008 (5.7%) and 2009 (6.4%), for each income quintile (see annual Census income data, Historical Income Table F3) in 2007 dollars. Elasticities, which correspond to each quintile, are from Timothy Bartik (2002) <www.upjohninst.org>.

F   *Growth in annual earnings by wage group.* See note for Table 3.10.

G   *Ratio of wages of highest earners to those of bottom 90%.* See note for Table 3.10.

H   *Productivity and compensation:* Four recoveries. See Figure 3O.

I   *How likely is it that a son of a low-wage father will attain higher earnings?*
         See Figure 2C. Based on unpublished data provided by Gary Solon.

J   *College completion by income status and test scores.* See also Figure 2N,
         accompanied by further analysis.

K   *Intergenerational correlations, father and son, U.S. and Europe.* See also
         Figure 2H, accompanied by further analysis.

Chapter 1

1A   Real median family income. See note to Table 1.1.

1B   Years for median family income to regain prior peak. Authors' analysis of data
         used for Table 1.1.

1C   Change in average real family income following peak years, by selected
         income quintiles. Authors' analysis of U.S. Census Bureau, Historical Income
         Tables, Families, Table F-3.

1D   Forecasted real income losses given predicted unemployment. Authors'
         analysis of data used for Table 1.2. Elasticities are from Bartik (2001).

1E   Ratio of black and Hispanic to white median family income. See note to Table 1.3.

1F   *Income growth for middle-income immigrant and non-immigrant families.*
         Authors' analysis of CPS ASEC data. See Appendix A. Values are for average
         of middle fifth.

1G   *Productivity and real median family income growth.* See note to Table 1.1 for
         income data. See BLS for Productivity (pertaining to nonfarm business).

1H   Real family income growth by quintile. Authors' analysis of U.S. Census
         Bureau, Historical Income Tables, Families, Table F-3.1947 value is
         unpublished and was provided by the Census.

1I   Ratio of family income of top 5% to lowest 20%. Authors' analysis of U.S.
         Census Bureau, Historical Income Tables, Families, Table F-3.

1J   *Low-, middle-, and high-income growth.* Authors' analysis of U.S. Census
         Bureau, Historical Income Tables, Families, Table F-1.

1K   Share of income held by top 1%, 1913-2006. Piketty and Saez (2003), updated
         to 2006 (available at http://elsa.berkeley.edu/~saez/).

1L   *Income share (investment and labor income)*, top 0.1%. See note to Figure 1K.

1M   Share of household income, bottom 99.5%. See note to Figure 1K.

1N   *Household income growth by income group, pre- and post-tax.* See note to Table 1.9.

1O   *Change in income shares, pre- and post-tax.* See note to Table 1.9.

1P   *Real expenditures by income fifth.* BLS data from Consumer Expenditure Survey on expenditures by income class, available at <http://data.bls.gov/PDQ/outside.jsp?survey=cx>.

1Q   *Increase in consumption inequality.* See Attanasio et al. (2006).

1R   *Consumption inequality among children.* See Johnson et al. (2005).

1S   *Inequality and income shares.* Authors' analysis of CPS ASEC data. See Appendix A.

1T   *Share of capital income received by income groups.* This is based on Congressional Budget Office data presented in the Share of Corporate Income Tax Liabilities section of Table 1B, Shares of Federal Tax Liabilities for All Households, by Comprehensive Household Income Quintile, 1979-2005. These data reflect shares of capital income by income group. These do not sum to 100% (because those with negative incomes are left out of the bottom decile), omitting about 2%. Therefore, the data were rescaled to 100%. These data were developed by CBO for "Historical Effective Federal Tax Rates: 1979 to 2005" (December 2007) and are available in the accompanying workbook at <http://www.cbo.gov/doc.cfm?index=8885 >.

1U   *Capital shares in the corporate sector.* See annual data developed for Table 1.20.

1V   *Before and after-tax return to capital.* See annual data developed for Table 1.20.

1W   *Trends in hours worked, weekly and annual.* Authors' analysis of CPS ASEC data. See Appendix A.

Chapter 2

2A   *Real median income growth by cohort.* Authors' analysis of Census homepage, Historical Income Tables, Families, Table F-11.

2B   *Intergenerational income persistence, sons and daughters.* Lee and Solon, 2006, Table 1 and 2.

2C   *Likelihood that low-income son ends up above various percentiles.* Unpublished
        data provided by Gary Solon.

2D   *Intergenerational mobility.* See Aaronson and Mazumder (2005), Table 1.

2E   *Income mobility, children by race.* See Hertz (2006).

2F   *Percent of children in bottom fifth as adults, based on parents' income fifth, by
        race.* Julia Isaacs in Haskins et al. (2008), Chapter 6.

2G   *Mobility in the United States vs. European Union.* Authors' analysis.

2H   *Intergenerational correlations, fathers and sons, U.S., U.K., Europe, and
        Scandanavia.* See Corak (2006), Table 1.

2I   *Mobility for sons of low-income fathers.* See Jantti et al. (2006), Table 12.

2J   *Mobility for daughters of low-income fathers.* See Jantti et al. (2006), Table 12.

2K   *Education correlations: parents and children.* See Hertz et al. (2008).

2L   *Intergenerational mobility: role of education.* See Blandon (2004).

2M   *Income position of the entering class at top colleges and community colleges.*
        See Carnevale and Rose (2003).

2N   *College completion by income status and test scores.* Fox, Connelly, and
        Snyder (2005).

2O   *Intergenerational mobility, by college education.* See Haskins et al. (2008),
        Chapter 8.

2P   Cumulative growth in family income volatility since 1973. See Hacker and
        Jacobs (2008), Figure 1.

2Q   Prevalence of a 50% or greater drop in family income. See Hacker and
        Jacobs (2008).

Chapter 3

3A   *Productivity and median wage by education.* Productivity measured as
        output per hour in the non-farm business sector. Wage measures are median
        hourly wages from Table 3.20 converted to compensation by scaling by the
        compensation/wage ratio in the data from Table 3.3.

3B   *Hourly wage and compensation growth for production/non-supervisory
        workers.* See note to Table 3.4. Hourly compensation was estimated based

on multiplying hourly wages by the ratio of compensation to wages for all workers in each year. The compensation/wage ratio is drawn from the NIPA data used in Table 3.3. The compensation/wage ratio for 2007 was set equal to 2006's level plus the percentage point change between 2006 and 2007 in the comparable ratio in the ECEC (Table 3.11).

3C   *Changes in real hourly wages for men by wage percentile.* See note to Table 3.6.

3D   *Changes in real hourly wages for women by wage percentile.* See note to Table 3.7.

3E   *Share of workers earning poverty-level wages, by gender.* See note to Table 3.8.

3F   *Share of workers earning poverty-level wages, by race/ethnicity.* See notes to Tables 3.8 and 3.9.

3G   *Top 1% share of total wages and salaries.* See note to Table 3.10.

3H   *Annual wage growth, by wage group.* See note to Table 3.10.

3I   *Private-sector employer-provided health insurance coverage.* See note to Table 3.12.

3J   *Share of pension participants in defined-contribution and defined-benefit plans.* From frequently requested data at the Center for Retirement Research at Boston College, "Private Workers with Pension Coverage, By Pension Type, 1980, 1992, and 2004," using data from the Current Population Survey and the Department of Labor's Annual Return/Report Form 5500 Series <http://crr. bc.edu/images/stories/Frequently_Requested_Data/cps_pension_coverage. xls>.

3K   *Men's wage inequality.* Based on ratios of wages by decile in annual data presented in Table 3.6.

3L   *Women's wage inequality.* Based on ratios of wages by decile in annual data presented in Table 3.7.

3M   *95/50 percentile wage inequality.* Based on ratios of wages by percentile presented in Tables 3.6 and 3.7.

3N   *College/high school wage premium.* Differentials estimated with controls for experience (as a quartic), region (4), marital status, race/ethnicity, and education, which are specified as dummy variables for less than high school, some college, college, and advanced degree. Estimates were made on the CPS ORG data as described in Appendix B, and presented in Table 3.14.

3O   *Productivity and hourly compensation growth.* Average hourly productivity and compensation are for the non-farm business sector and available from the

BLS Web site (see major sector productivity and cost index). The compensation series is deflated by the CPI-U-RS. The median compensation of female, male, and all workers is derived by multiplying the compensation/wage ratio (based on the NIPA data discussed in the note to Table 3.3 and Figure 3B) by the real median wage series for each in Tables 3.5, 3.6, and 3.7.

3P   *Entry-level wages of male and female high school graduates.* See note to Table 3.19.

3Q   *Entry-level wages of male and female college graduates.* See note to Table 3.19.

3R   *Health and pension coverage for recent high school graduates.* Computed from the same data as used in Tables 3.12 and 3.13.

3S   *Health and pension coverage for recent college graduates.* Computed from CPS March Survey data as used in Tables 3.12 and 3.13.

3T   *Log wage gap profile by cohort.* See Shierholz (2009).

3U   *Unemployment.* Data are from the U.S. Department of Labor, BLS (2008c).

3V   *Imports, exports, and trade balance as a share of GDP.* See Bivens (2008).

3W   *Manufacturing imports as a share of U.S. GDP.* See Bivens (2008).

3X   *Relative productivity of U.S. trading partners.* See Bivens (2008).

3Y   *Wage premium of offshorable jobs.* See note to Table 3.29.

3Z   *Union coverage rate in the United States.* Data are from Hirsch and Macpherson (2003), accessible through unionstats.com <http://unionstats.gsu.edu/UnionStats.pdf>. and BLS data on union representation. The data on union coverage begin in 1977 and are extended back to 1973, based on percentage point changes in union membership shares in Hirsh and Macpherson (2003).

3AA   *Real value of the minimum wage.* Series compiled from series in Table 3.38 (see note) and deflated using CPI-U-RS.

3AB   *Minimum wage as percentage of average hourly earnings.* Calculated from values of minimum wage (See note to Table 3.38) and average hourly earnings (Table 3.5).

3AC   *Value of federal minimum wage compared to share of workforce covered by higher state minimums.* Calculation provided by Liana Fox. See Fox (2007), "What a new federal minimum wage means for the states." <http://www.epi.org/content.cfm/ib234>.

3AD   *Relative demand for college graduates.* Authors' analysis of Goldin and Katz (2008), Table 1.

3AE   *Ratio of average and median CEO total direct compensation to average worker pay.* Calculated by dividing the CEO average annual pay (see note to Table 3.41) by production non-supervisory workers' average annual pay (hourly average earnings multiplied by 2,080 multiplied by the compensation/ wage ratio discussed in note to Table 3.2). The production non-supervisory workers' average hourly pay is available online from the BLS (2008b). CEO pay for the pre-1995 period based on the Pearl Meyers/*Wall Street Journal* survey scaled to the level of the Mercer CEO pay in 1995 (meaning the data rely on the levels of Mercer in 1995 and the growth between earlier years and 1995 as shown in the Pearl Meyer data).

3AF   *Education requirements of current and future jobs.* See note to Table 3.43.

Chapter 4

4A   *Labor force and total nonfarm employment.* Considers total employment through August 2008. Labor force data are from U.S. Department of Labor, BLS (2008c) and nonfarm employment is from BLS (2008b).

4B   *Number of months to regain peak-level employment after a recession, current and prior business cycles.* Data are from U.S. Department of Labor, BLS (2006b).

4C   *Annualized peak-to-peak growth in employment.* Data are from U.S. Department of Labor, BLS (2008b) data.

4D   *Gross jobs gains and losses.* Seasonally adjusted data from 1990q2 to 1992q2 are from Faberman (2004). Data from 1992q2 to 2007q4 are from U.S. Department of Labor, BLS (2008a), Business Employment Dynamics, Table 1, Private sector gross job gains and job losses, seasonally adjusted <http://www. bls.gov/news.release/cewbd.t01.htm>, based on quarterly state unemployment insurance records submitted by 6.9 million private sector employers.

4E   *Peak-to-peak annual growth rates by industry.* Data are from U.S. Department of Labor, BLS (2008b), Table B-1.

4F   *Good jobs as percent of total employment.* From Schmitt (2007), Table 1, *Job, quality over the business cycle,* 1979-2006 <http://www.cepr.net/documents/ publications/goodjobscycles.pdf>. Good jobs are defined as those that pay at least $17 per hour, have employer-provided health insurance where the employer pays at least some of the premium, and an employer-sponsored pension plan, including 401(k) and similar defined-contribution plans. GDP per capita is from the Bureau of Economic Analysis (2008), Table 7.1. "Selected Per Capita Product and Income Series in Current and Chained Dollars."

4G *Unemployment rate and its trend.* Unemployment data and trend are from U.S. Department of Labor, BLS (2008c). The trend is calculated by authors using kernel-weighted local polynomial smoothing.

4H *Actual and simulated unemployment rate.* Data from BLS (2008c), taken from January 1980 to August 2008. Simulated unemployment rate is what the unemployment rate would be if the distribution of the labor force across age categories had not changed from the first quarter of 1980, but if the unemployment rates within each age category changed as they actually did.

4I *Unemployment rates of foreign-born and native-born workers.* Authors' calculations of BLS (2008c) microdata, CPS ORG (see Appendix B).

4J *Long-term unemployment as a share of total unemployment, and the unemployment rate.* Data are from BLS (2008c), through the 2nd quarter of 2008.

4K *Unemployment rate and the 2000s recovery period.* "Prior to 2000s recovery" is the period from January 1948 to November 2001. "2000s recovery" is defined as the period from December 2001 to December 2007.

4L *Labor force participation rates.* Data are from BLS (2008c) through the first quarter of 2008.

4M *Annual labor force participation rate of college graduates.* Authors' calculation of BLS (2008c) micro data, CPS ORG (see Appendix B).

4N *Actual and simulated unemployment rates.* Author's analysis of BLS (2008c) data through the 2nd quarter of 2008, for people 25 to 54.

4O *Employment rates.* Data are from BLS (2008c), employment to population ratio for people 25 to 54, through the 2nd quarter of 2008.

4P *Peak-to-peak change in employment rate.* Data are from BLS (2008c) for people 25 to 54.

4Q *Peak-to-peak change in employment rates by race and ethnicity.* Authors' analysis of BLS (2008c) data.

4R *Annual employment rates of workers 55 years and older.* Data are from BLS (2008c) for people 55 years and older.

4S *Access to job-based retirement plan by work arrangement.* See note to Table 4.7.

4T   *Part-time status, as a share of total employment.* Authors' analysis of BLS (2008c), Table A-5. Employed persons by class of worker and part-time status, through August 2008. Considers share of workers (16+) working 1 to 34 hours during the reference week as a share of total employment. *Involuntary part-time* refers to those who want and are available for full-time work, but who work part-time for economic reasons, including slack work or unfavorable business conditions, inability to find full-time work, and/or seasonal declines in demand. *Voluntary part-time* refers to those who work part-time for non-economic reasons include medical reasons, personal obligations, retirement or Social Security limits on earnings, along with those who gave an economic reason for working part-time but did not want to work full-time and/or were unavailable to do so during the reference week. In 1994, new methodology was implemented that was stricter in determining whether a worker was involuntarily part-time, making the data before and after 1994 not directly comparable.

4U   *Employment in temporary help industry as share of non-farm employment.* From BLS (2008b) Current Employment Statistics, through August 2008. See Table B-1 series Historical data, "Employees on nonfarm payrolls by industry sector and selected industry detail," <http://www.bls.gov/ces/cesbtabs.htm>.

4V   *Labor force status post-displacement.* Authors' analysis of Farber (2005), supple-mented by unpublished updates provided to EPI by the author.

4W   *Average decline in weekly earnings for displaced full-time workers who find new full-time work.* See note to Figure 4V.

Chapter 5

5A   *Growth of household net worth.* Net worth and asset data are from the Federal Reserve Board (2008a), Table B.100, Balance Sheet of Households and Nonprofit Organizations. Data were converted to real dollars using the CPI-U-RS and divided by the number of U.S. households based on Bureau of the Census, Table HH-1 Households by type < http://www.census.gov/population/socdemo/hh-fam/hh1.xls>, updated through 2006. The total number of households in 2007 was estimated using growth rate of Total Occupied Units from 2006 to 2007, from the Bureau of the Census (2008a). Note: In 2007, 76% of tangible assets were in household real estate.

5B   *Distribution of wealth by wealth class.* Data are derived from Table 5.1. All data for 1986 are linear interpolations between 1983 and 1989.

5C   *Ratio of the wealthiest 1% to median wealth in the United States.* Data derived from Table 5.3.

5D   *Annual net worth of "Forbes 400" wealthiest individuals.* Data for 1982 to
        1999 adapted from Broom and Shay (2000) Table 2. "Forbes 400" Individual
        Fortunes. Data for 2000-07 are from Forbes (2008) annual lists of the richest
        Americans.

5E   *Growth of U.S. stock market.* Standard and Poor's Composite Index from
        Economic Report of the President (2008), Table B-95, "Historical stock prices
        and yields" for 1955 to 2003, and B-96, "Common stock prices and yields" for
        2004 to 2007, deflated by the CPI-U-RS in 2007 dollars and indexed to 1960.

5F   *Distribution of stock market wealth by wealth class.* Data derived from Table
        5.8.

5G   *Distribution of growth in stock market holdings by wealth class.* Data derived
        from Table 5.8.

5H   *Home ownership rates.* Yearly average of data published by the U.S. Census
        Bureau (2008b), Series H-111, Historical Tables, Table 14: "Homeownership
        Rates for the U.S. and Regions: 1965 to Present" accessible at: <http://www.
        census.gov/hhes/www/housing/hvs/historic/histt14.html>.

5I   *Home ownership rates by income.* See note to Table 5.10.

5J   *Home ownership rates by race.* See note to Table 5.10. Data between 1979 and
        1982 are unavailable, and substituted using linear interpolations.

5K   *Debt as a percentage of disposable personal income.* For "all debt and
        mortgage debt," see note to Table 5.12. For "consumer credit and home equity
        loans," see note to Table 5.13.

5L   *Distribution of growth in debt.* Calculated from Table 5.8.

5M   *Consumer bankruptcies per 1,000 adults.* Authors' analysis of the American
        Bankruptcy Institute (2008) data on annual non-business filing, from U.S.
        Bankruptcy Filings table. Data on the adult population, used to calculate
        bankruptcies per 1,000 adults, are from the Economic Report of the President
        (2008). The Financial obligations ratio (FOR) is from the Federal Reserve
        Board (2008b).

5N   *Home prices and home ownership rates.* Home prices are taken from S&P/
        Case-Shiller (2008) U.S. National Home Price Index, updated to the 2nd quarter
        of 2008. Note that the index is calculated monthly using a three-month moving
        average and published with a two-month lag. Data for homeownership is
        based on a five-quarter moving average of quarterly data published by the U.S.
        Census Bureau, Housing Vacancy Survey (2008b), Table 14: "Homeownership
        Rates for the U.S. and Regions: 1965 to Present."

5O   *Homeowners' equity as a percent of home value.* Data are taken from Federal
      Reserve Board (2008a), B.100 Balance Sheet of Households and Nonprofit
      Organizations accessible online (http://www.federalreserve.gov/datadownload/
      default.htm) and updated to the 2nd quarter of 2008.

5P   *Volume of prime and subprime mortgage originations.* Data are used with
      permission from the Joint Center for Political and Economic Studies. Based
      on Leigh and Huff (2007), Figure 1, attributed to Joint Center for Housing
      Studies, State of the Nation's Housing 2007. <http://www.jchs.harvard.edu/
      publications/markets/son2007/son2007.pdf >

5Q   *Subprime share of loans for home purchase by race.* Data are used with
      permission from the Joint Center for Political and Economic Studies. Based on
      Leigh and Huff (2007), Figure 4, with original tabulations of the 2006 Home
      Mortgage Disclosure Act's Loan Application Register (LAR) data, by staff of
      the Joint Center's DataBank.

5R   *Foreclosures per owner-occupied households.* Figure represents the number
      of foreclosure filings as a proportion of owner-occupied units. Number of
      foreclosure filings is taken from RealtyTrac (2008) current and previous issues
      updated to August 2008, and refers to total number of homes in some stage
      of foreclosure nationwide. RealtyTrac's report includes properties in all three
      phases of foreclosure: Pre-foreclosures; Foreclosures; and Real Estate Owned,
      or REO properties (that have been repurchased by a bank). Number of owner-
      occupied units is taken from the U.S. Department of Commerce, Bureau of the
      Census (2008b) quarterly data, Series H-111, Table 8. "Quarterly Estimates of
      Total Housing Inventory for the United States: 1965 – Present."

Chapter 6

6A   *Poverty and twice-poverty rate.* See U.S. Census Bureau, Historical Poverty
      Income Tables, Persons, Table 5.

6B   *Change in poverty and productivity.* U.S. Census Bureau, Historical Poverty
      Income Tables, Persons, Table 2, and BLS nonfarm business productivity.

6C   *Poverty rates by race/ethnicity.* See note to Table 6.2.

6D   *Family poverty gap and family poverty rates.* For poverty gap, see note to
      Table 6.5. For family poverty rates, see note to Table 6.4.

6E   *Percent of the poor below half the poverty line.* U.S. Census Bureau, Historical
      Poverty Income Tables, Persons, Table 5.

6F   *Poverty, native and foreign born.* See note to Table 6.6.

6G   *Poverty rates, official compared to NAS alternatives.* Alternative rates published by Census Bureau online (http://www.census.gov/hhes/www/povmeas/tables. html). See "Official and NAS based poverty rates."

6H   *Official versus alternative poverty rates.* See Garner and Short (2008).

6I   *Official and relative poverty.* Authors' analysis, see Appendix A.

6J   *Real low-wage growth, productivity, and unemployment: Three five-year periods.* Productivity and unemployment from BLS, low-wage growth from CPS-ORG series, described in Appendix B.

6K   *Poverty rate, actual and simulated.* Authors' adaptation of analysis by Sheldon Danziger (unpublished). Danziger's method was to regress the poverty rate of the growth of real per capita income, from BEA (2008) NIPA Table 2.1, and then predict poverty rates based on that simple model. We also add the share of mother-only families to the model.

6L   *The impact of family structure changes on poverty rates.* See note to Table 6.10.

6M   *Poverty determinants.* See note to Table 6.10.

6N   *Annual hours worked, low-income women with children.* Authors' analysis of ASEC data, see Appendix A.

6O   *Low-income growth, single-mother families with children.* See CBO (2007). Low-income refers to bottom fifth of the income scale; data are from Figure 6.

6P   *Diminished effect of safety net: Share of children lifted above deep poverty.* From a memo drafted for the Center for Budget and Policy Priorities June 3, 2008, by authors Sherman, Trisi, and Parrott. Used with authors' permission.

6Q   *Percent change in wage given 1 point decline in unemployment.* Authors' analysis of CPS ORG data. Phillips curve model regresses nominal wage changes on the gender-specific unemployment rate and CPI-RS inflation with one lag (with inflation coefficient constrained to equal one). We include a dummy for post-1995 intercept shift, as in Katz and Krueger (1999). Models for low-wage women include nominal minimum wage when it is significant.

6R   *Real hourly wages of low-wage workers.* Wages are based on analysis of CPS wage data as described in Appendix B. The poverty-level wage is the hourly wage that, at full-time, full-year work, would lift a family of four above the poverty line. This equals $10.20 in 2007 dollars.

Chapter 7

7A   *Employment-based health insurance and Medicaid/SCHIP for children under 18 in the United States.* Taken from Gould (2007b), Figure A, "Employment-based health insurance and Medicaid/SCHIP, 2000-06, children under 18, United States," based on an analysis of the March Current Population Survey, updated 2001-07.

7B   *Status of enrollees of the State Children's Health Insurance Program (SCHIP).* Taken from Somers et al. (2007), Exhibit 2, "Main Reason Coverage Ended Among Recent Enrollees with Private Coverage Prior to Enrollment in The State Children's Health Insurance Program (SCHIP), 2002."

7C   *Duration without coverage, between 2001 and 2003.* Data are from the Survey of Income and Program Participation, based on responses from a nationally representative sample of U.S. households, interviewed once every four months during the life of the panel.

7D   *Source of health insurance.* Nonstandard work refers to any work arrangement other than employment in a full-time, full-year wage and salary job. This includes part-time workers, self-employed independent contractors, direct-hire temporaries, on call workers and day laborers, temporary help agency workers, wage and salary independent contractors, and contract company workers. Data are from Ditsler and Fisher (2006), as an update to Fisher et al. (2006), based on an analysis of the 2005 Contingent Work Supplement of the February 2005 CPS.

7E   *Access to health insurance via own employer.* See note to Figure 7D.

7F   *Absolute difference in life expectancy between top and bottom decile socioeconomic deprivation groups.* See note to Table 7.2.

7G   *Life expectancy for male Social Security-covered workers (age 60) by earnings group.* Adapted from Waldron (2007), Table 4, "Remaining years of life expectancy for male Social Security–covered workers, by earnings group, age, and year of birth."

7H   *Racial disparities in infant mortality.* Infant mortality refers to children in the United States under 1 year of age. Both race groups include people of Hispanic and non-Hispanic origin. From DHHS (2005, 2007), based on data from Center for Disease Control and Prevention, National Center for Health Statistics (National Vital Statistics System of the Linked Birth/Infant Death Data Set).

7I   *Racial differences in health care insecurity.* From American Worker Survey, conducted in February of 2007 by the Rockefeller Foundation.

7J   *Growth rate index of health premiums, workers' earnings and overall inflation.* Taken from Kaiser Family Foundation / Health Research and Educational Trust (HRET) Annual Survey of Employer-Sponsored Health Benefits (2007) for selected years. Data on premium increases reflect the cost of health insurance premiums for a family of four, the average of which is weighted by covered workers.

7K   *Employer contributions to health insurance and wages as a share of total compensation.* Authors' analysis U.S. Department of Commerce, BEA (2008) National Income and Product Accounts (NIPA), Table 2.1, Personal Income and Its Disposition, and Table 6.11B, Employer Contributions for Employee Pension and Insurance Funds by Industry and by Type.

7L   *Public and private expenditures on health care spending.* OECD health expenditure data are accessible through OECD.stat, and taken as a share of GDP. Data for Netherlands are from 2002 (most recent available). Data for Australia and Japan are based on data from 2004.

7M   *Life expectancy at birth and health spending per capita.* Data for Australia, the U.S., Canada, Japan, and the Netherlands are from 2004, where data are unavailable for one or both variables in 2005. Data for Poland, Hungary and Belgium are OECD estimates. Country codes are as follows: AUS = Australia, AUT = Austria, BEL = Belgium, CAN = Canada, CZE = Czech Republic, DNK = Denmark, FIN = Finland, FRA = France, DEU = Germany, GRC = Greece, HUN = Hungary, ISL = Iceland, IRL = Ireland, ITA = Italy, JPN = Japan, KOR = Republic of Korea, LUX = Luxembourg, MEX = Mexico, NLD = Netherlands, NZL = New Zealand, NOR = Norway, POL = Poland, PRT = Portugal, SVK = Slovakia (Slovak Republic), ESP = Spain, SWE = Sweden, CHE = Switzerland, TUR = Turkey, UK = United Kingdom, and USA = United States.

7N   *Infant mortality, per 1,000 live births.* Data from OECD (2007g), accessible through OECD.stat. Variation between countries may be due to variations among countries in registering practices of premature infants (whether they are reported as live births or not).

7O   *Percent of adults going without needed health care due to costs.* The study measures the percent of adults reporting any of the following access problems due to cost: 1) had a medical problem but did not visit a doctor; 2) skipped a medical test, treatment, or follow-up recommended by a doctor; or 3) did not fill a prescription. Data are based on the 2004 Commonwealth Fund International Health Policy Survey.

Chapter 8

8A   *Annual growth rates of per capita income.* See table note for 8.1.

8B   *Productivity growth rates in G-7 countries.* See table note for Table 8.2.

8C   *Collective bargaining coverage.* See OECD (2004), Table 3.3, "Trade union density and collective bargaining coverage in the OECD countries, 1970-2000." Data are unavailable for Greece and Ireland. Correlations were made using productivity data cited in Table 8.2, and earnings data based on OECD annual supplement to the Labor Force Survey of Households <http://www.oecd.org/dataoecd/9/59/39606921.xls>, accessed through the Directorate for Employment, Labour and Social Affairs. 90-10 ratios are limited to countries with gross weekly, monthly, or annual earnings data available for full-time workers, for which the Current Population Survey is used for the United States. Note: In 2007, collective bargaining coverage in the United States was 13.3%, for all industries, both public and private sectors, according to an analysis of the Current Population Survey. See figure note to Figure 7M for country abbreviations.

8D   *Relative household income dispersion.* Estimates of earnings used in the calculations refer to gross earnings of full-time wage and salary workers. See OECD (2007c), page 268, Table H based on OECD database on Earnings Distribution.

8E   *Household income dispersion relative to the U.S. median.* Estimates of earnings used in the calculations refer to gross earnings of full-time wage and salary workers. Data on median earnings for each country is from the OECD, Directorate for Employment, Labour and Social Affairs (see figure notes to Figure 8C) and converted to U.S. dollars using purchasing power parities for GDP. Data for Denmark, New Zealand, Greece, Italy, Norway, Switzerland, and Spain is nonexistent or unavailable past 2002 for weekly, monthly, or annual gross earnings. Data for Finland, France, Ireland, Sweden, and Switzerland correspond to median earnings in 2004 compared to median earnings in the U.S. of the same year.

8F   *Top 0.1% income share in selected countries.* Country selection is based on available data. Income is defined as annual gross income reported on individual tax returns excluding capital gains and all government transfers, and before individual income taxes and employee's payroll taxes. Data for the U.S. is from Smeeding and Piketty (2006), updated in Atkinson and Piketty (2007); data for France, the UK, and Canada are from Smeeding and Piketty (2006), Figures 3A and 3B; data for Spain are from Smeeding and Alvaredo (2007), Table B6; data for Japan are from Smeeding and Moriguchi (2007), Table A1.

8G   *Child poverty rates before and after taxes and transfers.* See Corak (2005), Figure 7: "Child low income rates in the OECD based on market sources and disposable income: late 1990s and early 2000s." Data for the following countries in this study are attributed to Mira d'Ercole and Förster (2005): Denmark, Switzerland, France, Greece, Ireland, and New Zealand. Data for remaining countries in this study are attributed to the Luxembourg Income Study. Data for Austria, Belgium, and Denmark are for 1997, and data for the Netherlands and the UK are from 1999.

8H   *Social expenditure versus child poverty.* See OECD Social Expenditure Database 1980-2001 <www.oecd.org/els/social/expenditure>: Chart EQ5.1: "Public social expenditure by broad social policy area, in percentage of GDP, in 2001." For Child Poverty, see Table 8.16.

Bibliography

Aaronson, D and Mazumder, B. 2005. "Intergenerational Economic Mobility in the U.S., 1940 to 2000." Working Paper 2005-12, Federal Reserve Bank of Chicago.

Acs, Gregory and Seth Zimmerman 2008. *Like Watching Grass Grow? Assessing Changes in the U.S. Intragenerational Economic Mobility over the Past Two Decades.* Washington, D.C.: Economic Mobility Project, an initiative of The Pew Charitable Trusts.

American Bankruptcy Institute (ABI). 2008. *Annual U.S. Filings.* <http://www.abi-world.org/Content/NavigationMenu/NewsRoom/BankruptcyStatistics/Bankruptcy_Filings_1.htm >

Attanasio, Orazio, Erich Battistin and Hidehiko Ichimura. 2006. "What Really Happened to Consumption Inequality in the US?" National Bureau of Economic Research, Working Paper No. 10338. Cambridge, Mass.: NBER. <www.nber.org/papers/w10338>

Banthin and Bernard. 2006. "Changes in Financial Burdens for Health Care: National Estimates for the Population Younger Than 65 Years, 1996 to 2003". *Journal of the American Medical Association* (reprinted), Vol. 296, No.22.

Bartik, Timothy J. 2001. *Jobs for the Poor: Can Labor Demand Policies Help?* New York: New Press.

Bernstein, Jared, James Lin, and Lawrence Mishel. 2007. "The Characteristics of Off-shorable Jobs." Economic Policy Institute Viewpoints. <http://www.epi.org/content.cfm/webfeatures_viewpoints_characteristics_of_offshorable_jobs>

Bivens, Josh. 2008. *Everybody Wins, Except for Most of Us: What Economics Teaches About Globalization.* Washington, D.C.: Economic Policy Institute.

Blanden, Jo. 2004. "International Evidence on Education and Intergenerational Mobility" CEE Conference Paper. Centre for the Economics of Education, LSE. <http://cee.lse.ac.uk/conference_papers/15_10_2004/jo_blanden.pdf>.

Borjas, George J. and Lawrence F. Katz. 2005. "The Evolution of the Mexican-Born Workforce in the United States." National Bureau of Economic Research, Working Paper No. 11281. Cambridge, Mass.: NBER.

Broom and Shay. 2000. Working Paper No. 308, "Discontinuities in the Distribution of Great Wealth: Sectoral Forces Old and New". Prepared for the Conference on "Saving, Intergenerational Transfers, and the Distribution of Wealth", Jerome Levy Economics Institute, Bard College, June 2000.

Buchmueller, Thomas C., DiNardo, John, Valletta Robert G. 2001. "Union effects on health insurance provision and coverage in the United States." National Bureau of Economic Research, Working Paper No. 8238. Cambridge, Mass.: NBER.

Bucks, Brian K., Arthur B. Kennickell, and Kevin B. Moore. 2006. "Recent changes in U.S. family finances: Evidence from the 2001 and 2004 Survey of Consumer Finances." *Federal Reserve Bulletin.* January. <http://www.federalreserve.gov/pubs/bulletin/2006/financesurvey.pdf>

Card, David, T. Lemieux and W. Craig Riddell. 2002. "Unions and the Wage Structure." September 2002.

Carnevale, Anthony P. and Stephen J. Rose. 2003. "Socioeconomic Status, Race/Ethnicity, and Selective College Admissions." A Century Foundation Paper.

Cauthen, Nancy. 2007. Improving Work Supports: Closing the Financial Gap for Low-wage Workers and Their Families. EPI Briefing Paper, #198. <http://www.sharedprosperity.org/bp198.html >

Central Intelligence Agency (CIA). 2008. *The World Factbook.* < https://www.cia.gov/library/publications/the-world-factbook/fields/2172.html>

Charles, Kerwin K. and Erik Hurst. 2003. "The Correlation of Wealth Across Generations." *The Journal of Political Economy.* Dec., Vol. 111, No. 6, pp. 1155-82. University of Chicago Press.

The Conference Board and Groningen Growth and Development Centre. 2008. Total Economy Database, January 2008.

Cook, Frederic. 2006. "Research on CEO Compensation for Business Roundtable". Frederic W. Cook & Co., Inc./ Mercer Human Resource Consulting.

Congressional Budget Office (CBO). "Changes in the Economic Resources of Low-Income Households with Children." Publication No. 2602, May 2007. <http://www.cbo.gov/ftpdocs/81xx/doc8113/05-16-Low-Income.pdf>

Congressional Budget Office (CBO). 2008. "Sources of the Growth and Decline in Individual Income Tax Revenues Since 1994." May 2008.

Corak, Miles. 2005. "Principles and practicalities for measuring child poverty in rich countries." LIS working paper no.406. Luxembourg: Luxembourg Income Study.

Corak, Miles. 2006. "Do Poor Children Become Poor Adults?" Lessons from a Cross Country Comparison of Generational Earnings Mobility." Discussion Paper No. 1993. Bonn, Germany: Institute for the Study of Labor.

Danziger, Sheldon and Peter Gottschalk. 1996. America Unequal. Harvard University Press, Cambridge.

Ditsler, Elaine and Peter Fisher. 2006. *Nonstandard Jobs, Substandard Benefits, A 2005 Update.* The Iowa Policy Project, September 2006.

Dohm, Arlene and L. Shniper. 2007. "Occupational employment projections to 2016." *Monthly Labor Review.* November 2007, Vol. 130, No. 11. <http://www.bls.gov/opub/mlr/2007/11/art5full.pdf>

Economic Report of the President. 2008. *Annual.* Washington, D.C.: U.S. Government Printing Office.

Faberman, Jason. R. 2004. "Gross Jobs Flows over the Past Two Business Cycles: Not all 'Recoveries' are Created Equal." Bureau of Labor Statistics, Office of Employment and Unemployment Statistics. Working Paper 372. <http://www.bls.gov/ore/pdf/ec040020.pdf>

Farber, Henry S. 2005. "What do we know about job loss in the United States? Evidence from the Displaced Worker Survey, 1984-2004." *Economic Perspectives*, 2nd Quarter. Federal Reserve Bank of Chicago.

Farber, Henry S. 2007. "Is the company man an anachronism? Trends in long term employment in the U.S., 1973-2006". Working Paper #518, Princeton University Industrial Relations Section.

Federal Reserve Board. 2008a. *Flow of Funds Accounts of the United States: Annual Flows and Outstandings 2005-2007 (Z.1)*. Washington, D.C.: Board of Governors of the Federal Reserve System. <http://www.federalreserve.gov/datadownload/Choose.aspx?rel=Z.1 >

Federal Reserve Board. 2008b. "Household Debt Service and Financial Obligations Ratios." < http://www.federalreserve.gov/releases/housedebt/default.htm >

Fisher, Ditsler, Gordon, & West. 2006. *Nonstandard Jobs, Substandard Benefits*. The Iowa Policy Project. < http://www.iowapolicyproject.org/2005docs/051201-nonstd-jobs.pdf>

Forbes. 2008. "The 400 Richest Americans". < http://www.forbes.com/>

Förster and Mira D'Ercole. 2005. "Income distribution and poverty in OECD countries in the second half of the 1990s", OECD Social, Employment and Migration Working Papers. Paris: OECD.

Fox, Liana. 2007. "What a new federal minimum wage means for the states". Economic Policy Institute Issue Brief #234. Updated June 1, 2007. <http://www.epi.org/content.cfm/ib234>

Fox, M.A., B.A. Connolly, and T.D. Snyder. 2005. *Youth Indicators 2005: Trends in the Well-Being of American Youth*. Washington, D.C.: U.S. Department of Education, National Center for Education Statistics. <http://nces.ed.gov/pubs2005/2005050.pdf>

Freeman, Richard. 1991. "How Much Has De-unionization Contributed to the Rise in Male Earnings Inequality?" National Bureau of Economic Research, Working Paper No. 3826. Cambridge, Mass.: NBER.

Garner, Thesia I., and Kathleen S. Short. 2008. "Creating a Consistent Poverty Measure over Time Using NAS Procedures: 1996-2005." Unpublished research paper of the Bureau of Labor Statistics. < http://www.bls.gov/ore/abstract/ec/ec080030.htm>

Gittleman, Maury and Brooks Pierce. 2007. "New estimates of union wage effects in the U.S." *Economics Letters*. Elsevier, Vol. 95, pp. 198–202.

Goldin, Claudia and Lawrence F. Katz. 2008. "The Race between Education and Technology: The Evolution of U.S. Educational Wage Differentials, 1890 to 2005." Harvard University and the National Bureau of Economic Research. March 8, 2007.

Gould, Elise. 2007a. "The Erosion of Employment-Based Insurance: More working families left uninsured." Economic Policy Institute Briefing Paper #203. November 1, 2007.

Gould, Elise. 2007b. "California kids lose employment-based coverage: The impact on the community, business, and the public insurance system." Economic Policy Institute Briefing Paper #199. September 20, 2007.

Gundersen, Bethney. 2003. "Unions and the well-being of low-skill workers." George Warren Brown School of Social Work, Washington University. Ph.D. dissertation.

Hacker, Jacob and Elizabeth Jacobs. 2008. "The Rising Instability of American Family Incomes, 1969-2004: Evidence from the Panel Study of Income Dynamics." Economic Policy Institute Briefing Paper # 213. May 29, 2008.

Haskins, Ron, Julia B. Isaacs and Isabel V. Sawhill. 2008. *Getting Ahead or Losing Ground: Economic Mobility in America.* Washington, D.C.: Brookings Institution Press.

Hertz, Tom. 2006. Understanding Mobility in America. Center for American Progress. Hirsch, Barry T. and David A. Macpherson. 2003. "Union Membership and Coverage Database from the Current Population Survey: Note." *Industrial and Labor Relations Review*, Vol. 56, No. 2, January 2003, pp. 349-54.

Hertz, Tom, et al. 2008. "The Inheritance of Educational Inequality: International Comparisons and Fifty-Year Trends." *Berkeley Electronic Journal of Economic Analysis and Policy*, Vol. 7, No. 2, January 2008.

International Social Security Association. *Social Security Programs Throughout the World: Europe, 2006-2007.* Retrieved October 2007. < http://www.ssa.gov/policy/docs/progdesc/ssptw/2006-2007/europe/index.html>

Jaquette, Scott, Matthew Knittel and Karl Russo. 2003. "Recent Trends in Stock Options". Working Paper No. 89. Office of Tax Analysis. Washington, D.C.: U.S. Department of the Treasury.

Jäntti, Markus, Bernt Bratsberg, Knut Röed, Oddbjörn Raaum, Robin Naylor, Johnson D., Smeeding T. and Boyle Torrey B. 2005. "Economic Inequality through the Prisms of Income and Consumption." *Monthly Labor Review*, April 2005.

Kaiser Family Foundation. 2007. Employer Health Benefits Annual Survey 2007. <http://www.kff.org/insurance/7672/upload/76723.pdf>

Katz, Lawrence F., and Alan B. Krueger. 1999. "The High Pressure U.S. Labor Market of the 1990s." Brookings Papers on Economic Activity, 1999:1, pp. 1-65. Washington, D.C.: Brookings Institute.

Kopczuk, Wojciech, E. Saez and J. Song. 2007. "Uncovering the American Dream: Inequality and Mobility in Social Security Earnings Data since 1937." National Bureau of Economic Research, Working Paper No. 13345. Cambridge, Mass.: NBER.

Krugman, Paul. 1995. "Growing World Trade: Causes and Consequences." *Brookings Papers on Economic Activity*. Vol. 26(1), pp. 327-377.

Lee, Chul-In and Gary Solon. 2006. "Trends in Intergenerational Income Mobility", NBER Working Paper No. 12007, February 2006. Cambridge, Mass.: NBER. <http://www.nber.org/papers/w12007>

Leigh, Wilhelmina A. and Danielle Huff. 2007. "African Americans and Homeownership: The Subprime Lending Experience, 1995 to 2007" (Brief #2), Washington, DC: Joint Center for Political and Economic Studies, November 2007. < http://www.jointcenter. org/publications_recent_publications/economics_business/african_americans_and_ homeownership_the_subprime_lending_experience_1995_to_2007_november_2007_ brief_2 >

Luxembourg Income Study (LIS). 2007. *Key Figures*. Luxembourg: Luxembourg Income Study. <http://www.lisproject.org/keyfigures.htm>

Meara, Ellen R., Seth Richards and David M. Cutler. 2008. "The Gap Gets Bigger: Changes in Mortality and Life Expectancy, By Education, 1981-2000." *Health Affairs*, Vol. 27, No.2.

Mishel, Lawrence and Matthew Walters. 2003. "How unions help all workers." Economic Policy Institute Briefing Paper #143, August 2003. < http://www.epi.org/content. cfm/briefingpapers_bp143>

Moore, Quinn and Heidi Shierholz. 2007. "A Cohort Analysis of the Gender Wage Gap". Unpublished manuscript.

Murphy, Kevin, and Finis Welch. 1989. "Recent trends in real wages: Evidence from household data." Paper prepared for the Health Care Financing Administration of the U.S. Department of Health and Human Services. University of Chicago.

National Council of La Raza. 2008. "Employer-Sponsored Health Insurance: Already Poor Access Further Dwindles for Working Latino Families," Washington D.C.: National Council of La Raza.

Organization for Economic Cooperation and Development (OECD). 2004. *Employment Outlook*. Paris: OECD.

Organization for Economic Cooperation and Development (OECD). 2005. *Society at a Glance.* Paris: OECD.

Organization for Economic Cooperation and Development (OECD). 2007a. *Economic Outlook.* Paris: OECD. No 82: Annual and Quarterly data, Vol. 2007, Release 2.

Organization for Economic Cooperation and Development (OECD). 2007b. *Education at a Glance.* Paris: OECD.

Organization for Economic Cooperation and Development (OECD). 2007c. *OECD Employment Outlook.* Paris: OECD.

Organization for Economic Cooperation and Development (OECD). 2007d. *OECD Factbook 2007: Economic, Environmental and Social Statistics.* Paris: OECD.

Organization for Economic Cooperation and Development (OECD). 2007e."Factors explaining differences in hours worked across OECD countries", Working paper. ECO/CPE/WP1(2007)11.

Organization for Economic Cooperation and Development (OECD). 2007f. "Babies and Bosses - Reconciling Work and Family Life (Vol. 5): A Synthesis of Findings for OECD Countries," in OECD Family Database. <www.oecd.org/els/social/family/database>

Organization for Economic Cooperation and Development (OECD). 2007g. *OECD Health Data 2007, Statistics and Indicators for 30 Countries.* October 2007 edition.

Organization for Economic Cooperation and Development (OECD). 2007h. *Main Economic Indicators.* Paris: OECD.

Organization for Economic Cooperation and Development (OECD). 2008. *OECD Annual National Accounts.* Paris: OECD.

Österbacka, Eva, Anders Björklund and Tor Eriksson. 2006. "American Exceptionalism in a New Light: a Comparison of Intergenerational Earnings Mobility in the Nordic Countries, the United Kingdom and the United States", Discussion Paper No. 2006:1938 Institute for the Study of Labor.

Pierce, Brooks. 1999. "Compensation Inequality." Office of Compensation and Working Conditions, BLS Working Paper No.323. Washington, D.C.: Department of Labor. < http://www.bls.gov/ore/pdf/ec990040.pdf>

Piketty, Thomas and Emmanuel Saez. 2003. "Income Inequality in the United States, 1913-1998" with Thomas Piketty, *Quarterly Journal of Economics*, 118(1), 2003, pp. 1-39. Updated. < http://elsa.berkeley.edu/~saez/ >

Ray, Rebecca and John Schmitt. 2007. "No-vacation nation USA- a comparison of leave and holiday in OECD countries," European Economic and Employment Policy Brief No.3.

RealtyTrac. 2008. *RealtyTrends Newsletter*. < http://www.realtytrac.com/News-Trends/Newsletter/Current.html >

Rockefeller Foundation. 2007. *American Worker Survey.* New York: The Rockefeller Foundation.

S&P /Case-Shiller. 2008. "U.S. National Home Price Index," *S&P/Case-Shiller Home Price Indices*. <http://www2.standardandpoors.com/portal/site/sp/en/us/page.topic/indices_csmahp/0,0,0,0,0,0,0,0,0,1,1,0,0,0,0,0.html >

Schmitt, John. 2007. "The Good, the Bad, and the Ugly: Job Quality in the United States over the Three Most Recent Business Cycles." Center for Economic and Policy Research, November 2007.

Schmitt, John. 2008. "The Union Wage Advantage for Low-Wage Workers." Center for Economic Policy and Research, May 2008.

Schoen, Cathy, and Robin Osborn. 2004. "Primary care and health system performance: Adults' experiences in five countries," *Health Affairs* Web Exclusive, October 28, 2004. Accessible via The Commonwealth Fund. <http://www.cmwf.org/publications/publications_show.htm?doc_id=245178>

Shapiro, Isaac. 1987. "No Escape: The Minimum Wage and Poverty". Washington, D.C.: Center on Budget and Policy Priorities.

Singh, Gopal K. and Mohammad Siahpush. 2006. "Widening socioeconomic inequalities in US life expectancy, 1980-2000." *International Journal of Epidemiology*.

Smeeding, Timothy and Thomas Piketty. 2003. "Income Inequality in the United States, 1913-1998", *Quarterly Journal of Economics*, 118(1), pp. 1-39.

Smeeding, Timothy and Thomas Piketty. 2006. "The Evolution of Top Incomes: A Historical and International Perspective" in *American Economic Review*, Papers and Proceedings, 96(2), pp. 200-205.

Smeeding, Timothy and Chiaki Moriguchi. 2007. "The Evolution of Income Concentration in Japan, 1886-2005: Evidence from Income Tax Statistics", *Review of Economics and Statistics*. Revised June 2007.

Smeeding, Timothy and Facundo Alvaredo. 2007. "Income and Wealth Concentration in Spain in a Historical and Fiscal Perspective". Revised December 2007.

Sommers, Anna, Stephen Zuckerman, Lisa Dubay and Genevieve Kenney. 2007. "Substitution of SCHIP for private coverage: Results from a 2002 evaluation in ten states." *Health Affairs*, Vol. 26, No. 2, pp. 529-537.

Towers Perrin. Annual. "Worldwide Total Remuneration". Annual Reports for 1988, 2003 and 2005. <www.towersperrin.com >

United Nations. 2005a. The World's Women 2005: Progress in Statistics. <http://unstats.un.org/unsd/demographic/products/indwm/wwpub.htm>

United Nations Statistics Division. 2005b. Statistics and Indicators on Women and Men. <http://unstats.un.org/unsd/demographic/products/indwm/ww2005/tab5c.htm>

U.S. Department of Commerce, Bureau of Economic Analysis. 2008. *National Income and Product Accounts.* <http://www.bea.gov/national/nipaweb/Index.asp>

U.S. Department of Commerce, Bureau of the Census. 2001. *Survey of Income and Program Participation* (SIPP). < http://www.census.gov/sipp/>

U.S. Department of Commerce, Bureau of the Census. 2005. *American Housing Survey.*

U.S. Department of Commerce, Bureau of the Census. 2008a. *Housing Vacancy Survey*, Annual Statistics: 2007. <http://www.census.gov/hhes/www/housing/hvs/annual07/ann07ind.html>

U.S. Department of Commerce, Bureau of the Census. 2008b. *Housing Vacancy Survey*, Historical tables.< http://www.census.gov/hhes/www/housing/hvs/historic/index.html>

U.S. Department of Health and Human Services (DHHS), National Center for Health Statistics. 2005. *Health, United States, 2005.* Washington, D.C.: DHHS.

U.S. Department of Health and Human Services (DHHS), National Center for Health Statistics. 2007. *Health, United States, 2007.* Washington, D.C.: DHHS.

U.S. Department of Labor, BLS Foreign Labor Statistics. 2008. January.

U.S. Department of Labor, Bureau of Labor Statistics. 2008a. *Business Employment Dynamics*. < http://www.bls.gov/news.release/cewbd.toc.htm >

U.S. Department of Labor, Bureau of Labor Statistics. 2008b. Current Employment Statistics. < http://www.bls.gov/ces/home.htm >

U.S. Department of Labor, Bureau of Labor Statistics. 2008c. Current Population Survey (CPS). < http://www.bls.gov/cps/home.htm>
U.S. Department of Labor, Bureau of Labor Statistics. 2008d. Employer Cost for Employee Compensation Historical Listing. Washington, D.C.: Bureau of Labor Statistics.

Waldron, Hilary. 2007. "Trends in Mortality Differentials and Life Expectancy for Male Social Security-Covered Workers, by Socioeconomic Status." *Social Security Bulletin*, Vol. 678, No. 3.

Wolff, Edward. 2006. Unpublished analysis of the Survey of Consumer Finances data prepared in 2006 for the Economic Policy Institute.

Index

Jobs, generally. See Employment
Job stability, 256–60
Job tenure, 256–58
  long-term jobs, 258

Krugman, Paul, 192

Labor force. *See also* Employment
  age category, share by, 235–36
  growth, 1979-2008, 228
  participation rate, 19, 245–48
Labor income shares, 83–89, 95, 162
Less-educated workers
  high school education or less (*See*
    High school education or less,
    workers with)
  problems with designation, 164, 169
Life expectancy
  inequalities, 344–46
  infant mortality (*See* Infant mortality)
  international comparisons, 352
  men, 345
  per capita health care spending and, 352
  socioeconomic deprivation group, by,
    344–45
  women, 345
Low-wage labor market
  blacks, wages for, 122, 139–44
  demographic characteristics of
    workforce, 329–33
  full employment, impact of, 333
  gender disparities, 139–44
  Hispanics, wages for, 122, 139–44
  industries, 329–31
  industry shifts to, 183–86
  men's wages, 122, 139–44
  occupations, 329–31
  poverty, role in, 329–33
  racial/ethnic disparities, 139–44
  real hourly wages, 333
  shares of workers, 329–33
  unionization rate, 331
  whites, wages for, 122, 139–44
  women's wages, 122, 139–44

Manufacturing
  employment declines, 232
  trade, impact of, 186–92
  wages – international comparisons,
    378–79
Marginally attached workers, 244
Married-couple families
  hours of work, 91–94
  median income, 56–57
  minimum wage, impact of, 211–13
  poverty rate, 305–6
  retirement wealth, 282–83
Maternity leave
  Family and Medical Leave Act, 369
  international comparisons, 369
Median family income
  age of householder, by, 54–56
  blacks, 35, 50–53
  failure to grow in 2000s business cycle,
    44–50
  family type, by, 56–57
  growth, 1947-2007, 44–47
  Hispanics, 35, 50–52
  married-couple families, 56–57
  prior peak, years to regain, 44–50
  productivity and, 58–60
  racial/ethnic disparities, 50–53
  single-mother families, 56–57
  whites, 50–52
Medicaid, 339
Men
  educational attainment, 168–69
  employment rate – generally, 249–51
  employment rate – international
    comparisons, 369–72
  health insurance coverage, 148
  income class mobility; sons and parents,
    104–5
  job tenure, 256–58
  labor force participation rate, 246
  life expectancy, 345
  low-wage labor market shares, 329–33
  minimum wage, affected by, 211–13
  nonstandard work, 252
  pension coverage, 150–51

The Agenda for Shared Prosperity

The American people want and need an economic agenda that will spur growth, reduce insecurity, and provide broadly shared prosperity. The Economic Policy Institute's Agenda for Shared Prosperity initiative was born out of a belief that poor economic outcomesfor average Americans are not inevitable, and that a change in policy direction is needed to ensure that everyone can benefit from a growing economy. Collaborating with some of the nation's top progressive thinkers, EPI researchers have been exploring and refining solutions for the better part of two years. EPI has compiled the best of these proposals into a small, easy-to-read Policy Handbook called *A Plan to Revive the American Economy*.

A copy of the Plan can be downloaded at ***www.SharedProsperity.org***.

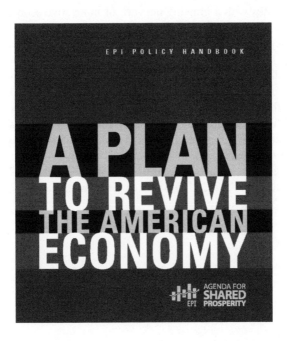

www.SharedProsperity.org

About EPI

The **Economic Policy Institute** was founded in 1986 to widen the debate about policies to achieve healthy economic growth, prosperity, and opportunity. Today, despite rapid growth in the U.S. economy in the latter part of the 1990s, inequality in wealth, wages, and income remains historically high. Expanding global competition, changes in the nature of work, and rapid technological advances are altering economic reality. Yet many of our policies, attitudes, and institutions are based on assumptions that no longer reflect real world conditions.

With the support of leaders from labor, business, and the foundation world, the Institute has sponsored research and public discussion of a wide variety of topics: globalization; fiscal policy; trends in wages, incomes, and prices; education; the causes of the productivity slowdown; labor market problems; rural and urban policies; inflation; state-level economic development strategies; comparative international economic performance; and studies of the overall health of the U.S. manufacturing sector and of specific key industries.

The Institute works with a growing network of innovative economists and other social science researchers in universities and research centers all over the country who are willing to go beyond the conventional wisdom in considering strategies for public policy.

Founding scholars of the Institute include Jeff Faux, former EPI president; Lester Thurow, Sloan School of Management, MIT; Ray Marshall, former U.S. secretary of labor, professor at the LBJ School of Public Affairs, University of Texas; Barry Bluestone, Northeastern University; Robert Reich, former U.S. secretary of labor; and Robert Kuttner, author, editor of *The American Prospect*, and columnist for *Business Week* and the *Washington Post* Writers Group.

For additional information about the Institute, contact EPI at 1333 H St. NW, Suite 300, Washington, DC 20005, (202) 775-8810, or visit www.epi.org.

About the authors

LAWRENCE MISHEL has been president of the Economic Policy Institute since 2002. Prior to that he was EPI's first research director (starting in 1987) and later became vice president. He is the co-author of all previous versions of *The State of Working America*. He holds a Ph.D. in economics from the University of Wisconsin-Madison, and his articles have appeared in a variety of academic and non-academic journals. His areas of research are labor economics, wage and income distribution, industrial relations, productivity growth, and the economics of education.

JARED BERNSTEIN joined the Economic Policy Institute in 1992. His latest book is *Crunch: Why Do I Feel So Squeezed? (And Other Unsolved Economic Mysteries)*, which follows *All Together Now: Common Sense for a Fair Economy*. His areas of research include income inequality and mobility, trends in employment and earnings, low-wage labor markets and poverty, international comparisons, and the analysis of federal and state economic policies. He is the co-author of nine editions of *The State of Working America* and has published extensively in popular and academic venues. Mr. Bernstein is on the Congressional Budget Office's advisory committee and is a contributor to the financial news station CNBC. He serves on the boards of the Coalition on Human Needs and the Mertz Gilmore Foundation and holds a Ph.D. in social welfare from Columbia University.

HEIDI SHIERHOLZ joined the Economic Policy Institute as a labor economist in 2007. Her areas of research include employment and unemployment, the gender wage and employment gaps, international comparisons, and the low-wage labor market. She previously worked as an assistant professor of economics at the University of Toronto, and she holds a Ph.D. in economics from the University of Michigan.